STUDIES ON THE ABUSE AND DECLINE OF REASON

F. A. HAYEK

THE COLLECTED WORKS OF

F. A. Hayek

STUDIES ON THE
ABUSE AND DECLINE
OF REASON

Text and Documents

Edited by Bruce Caldwell

Liberty Fund

This book is published by Liberty Fund, Inc., a foundation established to encourage study of the ideal of a society of free and responsible individuals

The cuneiform inscription that serves as our logo and as a design element in Liberty Fund books is the earliest-known written appearance of the word "freedom" (amagi), or "liberty." It is taken from a clay document written about 2300 B.C. in the Sumerian city-state of Lagash.

Studies on the Abuse and Decline of Reason is volume 13 of The Collected Works of F. A. Hayek, published by The University of Chicago Press.

This 2018 Liberty Fund paperback edition of *Studies on the Abuse and Decline of Reason* is published by arrangement with The University of Chicago Press and with Routledge, a member of the Taylor & Francis Group, an Informa Business.

Frontispiece: Friedrich Hayek © Bettmann/CORBIS
Cover photo: Friedrich August von Hayek © Dulton-Deutsch Collection/CORBIS

Printed in the United States of America

24   25   26   27   P   6   5   4   3   2

Library of Congress Cataloging-in-Publication Data

Names: Hayek, Friedrich A. von (Friedrich August), 1899-1992. |
Caldwell, Bruce, 1952- editor.
Title: Studies on the abuse and decline of reason : text and documents /
F. A. Hayek ; edited by Bruce Caldwell
Description: Carmel, Indiana : Liberty Fund, [2018] |
Series: The collected works of F. A. Hayek | Originally published
as hardback in 2010 by Routledge. |
Includes bibliographical references and index.
Identifiers: LCCN 2017052106 | ISBN 9780865979079 (pbk. : alk. paper)
Subjects: LCSH: Social sciences. | Social sciences—Philosophy. | Economics.
Classification: LCC H61 .H33664 2018 | DDC 300.1—dc23
LC record available at https://lccn.loc.gov/2017052106

Liberty Fund, Inc.
11301 North Meridian Street
Carmel, Indiana 46032
libertyfund.org

Printed on paper that is acid-free and meets the requirements of
the American National Standard for Permanence of Paper for
Printed Library Materials, Z39.48-1992. ♾

Cover design by Erin Kirk New, Watkinsville, Georgia
Printed and bound by Sheridan Books, Inc., Chelsea, Michigan

THE COLLECTED WORKS OF F. A. HAYEK

Founding Editor: W. W. Bartley III
General Editor: Bruce Caldwell

*The University of Chicago Press edition
was published with the support of*

The Hoover Institution on War, Revolution,
and Peace, Stanford University

The Cato Institute

The Earhart Foundation

The Pierre F. and Enid Goodrich Foundation

The Heritage Foundation

The Morris Foundation, Little Rock

CONTENTS

EDITORIAL FOREWORD

It is with considerable pleasure, pride, and relief that I present to the reader volume 13 of *The Collected Works of F. A. Hayek*. For reasons explained in the editor's introduction, *Studies on the Abuse and Decline of Reason* pairs the essays found in Hayek's 1952 book, *The Counter-Revolution of Science*, with his famous piece "Individualism: True and False". That one should feel both pride and pleasure in bringing out a new edition of these important texts is self-evident. The relief comes from the knowledge that no more footnotes need be checked!

The "Scientism and the Study of Society" and "The Counter-Revolution of Science" essays originally appeared in the journal *Economica* during World War II. Hayek frequently quoted from French and German sources, sometimes providing translations, and sometimes not. Typographical errors occasionally occurred, particularly in the spelling of foreign words. When the texts were reset for the Free Press edition of 1952, more errors crept in. Finally, quite apart from the question of French and German passages, Hayek himself was not always accurate in his citation practices. When he quoted others, sometimes the quotation he provided was different from what was found in the original. And sometimes the reference that accompanied the quotation was wrong in some way: for example, the author's name was misspelled, or the volume number of a journal or a page number was incorrect.

Given these multiple possible sources of errors, the following guidelines were followed in correcting the text. All typographical errors in the text proper were silently corrected. All misspellings in the French and German passages were similarly corrected silently, and when not provided by Hayek, translations for the passages were given.

When Hayek quoted others, any errors in a quotation were usually silently corrected. The exception was when Hayek made a small change to allow the quotation to fit better into his own surrounding prose. If there was any possibility that a correction of the text might introduce a meaning change, this was noted. Direct quotations by Hayek of others were indicated by the use of double quotation marks. Single quotation marks were used by Hayek for emphasis, and they have been retained.

Finally, in Hayek's citations, errors in the title of a book or journal were silently corrected. But for errors in the spelling of an author's name, wrong dates or volume numbers for journal articles, and wrong page numbers, the correction was indicated by putting the correct information in [brackets].

The organisations whose financial assistance has made possible the publication of this series are noted at the beginning of the volume. I am especially happy to report that the Pierre F. and Enid Goodrich Foundation has arranged with the University of Chicago Press to publish paperback editions of selected volumes in the *Collected Works* series. Liberty Fund is known for producing volumes of exceptional quality that are sold for almost unreasonably low prices, so this is very good news indeed for the series and for readers alike.

I also would like to thank the following individuals and institutions for granting permission to reproduce or quote from materials for which they hold copyright: the Estate of F. A. Hayek for permission to quote from his unpublished correspondence and papers; Stephen Kresge for permission to quote from transcripts of interviews conducted by W. W. Bartley III with F. A. Hayek; the University of Chicago and Princeton University Libraries for permission to quote from materials contained in their archives; the Hoover Institution on War, Revolution, and Peace for permission to quote from materials contained in the Hoover Institution Archives; and the Syndics of Cambridge University Library for permission to quote from the Lord Acton correspondence.

The British economics journal *Economica* first published Hayek's essays "The Counter-Revolution of Science" and "Scientism and the Study of Society" in 1941 and 1942–44, respectively. Revised versions of the essays were published by the Free Press in 1952 in a volume entitled *The Counter-Revolution of Science: Studies on the Abuse of Reason*, and those versions provided the basis for the present text. Our thanks to the Free Press for granting the rights for publishing these essays to the Estate of F. A. Hayek.

Bruce Caldwell
Greensboro, NC

INTRODUCTION

The Austrian economist Friedrich A. Hayek came to the London School of Economics (LSE) as a visiting professor in fall of 1931 and secured a permanent position as the Tooke Chair of Economic Science and Statistics the following year. From late 1933 onwards, he toiled fitfully over a big book on capital theory, an endeavour that was finally nearing completion in 1939. On August 27 of that year Hayek wrote a letter to Fritz Machlup, an old friend from university days.[1] He told him about his plans for his next big research project, a wide-ranging historical investigation that would incorporate intellectual history, methodology, and an analysis of social problems, all aimed at shedding light on the consequences of socialism:

> A series of case studies should come first, that would have as its starting point certain problems of methodology and especially the relationship between the method of natural science and social problems, leading to the fundamental scientific principles of economic policy and ultimately to the consequences of socialism. The series should form the basis of a systematic intellectual historical investigation of the fundamental principles of the social development of the last hundred years (from Saint-Simon to Hitler).[2]

---

[1] At the time, Machlup was teaching at the University of Buffalo in New York; he and Hayek had corresponded frequently throughout the 1930s about the book on capital theory. For more on this, see the editor's introduction to F. A. Hayek, *The Pure Theory of Capital*, ed. Lawrence H. White, vol. 12 (2007) of *The Collected Works of F. A. Hayek* (Chicago: University of Chicago Press, and London: Routledge), xviii–xxi. The correspondence between Hayek and Machlup was invaluable in reconstructing the evolution of the Abuse of Reason project.

[2] Es sollte zuerst eine Serie von Einzelstudien folgen, die von gewissen Problemen der Methodologie und besonders den Beziehungen zwischen naturwissenschaftlicher Methode und sozialen Problemen ausgehend über die wissenschaftlichen Grundlagen der Wirtschaftspolitik zu den Folgen des Sozialismus hinführen würde und die Grundlage einer systematischen geistesgeschichtlichen Untersuchung der Grundlagen der sozialen Entwicklung der letzten hundert Jahre (von Saint simon zu Hitler) bilden sollte. Letter, F. A. Hayek to Fritz Machlup, August 27, 1939, in the Fritz Machlup papers, box 43, folder 15, Hoover Institution Archives, Stanford University, Calif.

The date on the letter is significant. Four days earlier, the Molotov-Ribbentrop non-aggression pact between Germany and the Soviet Union had been signed. Five days later Hitler would invade Poland. On September 3, England and France would respond by declaring war on Germany. The Second World War had begun.

The war might well have stopped Hayek's grand project in its tracks. Within a week of England's declaration, Hayek drafted a letter to the director general of the British Ministry of Information offering his services to the war effort. Describing himself as an "ex-Austrian", a university professor, and someone who had "for some time" been a British subject (he had in fact been naturalised only the previous year), it was evident that he wanted to make crystal clear both his credentials and his allegiances. Accompanying the letter was a memo, "Some Notes on Propaganda in Germany", that contained a variety of suggestions about how to launch an effective propaganda campaign in the German-speaking countries.[3] Among the recommendations was an initiative that would seek to demonstrate to the German people, using German sources, that the principles of liberal democracy now being defended by England and France had also once been embraced by some of the great German poets and writers of the past, a fact that had been effectively written out of German history since Bismarck's time.[4] Evidently envisioning a rôle for himself in the propaganda effort, Hayek went on to say that "If such 'historical instruction' is to have a chance of success it is absolutely essential that all historical references should be scrupulously and even pedantically correct".[5]

Hayek would wait until December for his answer from the Ministry of Information. How different his personal history might have been had the director general accepted his offer! But it was not to be; the letter from the Ministry thanked him for his proposals but failed to ask for his assistance. Instead of working for the government as a propagandist, Hayek would begin writing the book that he had described to Machlup just days before the war began.

Only parts of that grand project would ever be finished. The "series of case studies" relating methodology and the scientific method to social problems that Hayek mentioned first would ultimately become his essay "Scientism and the Study of Society". The intellectual history part would never be com-

---

[3] Hayek's memo may be found in the Friedrich A. von Hayek papers, box 61, folders 4, Hoover Institution Archives, Stanford University, Calif. It is reproduced in the appendix to this volume.

[4] In this context it is interesting to note Hayek's remarks in an unpublished interview with W. W. Bartley III, dated "Summer 1984, at St. Blasien": "I was reading Schiller, and Goethe's friends and circle at a very early age. I got my liberalism from the great German poets". This and other unpublished interviews cited in the editor's introduction are used with the permission of the Hayek estate and Stephen Kresge.

[5] See this volume, appendix, p. 306.

pleted: only his study of the origins of scientism in France, which carried the title "The Counter-Revolution of Science", plus the short piece "Comte and Hegel", would be published. Hayek got sidetracked, first by the growth in scope of his "Scientism" essay, and then by his decision to transform the last part of his project, the part on "the consequences of socialism", into a separate full-length book. That volume would appear in 1944 and would be called *The Road to Serfdom*.

Hayek's larger book would have carried the provocative title *The Abuse and Decline of Reason*, and that title has been retained for this *Collected Works* edition, with the words "*Studies on*" added to emphasise that the originally envisioned volume was never completed. This introduction will tell the story of Hayek's greatest unfinished piece of work. It will document the sequence in which the essays were created, explore some of their major themes, and examine some aspects of Hayek's intellectual history that may help to explain why he made the arguments that he did. In the concluding sections, a brief assessment of Hayek's contribution will be offered, and the significance of the Abuse of Reason project for the later development of his ideas will be traced.

The Creation of the Essays

> The studies of which this book is the result have from the beginning been guided by and in the end confirmed the somewhat old-fashioned conviction of the author that it is human ideas which govern the development of human affairs.[6]

About ten months after his initial letter, in June 1940, Hayek wrote again to Machlup about his new endeavour. His enthusiasm is transparent:

> It is a great subject and one could make a great book of it. I believe indeed I have now found an approach to the subject through which one could exercise some real influence. But whether I shall ever be able to write it depends of course not only on whether one survives this but also on the outcome of it all. If things go really badly I shall certainly not be able to continue it here and since I believe that it is really important and the best I can do for the future of mankind, I should then have to try to transfer my activities elsewhere. Since at a later stage it may be difficult to write about it, I have already sent copies of the outline of the first part to Haberler and Lipmann

---

[6] This and subsequent aphorisms are taken from Hayek's notes on the project, some of which appear to have been for an intended, but never written, preface for the book. The notes may be found in the Hayek papers, box 107, folder 17, Hoover Institution Archives.

[*sic*][7] as a basis of any future application to one of the foundations for funds, and I am enclosing another copy with this letter. I am afraid it only gives the historical skeleton round which the main argument is to be developed, but I have not the peace of mind at the present moment to put the outline of the argument itself on paper. The second part would of course be an elaboration of the central argument of my pamphlet on Freedom and the Economic System.[8]

It is clear from this passage that, in addition to being enthusiastic, Hayek also thought that his project was a vitally important one: for a man not normally given to hyperbole, "the best I can do for the future of mankind" is certainly an unexpected phrasing. The dramatic choice of words presumably reflected his response to recent events. The 'phoney war' had ended dramatically on May 10, 1940, when Hitler invaded France and the Low Countries. Hayek was writing only three weeks after the British Expeditionary Force and its allies had barely avoided annihilation or capture on the beaches of Dunkirk. He was worried about whether he would survive the war, and perhaps even about which side would win, and was convinced that this was his best means for making a real contribution to the war effort.

The outline he included shows that he had established where he wanted to go with the book, even to the point of creating titles for the first eighteen chapters. The subtitle, as well as the title of part I, reveal his major theme: the abuse and decline of reason was caused by hubris, by man's pride in his ability to reason, which in Hayek's mind had been heightened by the rapid advance and multitudinous successes of the natural sciences, and the attempt to apply natural science methods in the social sciences. The letter also indicates that he had already decided that the second part of the book, to be titled "The Totalitarian Nemesis", was to be an expansion of the themes found in his 1939 article "Freedom and the Economic System".[9]

---

[7] Gottfried Haberler (1901–95) was another friend from his university days, who by then was on the faculty at Harvard University. Hayek should not have misspelled the name of the American newspaperman and author Walter Lippmann (1889–1974), given that he had attended a colloquium in Paris the year before honouring Lippmann's book, *An Inquiry into the Principles of the Good Society* (Boston: Little, Brown, 1937). Comments by some of those who attended the Colloque (unfortunately those of Hayek were not preserved) may be found in Louis Rougier, ed., *Compte-rendu des séances du colloque Walter Lippmann* (Paris: Editions politiques, économiques et sociologiques, Librarie de Médicis, 1938). The Colloque Lippmann led to the establishment of a research centre in France dedicated to the revival of liberalism, one that disappeared once the war began. It is plausible that Hayek viewed his book as his own contribution to the cause of defending liberalism.

[8] Letter, F. A. Hayek to Fritz Machlup, June 21, 1940, Machlup papers, box 43, folder 15, Hoover Institution Archives. The full text of the letter is reproduced in the appendix.

[9] There were two versions of "Freedom and the Economic System", one published in 1938, the other in 1939. They are both reproduced in F. A. Hayek, *Socialism and War*, ed. Bruce Caldwell, vol. 10 (1997) of The *Collected Works of F. A. Hayek*, chapters 8 and 9.

THE ABUSE AND DECLINE OF REASON.

The Reflections of an Economist on the Self-
Destructive Tendencies of our Scientific Civilization.

SYNOPSIS.

Preface and Plan.

Introduction: The Humility of Individualism.

Part I. - The Collectivist Hybris.

Section I. The French Phase.

Chapter 1. Scientism.
" 2. The Origin of the Scientistic Hybris:
L'Ecole Polytechnique.
" 3. L'Accoucheur d'idees: Saint-Simon.
" 4. The Feligion of the Engineers: The Saint-Simonians.
" 5. Saint-Simonian Influence.
" 6. Social Physics: Auguste Comte.

Section II. The German Phase.

Chapter 7. The Extremes Meet: Comte and Hegel.
" 8. Scientific Socialism and the Technological
Interpretation of History.
" 9. Historism and the Socialism of the Chair.
" 10. The "Social Empire".
" 11. Scientifically Organised Industry.
" 12. The Spiritual Bodyguard of the Hohenzollerns.

Section III. The English Phase.

Chapter 13. England's Lost Intellectual Leadership.
" 14. Evolutionism and English Positivism
" 15. "We are all Socialists now."
" 16. Fabianism.
" 17. Tory Socialism
" 18. The End of Free Trade.

Section IV. The American Phase.

(Will deal in succession with the influence of the
historical School, Pragmatism, Behaviourism, Institutionalism
Technocracy, and Econometrics.)

Part II. - The Totalitarian Nemesis.

An early outline of the book.

Hayek worked on the book throughout the summer of 1940, sending copies of chapters to Gottfried Haberler as he finished them. On September 7 the London Blitz began. As a result, the LSE was fully evacuated for the duration to Peterhouse, Cambridge, and during the coming academic year (1940–41) Hayek would spend three nights of each week in Cambridge, the other four in his London home in the Hampstead Garden Suburb, his own family having long since been evacuated to Lionel Robbins's country cottage. Hayek's letter to Machlup of October 13, 1940, gives a taste of what life was like in London, then goes on to detail the progress of his book:

> I have, in fact, done more work this summer than ever before in a similar period. After finishing with the proofs of my capital book (which Macmillan is now hesitating to bring out—it is all ready), I have completed five historical chapters of my new book and am now deep in the most difficult first theoretical chapters.[10]

We see here not only Hayek's progress but also how his plan for the volume was beginning to change. The "five historical chapters", chapters two through six on the original outline, contained Hayek's account of "the French Phase", detailing the origins of scientism, which he located in the writings of Henri Saint-Simon, his followers the Saint-Simonians, and the polymath scholar Auguste Comte. Hayek published these chapters the next year, in the February, May, and August 1941 issues of the LSE journal *Economica* under the title "The Counter-Revolution of Science". But instead of continuing on with the historical section, Hayek began working on chapter one, which was to be called "Scientism". The only other historical chapter that Hayek would finish was the first chapter of "the German Phase", titled "Comte and Hegel", which was finally published in 1951.[11]

As his letter suggests, Hayek's planned single chapter on scientism had expanded, and he was having difficulties with the topic. It would take him four more years to complete the essay: the first instalment would appear in *Economica* in August 1942, the second in February 1943, and the last in February 1944. Thus did the single chapter labelled "Scientism" ultimately become a major essay of ten chapters, "Scientism and the Study of Society".

The expanded scope and the inherent difficulties of the material covered in the "Scientism" essay were partly responsible for the slowdown, but it was also due to Hayek's decision to begin focusing on another project. He announced this in his holiday letter to Machlup, begun in December 1940 in Cambridge (where by this time Hayek had, with the assistance of John Maynard Keynes, secured rooms at King's College) and finished on New Year's Day 1941 in Tintagel on the Cornish coast: "at the moment I am mainly concerned with an enlarged and somewhat more popular exposition of the theme of my *Freedom and the Economic System* which, if I finish it, may come out as a sixpence Penguin

---

[10] Letter, F. A. Hayek to Fritz Machlup, October 13, 1940, Machlup papers, box 43, folder 15, Hoover Institution Archives. The full text of the letter is reproduced in the appendix.

[11] Hayek apparently used "Comte and Hegel" as his inaugural lecture at the University of Chicago.

volume".[12] By the summer Hayek would report that a "much enlarged" version of the pamphlet was "unfortunately growing into a full fledged book".[13] Finally, by October 1941 Hayek told Machlup that he had decided to devote nearly all of his time to what would become *The Road to Serfdom*:

> It [the "Scientism" essay] is far advanced, but at the moment I am not even getting on with that because I have decided that the applications of it all to our own time, which should some day form volume II of *The Abuse and Decline of Reason*, are more important. . . . If one cannot fight the Nazis one ought at least fight the ideas which produce Naziism; and although the well-meaning people who are so dangerous have of course no idea of it, the danger which comes from them is none the less serious. The most dangerous people here are a group of socialist scientists and I am just publishing a special attack on them in *Nature*—the famous scientific weekly which in recent years has been one of the main advocates of "planning".[14]

Hayek's change in course is understandable. He had begun his great book just as Europe was going to war. Western civilisation itself was at stake, and given that the British government would not allow him to participate directly, writing a treatise on how the world had come to such an awful state was to be Hayek's war effort, the best he could do "for the future of mankind". Two years later the prospects for the allies seemed brighter, but a new danger was looming. Hayek increasingly feared that the popular enthusiasm for planning, one that had only increased during the war, would affect postwar policy in England.[15] *The Road to Serfdom* was intended as a counterweight to these trends. Working on it became his first priority, even if it meant delaying his more

---

[12] Letter, F. A. Hayek to Fritz Machlup, December 14, 1940/January 1, 1941, Machlup papers, box 43, folder 15, Hoover Institution Archives. The full text of the letter is reproduced in the appendix.

[13] Letter, F. A. Hayek to Fritz Machlup, July 31, 1941, Machlup papers, box 43, folder 15, Hoover Institution Archives.

[14] Letter, F. A. Hayek to Fritz Machlup, October 19, 1941, Machlup papers, box 43, folder 15, Hoover Institution Archives. The full text of the letter is reproduced in the appendix. The article in *Nature* that Hayek refers to, titled "Planning, Science, and Freedom", is reprinted in F. A. Hayek, *Socialism and War*, chapter 10. We will learn more about these socialist (mostly natural) scientists later in this introduction.

[15] For a more detailed account of Hayek's decision, see the editor's introduction to F. A. Hayek, *The Road to Serfdom: Text and Documents*, ed. Bruce Caldwell, vol. 2 (2007) of *The Collected Works of F. A. Hayek*, pp. 9–15. Hayek expressed his concerns succinctly in a letter to Jacob Viner, in which he wrote "although I am fairly optimistic about the war, I am by no means so about the peace, or rather about the economic regime that will follow the war". Letter, F. A. Hayek to Jacob Viner, February 1, 1942, Jacob Viner papers, box 13, folder 26, Public Policy Papers, Department of Rare Books and Special Collections, Princeton University Library, Princeton, NJ.

scholarly treatment of the historical origins and eventual spread of the doctrines that had in his estimation led to the abuse and decline of reason.

The present volume includes an additional chapter, Hayek's famous essay "Individualism: True and False". According to his outline, the two-volume work was to have been introduced with this essay, which Hayek had originally titled "The Humility of Individualism". It has accordingly been placed in its intended position and labelled as a 'Prelude' to the other essays. It is not clear exactly when "Individualism: True and False" was written, but given that it was first delivered as an address in Ireland in December 1945, it was probably completed sometime after the publication of the "Scientism" and "Counter-Revolution" essays.[16]

After the war was over, Hayek undertook a number of disparate projects, among them writing *The Sensory Order*, putting together a volume on the correspondence between John Stuart Mill and Harriet Taylor, arranging for the first meeting of the Mont Pèlerin Society, and leaving the LSE for a new job at the Committee on Social Thought at the University of Chicago. In a letter in November 1948 replying to John Nef's invitation to come to Chicago, Hayek reiterated his plan to do further work on *The Abuse and Decline of Reason*.[17] But sometime during the next couple of years he evidently decided to abandon the project, for in 1952 he published *The Counter-Revolution of Science: Studies on the Abuse of Reason*.[18] The book contained all that he had finished of the project: "Scientism", "The Counter-Revolution of Science", and "Comte and Hegel". Hayek's prefaces to the 1952 English and 1959 German editions of that book are included in the appendix of the present volume.

As this history of the creation of the essays makes clear, they were actually written in the reverse order in which they appear in this volume: "Counter-Revolution" was completed first, then "Scientism", then "Individualism: True and False". In the preface to the German edition, Hayek noted that for "the reader who has little taste for abstract discussion", the historical account provided in "Counter-Revolution" makes for easier reading than does "Scientism", so that such readers may wish to start there first.[19]

---

[16] One can never know for sure why Hayek chose the title "Individualism: True and False" for his paper. Two titles that he may have been playing off were Sidney Webb, *Socialism: True and False* (London: The Fabian Society, 1894), a lecture that Webb gave before the Fabian Society in 1894, and John Dewey, *Individualism, Old and New* (New York: Minton, Balch, and Co., 1930). Alternatively, given his Irish audience, he may well have been responding to passages about true and false individualism that may be found in Oscar Wilde, "The Soul of Man under Socialism" [1891], reprinted in *The Writings of Oscar Wilde* (New York: Wise, 1931), pp. 12–13.

[17] Letter, F. A. Hayek to John Nef, November 6, 1948, Hayek papers, box 55, folder 1, Hoover Institution Archives.

[18] F. A. Hayek, *The Counter-Revolution of Science: Studies on the Abuse of Reason* (Glencoe, IL: Free Press, 1952; reprinted, Indianapolis, IN: LibertyPress, 1979).

[19] F. A. Hayek, Preface to the German Edition, this volume, pp. 322–23.

Major Themes of the "Scientism" Essay

> What has so far been the greatest achievement of the human mind (the tech-
> niques of commanding the forces of nature) applied to society may yet prove
> the cause of its destruction.[20]

The "Scientism" essay does contain some "abstract discussion", but the main lines of Hayek's argument are pretty straightforward. Hayek begins by noting that in the eighteenth and early nineteenth centuries, those who sought to examine economic and social phenomena scientifically usually followed methods that were dictated by the material under study. As the nineteenth century progressed, however, the term 'science' came more and more to be associated with the successes of the physical and biological sciences, with the rigour of their methods and the certainty of their results. A change gradually took place in the social sciences, as the "ambition to imitate Science in its methods rather than its spirit" became a dominant theme.[21] Hayek refers to this "slavish imitation of the method and language of Science" as *scientism*, or as the scientistic prejudice, an attitude that he felt was profoundly *un*scientific.[22] Scientism involves a prejudice because, even before considering the nature of a subject area, it presumes to know the best way to study it.

Hayek's next step, accordingly, is to offer a description of the social reality that we seek to understand. The social sciences concern themselves first and foremost with explaining human action. All human action is based on people's subjective perceptions and beliefs, or what Hayek calls 'opinions'. Because these opinions determine the actions we seek to explain, they constitute the 'data' of the social sciences. What can we say about them?

First, though each person knows by introspection that opinions drive his own actions, opinions are not observable, only the actions that follow from them are. The fact that we are able to communicate with other people about the world suggests, however, that our minds operate in a similar way. Though the structures of individual minds may be similar, humans have different subjective beliefs: our knowledge "only exists in the dispersed, incomplete, and inconsistent form in which it appears in many individual minds".[23] And as he

[20] Notes, F. A. Hayek papers, box 107, folder 17, Hoover Institution Archives.

[21] This volume, p. 78.

[22] Ibid., p. 80. As Hayek wrote on one of his notes for the project, "I use scientistic because it desires to be but is not scientific". See Notes, F. A. Hayek papers, box 107, folder 17, Hoover Institution Archives.

[23] Ibid., p. 93. That our beliefs are subjective and knowledge is dispersed is something that Hayek had first asserted in "Economics and Knowledge". See F. A. Hayek, "Economics and Knowledge", *Economica*, n.s., vol. 4, Feb. 1937, pp. 33–54, reprinted in F. A. Hayek, *Individualism and Economic Order* (Chicago: University of Chicago Press, 1948), pp. 33–56. The essay will appear in a forthcoming volume of *The Collected Works*.

indicates with the word "inconsistent", a further implication of the subjective nature of beliefs is that they may be false. Hayek sums up his discussion of the subject matter of the social sciences with the following words:

> we must start from what men think and mean to do: from the fact that the individuals which compose society are guided in their actions by a classifica- tion of things or events according to a system of sense qualities and of con- cepts which has a common structure and which we know because we, too, are men; and that the concrete knowledge which different individuals possess will differ in important respects. . . . Society as we know it is, as it were, built up from the concepts and ideas held by the people; and social phenomena can be recognised by us and have meaning to us only as they are reflected in the minds of men.[24]

Given this description of the nature of social reality, Hayek then outlines the appropriate method for its study. Simply put, the task of the social scien- tist is to show how the constitutive opinions of individual agents lead them to create through their actions the more complex structures that constitute the social world. The most interesting structures are those which are unintended: observed regularities that are not the results of anyone's design. Following Carl Menger, Hayek dubs the method by which such larger social phenom- ena are composed from the interaction of individual elements the *compositive* method.[25]

Hayek provides a simple example of what he means—the explanation of the formation of footpaths. Before a footpath is formed in a forest, each per- son travelling through makes his own path. But over time certain paths get used more often, and eventually, everyone starts using the same ones. This explanation, Hayek notes, has little to do with our powers of observation, but much to do with our understanding of how human beings act:

> it is not the observation of the actual growth of any particular track, and still less of many, from which this explanation derives its cogency, but from our general knowledge of how we and other people behave in the kind of situa- tion in which the successive people find themselves. . . . It is the elements of the complex of events which are familiar to us from everyday experience, but it is only by a deliberate effort of directed thought that we come to see the necessary effects of the combination of such actions by many people. We 'understand' the way in which the result we observe can be produced,

[24] This volume, p. 97.
[25] Ibid., p. 102.

although we may never be in a position to watch the whole process or to predict its precise course and result.[26]

The homely example gains significance when it is realised that many social and economic phenomena are susceptible to similar sorts of explanations. These include both the sort of institution formation that Menger had described, as well as the processes that underlie the everyday workings of markets:

> It makes no difference for our present purpose whether the process extends over a long period of time, as it does in such cases as the evolution of money or the formation of language, or whether it is a process which is constantly repeated anew, as in the case of the formation of prices or the direction of production under competition.[27]

Using the compositive method to explain how individual actions create larger social processes, structures, and institutions, then, is in Hayek's mind the chief rôle of the social scientist.

Hayek draws a further important conclusion from his discussion. Given the sometimes vast number of elements whose interactions create social structures and institutions, the social scientist will rarely be able to predict precise outcomes: one can accurately describe how a footpath will form, but one typically will not be able to predict its exact position. This leads him to distinguish between explanations that allow predictions and those that only can describe the principle by which a phenomenon is produced. Because of the nature of our materials, 'explanations of the principle' and 'pattern predictions' are often the best we can do in the social sciences.[28] This fundamental conclusion about the limits of the social sciences is one that Hayek would retain and emphasise throughout his life.

Having laid out his preferred approach, Hayek then turns to a critique of the various scientistic approaches. He identifies three broad types of scientistic thought. All apply methods that work well in the natural sciences to the material of the social sciences, and by so doing deny basic aspects of the phenomena under study.

Thus, those who demand a more 'objectivist' approach deny the *subjective* nature of the data of the social sciences. Among the proponents Hayek identifies are Auguste Comte, who disparaged the use of introspection; behaviour-

---

[26] Ibid., p. 104.
[27] Ibid., pp. 104–5.
[28] Ibid., pp. 105–6.

ists of various stripes, all of whom want to restrict their science to the identification of correlations between observable stimuli and behavioural responses; and physicalists like the philosopher Otto Neurath, whom Hayek interpreted as insisting that the terms of scientific theories should make reference only to observables.[29]

Those who tout 'collectivism' deny that the social sciences should start from the opinions of *individual* humans, preferring instead to begin with empirical regularities that exist at the levels of wholes like 'the economy' or 'society'. While Auguste Comte is again cited as a major offender, Hayek also discusses those who assert that the collection of massive amounts of statistical data might help us better to understand the relationships existing among social phenomena. While he names no names, his comments seem directed at people like the American institutionalist Wesley Clair Mitchell, and perhaps also at John Maynard Keynes.[30]

Finally, those who advocate 'historicism' deny that the social sciences are properly *theoretical* in nature. Hayek deals with two variants of historicism. One sees history as the gradual accumulation of statistics, which ultimately will be used to draw generalisations about society—this view is typically associated with Gustav Schmoller, the leader of the younger German historical school. Another variant is the search for laws of the development of human history. In this camp Hayek places various stage theories and philosophies of history, the "darling vice" of the nineteenth century, and among the guilty are Hegel, Comte, Marx ("particularly Marx"), and later, Werner Sombart and Oswald Spengler.[31] By claiming that various laws determine the development of history, these historicists deny the importance of human intentional action in shaping events—from Hayek's perspective they, like the collectivists, seek regularities and laws at the wrong level.

In his closing chapters Hayek details certain detrimental consequences of the scientistic worldview. One is the inability of its advocates to grasp the foundational idea that "the independent action of many men can produce coherent wholes, persistent structures of relationships which serve important

---

[29] Ibid., pp. 108–9. In correspondence with Hayek in 1945—see the Hayek papers, box 40, folder 7, Hoover Institution Archives—Otto Neurath claimed that Hayek had misrepresented his views, a point reiterated by some recent interpreters: see, e.g., John O'Neill, "Ecological Economics and the Politics of Knowledge: The Debate between Hayek and Neurath", *Cambridge Journal of Economics*, vol. 28, 2004, pp. 431–47. For the view that Neurath's interpreters have tended to impose coherence on the writings of an often messy thinker, see Bruce Caldwell, "Book Review: Elisabeth Nemeth, Stefan Schmitz, and Thomas Uebel, eds., *Otto Neurath's Economics in Context*", *Journal of the History of Economic Thought*, vol. 31, December 2009, forthcoming.

[30] Regarding Keynes, see, for example, Hayek's comments about the "macroscopic view" on p. 122.

[31] Ibid., pp. 135–36.

human purposes without having been designed for that end".[32] Those who take the scientistic view think that if something serves a human purpose, it must have been designed. From this idea, it is but a small step to the even more dangerous view that we possess the ability to refashion social institutions at will. All such views overvalue the power of human reason.[33] By way of contrast, the 'individualist approach' recognises the limits of the human mind:

> The individualist approach, in awareness of the constitutional limitations of the individual mind, attempts to show how man in society is able, by the use of various resultants of the social process, to increase his powers with the help of the knowledge implicit in them and of which he is never aware; it makes us understand that the only 'reason' which can in any sense be regarded as superior to individual reason does not exist apart from the inter-individual process in which, by means of impersonal media, the knowledge of successive generations and of millions of people living simultaneously is combined and mutually adjusted, and that this process is the only form in which the totality of human knowledge ever exists.[34]

The distinction between the hubris of the scientistic approach and the humility of individualism would be a major theme of Hayek's "Individualism: True and False", and would reappear in later writings as the contrast between constructivist rationalism and the evolutionary way of thinking.

Scientism, then, underpins the ubiquitous call for planning in modern society. It gives rise to the 'engineering point of view', in which all social problems are seen as identical to those faced by engineers, as well as the confidence that large-scale social planning can succeed. For Hayek, widespread enthusiasm for a variety of forms of economic planning revealed the pervasiveness of the engineering mentality, and was but a natural consequence of the steady ascendancy of the scientistic prejudice.

One can see how *The Road to Serfdom* made for a natural successor to this argument. Those in the West who called for extensive state planning recognised that it could be a handmaiden to totalitarianism, as the examples of the Soviet Union and the various fascist experiments made clear. But for the

---

[32] Ibid., p. 142.

[33] Though neither Hegel nor Marx should be accused of holding such views, at least some of them were endorsed by proponents of the variant of Marxism, Austro-Marxism, that Hayek encountered in Vienna, more about which below. As noted in note 84 below, Hayek could not stomach Hegel's thought and, it should be added, was not always on strong ground when interpreting it. To his credit, Hayek at least admitted that he does "not pretend to understand Hegel". See below p. 290.

[34] Ibid., p. 153.

Western democracies, the hope was held out that a democratic form of planning was also possible, a new system that would fully preserve individual freedom while remedying the failures of the capitalist system that had become so manifest in the years of the Great Depression. Hayek's message in *The Road to Serfdom* was that such a dream was a sham, that a democratic polity was incompatible with a fully planned socialist society, that, as he put it in 1944, "socialism can be put into practice only by methods of which most socialists disapprove".[35] This put the choice fairly starkly: if socialist planning were actually successfully implemented, both liberty and democracy would be lost. Hayek, of course, held out the hope that a reconstructed democratic but *liberal* polity provided a far better alternative.

Hayek's Theses in the Context of his Times

> . . . a number of independent experiences and observations which gradually proved to hang together[36]

In developing his theses about scientism, Hayek was principally responding to the intellectual milieu he experienced on coming to England in the 1930s. But the specific content of his arguments also very much reflected his own personal intellectual development. Hayek was raised within the Austrian school tradition in economics, one that had originated with Carl Menger and had come to international recognition with the ascendancy of Eugen von Böhm-Bawerk and Friedrich von Wieser. He was well schooled in the particulars of the famous *Methodenstreit*, or debate over methods, that had taken place between the Austrians and the German historical school economists in the generations that preceded him. As a student at the University of Vienna after the end of the First World War, he also had direct experience with Austro-Marxism. Drawing heavily on the ideas of the physicist Ernst Mach, Austro-Marxists blended socialist economics with positivist philosophy of science, in the hope of elucidating what Karl Marx always claimed to have discovered, a truly scientific socialism. Upon finishing his second degree Hayek spent fifteen months in the United States, and this trip also affected the way he viewed the world. All of these experiences would colour his response to the situation in which he found himself in inter-war Britain.

---

[35] F. A. Hayek, *The Road to Serfdom*, p. 159.

[36] Notes, Hayek papers, box 107, folder 17, Hoover Institution Archives. In this section I will link some of the headings in Hayek's proposed outline of chapters to certain "independent experiences and observations" that he had that he alludes to in this note.

The Austrian Background: Historicism, Socialism, and Positivism

What was the nature of the methodological dispute between the Austrian school economists and their rivals in Germany? At the most basic level, the German historical school economists rejected a theoretical approach to their subject as at best premature, and at worst wholly inappropriate. Noting that each country has its own unique history, with different social norms, institutions, and cultural values affecting its course of development, they concluded that the abstract theorising that had begun with David Ricardo and was taken to extremes by his followers was simply a mistaken generalisation from the experience of one nation during a certain period of its history, Great Britain since the late eighteenth century. They favoured instead the detailed study of the development of each nation's economic, social, cultural, and ethical institutions; this would then shed light on which policies were most appropriate. Some had stage theories of development, others urged the patient collection of facts, but all derided the classical economists' claim to have discovered a universal theory of economics.

Carl Menger agreed with the German historical school economists that the specific theory of value endorsed by Ricardo and the British classicals—most followed some variant of a cost of production theory—was wrong. But he disagreed that this implied that there could be *no* theoretical approach to economic phenomena. In the *Principles of Economics* he argued that a number of economic practices and institutions—these included the origins of money and exchange, the formation of prices, and the development of various market structures—could be explained as the unintended consequences of intentional human action. People in pursuing their own interests do not set out to create such institutions; they emerge, rather, as unintended, and in that sense spontaneous, orders.[37] Because he defended a theoretical approach, Menger's book was interpreted by the leader of the younger German historical school, Gustav Schmoller, as simply a continuation of the errors of Ricardo and other classicals. Disputes between two schools led eventually to the *Methodenstreit*—and it was in this debate that the label 'Austrian school of economics', originally meant as a term of derision, was coined by its opponents.

At least in terms of academic appointments, the battle over methods was initially won by the historical school economists. This was in part because the historical school professors also played the crucial rôle of educating those who would later fill the ranks of the German imperial bureaucracy. It was

---

[37] Carl Menger, *Principles of Economics*, translated by James Dingwall and Bert E. Hoselitz (New York: New York University Press, 1976). This theme is, of course, very much in evidence in Hayek's "Scientism" essay.

the age of imperialism, and the leaders of the German Empire (in existence only since 1871) were keen that it be able to compete effectively against its rivals. The professoriate, then, had the additional duty of providing intellectual support for the policies favoured by the empire, a rôle that allowed one of their number to claim that they constituted "the intellectual bodyguard of the Hohenzollerns".[38]

Paradoxically, even as Bismarck was attacking the socialists, his government was adopting many of their programs, the better to preserve order in the face of threats both from within (unrest among the workers, dubbed 'the social problem') and without. Their support of these specific policies earned the conservative German historical school professors the label 'socialists of the chair', given to them by a liberal newspaperman.

From Hayek's perspective, there was an unsettling consistency between the methodological and political positions embraced by the historical school economists. Their denial of the efficacy of theory, and their insistence that each country's unique history dictated the policies that were appropriate, allowed the professors considerable flexibility in picking among the policies they chose to support (and, of course, that they would support those policies that best promoted the interests of the empire was all but self-evident). The historical school economists also insisted that theirs was the only truly scientific approach to the study of social phenomena. Seeing this as a chief weakness, Menger launched a methodological attack against his opponents in the *Methodenstreit*. Hayek would follow a similar strategy in his Abuse of Reason project.

By the turn of the century, a new opponent for the Austrian economists, the Austro-Marxists, emerged on the scene. Böhm-Bawerk and Wieser, the 'second-generation' Austrian economists, were proponents of the marginalist approach to value theory, one that stood in direct opposition to the cost of production theories of value of the classicals. A prominent defender of one variant of the classical theory was Karl Marx, whose utilisation of a labour theory of value was central to his explanation of the origin of surplus value, itself a key part of his theory of the exploitation of the proletariat. Marxist value theory then became a natural target for the Austrians. After Böhm-Bawerk's devastating 1896 critique of the third and final volume of *Das Kapital*, the Austrian economists were evermore identified as the most prominent critics of Marxism.[39]

---

[38] In his outline Hayek referred to them as the spiritual, rather than the intellectual, bodyguard. The phrase "intellectual bodyguard of the Hohenzollerns" was used by the physiologist Emil du Bois-Reymond, who was also the rector of the University of Berlin and president of the Prussian Academy of Science, in a speech delivered in 1870. See Emil du Bois-Reymond, *A Speech on the German War* (London: Bentley, 1870), p. 31.

[39] See Eugen von Böhm-Bawerk, *Karl Marx and the Close of his System* (London: Fisher Unwin, 1898), reprinted in *Karl Marx and the Close of his System / Böhm-Bawerk's Criticism of Marx*, ed. Paul Sweezy (New York: Kelley, 1949; reprinted, 1975), pp. 3–118.

While Böhm-Bawerk's and others' criticisms of Marxist value theory caused some socialists to abandon the labour theory of value, others rose to its defence, and among them were the Austro-Marxists. This led to a famous debate in Böhm-Bawerk's economics seminar between Böhm-Bawerk and Otto Bauer, the brilliant young leader of the Austro-Marxists who would go on to lead the Austrian Social Democrats after the war. Other seminar participants included the Marxist theoretician Rudolf Hilferding, who had himself published a criticism of Böhm-Bawerk's position on Marx, as well as Joseph Schumpeter and Ludwig von Mises.[40] After participating in these debates on the transformation problem and the Marxian theory of value, the Austrian economists were thoroughly schooled in the nuances of Marxist theory, and indeed defined their own approach at least partly in contradistinction to it.

But the Austrian critique of socialism was ultimately to go far beyond the criticism of its value theory. This was due in part to another seminar participant, Otto Neurath. In the seminar Neurath propounded the doctrine of 'war economy', the idea that the massive central planning that typically characterises an economy in war should be extended into peacetime. Neurath further proposed that money should be abolished, that managers charged with directing the economy should rely instead on 'in natura' calculation, utilising an extensive body of social statistics to plan production and distribution. By the end of the war many others had joined Neurath in proposing alternative socialisation schemes for the reorganisation of society, though few were as radical as his. These proposals ultimately provoked Ludwig von Mises to write an article and later a book on socialism, thereby beginning the German language socialist calculation debate.[41]

Neurath's writings also strengthened the link in the Austrian mind between socialism and positivism, for in the 1920s he was to become the 'social science expert' of the Vienna Circle. As recent scholarship emphasises, the early days of the logical positivist movement had a distinctly political side, and Neurath played a central rôle in this. In advocating the unity of science, for example, he hoped to enlist all of the sciences to use them to refashion society along socialist lines.[42] He was also clear about the proper approach to the social

---

[40] See Rudolf Hilferding, *Böhm-Bawerk's Criticism of Marx*, in *Karl Marx and the Close of His System/ Böhm-Bawerk's Criticism of Marx*, pp. 121–96.

[41] See Ludwig von Mises, "Economic Calculation in the Socialist Commonwealth", translated by S. Adler, in *Collectivist Economic Planning*, ed. F. A. Hayek (London: George Routledge and Sons, 1935; reprinted, Clifton, NJ: Kelley, 1975), pp. 87–130; *Socialism: An Economic and Sociological Analysis*, translated by J. Kahane (London: Cape, 1936; reprinted, Indianapolis, IN: LibertyClassics, 1981). For more on this episode, see the "Introduction" to F. A. Hayek, *Socialism and War*, pp. 2–10. Hayek criticises 'in natura' calculation in the "Scientism" essay: see this volume, p. 159.

[42] See the discussions of Neurath in George A. Reisch, *How the Cold War Transformed Philosophy of Science: To the Icy Slopes of Logic* (Cambridge: Cambridge University Press, 2005).

sciences: "Of all the attempts at creating a strictly scientific unmetaphysical physicalist sociology, Marxism is the most complete".[43] Positivist philosophy of science was therefore always aligned in the minds of the Austrian school economists with socialist politics and economics.

Hayek was exposed to positivist thought as a student, and apparently even entertained the idea of joining the Vienna Circle, but his most intense exposure to the relevant debates doubtless occurred after he began participating in the Mises Circle, that is, directly after his return from America, more of which anon. His friend from student days Felix Kaufmann was a member of both the Mises Circle and the Vienna Circle, and he kept the Mises Circle members apprised of the latter's activities. In the late 1920s Mises was fashioning his own response to the positivists with his theory of human action, so logical positivism was much discussed in the seminar. Though Hayek appears never to have been comfortable with the *a priori* foundations that Mises claimed for his program, he imbibed and fully concurred with the view that the positivists were only pretenders to the mantle of science. And because their radically empiricist approach to science had much in common with the naïve empiricism of the German historical school economists, the arguments against them came naturally to the lips of anyone trained in the Austrian economic tradition.

By the time that Hayek came onto the scene, logical positivism was flourishing, but the battle between the Austrian and German historical schools was pretty much over. Schmoller had died during the war, and the historical school economists had proved of little assistance during that conflict, and even less in the hyperinflation that followed. Their whole approach was, in the eyes of many, discredited. Yet in 1933 Hayek would argue, in his inaugural lecture at the LSE and in a memo he sent to William Beveridge, the director of the LSE, that their influence was still to be felt. How could that be?

Hayek's American Experience

Hayek's experiences on his trip to America may help to provide an answer. Hayek left for the States in March 1923, and although he was armed with letters of introduction from Joseph Schumpeter addressed to all the leading American economic theorists, he was disappointed by what he found.[44] Few advances in theory had been made. The one economist that everyone was

---

[43] Otto Neurath, "Empirical Sociology: The Scientific Content of History and Political Economy", in *Empiricism and Sociology*, Marie Neurath and Robert S. Cohen, eds. (Dordrecht, Holland: D. Reidel, 1973), p. 349.

[44] F. A. Hayek, "Introduction", in *Money, Capital, and Fluctuations: Early Essays*, ed. Roy McCloughry (Chicago: University of Chicago Press, 1984), p. 2.

talking about was the one for whom he had no letter of introduction: Wesley Clair Mitchell.

Mitchell had studied under the iconoclastic and idiosyncratic economist Thorstein Veblen and the pragmatist philosopher John Dewey at the University of Chicago. A dominant figure in the American institutionalist movement, he had published in 1913 a major treatise on business cycles.[45] Mitchell's approach to his subject was radically empirical: rather than start with a theory of the cycle, he gathered historical records on the cyclical movement through time of a wide variety of economic variables to see what sorts of patterns in the timing of their amplitudes and rates of change might emerge. This sort of approach, though reminiscent of that of Schmoller and the German historical school economists, was much more systematic. It was also more useful: unlike his German counterparts, Mitchell had contributed to the war effort by serving as the head of the Price Section of the War Industries Board, where he witnessed firsthand how important the use of statistical data could be for planning the production and distribution of war materials. As a reform-minded progressive, he had hopes that such scientific techniques could be useful to the government in attacking the social problems of the day.

By the time Hayek appeared on the scene, Mitchell was the director of research at the newly founded National Bureau of Economic Research, as well as a professor at Columbia University, itself then becoming a hotbed of institutionalist thought.[46] During the 1923–24 academic year, he taught a class called "Types of Economic Theory" on Tuesday and Thursday afternoons. Since Hayek was spending most of his time in New York, he decided to 'gate-crash' Mitchell's course. It must have been an eye-opener.[47]

The course differed from a more standard class on the history of economic thought in two important ways. First, Mitchell's ambitious goal was to elucidate how changes in all sorts of institutions—political, economic, social, and

---

[45] Wesley Clair Mitchell, *Business Cycles* (Berkeley, CA: University of California Press, 1913).

[46] Among the Columbia economists sympathetic to institutionalism were J. M. Clark, Frederick C. Mills, Robert Hale, Paul Brissenden, and Rexford Tugwell. See Malcolm Rutherford, "Institutional Economics at Columbia University", *History of Political Economy*, vol. 36, Spring 2004, pp. 31–78.

[47] Lectures notes from the 1934–35 class were stenographically recorded by a student: see Wesley Clair Mitchell, *Lecture Notes on Types of Economic Theory*, 2 vols. (New York: Augustus M. Kelley, 1949); cf. Wesley Clair Mitchell, *Types of Economic Theory: From Mercantilism to Institutionalism*, ed. Joseph Dorfman, 2 vols. (New York: Kelley, 1967–69). The Dorfman edition contains a vast amount of additional material—course outlines, notes from other versions of the lectures, and so on—so is more comprehensive, but the additions also make it more difficult to follow Mitchell's narrative. I have used the 1934–35 notes as the basis for my remarks in the text. Evidently, there may have been some alterations in emphasis in the later lectures from the ones that Hayek would have heard in 1923–24, though as Rutherford, "Institutional Economics . . .", p. 64, points out, if anything Mitchell's expressed views had moderated somewhat by the 1930s.

legal—affected both the type of economic theory that developed and its reception. Thus, in explaining the acceptance of Adam Smith's teachings, he painted a picture of a community that had experienced a period of relative peace, one that had turned its attention to bettering its economic condition, one where there was more voluntary co-operation in the pursuit of enterprise and less government interference in local affairs: a community, in short, that was ready to hear Smith's message.[48] In a like manner, David Ricardo's analysis, which was used to support the repeal of the corn laws, was directed at, and promoted the interests of, the emerging capital-owning class.[49] The idea that social institutions and the phase of a country's development help to determine which theories are accepted had evident affinities with the historical school's claim that the stage of a nation's development determines which economic policies it should adopt.

A second unusual characteristic of the course was Mitchell's critical focus on the classical economists' 'theories of human nature'.[50] The ideas of Jeremy Bentham were singled out for intensive scrutiny. Bentham was an advocate of utilitarianism and the leader of the Philosophical Radicals, a group that used utilitarian analysis to press for all manner of reforms: political, legal, educational, even penal. Mitchell admired Bentham's zeal for reform, praising, for example, his criticisms in *Fragments on Government* of the jurist Sir William Blackstone's *Commentaries on the Laws of England*.[51] At the same time Mitchell was highly critical of Bentham's implicit theory of human nature which, based on hedonistic psychological foundations, portrayed humans as calculating creatures who constantly try to weigh the costs and benefits of their

[48] Mitchell, *Lecture Notes*, vol. 1, pp. 58–59.

[49] Ibid., pp. 178–79. Mitchell made the interesting point that, if one considers Ricardo's three classes, neither the landlords nor the workers read that much, which left only the capitalists as an audience!

[50] Mitchell originally called his course "History of Economic Thought and Economic Psychology". He described the goal of his course in a 1912 letter (that is, when he was first developing it) as follows: "What I am trying first is to study the character of the psychological assumptions present tacitly or explicitly in all economic writings and to see how far they are out of line with what we really know about the character of human activity". Lucy Sprague Mitchell, *Two Lives: The Story of Wesley Clair Mitchell and Myself* (New York: Simon and Schuster, 1952), p. 234; cf. p. 164.

[51] Whereas Blackstone extolled the virtues of the British constitution, Bentham saw it and the common law tradition as standing in the way of reform. Mitchell's antipathy towards Blackstone's views is evident in his statement that "Blackstone was a man who worshipped the British Constitution with an idolatry that no American lawyer can exceed when he contemplates our own fundamental instrument of government" Mitchell, *Lecture Notes*, vol. 1, p. 92. Mitchell had been a colleague of Charles Beard at the New School in 1919–22, so was familiar with, if not sympathetic towards, Beard's argument in *An Economic Interpretation of the Constitution of the United States* (New York: Macmillan, 1913) that the principal aim of the founders in creating the American Constitution was to protect the property interests of the upper classes.

actions. They were not always successful, but the associationist psychology that Bentham also embraced suggested that humans could be taught to make better associations: hence the possibilities for educational and penal reform.[52] Mitchell concluded that the Philosophical Radicals were successful in pushing through certain reforms not because of their theories of human nature (which were, in his estimation, wrong) but because their ideas matched up well with the sorts of changes that powerful, interested parties already favoured. Their ideas about human nature were, to Mitchell's chagrin, to persist in the writings of later economists.[53]

If Bentham provided a false theory of human nature, further damage was done by David Ricardo, who provided economists with their method of analysis. Mitchell praised Ricardo for his understanding of facts and reforming sympathies, but criticised his method of providing "abstract intellectual analyses" in which 'interests' were substituted for Bentham's 'pleasure and pain' in explaining the determination of distributive shares.[54] When this approach was copied by his less astute followers, who incautiously drew conclusions based on the simplified models, the science of political economy rightfully fell into disrepute. Mitchell lamented that Thomas Robert Malthus and other economists who were more empirically oriented were in general regarded as lesser economists when compared to Ricardo and his tradition.

Mitchell was likewise sceptical about the marginal revolution of the 1870s, in which the classical cost of production theories of value were replaced by a subjective theory of value. Despite changes in terminology (e.g., Alfred Marshall substituting 'gratification and sacrifice' for 'pleasure and pain'), Mitchell argued that the new theory was still based on the same, now discredited, hedonistic psychology of the classicals. Other missteps included transforming the theory of value into a theory of price formation, where only demand and supply schedules mattered, or into a pure logic of choice relating means to ends.[55] In both of these cases, the psychological foundations that Mitchell viewed as so essential were simply abandoned.

---

[52] The Panopticon, the novel prison that Bentham designed, was thus likened to a mill that would "grind rogues honest, and idle men industrious". Mitchell, *Lecture Notes*, vol. 1, p. 103.

[53] "It is because these notions about human nature have played so large a rôle in the building up of the kind of economic theory that we have had, and to a certain extent still have today, that it seems to me indispensable to dwell at such considerable length as I have done on Bentham's work". Mitchell, *Lecture Notes*, vol. 1, p. 112. Recall that it was Mitchell's teacher Veblen who provided the famous disparaging description of 'rational economic man': "The hedonistic conception of man is that of a lightning calculator of pleasures and pains, who oscillates like a homogeneous globule of desire of happiness under the impulse of stimuli that shift him about the area, but leave him intact". Thorstein Veblen, "Why Is Economics Not an Evolutionary Science?", *Quarterly Journal of Economics*, vol. 12, July 1898, p. 389.

[54] Mitchell, *Lecture Notes*, vol. 1, p. 153.

[55] Mitchell, *Lecture Notes*, vol. 2, chapter 19.

Mitchell, then, was a critic of 'rational economic man' and of Ricardo's theoretical approach, and he saw little difference between the classicals and the marginalists. In each of these opinions, he repeated interpretations that had been offered by Gustav Schmoller some fifty years earlier. And all this, we must assume, was duly noted by the young visitor from Vienna.

Mitchell only hinted at his preferred alternatives in the classroom but was more forthcoming in such publications as his opening essay for Rexford Tugwell's 1924 book, *The Trend of Economics*, a paper he would have written just around the time that Hayek was in New York.[56] As a first step, Mitchell recommended that the subjective value theory of the marginalists be replaced by the 'scientific psychology' of behaviourism. Once economists embraced such modern psychological underpinnings, the natural next step would be the study of institutions, because institutions affect behaviour: "'Institutions' is merely a convenient term for the more important among the widely prevalent, highly standardised social habits. And so it seems that the behaviourist viewpoint will make economic theory more and more a study of economic institutions".[57] The new focus of study would be, not the imaginary choices of rational economic man, but rather mass behaviour, which is best studied using sophisticated quantitative methods. In the future, economists would collaborate with natural scientists, psychologists, and engineers to build a better society. Behaviourism, the study of institutions, quantitative analysis, and co-operation among like-minded scientists—this was Mitchell's formula for a new, modern science of economics.

His encounter with the formidable and erudite Mitchell must have had a profound effect on Hayek.[58] We have seen that though Mitchell was a progressive reformer rather than a conservative imperialist, in his attacks on marginalist theory, his recommendation to study institutions, and his emphasis on the use of statistics, he would have reminded Hayek of the German historical school economists. It was doubtless as intriguing as it was disquieting to find that a group whose views had dominated German-speaking countries since the 1880s, but which had begun to go into eclipse, were not just still influ-

[56] Mitchell, "The Prospects of Economics", in *The Trend of Economics*, ed. Rexford Tugwell (New York: A. A. Knopf, 1924), pp. 3–34. The idea for the book was born at a session at the American Economic Association meetings in December 1922 in which Tugwell proposed that a number of economists write papers assessing the discipline. With a few exceptions, the resulting volume reads like an institutionalist manifesto.

[57] Ibid., p. 25.

[58] Among the earliest documents in the Hayek collection are his correspondence with Mitchell; see the Hayek papers, box 38, folder 28, Hoover Institution Archives. Stephen Kresge suggests that Hayek's concern with the implications of time in economic analysis, and possibly also the idea that economics studies complex phenomena, may have come from his interactions with Mitchell. See his introduction to F. A. Hayek, *Good Money, Part I: The New World*, ed. Stephen Kresge, vol. 5 (1999) of *The Collected Works of F. A. Hayek*, pp. 7–8.

encing ideas but indeed were apparently viewed as *avant-garde* in the United States.[59] Similarly, though Mitchell had no sympathy for the Marxism that underlay Neurath's positions, his advocacy of behaviourism (which could be viewed as the psychological analogue of physicalism) and his insistence on the scientific management of society were both reminiscent of arguments that had been made by that Vienna Circle philosopher. What would have been evident to Hayek, then, was that though men like Neurath, Mitchell, and the German historical school economists had very different political views and agendas, they all shared similar views about methods and about the rôle of science in shaping the society to come.[60]

We have yet to mention another way in which the trip to the United States may have affected Hayek. He would later say in interviews that his attraction to British liberalism was formed while he was in America, when during 'free evenings' he would read on his own:

> It was then that I discovered my sympathy with the British approach, a country I did not yet know but whose literature increasingly captivated me. It was this experience which, before I had ever set foot on English soil, converted me to a thoroughly English view on moral and political matters, which at once made me feel at home when I later first visited England three and a half years later. . . . In the sense of that Gladstonian liberalism, I am much more English than the English.[61]

Though there is no direct evidence, it is plausible that it was Mitchell's class that prompted Hayek to begin learning more about 'the British approach'. Mitchell had an extensive knowledge of British history—economic, political, social, even technological—and because of his emphasis on Bentham, Ri-

[59] Hence the first four entries in "The American Phase" of Hayek's outline are to the German influence, Pragmatism, Behaviourism, and Institutionalism. Hayek my have been expressing his reaction to all this when he wrote in one of his notes for his project, "If it does no more than to show how stale is all the current talk which is viewed as modern or progressive, how little there is original or radical in these ideas which were old to our grandfathers but are still rediscovered and rehashed as the latest novelties". Notes, Hayek papers, box 107, folder 17, Hoover Institution Archives.

[60] Nor was he alone in drawing such comparisons: Mitchell himself said of John R. Commons that his "contribution belongs to the institutional type of economics, the type represented in Germany by Sombart, in England by Mr. and Mrs. Webb, in America by Veblen and many of the younger men". Wesley Clair Mitchell, "Commons on the Legal Foundations of Capitalism", *American Economic Review*, vol. 14, June 1924, p. 253. Sombart at the time was viewed as a representative (one of the last) of the historical school. The Webbs will be introduced below.

[61] F. A. Hayek, in W. W. Bartley III, "Inductive Base", p. 64. Bartley was to have been Hayek's official biographer, but he died, the job unfinished, in 1990. Bartley playfully titled his unpublished set of interviews of Hayek the 'Inductive Base' because they were the 'facts' on which the biography would be built.

cardo, and their British followers, that knowledge was amply demonstrated in the course. His thorough coverage of Bentham's and others' theories of human nature, and his remarks on then current alternatives to association-ist psychology, doubtless would also have fascinated Hayek, who had train-ing in psychology. Because Hayek had also trained as a lawyer, Mitchell's re-marks on Blackstone and on British legal history would have further piqued his interest. Finally, Mitchell's interpretation of, and praise for, John Stuart Mill as a reform-minded socialist who had shown that questions of distribu-tion were subject to human control, may well have started Hayek on his long, and ultimately highly ambivalent, relationship with ideas of Mill and Harriet Taylor.[62] It was in any event an interpretation, having been popularised by Sidney Webb and the Fabian socialists, that was widely shared in Britain, and therefore one which Hayek would very soon be hearing again.[63]

We have focused here on Hayek's important encounter with Mitchell. But the idea that science could and should be used to transform society, some-times radically, was in fact ubiquitous in the States (as elsewhere) and gaining adherents. Perhaps the most notable mass movement carried the label 'Tech-nocracy', also mentioned by Hayek in his outline. Founded and promoted by the American engineer Howard Scott (1890–1970) following World War I, the Technocracy movement gained popularity in the 1920s and especially during the depression years of the 1930s. Technocracy was promoted by its advocates as the appropriate socioeconomic system in the new world of abun-dance that had replaced the old world of scarcity. Technological advances bring with them vast increases in productive efficiency, but the old economic system, based on scarcity, creates competition among workers and results in a falling standard of living. Through scientific management the technocratic state would guarantee that the benefits of technology would be shared by all. At its height there were Technocracy 'sections' in many American cities—and

[62] Mitchell referred to Mill as a "great emancipator", noting that he was viewed as "a great spiritual leader . . . who stood for all that was best and finest in the moral aspirations of those who pinned their faith on the use of human intelligence as a means for bettering the doubtful lot of mankind". Mitchell, *Lecture Notes*, vol. 1, pp. 183, 240. Cf. Mitchell, *Types of Economic Theory*, vol. 1, p. 600: "Those who think of Mill merely as a political economist usually neglect Mill the socialist and enlarge upon technical aspects of his work that he valued less than his discovery that institutional arrangements are subject to social control".

[63] E.g., "The publication of John Stuart Mill's 'Political Economy' in 1848 marks conveniently the boundary of the old individualist economics. Every edition of Mill's book became more and more socialistic. After his death the world learnt the personal history, penned by his own hand, of his development from a mere political democrat to a convinced Socialist". Sidney Webb, "Historic", in *Fabian Essays in Socialism*, ed. George Bernard Shaw (Garden City, NY: Doubleday, [1889] 1961), p. 80. Similar sentiments may be found in, for example, L. T. Hobhouse, *Liberal-ism* [1906], reprinted in *Liberalism and Other Writings*, ed. James Meadowcroft (Cambridge: Cam-bridge University Press, 1994), pp. 51–55; Harold Laski, *The Rise of Liberalism: The Philosophy of a Business Civilisation* (New York: Harper and Brothers, 1936), p. 293.

sometimes multiple sections, because membership in each was capped at fifty individuals.[64]

Déjà Vu: Hayek Comes to London

When Hayek came to London he felt immediately at home in British society, but he also realised that the Liberal England that he had read about in New York had nearly vanished.[65] In its place was a new and widely shared (at least among the intelligentsia) vision, one that anticipated the creation, with the assistance of science, of a planned socialist society.

It is no small irony that Hayek should win a position at the LSE, for it had been founded in 1895 by Fabian socialists. The Fabians believed in 'socialism of the ballot box', that once the masses had been educated to the benefits of socialism, their proposed reforms would easily be put into place through the electoral process. Sidney Webb was so convinced that the truth of socialism would win out that he imposed no ideological litmus tests on those hired to teach at the LSE. He was, however, insistent that (as the LSE prospectus stated) the "special aim" of the School would be "the study and investigation of the concrete facts of industrial life", a view that gave 'facts' pride of place over 'theory' in the investigation of social phenomena.[66] In short, Sidney Webb was both a positivist and a socialist.

That socialism was popular should come as no surprise. The economic and political situation was bleak when Hayek arrived in London in the fall of 1931. The Great Depression was already underway and, induced by a financial crisis that afflicted all of Europe, England had that summer abandoned the gold standard. The Labour government collapsed in September, and the new coalition government soon thereafter imposed a protective tariff.[67] The intensity and duration of the Great Depression after the miserable performance of the British economy in the 1920s provided powerful and widely persuasive new economic arguments against capitalism.

---

[64] The similarities between Technocracy and energetics movements in Germany and elsewhere is noted by Hayek in the "Scientism" essay, this volume, p. 159, note 7.

[65] In another unpublished interview, Hayek concluded his description of how he quickly felt himself becoming English after arriving in London with the words, "but the tragedy of it is, I became a nineteenth century Englishman". F. A. Hayek, in W. W. Bartley III, "Interview, Summer 1984, at St. Blasien". From his book outline it appears that Hayek was planning to trace the changes that took place in Britain to "Tory Socialism", which refers to the reform-minded activism associated with the Conservative Prime Minister Benjamin Disraeli, as well as to the nearly contemporaneous emergence of evolutionary thought, Fabian socialism, and English variants of positivism in the mid-to-late nineteenth century.

[66] For more on this see Ralf Dahrendorf, *LSE: A History of the London School of Economics and Political Science, 1895–1995* (Oxford: Oxford University Press, 1995), p. 20.

[67] Hence the rationale for a chapter entitled "The End of Free Trade" in Hayek's outline.

Given that virtually all of the intelligentsia agreed that a liberal free market society no longer seemed viable, the logical next question was, what would replace it? Though advocates of full-fledged communism and of fascism were to be found, those who occupied the broad middle ground favoured some form of socialist planning. In the phrase that was then so often employed, socialist planning provided a 'middle way' between a failed capitalism and totalitarianisms of the left and right.

Hayek started publicly to attack these ideas in his inaugural lecture, "The Trend of Economic Thinking", which he delivered on March 1, 1933, soon after Adolf Hitler had become Chancellor of Germany.[68] He began his talk by lamenting the current low state of public confidence in the writings of economists. It is of considerable interest that he linked this development to the pernicious influence of the German historical school economists, whose attacks on theory sixty years earlier had undermined confidence that anyone could gain a theoretical understanding of the complex workings of the economic system. This had made it much easier for socialists to put forward bold, but in Hayek's view utopian, plans for a new social order. In his first public address in England, then, Hayek began linking the methodological views of the German historical school economists to the emergence of socialism.

He added another element to the argument when, shortly after delivering the lecture, he sent a memo to the director of the LSE, William Beveridge, in which he discussed the origins of Naziism in Germany. Here Hayek defended the view that, in terms of intervention in the economy and restrictions on individual liberty, National Socialism had much more in common with socialism than either one had with liberalism.[69] This directly opposed the then common view that fascism was the last dying gasp of a failed capitalist system.[70]

In the mid-1930s Hayek continued his attack on socialism with the publication of *Collectivist Economic Planning*.[71] The book was aimed at academic econo-

---

[68] F. A. Hayek, "The Trend of Economic Thinking", in *The Trend of Economic Thinking*, W. W. Bartley III and Stephen Kresge, eds, vol. 3 (1991) of *The Collected Works of F. A. Hayek*, pp. 17–34. It is no accident that Hayek's title echoes that of Rexford Tugwell's 1924 edited book, *The Trend of Economics*.

[69] In the opening paragraph of the memo we find these words: "The persecution of the Marxists, and of democrats in general, tends to obscure the fundamental fact that National Socialism is a genuine socialist movement, whose leading ideas are the final fruit of the anti-liberal tendencies which have been steadily gaining ground in Germany since the later part of the Bismarckian era, and which led the majority of the German intelligentsia first to 'socialism of the chair' and later to Marxism in its social-democratic or communist form". The memo to Beveridge is reproduced in F. A. Hayek, *The Road to Serfdom: Text and Documents*, pp. 245–48. The editor's introduction for the volume, pp. 4–5, provides more background on the Beveridge memo.

[70] See, e.g., Harold Laski, *The Rise of Liberalism*, p. 283, "Fascism, in short, emerges as the institutional technique of capitalism in its phase of contraction".

[71] Hayek, ed. *Collectivist Economic Planning*. Hayek's two essays in the book are reprinted in F. A. Hayek, *Socialism and War*, chapters 1 and 2.

mists and soon provoked a response.[72] But as the decade progressed it became clear that an even more important foe than the socialists of the academy was emerging: this was the popular enthusiasm for planning that had gripped the nation. This posed a more formidable threat because advocates for planning could be found all across the political spectrum.[73]

There is plentiful evidence for Hayek's thesis that the 'planning mentality' was repeatedly linked to the scientistic impulse in inter-war Britain. For some, like Sidney and Beatrice Webb, the model of how science was to be pursued was provided by the Soviet Union. Praising the "Cult of Science" that they found when they visited there, the Webbs reported that

> the administrators in the Moscow Kremlin genuinely believe in their professed faith in science. No vested interests hinder them from basing their decisions and their policy on the best science they can obtain. . . . The whole community is eager for new knowledge.[74]

The Webbs were not unique in their enthusiasm for the Soviet model. In July 1931 the International Congress of the History of Science and Technology was held at the Science Museum in London. Organised by British academics Lancelot Hogben and Joseph Needham, it was attended by a Soviet delegation led by Nikolai Bukharin. The program became a showcase for Soviet science and the Marxist interpretation of the history of science.

The final ingredient—the active promotion of the application of methods that had succeeded in the natural sciences to the more backwards social sciences—was provided by an assortment of British natural scientists whom Hayek would dub the 'men of science'.[75] One of their principal claims was that science could no longer be effectively harnessed to work for the social

---

[72] E.g., Oskar Lange, "On the Economic Theory of Socialism", in *On the Economic Theory of Socialism*, ed. Benjamin E. Lippincott (Minneapolis: University of Minnesota Press, 1938; reprinted, New York: McGraw Hill, 1956), pp. 57–143. Lange's piece was originally published in two parts in the journal *Review of Economic Studies* in 1936 and 1937.

[73] The ubiquity of the call for planning is emphasised in Arthur Marwick, "Middle Opinion in the Thirties: Planning, Progress and Political 'Agreement'", *English Historical Review*, vol. 79, April 1964, pp. 285–98.

[74] Sidney and Beatrice Webb, *Soviet Communism: A New Civilisation*, 2nd ed. (London: Longmans, Green, 1937), p. 1133.

[75] As Hayek would later write to Michael Polanyi, "I attach very great importance to these pseudo-scientific arguments on social organisation being effectively met and I am getting more and more alarmed by the effect of the propaganda of the Haldanes, Hogbens, Needhams, etc., etc". Letter, F. A. Hayek to Michael Polanyi, July 1, 1941, Michael Polanyi papers, box 4, folder 7, Special Collections Research Center, University of Chicago Library. For more on the 'men of science' see Gary Werskey, *The Visible College: The Collective Biography of British Scientific Socialists of the 1930s* (New York: Holt, Rinehart and Winston, 1978), Caldwell, *Hayek's Challenge*, pp. 232–41, and also this introduction, note 14.

good in a mature capitalist society in which monopolistic firms suppressed inventions to keep profits high and the cyclical crises of capitalism led to under-investment in new research and technology. Were science itself managed and planned, however, such distorting effects of late capitalism could be avoided.

Hayek began focusing on the scientism of his socialist opponents in his 1936 review of the Webbs' book on the Soviet Union, writing that it is "probably true that Soviet Communism approaches more closely than anything we have yet seen to that synthetic, scientific civilisation which appealed to the peculiar brand of late nineteenth-century rationalism of which the authors are among the most distinguished exponents".[76] By 1939, in the second version of "Freedom and the Economic System", he would write, "It would be interesting, but it is not possible within the space available, to show how this belief [i.e., the demand for planning] is largely due to the intrusion into the discussion of social problems of the pre-conceptions of the pure scientist and the engineer, which have dominated the outlook of the educated man during the past hundred years".[77] This would finally become the dominating theme of his Abuse of Reason project.

Hayek's experience, then, was that though (as the historical school economists had always insisted!) each nation had its own unique historical evolution, certain recurrent themes were evident in the thought of the intelligentsia and of the scientific elite of western Europe, Britain, and the United States during the inter-war years, themes that had begun to filter into public discourse at large. A key assumption was that the failures of old-style liberalism were irreversible: that in a world of large scale production, cartels, and monopoly capitalism, one could no longer depend on the forces of competition to constrain the power of big business; that in a world of cyclical crises of enduring length, the notion of self-stabilising market forces seemed demonstrably false. This was everywhere taken to imply that planning of some sort, with proposals ranging from piecemeal intervention to full-fledged nationalisation to the Technocratic vision, was necessary to rationalise production and distribution decisions in the new age of plenty. It was next observed that our knowledge of social processes and phenomena had lagged far behind the sorts of knowledge produced in the natural sciences, with blame again placed (especially by the natural scientists of Britain) at capitalism's door. In the new epoch that was at hand, however, scientists and engineers would play an integral rôle,

---

[76] F. A. Hayek, "A 'Scientific' Civilisation: The Webbs on Soviet Communism", *Times* (London), Sunday, January 5, 1936, p. 11. Hayek's review is reprinted in Hayek, *Socialism and War*, pp. 239–42.

[77] Hayek, "Freedom and the Economic System", p. 197.

both in facilitating the transition to the new planned society and in providing the expertise to make it all work. Finally, the communist and fascist 'experiments' that had taken place in Russia and on the continent coupled with the depth and intensity of the Great Depression had created a dramatic sense of urgency.

It was evident that people like Neurath, the Webbs, and Mitchell differed rather radically from one another politically, spanning the spectrum from Marxism to Fabian socialism to American progressivism. That they could so differ about politics but still all agree that planning was the best hope for constructing a world in which freedom and prosperity could coexist was Hayek's whole point. No matter where they started from or where they hoped to go, 'planning for freedom' and 'freedom under planning' were the slogans of progressive intellectuals everywhere.[78]

From Hayek's perspective, the idea that individual freedom was compatible with a fully planned society was logically flawed. The notion that science itself could be planned, and that such a science would permit the rationalisation of society, was further evidence of the hubris of reason. Hayek's project became to show how such ideas got started and how they had become so well accepted everywhere.

We do not know when Hayek finally conceived the plan to trace the dual origins of socialism and scientism back to the writings of Saint-Simon. He justified his starting point in the notes he made for the project as follows: "The reason why I begin so late is that though all these attitudes can already be found in the eighteenth century, they are not yet systematised or, for that reason, systematically developed".[79] That Saint-Simon was the logical starting point would have been reinforced by writers like Emile Durkheim (whom rather surprisingly he does not cite), who had argued that Saint-Simon, rather than Comte, was the true father of positivism and also a founder of modern socialism.[80] Elie Halévy, whom he does cite, might also be mentioned: in his

---

[78] Thus Barbara Wootton's book, offered in reply to Hayek's *The Road to Serfdom*, would carry the title *Freedom under Planning* (Chapel Hill: University of North Carolina Press, 1945). For his part, Wesley Clair Mitchell served on Roosevelt's National Planning Board (later called the National Resources Board). Writing in the early 1950s, his wife would note that Mitchell "had faith in the principle of 'planning' provided it was based on factual knowledge of the situations planned for and of the consequences that would result in other related situations". Mitchell, *Two Lives*, p. 367.

[79] Notes, Hayek papers, box 107, folder 17, Hoover Institution Archives.

[80] See Emile Durkheim, *Socialism and Saint-Simon*, ed. Alvin Gouldner, translated by Charlotte Sattler (Yellow Springs, OH: Antioch Press, 1958), pp. 104–5. The latter is a translation of lectures given by Durkheim and first published in 1928 as *Le socialisme*, edited by Marcel Mauss. Hayek also did not cite Max Weber, though he clearly made use of the latter's criticisms of historicism in chapter 7. This brings to mind the barb, attributed to the Popperian philosopher, Hayek biographer, and first General Editor of *The Collected Works of F. A. Hayek* Bill Bartley,

two masterful essays on the economic doctrines of Saint-Simon and the Saint-Simonians that great French historian concluded that their ideas are still influential today, and not just among socialists.[81] As he began examining in depth the writings of men like Condorcet, Saint-Simon, and Comte, Hayek saw that they, like he, lived in extraordinary times, and that many of their responses rather eerily mimicked those of others in his own day. The germ of a book was born, one that he would tell his friend Fritz Machlup about a few days before the start of the war.

Hayek's chief purpose in undertaking the Abuse and Decline of Reason project was to show the origins of ideas that he thought were leading us astray and to criticise them.[82] But in the longer run, it is clear that criticism was not his only goal; he ultimately sought also to offer an alternative to the planned society. In his original formulation for his book, the hubris of reason was to be contrasted to the humility of individualism. By 1945 he would contrast the 'false' individualism of the French enlightenment philosophers with the 'true' individualism of such Scottish enlightenment figures as Adam Ferguson, Josiah Tucker, David Hume, and Adam Smith. In his later work, the writings of these scholars (together with those of such disparate thinkers as Edmund Burke, Alexis de Tocqueville, and Lord Acton) would provide the intellectual underpinnings of his effort to create a liberal philosophy for the twentieth century and beyond.

How Well Have Hayek's Ideas Stood Up?

. . . describing the spirit of an epoch by the examples of particular persons[83]

Thus far we have traced the probable origins of Hayek's ideas, ideas that, when seen within the context of his times, appear both understandable and

---

that Hayek was less than generous to his predecessors, and Popper less than generous to his followers.

[81] Elie Halévy, L'ère des tyrannies: Etudes sur le socialisme et la guerre (Paris: Librarie Gallimard, 1938), translated as The Era of Tyrannies, translated by R. K. Webb (New York: New York University Press, 1965), pp. 99–104. Hayek published a translation of a discussion piece by Halévy in the same issue of Economica that the first instalment of his own "Counter-Revolution" article appeared. There Halévy argued, as Hayek would, that "Socialism, in its original form, is neither liberal nor democratic, but stands for an organised and hierarchical society. This is especially true of Saint-Simonian Socialism". See Elie Halévy, "The Era of Tyrannies", translated by May Wallas, Economica, n.s., vol. 8, February 1941, pp. 77–93.

[82] As he himself put it in the penultimate sentence of his final chapter, "it is our special duty to recognise the currents of thought which still operate in public opinion, to examine their significance, and, if necessary, to refute them". See chapter 17, p. 304.

[83] Notes, Hayek papers, box 107, folder 17, Hoover Institution Archives.

reasonable. But other questions may be raised about his theses. In particular, we will inquire here about the adequacy of his historical account, his changing definition of 'scientism', and finally, the extent to which his claims have any continuing resonance today.

Hayek's Historical Account

Let us begin with "Counter-Revolution", and consider only the sections he actually completed, that is, his historical treatment of the joint appearance of scientism and socialism in the writings of Saint-Simon and his followers. It is evident, in the first instance, that Hayek did a meticulous job in his research. His footnotes indicate that he read nearly everything that was then available in German, English, and French about Saint-Simon, Comte, and their followers, including among his primary sources the forty volumes that comprise the collected works of Saint-Simon and Barthélemy Prosper Enfantin, and the multiple volumes of Comte's two major works, the *Cours de philosophie positive* and the *Système de politique positive*.[84] He appears to have been relentless in trying to track down sources. Early on in the project he wrote to William Rappard, imploring him to send him some titles from Switzerland, and later he would complain to Machlup about not being able to get all the books that he needed.[85] His determination in this regard is demonstrated by a list (discovered among his papers relating to the project) of twenty-five books and two

[84] *Oeuvres de Saint-Simon et d'Enfantin* (Paris: E. Dentu, 1865–78); Auguste Comte, *Cours de philosophie positive*, 6 vols. (Paris: Bachelier, 1830–42); *Système de politique positive*, 4 vols. (Paris: L. Mathias, 1851–54). As will be evident in his recounting of their content, it is a testimony to Hayek's scholarly self-discipline and stamina that he was actually capable of working through these volumes. His acute observation at the end of chapter 16, p. 281, that, "Why this influence of Comte should so frequently have been much more effective in an indirect manner, those who have attempted to study his work will have no difficulty in understanding", reveals considerable self-restraint. It is perhaps understandable, too, that after having plowed through the French writers Hayek would find the next step too much to take: in an interview he said he stopped working on the historical account because "the next historical chapter would have had to deal with Hegel and Marx, and I couldn't stand then once more diving into that dreadful stuff". F. A. Hayek, "Nobel Prize-Winning Economist", ed. Armen Alchian. Transcript of an interview conducted in 1978 under the auspices of the Oral History Program, University Library, UCLA, 1983. Oral History transcript no. 300/224, Department of Special Collections, Charles E. Young Research Library, UCLA, p. 279. For more on his reaction to Hegel, see his comments in chapter 17, p. 290.
[85] Letter, Hayek to Rappard, December 12, 1940, William Rappard papers, J. I. 149, 1977/ 135, box 23, Swiss Federal Archive, Bern; Letters, Hayek to Machlup, April 7, 1941, and October 19, 1941, Machlup papers, box 43, folder 15, Hoover Institution Archives. The October 19, 1941, letter is reproduced in the appendix to this volume.

journals that was headed, "All these works seem not to be in the libraries of London or Cambridge".

What about the results of his efforts? At least one very discriminating contemporary reader was generous with his praise. The eminent economic theorist and historian of thought Jacob Viner wrote to Hayek as follows, "I have just finished reading your 'The Counter-Revolution of Science' and want to tell you how much I enjoyed it. Most of the contents were wholly new to me, and you have handled a great mass of difficult material in masterly manner".[86] Viner went on to ask for an offprint to give to a colleague who was working on the history of ideas: "I am lending him my copy to read, but he would very much like one to keep".[87]

It is also probably appropriate to point out that Hayek's decision to begin his account with Saint-Simon would have made sense to readers of his own day, if only because of the startling number of similarities between the days of Saint-Simon and Comte and those of their own.[88] The huge economic, social, political, juridical, and cultural transformations that the French Revolution, Napoleonic Empire, and the Restoration had produced created a generation longing for order and stability. World War I, the communist and fascist revolutions, and the Great Depression had had a similar effect on Hayek's own generation. In search of a new way forward, advocates of liberalism and of a nascent socialism (both of whom opposed the royalist and Catholic reactions) had contended with each other in France and elsewhere in the 1820s and 1830s, just as liberals like Hayek sought to compete with the socialists of his day to provide a path that would avoid the horrors of communism and fascism. In both periods there existed a distinct 'spirit of the age', the widespread feeling that these were momentous times, that historic changes in society were in the offing.[89] There were other more specific similarities.[90] Saint-Simon's proposal for an encyclopedia of scientific knowledge anticipated Otto

---

[86] Letter, Jacob Viner to F. A. Hayek, December 7, 1941, Jacob Viner papers, box 13, folder 26, Public Policy Papers, Department of Rare Books and Special Collections, Princeton University Library, Princeton, NJ.

[87] Ibid.

[88] As Harold Laski, *The Rise of Liberalism*, p. 282, put it: "To understand our own epoch, in short, we must think ourselves back either to the epoch of the Reformation or to the period of the French Revolution".

[89] The 'Spirit of the Age' was the title of a collection of essays written by John Stuart Mill for the *Examiner* in 1831. These were reprinted as John Stuart Mill, *The Spirit of the Age* (Chicago: University of Chicago Press, 1942), and Hayek provided an introductory essay for the book, titled "John Stuart Mill at the Age of Twenty-Five". Hayek uses the phrase at the beginning of chapter 9 of the "Scientism" essay, where he says that the demand for the conscious control of social processes "expresses perhaps more clearly than any of its other clichés the peculiar spirit of the age". See this volume, p. 149.

[90] See chapter 12, p. 195.

Neurath's plan for an 'encyclopedia of unified science'. The Saint-Simonian theory of art, which Léon Halévy (Elie Halévy's grandfather!) among others had developed, were echoed in the Soviet realism of Lenin and Stalin. Hayek even claimed to have seen certain similarities in attitude when he compared the words and the personal descriptions of the earlier writers against the writings and behaviour of some of his peers.[91]

Hayek sought to write a very specific type of historical account. His goal was to locate the origins of certain fundamental ideas and ultimately to make an argument about the effects of these ideas on later generations. His was history with a point. He did not provide, nor did he aim to provide, what might be called a 'thick' historical description of the periods he covered.[92] Hayek's illustrative approach to history may not be to everyone's taste, though some, at least, have been prepared to defend it, and it was in any event a common approach among economists writing about the history of ideas.[93]

In his historical reconstruction, Hayek accordingly concentrated on certain key episodes that best illustrated his themes. In both its broad outlines—for example, the mutual rise of socialism and positivism in French writings[94]—as well as in his more specific claims, what he wrote was certainly accurate, usually uncontroversial, and always well documented. At times he broke new ground, as with his suggestion that the impact of the ideas of the Saint-Simonians on the Young Hegelians was an under-examined area that was ripe for further study.[95]

But it is also evident that, when one undertakes this sort of history, it is inev-

[91] "The Saint-Simonians seemed to me such a beautiful illustration of the kind of attitude I found in the Vienna Circle . . . the similarity between Carnap and some of these people was amazing". F. A. Hayek, in an unpublished interview by W. W. Bartley III, Freiburg, March 28, 1984. In the unpublished interview with Bartley dated "Summer 1984, at St. Blasien", Hayek said that J. D. Bernal "became to me representative of a new view, which I tried to analyse in 'The Counter-Revolution of Science', and that was so dominating" in Cambridge.

[92] Thus in his notes Hayek stated, "We are concerned entirely with the history of ideas . . . the men only as representative figures in whose ideas manifest themselves but shall neither attempt to discuss systems of thought of individuals nor do we mean to assert that ideas operated only through them". Notes, Hayek papers, box 107, folder 17, Hoover Institution Archives.

[93] For a defence of the approach, see, e.g., R. K. Webb, the translator of Elie Halévy's The Era of Tyrannies, who said in his preface to the book, p. xiii, that "Halévy's work is conclusive justification for the centrality of thesis and argument in historical writing". Hayek's approach shared common elements with those of Schmoller and Mitchell in their explanations of the history of their discipline, and with that of Sidney Webb when he traced the rise of British socialism. Hayek probably viewed his own account as an antidote to them.

[94] This was a view that had been established, for example, by Durkheim in his 1928 lectures. See Durkheim, Socialism and Saint-Simon.

[95] More work has since been done on this topic; see, e.g., Warren Breckman, Marx, the Young Hegelians, and the Origins of Radical Social Theory: Dethroning the Self (Cambridge: Cambridge University Press, 1999), especially chapters 4 and 5. In general, since then, considerably more has been discovered and written about Karl Marx.

itable that certain interpretations though not technically incorrect will end up being somewhat one-sided when considered in the light of more full-blown historical accounts. For example, in an effort to show the origins of the scientistic prejudice in the works of Saint-Simon, the Saint-Simonians, and Comte, Hayek glosses over the intense rivalry that existed between Comte and the Saint-Simonians in the late 1820s, mentioning only in passing their competing lectures of 1828 and 1829. This fascinating and complex episode may help to explain (at least in part) the latter group's strange decision to make themselves over into a religious cult, as well as some of the new directions that Comte took in his later work.[96] The rivalry also helps to explain why the Saint-Simonians specifically sought to attract students from the *Ecole Polytechnique*, who were seen by them as falling under the influence of Comte, which was an important part of Hayek's story.

In a like manner, the Marquis de Condorcet is chiefly portrayed as the quintessential enlightenment philosopher in whose final book, the *Esquisse*, "the unbounded optimism of the age found its last and greatest expression".[97] Now it is certainly true that Condorcet embraced what was, as one historian put it, "in effect, a technocratic creed: the creed of men confident in their expertise, easy in the tradition of power, convinced that the problems of politics are susceptible of rational answers and systematic solutions", and that he was accordingly viewed as a precursor by both Saint-Simon and Comte.[98] But it is equally evident that Condorcet differed from them in many fundamental ways.[99] Hayek was careful to distinguish the early from the late Condorcet in his own account, and also to suggest that later writers often misinterpreted him, so he was not unfair in his portrayal. Still, one would never guess from it that Condorcet had also influenced the Ideologues, or that his widowed spouse would run a salon that attracted many French liberals, or that she in 1798 would provide the French translation of Adam Smith's *The Theory of Moral Sentiments*.

In short, Hayek does not always provide the full historical background that lies behind the episodes he discusses, and some of the figures he portrays come across as somewhat one-dimensional. One reason for this might be that the essays began as journal articles, published in a journal of which Hayek was

[96] For a thorough exploration of the episode, see Mary Pickering, "Auguste Comte and the Saint-Simonians", *French Historical Studies*, vol. 18, Spring 1993, pp. 211–36.

[97] Hayek, this volume, chapter 11, p. 174.

[98] Keith Michael Baker, Condorcet: From *Natural Philosophy to Social Mathematics* (Chicago: University of Chicago Press, 1975), p. 57.

[99] Throughout his book Baker portrays Condorcet as a theorist of liberal democracy. In chapter 6 he also plausibly suggests that the *Esquisse*, completed by Condorcet in 1793 but amended while he was in hiding from the Revolutionary authorities in the early months of 1794, may well have been an expression of a desperate man's hope for the future rather than a prediction of what was to come, no matter how the piece may have been interpreted by later generations.

the editor: under the circumstances, it would have taken considerable arrogance to enlarge them much beyond their current size. But more fundamentally, Hayek's goal was to tell a story about the origins of certain specific ideas. Given that goal, his account as it stands is a coherent and, indeed, a compelling one.

One final aspect of Hayek's historical narrative must be addressed. It is one thing to point out the origins of certain ideas, or to note similarities between the ideas of different men who are separated in time. It is quite another to speak of influence. Sometimes lines of influence are not so difficult to establish: for example, the influence of positivism and of the Saint-Simonians on John Stuart Mill had been identified by Mill himself in his *Autobiography*, so Hayek made use of this in his narrative. But in other circumstances it is difficult, if not impossible, to do.

Hayek was fully aware of the problem. He recognised, for example, that though it might be easy enough to find similarities between the ideas of Auguste Comte and Friedrich Hegel, and to document the scholarly consensus regarding the existence of such similarities, establishing whether either one had actually influenced the other was problematical.[100] This is why Hayek stated at the end of his chapter "Comte and His Successors" that "The tracing of influences is the most treacherous ground in the history of thought".[101] Any competent intellectual historian would immediately assent, and indeed, one may rightly wonder whether his recognition of this difficulty may have been another reason why Hayek decided not to carry on with his historical account.[102]

Hayek's Definition of Scientism

Moving to the "Scientism" essay, recall that Hayek characterised scientism as the unthinking application of the methods of the natural sciences in areas where they did not apply. He then introduced the terms objectivism, collectivism, and historicism to identify certain representative features of 'the scientistic prejudice'. Such categories were sufficiently broad to encompass all the views that he disdained, from physicalism in philosophy to behaviourism

---

[100] Thus in chapter 17, notes 8–16, Hayek lists the many scholars who had commented on similarities in their views, but he also notes that "there would be about as much justification for thinking that Hegel might have been influenced by Comte, as that Comte was influenced by Hegel". See also his qualifications at the beginning of chapter 15 on the "Saint-Simonian Influence".

[101] This volume, p. 277. He went on to admit that he had "much sinned against the canons of caution".

[102] Hayek nowhere offers this as a reason. The reasons he did offer included wanting to work on something entirely new and scientific (*The Sensory Order*) after having completed *The Road to Serfdom*, and, as we have noted earlier, his not wanting to have to read systematically Marx and Hegel. For more on this, see Caldwell, *Hayek's Challenge*, pp. 257–59.

in psychology, from German historicism to the positing of a 'collective mind'. And it is no coincidence, of course, that the opposite of these terms—which taken together implies a subjectivist, individualist, and theoretical approach to the social sciences—precisely characterises the approach long recommended by the Austrian school economists.

The claim that there are fundamental differences in the appropriate methods for studying natural versus social phenomena has a venerable history.[103] Given that one of the groups that most agitated him were the British 'men of science' who were repeatedly insisting in the public forum on the necessity of applying (natural) scientific methods to the problems of society, it is understandable that Hayek should make recourse to it. Yet it was this very claim that Hayek would soon modify. It appears that he did so in response to criticism he received from a philosopher from Vienna. The philosopher was not, as one might first guess, Otto Neurath, but Karl Popper.

Popper and Hayek had met before war, when Popper gave a presentation of an early version of his *The Poverty of Historicism* in Hayek's seminar at the LSE.[104] Popper spent the war in New Zealand, and the two men carried on an active correspondence throughout the hostilities. Hayek subsequently aided Popper in a number of ways: he published *The Poverty of Historicism* in three parts in the journal *Economica*, he helped find a publisher for Popper's *The Open Society and Its Enemies*, and he helped to get Popper an invitation to join the Philosophy Department at the LSE after the war.[105]

Popper discussed Hayek's "Scientism" essay in *The Poverty of Historicism* in a section titled "The Unity of Method". He argued there that all real sciences follow the same method, and that this method (which Popper described as hypothetical, deductive, and controlled by attempts to falsify proposed theories) was in fact similar to the one that Hayek had defended as the proper method for the social sciences.[106] On this reading, what Hayek had described as 'scientism' was not really the method of the natural sciences, but rather the

---

[103] That Hayek appears to have endorsed the distinction, and his insistence on the central rôle of interpretation in the social sciences, has provided grist for many, often conflicting, interpretations of the essay. Suffice it to say that "Scientism" has been variously interpreted as revealing that Hayek was a critical realist, a hermeneutician, and a post-modernist. Such readings may tell us more about the problems that plague the interpretative enterprise than they do about Hayek's actual views. I address some of this literature in Appendix D of *Hayek's Challenge*.

[104] Karl Popper, *The Poverty of Historicism*, 2nd ed. (London: Routledge, 1957).

[105] Karl Popper, *The Open Society and Its Enemies* (London: Routledge, 1945).

[106] Popper, *The Poverty of Historicism*, pp. 130–43. Whether this claim is true or not, and the larger question of the compatibility of Popper's and Hayek's methodological pronouncements, are subjects that have given rise to considerable discussion and debate. See for example Bruce Caldwell, "Hayek the Falsificationist? A Refutation", *Research in the History of Economic Thought and Methodology*, vol. 10, 1992, pp. 1–15; Terence Hutchison, "Hayek and 'Modern Austrian' Methodology: Comment on a Non-Refuting Refutation", *Research in the History of Economic Thought and Methodology*, vol. 10, 1992, pp. 17–32; Caldwell, *Hayek's Challenge*, pp. 311–12.

misguided advice of the 'men of science'. That Hayek rather quickly accepted Popper's proposed emendation is seen by the fact that in the 1952 version of "Scientism" Hayek added a wholly new paragraph in which he noted that the methods that natural scientists "have so often tried to force upon the social sciences were not always necessarily those which the scientists in fact followed in their own field".[107] In the Preface to his 1967 collection of essays titled *Studies in Philosophy, Politics, and Economics*, Hayek credited Popper with having influenced him to make the change:

> Readers of some of my earlier writings may notice a slight change in the tone of my discussion of the attitude which I then called 'scientism'. The reason for this is that Karl Popper has taught me that natural scientists did not really do what most of them not only told us that they did but also urged the representatives of other disciplines to imitate.[108]

How important was this change for Hayek's argument? In one respect it mattered little. If in fact the objectivism, collectivism, and historicism that Hayek had criticised were not really practised by natural scientists, but were only caricatures that had been offered up by the 'men of science', it would strengthen his argument that such methods were inappropriate: if they are not followed anywhere, why use them? On the other hand, Hayek's strict delineation between the methods of the social and natural sciences played a key rôle in his own argument that there were special problems in the social sciences that made prediction there more difficult. It was because of these problems that Hayek had drawn the conclusion that often the best that we can do in the social sciences is to make pattern predictions, or to provide explanations of the principle by which social phenomena occur, as in his footpath example. If all sciences follow the same method, on what grounds could one say that prediction was more difficult in certain of them?

Hayek hit on a solution to the problem in the 1950s. From then on he seldom distinguished sciences according to the social science–natural science distinction that he had used in the "Scientism" essay. Drawing on the work of Warren Weaver and others, his dividing line would instead usually be between those sciences that studied simple and those that studied complex phenomena.[109] Crucially, the major conclusion that he had drawn in the "Sci-

---

[107] This volume, chapter 1, p. 79.

[108] F. A. Hayek, *Studies in Philosophy, Politics and Economics* (Chicago: University of Chicago Press, 1967), p. viii. Though Hayek credits Popper, criticisms by men like Ernest Nagel in his "Book Review: *The Counter-Revolution of Science*", *Journal of Philosophy*, vol. 49, August 14, 1952, pp. 560–65, may also have played a rôle in changing Hayek's mind.

[109] Warren Weaver, "Science and Complexity", *American Scientist*, vol. 36, October 1948, pp. 536–44. For a fuller discussion of Hayek's change in position, see Caldwell, *Hayek's Challenge*, pp. 297–306.

entism" essay—that when dealing with certain phenomena, pattern predictions or explanations of the principle are often the best that one can do—remained in effect. But these limitations plagued the sciences that studied *complex* phenomena (among them economics), rather than *the social sciences* in general.

That Hayek always emphasised these limitations constituted his great source of disagreement with Milton Friedman, for whom ability to predict was the key to any successful science. Friedman of course shared Hayek's antipathy towards socialist planning and was an outspoken advocate of a liberal free market regime. But he was also, in Hayek's eyes at least, a positivist. Friedman had been an undergraduate student of Arthur Burns (who would later succeed Wesley Clair Mitchell as the director of research at the National Bureau for Economic Research) and had worked at the NBER in the late 1930s, where Mitchell had supported and advised him.[110] Though their politics were very different, Friedman's views on the uses of empirical work in economics were nearly identical to those of Mitchell.[111] Friedman's effective advocacy of 'the methodology of positive economics' cut the cord tying positivist methodology to socialism and helped to ensure the preservation of the former in economics long after the enthusiasm for socialism had waned.

The Planning Mentality and Science

Let us turn finally to Hayek's critique of the planning mentality and the attendant hope that science will allow us to refashion society. The planning mania that Hayek was attacking reached its peak in the inter-war years and then dissipated following the war. This is not to say that it wholly disappeared. Experiments in planning continued to crop up over the years, from indicative plan-

[110] See Milton and Rose D. Friedman, *Two Lucky People: Memoirs* (Chicago: University of Chicago Press, 1998), pp. 69–75.

[111] See Mitchell, *Two Lives*, p. 351, where in notes recounting the founding of the NBER Mitchell wrote, "Group interested found certain differences in opinions on public policies based on different views concerning fundamental facts rather than on differences of our economic interests. No one could be sure his views were sound or that other fellow's were mistaken. None of us had time and facilities for making sure—though the facts could be ascertained with substantial accuracy. We believed many other men felt same need of a fact-finding agency. . . . National Bureau of Economic Research chartered January 1920 as such". Compare this to the rationale for empirical work—to settle disagreements among people—that Friedman offered: "you have a set of personal probabilities about events of the world. . . . I have a set of personal probabilities. Those personal probabilities differ. That's why we argue. The rôle of statistical analysis is to lead us to reconsider our personal probabilities in the hope that our personal probabilities will come closer and closer together". Milton Friedman, quoted in Daniel Hammond, "An Interview with Milton Friedman", in *Research in the History of Economic Thought and Methodology*, Warren Samuels and Jeff Biddle, eds, vol. 10 (Greenwich, CT: JAI Press, 1994), p. 101.

ning in France in the 1960s, to calls for industrial policy in the United States, to the establishment in 2005 of a Network of European Technocrats, the last seeking to transplant a revitalised Technocracy movement on a new continent. But at least at the present writing, the vision of a rationally and fully planned society seems more like an artefact of a simpler time, or perhaps even a warning of a coming dystopia, than anything else.[112]

One can think of a variety of reasons for why the change took place. The faith that science, once freed from the shackles of capitalism, was an unmitigated force for good was harder to maintain after Hiroshima, the start of the Cold War, and the subsequent arms race. 'Learning how to live with the bomb' led intellectuals to Existentialism, not Technocracy. The Soviet and Chinese examples eroded faith in the efficacy of the more extreme forms of central planning and of nationalisation schemes. In the West at least, the new 'middle way' was no longer socialism but some sort of mixed economy, variously labelled 'the welfare state', 'the social market economy', 'the Keynesian consensus', 'Butskellism', and the like. Hayek himself recognised the changes, which may be yet another reason why he decided not to continue with his big book.[113] He would be a critic of these modifications in his later years, when he would develop new arguments to engage them.

In any event, it is evident that certain parts of Hayek's arguments will seem somewhat dated. This is, of course, less a criticism of Hayek than a recognition of just how much the world has changed since the inter-war years. Nonetheless, some on the left may view Hayek's specific criticisms of the planning mentality as having little relevance for their own positions.[114]

There is certainly some truth to the charge. Part of the problem is that Hayek's neat bifurcation of the West's great political and economic thinkers into those whose ideas are in accord with the Scottish enlightenment heritage and those whose fit in better with the continental constructivist rationalist tradition, as fruitful and illuminating as it sometimes is, simply fails to make

---

[112] The possibility that the enthusiasm for scientific control of the social environment may come in waves should not be ignored.

[113] By 1956 Hayek could write, in his introduction to the American paperback edition of *The Road to Serfdom*, p. 44, that the "hot socialism against which it was mainly directed . . . is nearly dead in the Western world". Of course, as his emphasis on "the Western world" makes clear, for the hundreds of millions of people living in the Soviet Union, the East Bloc countries, China, North Korea, and other places where communist 'experiments' were attempted, the reality was decidedly different.

[114] Note for example Jeffrey Friedman's statement regarding Hayek's critique of the planning mentality: "the persistence of this polemic even after the advent of the New Left must have seemed to any left-wing reader of Hayek like a well-honed obsession, as it completely ignored the postwar left's revulsion against authority, planning, and 'conscious control'". Jeffrey Friedman, "Popper, Weber, and Hayek: The Epistemology and Politics of Ignorance", *Critical Review*, vol. 17, 2005, p. xl.

sense of certain cases.[115] For example, the distinction is unhelpful if one seeks to understand the positions of nineteenth century anarchists like Peter Kropotkin, who was a proponent of both a voluntaristic communism and positivism, but also a virulent anti-statist, or Michael Bakunin, whose writings carry the epigraph, "Liberty without socialism is privilege, injustice; socialism without liberty is slavery and brutality".[116] Moving to more recent times, members or followers of what became known as the Frankfurt School were virulent critics of authoritarian planning, positivism, and the alienation that permeated a technology-dominated society, all of which they depicted as a legacy of the enlightenment.[117] Certain scholars who were affiliated with the Frankfurt School went on to become iconic figures for the New Left.

And indeed, many modern critics of scientism are to be found on the left. These critics are opponents of the technological imperatives of a developed society and advocates of personal freedom and self-determination, which in their eyes can only come about by bringing an end to social and economic injustice. But as virtuous as such calls for reform may sound, they are not in the end that helpful. As Hayek always emphasised, both he and his opponents typically seek similar ends and differ principally on the means that they think are best to achieve them. So it is only after one gets beyond such vague gener-

---

[115] A number of scholars have challenged Hayek's placement of several writers within the two camps. See, e.g., R. F. Harrod, "Professor Hayek on Individualism", *Economic Journal*, vol. 56, September 1946, pp. 435–42; Lionel Robbins, "Hayek on Liberty", *Economica*, n.s., vol. 28, February 1961, pp. 66–81; Arthur Diamond, "F. A. Hayek on Constructivism and Ethics", *Journal of Libertarian Studies*, vol. 4, Fall 1980, pp. 354–58; and Christina Petsoulas, *Hayek's Liberalism and Its Origins: His Idea of Spontaneous Order and the Scottish Enlightenment* (London: Routledge, 2001). As we saw earlier, Milton Friedman also did not fit the mould.

[116] See Marshall S. Shatz's introduction to *Kropotkin: The Conquest of Bread and Other Writings*, in the series *Cambridge Texts in the History of Political Thought* (Cambridge: Cambridge University Press, 1995), pp. xvii–xviii; *Bakunin on Anarchy: Selected Works by the Activist-Founder of World Anarchism*, edited and translated by Sam Dolgoff (New York: Knopf, 1972). Hayek's characterisation in chapter 15, p. 249, of the "strong democratic and anarchistic elements" that had entered socialism by 1848 as "new and alien elements" shows that he recognised that his categorisation scheme did not fit them, but his decision simply to define positions that do not fit his scheme as "alien" is hardly satisfactory.

[117] Thus in a chapter titled "The Concept of Enlightenment" we find Max Horkheimer and Theodor Adorno writing such passages as "the fully enlightened earth radiates disaster triumphant" (p. 3), "Enlightenment is totalitarian" (p. 6), and "To the Enlightenment, that which does not reduce to numbers, and ultimately to the one, becomes illusion; modern positivism writes it off as literature" (p. 7). See their *Dialectic of Enlightenment*, translated by John Cumming (New York: Herder and Herder, 1972). Hayek apparently had little patience with the Frankfurt School, especially the writings of Herbert Marcuse: "It's the kind of Marxism which I dislike the most. It's a combination of Marxism and Freudianism. I am equally opposed to both of the sources, and in its combined form I find it particularly repulsive". F. A. Hayek, quoted in Dahrendorf, *LSE*, p. 291.

alisations as 'ending injustice' that one encounters the real issue: as Lenin put it, what is to be done?

It is here that Hayek and the New Left would presumably offer quite different answers.[118] If one wanted to have a meaningful comparison of positions, the right questions to move the discussion forward might be: What workable proposals have members of the New Left put forth? And how do they compare to Hayek's? On this score, we might find some fault with both camps, for neither has been particularly good at moving from the philosophical to the policy level.

Proponents of 'critical theory', as is evident by the name, have always been much better at thoroughgoing critique than at explaining how a new and more just society is to be formed. Indeed, for most critical theorists, trying to define a set of concrete proposals for social change would itself be a positivistic violation of the sort of fully Hegelianised vision of social evolution that they embrace, as well as simply a waste of time, given the complexity of social reality.[119] As a result, intricate and often quite nuanced cultural critiques are what one typically received from those associated with the Frankfurt School. If the point is to change the world, however, criticism is not enough.[120] The challenge that faces critics on the left is to come up with a set of operational proposals for how to change society for the better, ones that take into account all that we have learned about how market and planned systems typically work and how and when they fail to work.

As for Hayek, he too can be faulted for seldom getting to the operational level, though he did at least provide some concreteness in the last third of *The Constitution of Liberty*.[121] Others have risen to the task, however. Modern day economists working within the Austrian tradition, as well as public choice theorists, those who study property rights and transactions cost economics, some experimental economists, and participants in the New Institutionalist Eco-

[118] Hayek in fact hoped to engage the left in a grand debate over these matters in the late 1970s, and though the debate never took place, it led him to write his final book, *The Fatal Conceit: The Errors of Socialism*, ed. W. W. Bartley III, vol. 1 (1988) of *The Collected Works of F. A. Hayek*.

[119] For more on the Frankfurt School and critical theory, see Martin Jay, *The Dialectical Imagination: A History of the Frankfurt School and the Institute of Social Research 1923–1950* (Boston: Little, Brown and Co., 1973), and Zoltán Tar, *The Frankfurt School: The Critical Theories of Max Horkheimer and Theodor W. Adorno* (New York: Schocken Books, 1985). As Jay, pp. 63, 152, notes, most of those affiliated with the Institute of Social Research did not have much interest in economics and indeed accused members who sought to undertake purely economic analyses, like the Marxist economist Henryk Grossmann, of fetishisation: to separate out purely economic causal mechanisms was repellant to proponents of a fully dialectical approach.

[120] "The philosophers have only interpreted the world, in various ways; the point, however, is to change it". Karl Marx, "Theses on Feuerbach", in *The Marx-Engels Reader*, ed. Robert Norton, 2nd ed. (New York: Norton, 1978), p. 145.

[121] F. A. Hayek, *The Constitution of Liberty* (Chicago: University of Chicago Press, 1960). A *Collected Works* edition of this title is anticipated.

nomics movement, may all in varying degrees be viewed as trying to fill in the blanks that Hayek left in his always very general framework.

There was another important difference between Hayek and some of his more recent opponents on the left. Like the 'men of science' whom he had criticised in the 1940s, Hayek was a full participant in the modernist scientific project: he saw himself as a scientist and believed in the power of scientific argument.[122] His complaint was that many other believers (especially those so ready to label their opponent's beliefs as 'metaphysics') were, from his perspective, not practising what they preached. Hayek was a modernist through and through, but one who recognized the importance of interpretation. As a subjective value theorist raised within the Austrian tradition, he was in this sense a fully representative member.

Where Hayek Went Instead

Hayek never completed the Abuse and Decline of Reason project, instead moving on to other endeavours. In many cases, however, the new research that he undertook in its stead had links, sometimes very direct links, to his great unfinished work.

As noted earlier, the first 'delay' was caused by his decision to focus on writing and publishing the second part of the book, which became *The Road to Serfdom*. He might well initially have planned to return to the larger project, but the *Reader's Digest* condensation of *The Road to Serfdom* caused further delays by turning him into an internationally known figure virtually overnight. This led in its turn to an invitation from Harold Luhnow of the Volker Fund to write an American version of the book, which he did not do, but Luhnow did help Hayek to fulfil a dream to create an international liberal society, one that had its first meeting in Mont Pèlerin, Switzerland, in April 1947. The Luhnow connection also ultimately led to Hayek's appointment to the Committee on Social Thought at the University of Chicago in 1950.[123]

After finishing *The Road to Serfdom*, Hayek began in the summer of 1945 to write an essay on psychology. Tentatively titled "What Is Mind?" and based on a paper he had written in his student days, he hoped that it would be completed quickly. It was not. Though he had a first draft done in 1945, the essay

---

[122] "Some readers may feel that I myself in many respects hold views so closely related to those I criticise that I am hardly entitled to reject them. Yet fertile criticisms will always only come from persons holding somewhat similar views and the apparently small differences may indeed make all the difference between truth and error". Notes, Hayek papers, box 107, folder 17, Hoover Institution Archives.

[123] For more on this, see the editor's introduction to F. A. Hayek, *The Road to Serfdom*, pp. 18–21. The Volker Fund provided the monies for Hayek's appointment.

•

ultimately turned into a book, one that would not finally be published until 1952 under the title, *The Sensory Order*.[124]

The link between the "Scientism" essay and *The Sensory Order* is a direct one. Chapter 5 on the objectivism of the scientistic approach contains a lengthy critique of physicalism in philosophy and behaviourism in psychology, one that is based on a theory of sense perception that Hayek alludes to but does not fully describe.[125] The theory that he was referring to was one that he had developed in a paper that he had written as a student at the University of Vienna but had never published. The initial motivation behind "What Is Mind?", then, was to sketch out the foundation which underlay his critique. The book that resulted, of course, went far beyond a critique, but that was evidently why Hayek initially began the project.[126]

In 1951 Hayek published another book that had direct ties to the Abuse of Reason project. *John Stuart Mill and Harriet Taylor: Their Correspondence and Subsequent Marriage*[127] collects letters between Mill and Taylor from the early 1830s until her death in 1858. Hayek provided the requisite historical background to the letters in his introduction and first chapter and then interspersed additional background commentary among the letters. He would later report in an interview that it was his work on the Saint-Simonians for the Abuse of Reason project that had "led unexpectedly to my devoting a great deal of time to John Stuart Mill, who in fact never particularly appealed to me, though I achieved unintentionally the reputation of being one of the foremost experts on him".[128] In his research on Mill Hayek had come across a considerable amount of unpublished correspondence. He found the letters between Mill and Taylor to be "peculiarly fascinating",[129] ultimately prompting him to gather the most important of them together in a book.

Turning next to "Individualism: True and False", which was to have been the introduction to *The Abuse and Decline of Reason*, it would not I think be over-reaching to suggest that many of the most important themes that one finds in

---

[124] F. A. Hayek, *The Sensory Order: An Inquiry into the Foundations of Theoretical Psychology* (Chicago: University of Chicago Press, 1952). A *Collected Works* edition of this book is anticipated.

[125] This volume, pp. 108–14.

[126] Though criticisms of behaviourism and physicalism may still be found in *The Sensory Order*, they were much more prominent in the first draft of "What Is Mind?". Indeed, the criticism of behaviourism begins on the first page of the draft, under the heading "Views Which Deny or Disregard the Problem", that is, the problem with which the book would deal, that of a sensory order that differs from the natural order that science has revealed to us.

[127] F. A. Hayek, *John Stuart Mill and Harriet Taylor: Their Correspondence and Subsequent Marriage* (Chicago: University of Chicago Press, 1951). A *Collected Works* edition of this volume is anticipated.

[128] F. A. Hayek, *Hayek on Hayek: An Autobiographical Dialogue*, Stephen Kresge and Leif Wenar, eds (Chicago: University of Chicago Press, and London: Routledge, 1994), p. 128.

[129] Ibid., p. 129.

his later political writings, both *The Constitution of Liberty* and *Law, Legislation, and Liberty*, are present somewhere in the essay.[130] Thus we find him discussing there the differences between the French and the Scottish enlightenment; the importance of limiting the coercive power of the state to only those circumstances in which it is indispensable for reducing coercion by others; the limits of human knowledge and its implication that one should use general rules and abstract principles in designing a suitable legal framework; the tension that exists between preserving individual freedom within a market order and achieving distributive justice; and the importance for the smooth functioning of society of individuals submitting to moral rules and conventions that may appear to them unintelligible and irrational. Not everything is there— for example, evolutionary themes and the linking of spontaneous orders to rule-following would be added later—but "Individualism: True and False" still provides a précis or thumbnail sketch of much of Hayek's future work in political philosophy.

As we saw above, though Hayek changed his definition of scientism (to the methods *purportedly* followed in the natural sciences and which were advocated by the men of science), he never changed his bedrock methodological claim about the limitations that social scientists face. And ironically it was in being forced to modify his argument that Hayek came finally to realise exactly what caused the limitations: we face limits in sciences like economics because we study phenomena of organised complexity. This allowed Hayek to provide a foundation for his fundamental conclusion that when dealing with complex phenomena, the scientistic hope that scientific advances will one day permit us to control and predict them is a false and dangerous one. Hayek's subsequent important work on the theory of complex phenomena (and on the related area of spontaneously forming orders) was certainly linked to his movement from the natural science–social science distinction to the simple phenomena– complex phenomena one.

Finally, in his own mind at least, Hayek saw a connection between the Abuse and Decline of Reason project and his last book, *The Fatal Conceit*, which was published in 1988, only four years before his death. On a file card dated May 22, 1985, Hayek described the manuscript on which he was then working as follows: "This is to be the final outcome of what I planned about 1938 as *The Abuse and Decline of Reason* and of the conclusions which I published in 1944, the sketch on *The Road to Serfdom*. It is a work for which one has to be an economist but this is not enough!"[131]

---

[130] F. A. Hayek, *Law, Legislation, and Liberty*, 3 vols. (Chicago: University of Chicago Press, 1973–79). A *Collected Works* edition of this work is anticipated.

[131] File card dated May 22, 1985, provided by Stephen Kresge. Hayek made literally thousands of file cards while working on various projects, which contained his own thoughts or quotations from others that he would use in his books.

This allows us to conclude by pointing out a final irony. As we have shown, a great deal of Hayek's subsequent work, either directly or indirectly, had a connection to his great unfinished war effort. The book was, it would seem, left uncompleted in name only.

Bruce Caldwell
Greensboro, NC
February 2007

PRELUDE

Individualism: True And False[1]

Du dix-huitième siècle et de la révolution, comme d'une source commune,
étaient sortis deux fleuves: le premier conduisait les hommes aux institutions
libres, tandis que le second les menait au pouvoir absolu.

—Alexis de Tocqueville[2]

I

To advocate any clear-cut principles of social order is today an almost certain
way to incur the stigma of being an unpractical doctrinaire. It has come to be
regarded as the sign of the judicious mind that in social matters one does not
adhere to fixed principles but decides each question 'on its merits'; that one is
generally guided by expediency and is ready to compromise between opposed
views. Principles, however, have a way of asserting themselves even if they are
not explicitly recognised but are only implied in particular decisions, or if they
are present only as vague ideas of what is or is not being done. Thus it has
come about that under the sign of 'neither individualism nor socialism' we
are in fact rapidly moving from a society of free individuals towards one of a
completely collectivist character.

[1] The twelfth Finlay Lecture, delivered at University College, Dublin, on December 17, 1945.
Published by Hodges, Figgis & Co., Dublin, and Basil Blackwell, Oxford, 1946. [Reprinted
in F. A. Hayek, *Individualism and Economic Order* (Chicago: University of Chicago Press, 1948),
pp. 1–32. The essay is titled a 'prelude' because in Hayek's original plan for his book *The Abuse
and Decline of Reason*, this was to have been the introductory chapter, titled "The Humility of
Individualism". See the editor's introduction to this volume, p. 8. In what follows, all editorial
comments are in brackets. Brackets around a page or volume number correct Hayek's citation
errors; the bracketed information is correct.—Ed.]

[2] [From the eighteenth century and the Revolution, two rivers had emerged as from a common source: the first one drove men towards free institutions, whilst the second led them to
absolute power. Alexis de Tocqueville, "Discours de réception à l'académie française", in *Etudes
économiques, politiques et littéraires*, vol. 9 (1866) of *Œuvres complètes d'Alexis de Tocqueville* (Paris: Michel
Lévy Frères, 1864–67), p. 16.—Ed.]

I propose not only to undertake to defend a general principle of social organisation but shall also try to show that the aversion to general principles, and the preference for proceeding from particular instance to particular instance, is the product of the movement which with the 'inevitability of gradualness' leads us back from a social order resting on the general recognition of certain principles to a system in which order is created by direct commands.[3]

After the experience of the last thirty years, there is perhaps not much need to emphasise that without principles we drift. The pragmatic attitude which has been dominant during that period, far from increasing our command over developments, has in fact led us to a state of affairs which nobody wanted; and the only result of our disregard of principles seems to be that we are governed by a logic of events which we are vainly attempting to ignore. The question now is not whether we need principles to guide us but rather whether there still exists a body of principles capable of general application which we could follow if we wished. Where can we still find a set of precepts which will give us definite guidance in the solution of the problems of our time? Is there anywhere a consistent philosophy to be found which supplies us not merely with the moral aims but with an adequate method for their achievement?

That religion itself does not give us definite guidance in these matters is shown by the efforts of the church to elaborate a complete social philosophy and by the entirely opposite results at which many arrive who start from the same Christian foundations. Though the declining influence of religion is undoubtedly one major cause of our present lack of intellectual and moral orientation, its revival would not much lessen the need for a generally accepted principle of social order. We still should require a political philosophy which goes beyond the fundamental but general precepts which religion or morals provide.

The title which I have chosen for this chapter shows that to me there still seems to exist such a philosophy—a set of principles which, indeed, is implicit in most of Western or Christian political tradition but which can no longer be unambiguously described by any readily understood term. It is therefore necessary to restate these principles fully before we can decide whether they can still serve us as practical guides.

The difficulty which we encounter is not merely the familiar fact that the current political terms are notoriously ambiguous or even that the same term often means nearly the opposite to different groups. There is the much more serious fact that the same word frequently appears to unite people who in fact believe in contradictory and irreconcilable ideals. Terms like 'liberalism'

---

[3] ['The inevitability of gradualness' was a phrase used by the Fabians, English socialists led by Sidney and Beatrice Webb. See the editor's introduction to F. A. Hayek, *Socialism and War: Essays, Documents, Reviews*, ed. Bruce Caldwell, vol. 10 (1997) of *The Collected Works of F. A. Hayek* (Chicago: University of Chicago Press and London: Routledge), p. 11.—Ed.]

or 'democracy', 'capitalism' or 'socialism', today no longer stand for coherent systems of ideas. They have come to describe aggregations of quite heterogeneous principles and facts which historical accident has associated with these words but which have little in common beyond having been advocated at different times by the same people or even merely under the same name.

No political term has suffered worse in this respect than 'individualism'. It not only has been distorted by its opponents into an unrecognisable caricature—and we should always remember that the political concepts which are today out of fashion are known to most of our contemporaries only through the picture drawn of them by their enemies—but has been used to describe several attitudes towards society which have as little in common among themselves as they have with those traditionally regarded as their opposites. Indeed, when in the preparation of this paper I examined some of the standard descriptions of 'individualism', I almost began to regret that I had ever connected the ideals in which I believe with a term which has been so abused and so misunderstood. Yet, whatever else 'individualism' may have come to mean in addition to these ideals, there are two good reasons for retaining the term for the view I mean to defend: this view has always been known by that term, whatever else it may also have meant at different times, and the term has the distinction that the word 'socialism' was deliberately coined to express its opposition to individualism.[4] It is with the system which forms the alternative to socialism that I shall be concerned.

II

Before I explain what I mean by true individualism, it may be useful if I give some indication of the intellectual tradition to which it belongs. The true individualism which I shall try to defend began its modern development with John Locke, and particularly with Bernard Mandeville and David Hume, and achieved full stature for the first time in the work of Josiah Tucker, Adam Ferguson, and Adam Smith and in that of their great contemporary, Edmund Burke—the man whom Smith described as the only person he ever knew who thought on economic subjects exactly as he did without any previous com-

---

[4] Both the term 'individualism' and the term 'socialism' are originally the creation of the Saint-Simonians, the founders of modern socialism. They first coined the term 'individualism' to describe the competitive society to which they were opposed and then invented the word 'socialism' to describe the centrally planned society in which all activity was directed on the same principle that applied within a single factory. See on the origin of these terms the present author's article on "The Counter-Revolution of Science", *Economica*, n.s., vol. 8, May 1941, p. 146. [See this volume, chapter 14, p. 229.—Ed]

munication having passed between them.[5] In the nineteenth century I find it represented most perfectly in the work of two of its greatest historians and political philosophers: Alexis de Tocqueville and Lord Acton.[6] These two men

[5] Robert Bisset, *Life of Edmund Burke*, 2nd ed. (London: G. Cawthorn, 1800), vol. 2, p. 429. Cf. also William C. Dunn, "Adam Smith and Edmund Burke: Complementary Contemporaries", *Southern Economic Journal*, vol. 7, January, 1941, pp. 330–46. [English philosopher John Locke (1632–1704) was the author of *Two Treatises of Government* (1690), where he developed the notion of a social contract between the government and the people; when this contract is violated, the people have a right to revolt. This theory influenced the authors of the American Declaration of Independence. Dutch physician Bernard Mandeville (1670–1733) scandalised his readers with *The Fable of the Bees* (1714–29), which carried the subtitle *Private Vices, Publick Benefits*, in which he argued that the selfish pursuit of gain, though a vice, brings with it prosperity. In his essay "Dr. Bernard Mandeville (1670–1733)", chapter 6 of *The Trend of Economic Thinking: Essays on Political Economists and Economic History*, W. W. Bartley III and Stephen Kresge, eds, vol. 3 (1991) of *The Collected Works of F. A. Hayek*, Hayek credited Mandeville with raising at just the right moment the question of how an undesigned order might arise in society. Political economist Adam Smith (1723–90), philosopher David Hume (1711–76), and moral philosopher and historian Adam Ferguson (1723–1816) were prominent figures in the Scottish Enlightenment; all identified in their work social institutions that arose, in Ferguson's phrase, as "the result of human action, but not the execution of any human design". See F. A. Hayek, "The Results of Human Action but not of Human Design", *Studies in Philosophy, Politics and Economics* (Chicago: University of Chicago Press, 1967), chapter 6, as well as his "The Legal and Political Philosophy of David Hume (1711–76)" and "Adam Smith (1723–90): His Message in Today's Language", chapters 7 and 8 of *The Trend of Economic Thinking*. For a study of this movement, see Ronald Hamowy, "The Scottish Enlightenment and the Theory of Spontaneous Order" [1987], reprinted in *The Political Sociology of Freedom: Adam Ferguson and F. A. Hayek* (Cheltenham, UK: Elgar, 2005), chapter 3. English rector, pamphleteer and controversialist Josiah Tucker (1712–99) was in his time a well-known figure who wrote on a wide range of subjects, from religion to economics to politics. In his economic writings, he anticipated certain of Adam Smith's contributions. For example, he began his study by positing that man acts out of self-interest; he opposed monopolistic restraints on trade; and he criticised the mercantilist belief that bullion is wealth. Irish statesman and conservative political philosopher Edmund Burke's (1729–97) most famous work was *Reflections on the Revolution in France* (1790). Like Hayek, he emphasised the importance of gradually evolved customs and traditions as the most solid foundations of order and liberty, and thus disdained grand social experiments like the French Revolution that sought the radical transformation of society.—Ed.]

[6] [John Emerich Edward Dalberg-Acton, First Baron Acton (1834–1902) was a Liberal MP from 1859 to 1864, leader of the Liberal Roman Catholics in England, and founder-editor of the *Cambridge Modern History*, to which he contributed the first two volumes. His projected life's work on the history of liberty was never finished, but passages from his published lectures and reviews were frequently invoked by Hayek. French historian Alexis Charles Henri Clérel de Tocqueville (1805–59) argued in *Democracy in America* (1835, 1840) and *The Old Regime and the French Revolution* (1856) that the quest for social equality under democracy brings with it a growth in the centralisation of government, and that administrative centralisation and bureaucratisation lead inevitably to a reduction of individual liberties. Hayek once thought of naming the Mont Pèlerin Society the Acton-Tocqueville Society, but others objected to naming a liberal movement after two Catholics. For more of Hayek's views on Tocqueville (whom he often referred to as 'de Tocqueville'—this has been changed in the text for the *Collected Works*) and Acton, see his essays "Historians and the Future of Europe" and "The Actonian Revival", chapters 8 and 9,

seem to me to have more successfully developed what was best in the political philosophy of the Scottish philosophers, Burke, and the English Whigs than any other writers I know; while the classical economists of the nineteenth century, or at least the Benthamites or philosophical radicals among them, came increasingly under the influence of another kind of individualism of different origin.[7]

This second and altogether different strand of thought, also known as individualism, is represented mainly by French and other Continental writers—a fact due, I believe, to the dominant rôle which Cartesian rationalism plays in its composition.[8] The outstanding representatives of this tradition are the Encyclopedists, Rousseau, and the physiocrats; and, for reasons we shall presently consider, this rationalistic individualism always tends to develop into the opposite of individualism, namely, socialism or collectivism. It is because only the first kind of individualism is consistent that I claim for it the name of true individualism, while the second kind must probably be regarded as a source of modern socialism as important as the properly collectivist theories.[9]

---

respectively, of *The Fortunes of Liberalism*, ed. Peter Klein, vol. 4 (1992) of *The Collected Works of F. A. Hayek.*—Ed.]

[7] [By 'philosophical radicals' Hayek refers to the nineteenth century political radicals who based their doctrines on the writings of Jeremy Bentham (1748–1822) and James Mill (1773–1836). Hayek felt that these doctrines made it easier for socialist ideas to spread in Britain later in the century: "It was, in the end, the victory of the Benthamite Philosophical Radicals over the Whigs in England that concealed the fundamental difference which in more recent years has reappeared as the conflict between liberal democracy and 'social' or totalitarian democracy". F. A. Hayek, *The Constitution of Liberty* (Chicago: University of Chicago Press, 1960), p. 55. —Ed.]

[8] [In his later works, Hayek would refer to 'Cartesian rationalism' variously as 'constructivism', 'rationalist constructivism', or 'constructivist rationalism'. See, for example, F. A. Hayek, "Kinds of Rationalism" [1965], reprinted in *Studies in Philosophy, Politics and Economics*, chapter 5.—Ed.]

[9] Carl Menger, who was among the first in modern times consciously to revive the methodological individualism of Adam Smith and his school, was probably also the first to point out the connection between the design theory of social institutions and socialism. See his *Untersuchungen über die Methode der Socialwissenschaften und der politischen Oekonomie inbesondere* (Leipzig: Duncker & Humblot, 1883), especially book 4, chapter 2, towards the end of which (p. 208) he speaks of "a pragmatism which, against the intention of its representatives, leads inevitably to socialism". [Hayek refers to Menger's statement, "einen Pragmatismus, der gegen die Absicht seiner Vertreter unausweichbar zum Socialismus führt". Menger's book on methodology was translated into English and published under the title *Problems of Economics and Sociology* in 1963; the translation there formed the basis for a new re-titled edition, *Investigations into the Method of the Social Sciences with Special Reference to Economics*, ed. Louis Schneider, translated by Francis Nock (New York: New York University Press, 1985), p. 177. Carl Menger (1840–1921) was the founder of the Austrian School of Economics; for Hayek's views on Menger's contributions, see chapter 2 of Hayek, *Fortunes of Liberalism.*—Ed.]

It is significant that the physiocrats already were led from the rationalistic individualism from which they started, not only close to socialism (fully developed in their contemporary Morelly's

I can give no better illustration of the prevailing confusion about the meaning of individualism than the fact that the man who to me seems to be one of the greatest representatives of true individualism, Edmund Burke, is commonly (and rightly) represented as the main opponent of the so-called 'individualism' of Rousseau, whose theories he feared would rapidly dissolve the commonwealth "into the dust and powder of individuality",[10] and that the term 'individualism' itself was first introduced into the English language through the translation of one of the works of another of the great representatives of true individualism, Tocqueville, who uses it in his *Democracy in America* to describe an attitude which he deplores and rejects.[11] Yet there can be no doubt that both Burke and Tocqueville stand in all essentials close to Adam Smith, to whom nobody will deny the title of individualist, and that the 'individualism' to which they are opposed is something altogether different from that of Smith.

Code de la nature (Par-tout [the Netherlands]: Le vrai sage, 1755), but to advocate the worst despotism. "L'Etat fait des hommes tout ce qu'il veut", wrote Baudeau.

[Baudeau's statement may be translated as, "The state turns men into whatever it wants". The Encyclopedists were those associated with the publication of the French *Encyclopédie, ou dictionnaire raisonné des sciences, des arts et des métiers* (Paris: Briasson, 1751), namely Denis Diderot (1713–84) and Jean Le Rond d'Alembert (1717–83), but also Rousseau (1712–78), Voltaire (1694–1778), and Claude-Adrien Helvétius (1715–71). Perhaps the first organised school of economic thought, the physiocrats included François Quesnay (1694–1774), Victor Riqueti, the Marquis de Mirabeau (1715–89), Pierre-Samuel Du Pont de Nemours (1739–1817), as well as, after an initial period of dissent, the above mentioned Abbé Nicolas Baudeau (1730–92). Little biographical detail exists on Etienne-Gabriel Morelly. His book *Code of Nature* was a philosophical defence of ideas he had expressed in "Basiliad", a poem about a communist utopia.—Ed.]

[10] Edmund Burke, *Reflections on the Revolution in France* [1790], in *The Works of the Right Honourable Edmund Burke* (World's Classics ed., London and New York: Oxford University Press, 1906), vol. 4, p. 105: "Thus the commonwealth itself would, in a few generations, crumble away, be disconnected into the dust and powder of individuality, and at length dispersed to all the winds of heaven". That Burke (as Annie Marion Osborn points out in her book on *Rousseau and Burke* (London and New York: Oxford University Press, 1940), p. 23), after he had first attacked Rousseau for his extreme 'individualism', later attacked him for his extreme collectivism was far from inconsistent but merely the result of the fact that in the case of Rousseau, as in that of all others, the rationalistic individualism which they preached inevitably led to collectivism.

[11] Alexis de Tocqueville, *Democracy in America* [1840], translated by Henry Reeve (London: Longman, Greene, Longman, and Roberts, 1862), vol. 2, book 2, chapter 2, p. 119, where Tocqueville defines individualism as "a mature and calm feeling, which disposes each member of the community to sever himself from the mass of his fellows, and to draw apart with his family and his friends; so that, after he has thus formed a little circle of his own, he willingly leaves society at large to itself". The translator in a note to this passage apologises for introducing the French term 'individualism' into English and explains that he knows "no English word exactly equivalent to the expression". As Albert Schatz pointed out in the book mentioned below, Tocqueville's use of the well-established French term in this peculiar sense is entirely arbitrary and leads to serious confusion with the established meaning.

III

What, then, are the essential characteristics of true individualism? The first thing that should be said is that it is primarily a *theory* of society, an attempt to understand the forces which determine the social life of man, and only in the second instance a set of political maxims derived from this view of society. This fact should by itself be sufficient to refute the silliest of the common misunderstandings: the belief that individualism postulates (or bases its arguments on the assumption of) the existence of isolated or self-contained individuals, instead of starting from men whose whole nature and character is determined by their existence in society.[12] If that were true, it would indeed have nothing to contribute to our understanding of society. But its basic contention is quite a different one; it is that there is no other way towards an understanding of social phenomena but through our understanding of individual actions directed towards other people and guided by their expected behaviour.[13] This argument is directed primarily against the properly collectivist theories of society which pretend to be able directly to comprehend social wholes like society, etc., as entities *sui generis* which exist independently of the individuals which compose them. The next step in the individualistic analysis of society, however, is directed against the rationalistic pseudo-individualism which also leads to practical collectivism. It is the contention that, by tracing the combined effects of individual actions, we discover that many of the institutions on which human achievements rest have arisen and are functioning without a designing and directing mind; that, as Adam Ferguson expressed it, "nations

[12] In his excellent survey of the history of individualist theories the late Albert Schatz rightly concludes that "nous voyons tout d'abord avec évidence ce que l'individualisme n'est pas. C'est précisément ce qu'on croit communément qu'il est: un système d'isolement dans l'existence et une apologie de l'égoïsme". *L'Individualisme économique et social* (Paris: A. Colin, 1907), p. 558. This book, to which I am much indebted, deserves to be much more widely known as a contribution not only to the subject indicated by its title but to the history of economic theory in general. [Schatz's observation might be translated as: "We commonly assume individualism to be precisely what it is not: a system promoting an isolated existence and an apology for selfishness". —Ed.]

[13] In this respect, as Karl Pribram has made clear, individualism is a necessary result of philosophical nominalism, while the collectivist theories have their roots in the 'realist' or (as K. R. Popper now more appropriately calls it) 'essentialist' tradition (Karl Pribram, *Die Entstehung der individualistichen Sozialphilosophie* (Leipzig: C. L. Hirschfield, 1912). But this 'nominalist' approach is characteristic only of true individualism, while the false individualism of Rousseau and the physiocrats, in accordance with the Cartesian origin, is strongly 'realist' or 'essentialist'. [Hayek's friend the philosopher Karl Popper (1902–94) distinguished between nominalism and essentialism in his essay, *The Poverty of Historicism* (London: Routledge, 1957), pp. 26–34, an early version of which first appeared in 1944–45 in *Economica*, of which Hayek was then editor. For more on Hayek's relationship to Popper, see the editor's introduction, this volume, pp. 36–37.—Ed.]

stumble upon establishments, which are indeed the result of human action but not the result of human design";[14] and that the spontaneous collabora-

[14] Adam Ferguson, *An Essay on the History of Civil Society* (Edinburgh: Printed for A. Millar and T. Caddel, London, and A. Kincaid and J. Bell, Edinburgh, 1767), p. 187. Cf. also ibid.: "The forms of society are derived from an obscure and distant origin; they arise, long before the date of philosophy, from the instincts, not from the speculations, of men. . . . We ascribe to a previous design, what came to be known only by experience, what no human wisdom could foresee, and what, without the concurring humour and disposition of his age, no authority could enable an individual to execute" (pp. 187 and 188). [The phrase quoted in the text actually reads, "nations stumble upon establishments, which are indeed the result of human action, but not the execution of any human design". Perhaps Hayek's modification was intended to make Ferguson's point easier for a modern reader to understand.—Ed.]

It may be of interest to compare these passages with the similar statements in which Ferguson's contemporaries expressed the same basic idea of the eighteenth-century British economists:

Josiah Tucker, *The Elements of Commerce*, 1756 [1755], reprinted in *Josiah Tucker: A Selection from His Economic and Political Writings*, ed. R. L. Schuyler (New York: Columbia University Press, 1931), pp. 31 [59] and 92: "The main point to be aimed at, is neither to extinguish nor enfeeble self-love, but to give it such a direction, that it may promote the public interest by pursuing its own. . . . The proper design of this chapter is to show that the universal mover in human nature, self-love, may receive such a direction in this case (as in all others) as to promote the public interest by those efforts it shall make towards pursuing its own". [Hayek incorrectly listed the date of Tucker's book as 1756. As Schuyler noted in his introduction, a substantial part of Tucker's book was privately printed, but never published, in 1755. The Schuyler edition actually published it for the first time.—Ed.]

Adam Smith, *An Inquiry into the Nature and Causes of the Wealth of Nations* [1776], ed. Edwin Cannan (London: Methuen and Co., 1904), vol. 1, p. 421: "By directing that industry in such a manner as its produce may be of the greatest value, he intends only his own gain, and he is in this, as in many other cases, led by an invisible hand to promote an end which was no part of his intention. Nor is it always the worse for the society that it was no part of it. By pursuing his own interest he frequently promotes that of the society more effectually than when he really intends to promote it". Cf. also *The Theory of Moral Sentiments* [1759], (London: Printed by A. Strahan for T. Caddel, Jr., and W. Davies, W. Creech, and J. Bell and Co., 1801), chapter 1, part 4, p. 386. [Hayek's references may also now be found in *The Glasgow Edition of the Works and Correspondence of Adam Smith*, R. H. Campbell, A. S. Skinner, et. al., eds (Oxford: Clarendon Press, 1976; reprinted, Indianapolis, IN: LibertyClassics, 1981). See Smith, *Wealth of Nations*, ed. W. B. Todd, vol. 2, p. 456; and Smith, *Theory of Moral Sentiments*, D. D. Raphael and A. L. Macfie, eds, vol. 1, pp. 184–85.—Ed.]

Edmund Burke, *Thoughts and Details on Scarcity* [1795], in *Works of the Right Honourable Edmund Burke*, vol. 6, p. 9: "The benign and wise Disposer of all things, who obliges men, whether they will or not, in pursuing their own selfish interests, to connect the general good with their own individual success".

After these statements have been held up for scorn and ridicule by the majority of writers for the last hundred years (Charles E. Raven not long ago called the last-quoted statement by Burke a "sinister sentence"—see his *Christian Socialism, 1848–1854* (London: Macmillan, 1920 [reprinted, New York: A. M. Kelley, 1968]), p. 34), it is interesting now to find one of the leading theorists of modern socialism adopting Adam Smith's conclusions. According to Abba P. Lerner, in *The Economics of Control* (New York: Macmillan, 1944 [reprinted, New York: Kelley, 1970]), p. 67, the essential social utility of the price mechanism is that "If it is appropriately

tion of free men often creates things which are greater than their individual minds can ever fully comprehend. This is the great theme of Josiah Tucker and Adam Smith, of Adam Ferguson and Edmund Burke, the great discovery of classical political economy which has become the basis of our understanding not only of economic life but of most truly social phenomena.

The difference between this view, which accounts for most of the order which we find in human affairs as the unforeseen result of individual actions, and the view which traces all discoverable order to deliberate design is the first great contrast between the true individualism of the British thinkers of the eighteenth century and the so-called 'individualism' of the Cartesian school.[15] But it is merely one aspect of an even wider difference between a view which in general rates rather low the place which reason plays in human affairs, which contends that man has achieved what he has in spite of the fact that he is only partly guided by reason, and that his individual reason is very limited and imperfect, and a view which assumes that Reason, with a capital R, is always fully and equally available to all humans and that everything which man achieves is the direct result of, and therefore subject to, the control of individual reason. One might even say that the former is a product of an acute consciousness of the limitations of the individual mind which induces an attitude of humility towards the impersonal and anonymous social processes by which individuals help to create things greater than they know, while the latter is the product of an exaggerated belief in the powers of individual reason and of a consequent contempt for anything which has not been consciously designed by it or is not fully intelligible to it.

---

used it induces each member of society, while seeking his own benefit, to do that which is in the general social interest. Fundamentally this is the great discovery of Adam Smith and the Physiocrats". [Market socialist Abba Lerner (1905–82) thanked his teachers Hayek and Lionel Robbins in the preface of his book for providing his original training in economics. Market socialism is an attempt to combine a market pricing mechanism with social control of the economy.—Ed.]

[15] Cf. Schatz, *L'Individualisme économique et social*, pp. 41–42, 81, 378, 568–69, especially the passage quoted by him (p. 41, n. 1) from an article by Albert Sorel ("Comment j'ai lu la 'Réforme sociale'", in *Réforme sociale*, November 1, 1906, p. 614): "Quel que fût mon respect, assez commandé et indirect encore pour le *Discours de la méthode*, je savais déjà que de ce fameux discours il était sorti autant de déraison sociale et d'aberrations métaphysiques, d'abstractions et d'utopies que de données positives, que s'il menait à Comte il avait aussi mené à Rousseau". [Whatever respect—for the most part ordered and mediated by others—I then had for the *Discourse on Method*, I was nonetheless aware that the famous *Discourse* had given vent as much to social unreasonableness, metaphysical aberration, and abstract utopian speculation as to positive data, and that if it led to Comte it had led to Rousseau as well.—Ed.] On the influence of Descartes on Rousseau see further Paul Janet, *Histoire de la science politique, dans ses rapports avec la morale*, 3rd ed. (Paris: F. Alcan, 1887), p. 423; Francisque Bouillier, *Histoire de la philosophie cartésienne*, 3rd ed. (Paris: C. Delagrave et cie, 1868), vol. 2, p. 643; and Henry Michel, *L'idée de l'état*, 3rd ed. (Paris: Hachette, 1898), p. 68.

The anti-rationalistic approach, which regards man not as a highly rational and intelligent but as a very irrational and fallible being, whose individual errors are corrected only in the course of a social process, and which
aims at making the best of a very imperfect material, is probably the most
characteristic feature of English individualism. Its pre-dominance in English
thought seems to me due largely to the profound influence exercised by Bernard Mandeville, by whom the central idea was for the first time clearly formulated.[16]

I cannot better illustrate the contrast in which Cartesian or rationalistic
'individualism' stands to this view than by quoting a famous passage from part
II of the *Discourse on Method*. Descartes argues that "there is seldom so much
perfection in works composed of many separate parts, upon which different
hands had been employed, as in those completed by a single master". He
then goes on to suggest (after, significantly, quoting the instance of the engineer drawing up his plans) that "those nations which, starting from a semi-
barbarous state and advancing to civilisation by slow degrees, have had their
laws successively determined, and, as it were, forced upon them simply by
experience of the hurtfulness of particular crimes and disputes, would by this
process come to be possessed of less perfect institutions than those which,
from the commencement of their association as communities, have followed
the appointments of some wise legislator". To drive this point home, Descartes adds that in his opinion "the past pre-eminence of Sparta was due not

---

[16] The decisive importance of Mandeville in the history of economics, long overlooked or
appreciated only by a few authors (particularly Edwin Cannan and Albert Schatz), is now beginning to be recognised, thanks mainly to the magnificent edition of the *Fable of the Bees* which we
owe to the late F. B. Kaye. Although the fundamental ideas of Mandeville's work are already
implied in the original poem of 1705, the decisive elaboration and especially his full account
of the origin of the division of labour, of money, and of language occur only in part II of the
Fable which was published in 1728. See Bernard Mandeville, *The Fable of the Bees*, ed. F. B. Kaye
(Oxford: Clarendon Press, 1924), vol. 2, pp. 142, 287–88, 349–50. There is space here to quote
only the crucial passage from his account of the development of the division of labour where he
observes that "we often ascribe to the excellency of man's genius, and the depth of his penetration, what is in reality owing to length of time, and the experience of many generations, all of
them very little differing from one another in natural parts and sagacity" (ibid., p. 142).

It has become usual to describe Giambattista Vico and his (usually wrongly quoted) formula, *homo non intelligendo fit omnia*, in *Opere* [1834], ed. Guiseppe Ferrari, 2nd ed. (Milan: Soci-
età tipografica de' classici italiani, 1854), vol. 5, p. 183, as the beginning of the anti-rationalistic
theory of social phenomena, but it would appear that he has been both preceded and surpassed
by Mandeville. [Vico's aphorism may be translated as "Man becomes all things by *not* understanding them".—Ed.]

Perhaps it also deserves mention that not only Mandeville but also Adam Smith occupy honourable places in the development of the theory of language which in so many ways raises problems of a nature kindred to those of the other social sciences.

to the goodness of each of its laws in particular . . . but to the circumstance that, originated by a single individual, they all tended to a single end".[17]

It would be interesting to trace further the development of this social contract individualism or the 'design' theories of social institutions, from Descartes through Rousseau and the French Revolution down to what is still the characteristic attitude of the engineers to social problems.[18] Such a sketch would show how Cartesian rationalism has persistently proved a grave obstacle to an understanding of historical phenomena and that it is largely responsible for the belief in inevitable laws of historical development and the modern fatalism derived from this belief.[19]

All we are here concerned with, however, is that this view, though also known as 'individualism', stands in complete contrast to true individualism on two decisive points. While it is perfectly true of this pseudo-individualism that "belief in spontaneous social products was logically impossible to any philosophers who regarded the individual man as the starting point, and supposed him to form societies by the union of his particular will with another in a formal contract",[20] true individualism is the only theory which can claim to make the formation of spontaneous social products intelligible. And, while the design theories necessarily lead to the conclusion that social processes can be made to serve human ends only if they are subjected to the control of individual human reason, and thus lead directly to socialism, true individualism believes on the contrary that, if left free, men will often achieve more than individual human reason could design or foresee.

This contrast between the true, anti-rationalistic and the false, rationalistic individualism permeates all social thought. But because both theories have

---

[17] René Descartes, *A Discourse on Method* [1658], Everyman's ed. (London: J. M. Dent and Sons, 1912), pp. 10–11. [Hayek had mistakenly left off the "s" on "appointments" and, about Sparta, had written "the pre-eminence" rather than "the goodness" of each of its laws.—Ed.]

[18] On the characteristic approach of the engineer type of mind to economic phenomena compare the present author's study on "Scientism and the Study of Society", *Economica*, n.s., vols. 9–11, 1942–44, esp. vol. 11, pp. 34ff. [See this volume, part 2, especially chapter 10, "Engineers and Planners", pp. 156–66.—Ed.]

[19] Since this lecture was first published I have become acquainted with an instructive article by Jerome Rosenthal on "Attitudes of Some Modern Rationalists to History", *Journal of the History of Ideas*, vol. 4, October, 1943, pp. 429–56, which shows in considerable detail the anti-historical attitude of Descartes and particularly his disciple Malebranche and gives interesting examples of the contempt expressed by Descartes in his *Recherche de la vérité par la lumière naturelle* for the study of history, languages, geography, and especially the classics. [French cleric and philosopher Nicolas Malebranche (1638–1715) utilised Descartes' concept of 'clear and distinct ideas' to analyse a number of theological issues. As Rosenthal, p. 431, noted, "Malebranche does not hesitate to assert that a single principle of physics contains more truth than can be found in all the books of history".—Ed.]

[20] James Bonar, *Philosophy and Political Economy in Some of their Historical Relations* (London: Swan Sonnenschein and Co., 1893), p. 85.

become known by the same name, and partly because the classical economists of the nineteenth century, and particularly John Stuart Mill and Herbert Spencer, were almost as much influenced by the French as by the English
tradition, all sorts of conceptions and assumptions completely alien to true
individualism have come to be regarded as essential parts of its doctrine.[21]

Perhaps the best illustration of the current misconceptions of the individualism of Adam Smith and his group is the common belief that they have
invented the bogey of the 'economic man' and that their conclusions are viti-
ated by their assumption of a strictly rational behaviour or generally by a false
rationalistic psychology. They were, of course, very far from assuming anything of the kind. It would be nearer the truth to say that in their view man
was by nature lazy and indolent, improvident and wasteful, and that it was
only by the force of circumstances that he could be made to behave economi-
cally or carefully to adjust his means to his ends. But even this would be unjust
to the very complex and realistic view which these men took of human nature.
Since it has become fashionable to deride Smith and his contemporaries for
their supposedly erroneous psychology, I may perhaps venture the opinion
that for all practical purposes we can still learn more about the behaviour of
men from the *Wealth of Nations* than from most of the more pretentious modern treatises on 'social psychology'.

However that may be, the main point about which there can be little doubt
is that Smith's chief concern was not so much with what man might occasionally achieve when he was at his best but that he should have as little opportunity as possible to do harm when he was at his worst. It would scarcely be
too much to claim that the main merit of the individualism which he and his
contemporaries advocated is that it is a system under which bad men can do
least harm. It is a social system which does not depend for its functioning on
our finding good men for running it, or on all men becoming better than they
now are, but which makes use of men in all their given variety and complexity, sometimes good and sometimes bad, sometimes intelligent and more often
stupid. Their aim was a system under which it should be possible to grant
freedom to all, instead of restricting it, as their French contemporaries wished,
to 'the good and the wise'.[22]

---

[21] [Hayek's views on the eminent British philosopher and political economist John Stuart Mill
(1806–73) were complex, but he frequently blamed him for paving the way for the acceptance
of socialism among the British intelligentsia in the late nineteenth century and subsequently.
For more on this, see Bruce Caldwell, "Hayek on Mill", *History of Political Economy*, vol. 40, Winter 2008, pp. 689–704. British biologist and social philosopher Herbert Spencer (1820–1903)
coined the phrase 'survival of the fittest'. Rivalling Darwin in importance as a proponent of evolutionary thinking during the Victorian period, his variant of social Darwinism posited the progressive improvement of mankind via social evolution.—Ed.]

[22] Alfred William Benn, in his *The History of English Rationalism in the Nineteenth Century* (London:
Longmans, Green, and Co., 1906), vol. 1, p. 289, says rightly: "With Quesnay following nature

The chief concern of the great individualist writers was indeed to find a set of institutions by which man could be induced, by his own choice and from the motives which determined his ordinary conduct, to contribute as much as possible to the need of all others; and their discovery was that the system of private property did provide such inducements to a much greater extent than had yet been understood. They did not contend, however, that this system was incapable of further improvement and, still less, as another of the current distortions of their arguments will have it, that there existed a 'natural harmony of interests' irrespective of the positive institutions. They were more than merely aware of the conflicts of individual interests and stressed the necessity of "well-constructed institutions" where the "rules and principles of con-

---

meant ascertaining by a study of the world about us and of its laws what conduct is most conducive to health and happiness; and natural rights [right] meant liberty to pursue the course so ascertained. Such liberty only belongs to the wise and good, and can only be granted to those whom the tutelary authority in the state is pleased to regard as such. With Adam Smith and his disciples, on the other hand, nature means the totality of impulses and instincts by which the individual members of a society are animated; and their contention is that the best arrangements result from giving free play to those forces, in the confidence that partial failure will be far more than compensated by successes elsewhere, and that the pursuit of his own interest by each will work out in the greatest happiness of all".

On this whole question see Elie Halévy, *The Growth of Philosophic Radicalism*, translated by Mary Morris (London: Faber and Gwyer, 1928), esp. pp. 266–70.

The contrast of the Scottish philosophers of the eighteenth century with their French contemporaries is also brought out in Gladys Bryson's recent study on *Man and Society: The Scottish Inquiry of the Eighteenth Century* (Princeton: Princeton University Press, 1945), p. 145 [pp. 145–46]. She emphasises that the Scottish philosophers "all wanted to break away from Cartesian rationalism, with its emphasis on abstract intellectualism and innate ideas", and repeatedly stresses the "anti-individualistic" tendencies of David Hume (pp. 106, 155)—using "individualistic" in what we call here the false, rationalistic sense. But she occasionally falls back into the common mistake of regarding them as "representative and typical of the thought of the century" (p. 176). There is still, largely as a result of an acceptance of the German conception of 'the Enlightenment', too much inclination to regard the views of all the eighteenth-century philosophers as similar, whereas in many respects the differences between the English and the French philosophers of the period are much more important than the similarities. The common habit of lumping Adam Smith and Quesnay together, caused by the former belief that Smith was greatly indebted to the physiocrats, should certainly cease, now that this belief has been disproved by William Robert Scott's recent discoveries in *Adam Smith as Student and Professor* (Glasgow: Jackson, 1937 [reprinted, New York: Kelley, 1965]), p. 124. It is also significant that both Hume and Smith are reported to have been stimulated to their work by their opposition to Montesquieu. [For Hayek's review of the Scott volume, see *The Trend of Economic Thinking*, addendum to chapter 8, pp. 122–24.—Ed.]

Some suggestive discussion of the differences between the British and the French social philosophers of the eighteenth century, somewhat distorted, however, by the author's hostility towards the 'economic liberalism' of the former, will be found in Rudolf Goldscheid, *Grundlinien zu einer Kritik der Willenskraft* (Vienna: W. Braumüller, 1905), pp. 32–37.

tending interests and compromised advantages"[23] would reconcile conflicting interests without giving any one group power to make their views and interests always prevail over those of all others.

IV

There is one point in these basic psychological assumptions which it is necessary to consider somewhat more fully. As the belief that individualism approves and encourages human selfishness is one of the main reasons why so many people dislike it, and as the confusion which exists in this respect is caused by a real intellectual difficulty, we must carefully examine the meaning of the assumptions it makes. There can be no doubt, of course, that in the language of the great writers of the eighteenth century it was man's 'self-love', or even his 'selfish interests', which they represented as the 'universal mover', and that by these terms they were referring primarily to a moral attitude, which they thought to be widely prevalent. These terms, however, did not mean egotism in the narrow sense of concern with only the immediate needs of one's proper person. The 'self', for which alone people were supposed to care, did as a matter of course include their family and friends; and it would have made no difference to the argument if it had included anything for which people in fact did care.

Far more important than this moral attitude, which might be regarded as changeable, is an indisputable intellectual fact which nobody can hope to alter and which by itself is a sufficient basis for the conclusions which the individualist philosophers drew. This is the constitutional limitation of man's knowledge and interests, the fact that he *cannot* know more than a tiny part of the whole of society and that therefore all that can enter into his motives are the immediate effects which his actions will have in the sphere he knows. All the possible differences in men's moral attitudes amount to little, so far as their significance for social organisation is concerned, compared with the fact that all man's mind can effectively comprehend are the facts of the narrow circle of which he is the centre; that, whether he is completely selfish or the most perfect altruist, the human needs for which he *can* effectively care are an almost negligible fraction of the needs of all members of society. The real question, therefore, is not whether man is, or ought to be, guided by selfish motives but whether we can allow him to be guided in his actions by those immediate consequences which he can know and care for or whether he ought to be

[23] Edmund Burke, *Thoughts and Details on Scarcity* [1795], in *Works of the Right Honourable Edmund Burke*, vol. 6, p. 15.

made to do what seems appropriate to somebody else who is supposed to possess a fuller comprehension of the significance of these actions to society as a whole.

To the accepted Christian tradition that man must be free to follow *his* conscience in moral matters if his actions are to be of any merit, the economists added the further argument that he should be free to make full use of *his* knowledge and skill, that he must be allowed to be guided by his concern for the particular things of which *he* knows and for which *he* cares, if he is to make as great a contribution to the common purposes of society as he is capable of making. Their main problem was how these limited concerns, which did in fact determine people's actions, could be made effective inducements to cause them voluntarily to contribute as much as possible to needs which lay outside the range of their vision. What the economists understood for the first time was that the market as it had grown up was an effective way of making man take part in a process more complex and extended than he could comprehend and that it was through the market that he was made to contribute 'to ends which were no part of his purpose'.

It was almost inevitable that the classical writers in explaining their contention should use language which was bound to be misunderstood and that they thus earned the reputation of having extolled selfishness. We rapidly discover the reason when we try to restate the correct argument in simple language. If we put it concisely by saying that people are and ought to be guided in their actions by *their* interests and desires, this will at once be misunderstood or distorted into the false contention that they are or ought to be exclusively guided by their personal needs or selfish interests, while what we mean is that they ought to be allowed to strive for whatever *they* think desirable.

Another misleading phrase, used to stress an important point, is the famous presumption that each man knows his interests best. In this form the contention is neither plausible nor necessary for the individualist's conclusions. The true basis of his argument is that nobody can know *who* knows best and that the only way by which we can find out is through a social process in which everybody is allowed to try and see what he can do. The fundamental assumption, here as elsewhere, is the unlimited variety of human gifts and skills and the consequent ignorance of any single individual of most of what is known to all the other members of society taken together. Or, to put this fundamental contention differently, human Reason, with a capital R, does not exist in the singular, as given or available to any particular person, as the rationalist approach seems to assume, but must be conceived as an inter-personal process in which anyone's contribution is tested and corrected by others. This argument does not assume that all men are equal in their natural endowments and capacities but only that no man is qualified to pass final judgement on the capacities which another possesses or is to be allowed to exercise.

Here I may perhaps mention that only because men are in fact unequal can we treat them equally. If all men were completely equal in their gifts and inclinations, we should have to treat them differently in order to achieve any sort of social organisation. Fortunately, they are not equal; and it is only owing to this that the differentiation of functions need not be determined by the arbitrary decision of some organising will but that, after creating formal equality of the rules applying in the same manner to all, we can leave each individual to find his own level.

There is all the difference in the world between treating people equally and attempting to make them equal. While the first is the condition of a free society, the second means, as Tocqueville described it, "a new form of servitude".[24]

V

From the awareness of the limitations of individual knowledge and from the fact that no person or small group of persons can know all that is known to somebody, individualism also derives its main practical conclusion: its demand for a strict limitation of all coercive or exclusive power. Its opposition, however, is directed only against the use of *coercion* to bring about organisation or association and not against association as such. Far from being opposed to voluntary association, the case of the individualist rests, on the contrary, on the contention that much of what in the opinion of many can be brought about only by conscious direction, can be better achieved by the voluntary and spontaneous collaboration of individuals. The consistent individualist ought therefore to be an enthusiast for voluntary collaboration—wherever and whenever it does not degenerate into coercion of others or lead to the assumption of exclusive powers.

True individualism is, of course, not anarchism, which is but another product of the rationalistic pseudo-individualism to which it is opposed. It does not deny the necessity of coercive power but wishes to limit it—to limit it to those fields where it is indispensable to prevent coercion by others and in order to

[24] This phrase is used over and over again by Tocqueville to describe the effects of socialism, but see particularly "Discours prononcé à l'assemblée constituante dans la discussion du projet de constitution (12 septembre 1848) sur la question du droit au travail", in *Etudes économiques, politiques et littéraires*, p. 541, where he says: "Si, en définitive, j'avais à trouver une formule générale pour exprimer ce que m'apparaît le socialisme dans son ensemble, je dirais que c'est une nouvelle formule de la servitude". [Should I finally express in a general formula what socialism as a whole means to me, I should say it is a new form of servitude.—Ed.] Perhaps I may be allowed to add that it was this phrase of Tocqueville's which suggested to me the title of a recent book of mine. [Hayek here refers to his book *The Road to Serfdom* [1944], see F. A. Hayek, *The Road to Serfdom: Text and Documents*, ed. Bruce Caldwell, vol. 2 (2007) of *The Collected Works of F. A. Hayek*. —Ed.]

reduce the total of coercion to a minimum. While all the individualist philosophers are probably agreed on this general formula, it must be admitted that they are not always very informative on its application in specific cases. Neither the much abused and much misunderstood phrase of 'laissez faire' nor the still older formula of 'the protection of life, liberty, and property' are of much help. In fact, in so far as both tend to suggest that we can just leave things as they are, they may be worse than no answer; they certainly do not tell us what are and what are not desirable or necessary fields of government activity. Yet the decision whether individualist philosophy can serve us as a practical guide must ultimately depend on whether it will enable us to distinguish between the agenda and the non-agenda of government.

Some general rules of this kind which are of very wide applicability seem to me to follow directly from the basic tenets of individualism: If each man is to use *his* peculiar knowledge and skill with the aim of furthering the aims for which *he* cares, and if, in so doing, he is to make as large a contribution as possible to needs which are beyond his ken, it is clearly necessary, first, that he should have a clearly delimited area of responsibility and, second, that the relative importance to him of the different results he can achieve must correspond to the relative importance to others of the more remote and to him unknown effects of his action.

Let us first take the problem of the determination of a sphere of responsibility and leave the second problem for later. If man is to remain free to make full use of his knowledge or skill, the delimitation of spheres of responsibility must not take the form of an assignation to him of particular ends which he must try to achieve. This would be imposing a specific duty rather than delimiting a sphere of responsibility. Nor must it take the form of allocating to him specific resources selected by some authority, which would take the choice almost as much out of his hands as the imposition of specific tasks. If man is to exercise his own gifts, it must be as a result of his activities and planning that his sphere of responsibility is determined. The solution to this problem which men have gradually developed and which antedates government in the modern sense of the word is the acceptance of formal principles, "a standing rule to live by, common to every one of that society"[25]—of rules which, above all, enable man to distinguish between mine and thine, and from which he and his fellows can ascertain what is his and what is somebody else's sphere of responsibility.

The fundamental contrast between government by rules, whose main pur-

[25] John Locke, *Two Treatises of Government* [1690] book 2, chapter 4, § 22: "Freedom of men under government, is, to have a standing rule to live by, common to every one of that society, and made by the legislative power erected in it". [Locke's *Two Treatises* has been frequently reprinted; see, e.g., John Locke, *Two Treatises of Government*, ed. Peter Laslett (Cambridge: Cambridge University Press, 1988), p. 284.—Ed.]

pose is to inform the individual what is his sphere of responsibility within which he must shape his own life, and government by orders which impose specific duties has become so blurred in recent years that it is necessary to consider it a little further. It involves nothing less than the distinction between freedom under the law and the use of the legislative machinery, whether democratic or not, to abolish freedom. The essential point is not that there should be some kind of guiding principle behind the actions of the government but that government should be confined to making the individuals observe principles which *they* know and can take into account in *their* decisions. It means, further, that what the individual may or may not do, or what he can expect his fellows to do or not to do, must depend not on some remote and indirect consequences which his actions may have but on the immediate and readily recognisable circumstances which he can be supposed to know. He must have rules referring to typical situations, defined in terms of what can be known to the acting persons and without regard to the distant effects in the particular instance—rules which, if they are regularly observed, will in the majority of cases operate beneficially—even if they do not do so in the proverbial 'hard cases which make bad law'.

The most general principle on which an individualist system is based is that it uses the universal acceptance of general principles as the means to create order in social affairs. It is the opposite of such government by principles when, for example, a recent blueprint for a controlled economy suggests as the "fundamental principle of organisation . . . that in any particular instance the means that serves society best should be the one that prevails".[26] It is a serious confusion thus to speak of principle when all that is meant is that no principle but only expediency should rule; when everything depends on what authority decrees to be 'the interests of society'. Principles are a means to prevent clashes between conflicting aims and not a set of fixed ends. Our submission to general principles is necessary because we cannot be guided in our practical action by full knowledge and evaluation of all the consequences. So long as men are not omniscient, the only way in which freedom can be given to the individual is by such general rules to delimit the sphere in which the decision is his. There can be no freedom if the government is not limited to particular kinds of action but can use its powers in any ways which serve particular ends. As Lord Acton pointed out long ago: "Whenever a single definite object is made the supreme end of the State, be it the advantage of a class, the safety or the power of the country, the greatest happiness of the greatest number, or the support of any speculative idea, the State becomes for the time inevitably absolute".[27]

[26] Lerner, *The Economics of Control*, p. 5.

[27] John Emerich Edward Dalberg-Acton, First Baron Acton, "Nationality" [1862], reprinted in *The History of Freedom and Other Essays* (London: Macmillan, 1907), p. 288. [For a more recent

VI

But, if our main conclusion is that an individualist order must rest on the enforcement of abstract principles rather than on the enforcement of specific orders, this still leaves open the question of the kind of general rules which we want. It confines the exercise of coercive powers in the main to one method, but it still allows almost unlimited scope to human ingenuity in the designing of the most effective set of rules; and, though the best solutions of the concrete problems will in most instances have to be discovered by experience, there is a good deal more that we can learn from the general principles of individualism with regard to the desirable nature and contents of these rules. There is, in the first instance, one important corollary of what has already been said, namely, that the rules, because they are to serve as signposts to the individuals in making their own plans, should be designed to remain valid for long periods. Liberal or individualist policy must be essentially long-run policy; the present fashion to concentrate on short-run effects, and to justify this by the argument that "in the long run we are all dead", leads inevitably to the reliance on orders adjusted to the particular circumstances of the moment in the place of rules couched in terms of typical situations.[28]

We need, and get from the basic principles of individualism, however, much more definite aid than this for the construction of a suitable legal system. The endeavour to make man by the pursuit of his interests contribute as much as possible to the needs of other men leads not merely to the general principle of 'private property'; it also assists us in determining what the contents of property rights ought to be with respect to different kinds of things. In order that the individual in his decisions should take account of all the physical effects caused by these decisions, it is necessary that the 'sphere of responsibility' of which I have been speaking be made to comprise as fully as possible all the direct effects which his actions have on the satisfactions which other people derive from the things under his control. This is achieved on the whole by the simple conception of property as the exclusive right to use a particular thing where mobile effects, or what the lawyer calls 'chattels', are concerned. But it raises much more difficult problems in connection with land, where the recognition of the principle of private property helps us very little until we know precisely what rights and obligations ownership includes. And when we turn

edition, see *Essays in the History of Liberty*, ed. J. Rufus Fears, vol. 1 of *Selected Writings of Lord Acton* (Indianapolis, IN: LibertyClassics, 1985), p. 424.—Ed.]

[28] [John Maynard Keynes famously observed "In the long run we are all dead" in *A Tract on Monetary Reform* [1923], reprinted as volume 4 (1971) of *The Collected Writings of John Maynard Keynes*, Austin Robinson and Donald Moggridge, eds, 30 vols. (London: Macmillan (for the Royal Economic Society), 1971–89), p. 376.—Ed.]

to such problems of more recent origin as the control of the air or of electric power, or of inventions and of literary or artistic creations, nothing short of going back to the *rationale* of property will help us to decide what should be in the particular instance the sphere of control or responsibility of the individual.

I cannot here go further into the fascinating subject of a suitable legal framework for an effective individualist system or enter into discussion of the many supplementary functions, such as assistance in the spreading of information and in the elimination of genuinely avoidable uncertainty,[29] by which the government might greatly increase the efficiency of individual action. I mention them merely in order to stress that there are further (and non-coercive!) functions of government beyond the mere enforcement of civil and criminal law which can be fully justified on individualist principles.

There is still, however, one point left, to which I have already referred, but which is so important that I must give it further attention. It is that any workable individualist order must be so framed not only that the relative remunerations the individual can expect from the different uses of his abilities and resources correspond to the relative utility of the result of his efforts to others but also that these remunerations correspond to the objective results of his efforts rather than to their subjective merits. An effectively competitive market satisfies both these conditions. But it is in connection with the second that our personal sense of justice so frequently revolts against the impersonal decisions of the market. Yet, if the individual is to be free to choose, it is inevitable that he should bear the risk attaching to that choice and that in consequence he be rewarded, not according to the goodness or badness of his intentions, but solely on the basis of the value of the results to others. We must face the fact that the preservation of individual freedom is incompatible with a full satisfaction of our views of distributive justice.

---

[29] The actions a government can expediently take to reduce really avoidable uncertainty for the individuals are a subject which has given rise to so many confusions that I am afraid to let the brief allusion to it in the text stand without some further explanation. The point is that, while it is easy to protect a particular person or group against the loss which might be caused by an unforeseen change, by preventing people from taking notice of the change after it has occurred, this merely shifts the loss onto other shoulders but does not prevent it. If, e.g., capital invested in a very expensive plant is protected against obsolescence by new inventions by prohibiting the introduction of such new inventions, this increases the security of the owners of the existing plant but deprives the public of the benefit of the new inventions. Or, in other words, it does not really reduce uncertainty for society as a whole if we make the behaviour of the people more predictable by preventing them from adapting themselves to an unforeseen change in their knowledge of the world. The only genuine reduction of uncertainty consists in increasing its knowledge, but never in preventing people from making use of new knowledge.

VII

While the theory of individualism has thus a definite contribution to make to the technique of constructing a suitable legal framework and of improving the institutions which have grown up spontaneously, its emphasis, of course, is on the fact that the part of our social order which can or ought to be made a conscious product of human reason is only a small part of all the forces of society. In other words, that the state, the embodiment of deliberately organised and consciously directed power, ought to be only a small part of the much richer organism which we call 'society', and that the former ought to provide merely a framework within which free (and therefore not 'consciously directed') collaboration of men has the maximum of scope.

This entails certain corollaries on which true individualism once more stands in sharp opposition to the false individualism of the rationalistic type. The first is that the deliberately organised state on the one side, and the individual on the other, far from being regarded as the only realities, while all the intermediate formations and associations are to be deliberately suppressed, as was the aim of the French Revolution, the non-compulsory conventions of social intercourse are considered as essential factors in preserving the orderly working of human society. The second is that the individual, in participating in the social processes, must be ready and willing to adjust himself to changes and to submit to conventions which are not the result of intelligent design, whose justification in the particular instance may not be recognisable, and which to him will often appear unintelligible and irrational.

I need not say much on the first point. That true individualism affirms the value of the family and all the common efforts of the small community and group, that it believes in local autonomy and voluntary associations, and that indeed its case rests largely on the contention that much for which the coercive action of the state is usually invoked can be done better by voluntary collaboration need not be stressed further. There can be no greater contrast to this than the false individualism which wants to dissolve all these smaller groups into atoms which have no cohesion other than the coercive rules imposed by the state, and which tries to make all social ties prescriptive, instead of using the state mainly as a protection of the individual against the arrogation of coercive powers by the smaller groups.

Quite as important for the functioning of an individualist society as these smaller groupings of men are the traditions and conventions which evolve in a free society and which, without being enforceable, establish flexible but normally observed rules that make the behaviour of other people predictable in a high degree. The willingness to submit to such rules, not merely so long as one understands the reason for them but so long as one has no definite reasons to the contrary, is an essential condition for the gradual evolution and improvement of rules of social intercourse; and the readiness ordinarily to submit to the products of a social process which nobody has designed and the reasons for which nobody may understand is also an indispensable condition if it is to be possible to dispense with compulsion.[30] That the existence of common conventions and traditions among a group of people will enable them to work together smoothly and efficiently with much less formal organisation and compulsion than a group without such common background, is, of course, a commonplace. But the reverse of this, while less familiar, is probably not less true: that coercion can probably only be kept to a minimum in a society where conventions and tradition have made the behaviour of man to a large extent predictable.[31]

This brings me to my second point: the necessity, in any complex society in which the effects of anyone's action reach far beyond his possible range of vision, of the individual submitting to the anonymous and seemingly irrational forces of society—a submission which must include not only the acceptance of rules of behaviour as valid without examining what depends in the particular instance on their being observed but also a readiness to adjust himself to changes which may profoundly affect his fortunes and opportunities and the causes of which may be altogether unintelligible to him. It is against these that modern man tends to revolt unless their necessity can be shown to rest upon 'reason made clear and demonstrable to every individual'. Yet it is just here that the understandable craving for intelligibility produces illusory demands which no system can satisfy. Man in a complex society can have no choice but between adjusting himself to what to him must seem the blind

---

[30] The difference between the rationalistic and the true individualistic approach is well shown in the different views expressed by French observers on the apparent irrationality of English social institutions. While Henri de Saint-Simon, e.g., complains that "cent volumes *in folio*, du caractère plus fin, ne suffiraient pas pour rendre compte de toutes les inconséquences organiques qui existent en Angleterre" (*Œuvres de Saint-Simon et d'Enfantin* (Paris: E. Dentu, 1865–78), vol. 38 [37], p. 179 [89], Tocqueville retorts "que ces bizarreries des Anglais pussent avoir quelques rapports avec leurs libertés, c'est ce qui ne lui tombe point dans l'esprit" (*L'Ancien régime et la révolution*, 5th ed. (Paris: M. Lévy, 1866), p. 103). [Saint-Simon's outburst might be rendered, "one hundred folio volumes, with the thinnest characters, would not suffice to account for all the organic inconsistencies that exist in England", and Tocqueville's retort as "that such oddities of the English might be in some way related to their liberties, that is precisely what does not come to his mind". In the Saint-Simon quotation, "thinnest characters" refers to thin printed letters.—Ed.]

[31] Is it necessary to quote Edmund Burke once more to remind the reader how essential a condition for the possibility of a free society was to him the strength of moral rules? "Men are qualified for civil liberty", he wrote, "in exact proportion to their disposition to put moral chains upon their own appetites; in proportion as their love of justice is above their rapacity; in proportion as their soundness and sobriety of understanding is above their vanity and presumption; in proportion as they are more disposed to listen to the counsels of the wise and good, in preference to the flattery of knaves" (Edmund Burke, "A Letter to a Member of the National Assembly" [1791], in *Works of the Right Honourable Edmund Burke*, vol. 4, p. 319).

forces of the social process and obeying the orders of a superior. So long as he knows only the hard discipline of the market, he may well think the direction by some other intelligent human brain preferable; but, when he tries it, he soon discovers that the former still leaves him at least some choice, while the latter leaves him none, and that it is better to have a choice between several unpleasant alternatives than being coerced into one.

The unwillingness to tolerate or respect any social forces which are not recognisable as the product of intelligent design, which is so important a cause of the present desire for comprehensive economic planning, is indeed only one aspect of a more general movement. We meet the same tendency in the field of morals and conventions, in the desire to substitute an artificial for the existing languages, and in the whole modern attitude towards processes which govern the growth of knowledge. The belief that only a synthetic system of morals, an artificial language, or even an artificial society can be justified in an age of science, as well as the increasing unwillingness to bow before any moral rules whose utility is not rationally demonstrated, or to conform with conventions whose rationale is not known, are all manifestations of the same basic view which wants all social activity to be recognisably part of a single coherent plan. They are the results of that same rationalistic 'individualism' which wants to see in everything the product of conscious individual reason. They are certainly not, however, a result of true individualism and may even make the working of a free and truly individualistic system difficult or impossible. Indeed, the great lesson which the individualist philosophy teaches us on this score is that, while it may not be difficult to destroy the spontaneous formations which are the indispensable bases of a free civilisation, it may be beyond our power deliberately to reconstruct such a civilisation once these foundations are destroyed.

VIII

The point I am trying to make is well illustrated by the apparent paradox that the Germans, though commonly regarded as very docile, are also often described as being particularly individualistic. With some truth this so-called German individualism is frequently represented as one of the causes why the Germans have never succeeded in developing free political institutions. In the rationalistic sense of the term, in their insistence on the development of 'original' personalities which in every respect are the product of the conscious choice of the individual, the German intellectual tradition indeed favours a kind of 'individualism' little known elsewhere. I remember well how surprised and even shocked I was myself when as a young student, on my first contact with English and American contemporaries, I discovered how much they were disposed to conform in all externals to common usage rather than, as seemed natural to me, to be proud to be different and original in most respects. If you doubt the significance of such an individual experience, you will find it fully confirmed in most German discussions of, for example, the English public school system, such as you will find in Dibelius's well-known book on England.[32] Again and again you will find the same surprise about this tendency towards voluntary conformity and see it contrasted with the ambition of the young German to develop an 'original personality', which in every respect expresses what he has come to regard as right and true. This cult of the distinct and different individuality has, of course, deep roots in the German intellectual tradition and, through the influence of some of its greatest exponents, especially Goethe and Wilhelm von Humboldt, has made itself felt far beyond Germany and is clearly seen in J. S. Mill's *Liberty*.[33]

This sort of 'individualism' not only has nothing to do with true individualism but also may indeed prove a grave obstacle to the smooth working of an individualist system. It must remain an open question whether a free or individualistic society can be worked successfully if people are too 'individualistic' in the false sense, if they are too unwilling voluntarily to conform to traditions and conventions, and if they refuse to recognise anything which is not consciously designed or which cannot be demonstrated as rational to every individual. It is at least understandable that the prevalence of this kind of 'individualism' has often made people of good will despair of the possibility of achieving order in a free society and even made them ask for a dictatorial government with the power to impose on society the order which it will not produce itself.

In Germany, in particular, this preference for the deliberate organisation and the corresponding contempt for the spontaneous and uncontrolled was strongly supported by the tendency towards centralisation which the struggle for national unity produced. In a country where what traditions it possessed were essentially local, the striving for unity implied a systematic opposition to almost everything which was a spontaneous growth and its consistent replacement by artificial creations. That, in what a recent historian has well described

[32] Wilhelm Dibelius, *England* [1923], translated by Mary Agnes Hamilton (London: J. Cape, 1934), pp. 464–68. [The German historian Wilhelm Debelius (1876–1931) was the author of numerous books on Britain.—Ed.]

[33] [Hayek refers to John Stuart Mill's *On Liberty* [1859], reprinted in *Essays on Politics and Society I*, ed. J. M. Robson, vol. 18 (1977) of *Collected Works of John Stuart Mill* (Toronto: University of Toronto Press, 1963–91), pp. 213–310. In the book Mill defended the freedom of the individual in the face of social and political control. German poet, playwright, and scientist Johann Wolfgang von Goethe (1749–1832) was the author of *Faust* (1808, 1832) and *The Sorrows of Young Werther* (1774). Philologist and statesman Karl Wilhelm von Humboldt (1767–1835) was the first Prussian minister of education and founder of the University of Berlin. Hayek noted Mill's debt to Goethe and Humboldt in the introduction to *The Road to Serfdom*, p. 61, note 4.—Ed.]

as a "desperate search for a tradition which they did not possess",[34] the Germans should have ended by creating a totalitarian state which forced upon them what they felt they lacked should perhaps not have surprised us as much as it did.

IX

If it is true that the progressive tendency towards central control of all social processes is the inevitable result of an approach which insists that everything must be tidily planned and made to show a recognisable order, it is also true that this tendency tends to create conditions in which nothing but an all-powerful central government can preserve order and stability. The concentration of all decisions in the hands of authority itself produces a state of affairs in which what structure society still possesses is imposed upon it by government and in which the individuals have become interchangeable units with no other definite or durable relations to one another than those determined by the all-comprehensive organisation. In the jargon of the modern sociologists this type of society has come to be known as 'mass society'—a somewhat misleading name, because the characteristic attributes of this kind of society are not so much the result of mere numbers as they are of the lack of any spontaneous structure other than that impressed upon it by deliberate organisation, an incapacity to evolve its own differentiations, and a consequent dependence on a power which deliberately moulds and shapes it. It is connected with numbers only in so far as in large nations the process of centralisation will much sooner reach a point where deliberate organisation from the top smothers those spontaneous formations which are founded on contacts closer and more intimate than those that can exist in the large unit.

It is not surprising that in the nineteenth century, when these tendencies first became clearly visible, the opposition to centralisation became one of the main concerns of the individualist philosophers. This opposition is particularly marked in the writings of the two great historians whose names I have before singled out as the leading representatives of true individualism in the nineteenth century, Tocqueville and Lord Acton; and it finds expression in their strong sympathies for the small countries and for the federal organisation of large units. There is even more reason now to think that the small countries may before long become the last oases that will preserve a free society. It may already be too late to stop the fatal course of progressive centralisation

---

[34] Edmond Vermeil, *Germany's Three Reichs, their History and Culture*, translated by E. W. Dickes (London: A. Dakers, 1944), p. 224. [For more on Germany in this connection see Hayek's review of Vermeil's book in chapter 10 of *The Fortunes of Liberalism*.—Ed.]

in the bigger countries which are well on the way to produce those mass societies in which despotism in the end comes to appear as the only salvation. Whether even the small countries will escape will depend on whether they keep free from the poison of nationalism, which is both an inducement to, and a result of, that same striving for a society which is consciously organised from the top.

The attitude of individualism to nationalism, which intellectually is but a twin brother of socialism, would deserve special discussion. Here I can only point out that the fundamental difference between what in the nineteenth century was regarded as liberalism in the English-speaking world and what was so called on the Continent is closely connected with their descent from true individualism and the false rationalistic individualism, respectively. It was only liberalism in the English sense that was generally opposed to centralisation, to nationalism and to socialism, while the liberalism prevalent on the Continent favoured all three. I should add, however, that, in this as in so many other respects, John Stuart Mill, and the later English liberalism derived from him, belong at least as much to the Continental as to the English tradition; and I know no discussion more illuminating of these basic differences than Lord Acton's criticism of the concessions Mill had made to the nationalistic tendencies of Continental liberalism.[35]

X

There are two more points of difference between the two kinds of individualism which are also best illustrated by the stand taken by Lord Acton and Tocqueville by their views on democracy and equality towards trends which became prominent in their time. True individualism not only believes in democracy but can claim that democratic ideals spring from the basic principles of individualism. Yet, while individualism affirms that all government

[35] Acton, "Nationality", pp. 270–300. [See *Essays in the History of Liberty*, pp. 409–33. In the essay Acton argued that having various nationalities within a nation helps to protect individual freedom: "If we take the establishment of liberty for the realisation of moral duties to be the end of civil society, we must conclude that those states are substantially the most perfect which, like the British and Austrian Empires, include various distinct nationalities without oppressing them. . . . That intolerance of social freedom which is natural to absolutism is sure to find a corrective in the national diversities, which no other force could so efficiently provide. The coexistence of several nations under the same State is a test, as well as the best security of its freedom" (*Essays*, pp. 432, 425). This Acton contrasts with Mill's view that, "It is in general a necessary condition of free institutions, that the boundaries of governments should coincide in the main with those of nationalities" (*Essays*, p. 422). See John Stuart Mill, *Considerations on Representative Government* (1861), reprinted in *Essays on Politics and Society, II*, ed. J. M. Robson, vol. 19 (1977) of *Collected Works of John Stuart Mill*, p. 548.—Ed.]

should be democratic, it has no superstitious belief in the omni-competence of majority decisions, and in particular it refuses to admit that "absolute power may, by the hypothesis of a popular origin, be as legitimate as constitutional freedom".[36] It believes that under a democracy, no less than under any other form of government, "the sphere of enforced command ought to be restricted within fixed limits";[37] and it is particularly opposed to the most fateful and dangerous of all current misconceptions of democracy—the belief that we must accept as true and binding for future development the views of the majority. While democracy is founded on the convention that the majority view decides on common action, it does not mean that what is today the majority view ought to become the generally accepted view—even if that were necessary to achieve the aims of the majority. On the contrary, the whole justification of democracy rests on the fact that in course of time what is today the view of a small minority may become the majority view. I believe, indeed, that one of the most important questions on which political theory will have to discover an answer in the near future is that of finding a line of demarcation between the fields in which the majority views must be binding for all and the fields in which, on the contrary, the minority view ought to be allowed to prevail if it can produce results which better satisfy a demand of the public. I am, above all, convinced that, where the interests of a particular branch of trade are concerned, the majority view will always be the reactionary, stationary view and that the merit of competition is precisely that it gives the minority a chance to prevail. Where it can do so without any coercive powers, it ought always to have the right.

I cannot better sum up this attitude of true individualism towards democracy than by once more quoting Lord Acton: "The true democratic principle", he wrote, "that none shall have power over the people, is taken to mean that none shall be able to restrain or to elude its power. The true democratic principle, that the people shall not be made to do what it does not like, is taken to mean that it shall never be required to tolerate what it does not like. The true democratic principle, that every man's free will shall be as unfettered as possible, is taken to mean that the free will of the collective people shall be fettered in nothing".[38]

When we turn to equality, however, it should be said at once that true individualism is not equalitarian in the modern sense of the word. It can see no

---

[36] Lord Acton, "Sir Erskine May's Democracy in Europe" [1878], reprinted in *The History of Freedom and Other Essays*, p. 78. [See *Essays in the History of Liberty*, p. 68.—Ed.]

[37] Lord Acton, "The Study of History", in *Lectures on Modern History* (London: Macmillan, 1906), p. 10. [See *Essays in the Study and Writing of History*, ed. J. Rufus Fears, vol. 2 of *Selected Writings of Lord Acton*, p. 516.—Ed.]

[38] Lord Acton, "Sir Erskine May's *Democracy in Europe*", pp. 93–94. [See *Essays in the History of Liberty*, p. 80.—Ed.]

reason for trying to make people equal as distinct from treating them equally. While individualism is profoundly opposed to all prescriptive privilege, to all protection, by law or force, of any rights not based on rules equally applicable to all persons, it also denies government the right to limit what the able or fortunate may achieve. It is equally opposed to any rigid limitation of the position individuals may achieve, whether this power is used to perpetuate inequality or to create equality. Its main principle is that no man or group of men should have power to decide what another man's status ought to be, and it regards this as a condition of freedom so essential that it must not be sacrificed to the gratification of our sense of justice or of our envy.

From the point of view of individualism there would not appear to exist even any justification for making all individuals start on the same level by preventing them from profiting by advantages which they have in no way earned, such as being born to parents who are more intelligent or more conscientious than the average. Here individualism is indeed less 'individualistic' than socialism, because it recognises the family as a legitimate unit as much as the individual; and the same is true with respect to other groups, such as linguistic or religious communities, which by their common efforts may succeed for long periods in preserving for their members material or moral standards different from those of the rest of the population. Tocqueville and Lord Acton speak with one voice on this subject. "Democracy and socialism", Tocqueville wrote, "have nothing in common but one word, equality. But notice the difference: While democracy seeks equality in liberty, socialism seeks equality in restraint and servitude".[39] And Acton joined him in believing that "the deepest cause which made the French revolution so disastrous to liberty was its theory of equality"[40] and that "the finest opportunity ever given to the world was thrown away, because the passion for equality made vain the hope of freedom".[41]

XI

It would be possible to continue for a long time discussing further differences separating the two traditions of thought which, while bearing the same name, are divided by fundamentally opposed principles. But I must not allow myself to be diverted too far from my task of tracing to its source the confusion which

[39] Tocqueville, "Discours prononcé à l'assemblée constituante dans la discussion de projet de constitution (12 Septembre 1848) sur la question du droit au travail", in *Etudes économiques, politiques et littéraires*, p. 546.

[40] Lord Acton, "Sir Erskine May's *Democracy in Europe*", p. 88. [See *Essays in the History of Liberty*, p. 76.—Ed.]

[41] Lord Acton, "The History of Freedom in Christianity" [1877], reprinted in *The History of Freedom*, p. 57. [See *Essays in the History of Liberty*, p. 51.—Ed.]

has resulted from this and of showing that there is one consistent tradition which, whether you agree with me or not that it is 'true' individualism, is at any rate the only kind of individualism which I am prepared to defend and, indeed, I believe, the only kind which can be defended consistently. So let me return, in conclusion, to what I said in the beginning: that the fundamental attitude of true individualism is one of humility towards the processes by which mankind has achieved things which have not been designed or understood by any individual and are indeed greater than individual minds. The great question at this moment is whether man's mind will be allowed to continue to grow as part of this process or whether human reason is to place itself in chains of its own making.

What individualism teaches us is that society is greater than the individual only in so far as it is free. In so far as it is controlled or directed, it is limited to the powers of the individual minds which control or direct it. If the presumption of the modern mind, which will not respect anything that is not consciously controlled by individual reason, does not learn in time where to stop, we may, as Edmund Burke warned us, "be well assured that everything about us will dwindle by degrees, until at length our concerns are shrunk to the dimensions of our minds".[42]

---

[42] [Edmund Burke, "Speech on the Nabob of Arcot's Debts" [1785], in *Works of the Right Honourable Edmund Burke* (Boston: Little, Brown and Co., 1889), vol. 3, p. 16.—Ed.]

PART I

SCIENTISM AND THE STUDY OF SOCIETY

Systems which have universally owed their origin to the lucubrations of those who were acquainted with one art, but ignorant of the other; who therefore explained to themselves the phenomena, in that which was strange to them, by those in that which was familiar; and with whom, upon that account, the analogy, which in other writers gives occasion to a few ingenious similitudes, became the great hinge upon which every thing turned.

—Adam Smith, *Essay on the History of Astronomy*

[An initial version of "Scientism and the Study of Society" was published in three parts in *Economica*, n.s., vol. 9, August 1942, pp. 267–91; vol. 10, February 1943, pp. 34–63; and vol. 11, February 1944, pp. 27–39. A slightly revised version, which serves as the basis of this edition, was published in F. A. Hayek, *The Counter-Revolution of Science: Studies on the Abuse of Reason* (Glencoe, IL: Free Press, 1952; reprinted, Indianapolis, IN: Liberty Fund, 1979), pp. 17–182. Most of the differences between the two versions involve either Hayek changing phrasing to make a passage more clear, or the addition of new citations of pieces that appeared in the intervening period. Any significant differences between the two versions are noted in bracketed comments.—Ed.]
[Adam Smith, "The History of Astronomy", reprinted in *Essays on Philosophical Subjects*, vol. 3, *The Glasgow Edition of the Works and Correspondence of Adam Smith*, p. 47.—Ed.]

ONE

THE INFLUENCE OF THE NATURAL SCIENCES ON THE SOCIAL SCIENCES

In the course of its slow development in the eighteenth and early nineteenth centuries the study of economic and social phenomena was guided in the choice of its methods in the main by the nature of the problems it had to face.[1] It gradually developed a technique appropriate to these problems without much reflection on the character of the methods or on their relation to that of other disciplines of knowledge. Students of political economy could describe it alternatively as a branch of science or of moral or social philosophy without the least qualms whether their subject was scientific or philosophical. The term *science* had not yet assumed the special narrow meaning it has today,[2] nor

---

[1] This is not universally true. The attempts to treat social phenomena 'scientistically', which became so influential in the nineteenth century, were not completely absent in the eighteenth. There is at least a strong element of it in the work of Montesquieu and the Physiocrats. But the great achievements of the century in the theory of the social sciences, the works of Cantillon and Hume, of Turgot and Adam Smith, were on the whole free from it. [French social and political theorist Charles de Secondat, Baron de la Brède et de Montesquieu (1689–1755) is remembered today not for the elements of scientism in his work, but for enunciating in his *Spirit of the Laws* (1748) the idea of the inevitability of conflict among interests in democratic and monarchical regimes, and hence of the importance of the separation and balance of powers for their survival. François Quesnay (1694–1774), the leader of the physiocrats, was also the court physician for Louis XV, and in his economic writings drew analogies between the circulation of money and the circulation of the blood. While serving as the comptroller-general of finance from 1774–76 under Louis XVI, Anne Robert Jacques Turgot (1727–81) attempted to reduce barriers to trade among the French provinces and to abolish privileges of corporations, but these reforms were so unpopular among the upper classes that he was removed from office. The Irish-born French economist Richard Cantillon (c. 1680–1734) was author of *Essai sur la nature du commerce en général* (1755). Though influential in eighteenth-century France, his work had to be rediscovered in the nineteenth by William Stanley Jevons, who lauded his book as the first treatise on economics. For a translation of an early essay by Hayek on Cantillon, see chapter 13 of his *The Trend of Economic Thinking*.—Ed.]

[2] The earliest example of the modern narrow use of the term 'science' given in Murray's *New English Dictionary* (Oxford: Clarendon Press, 1888–1928) dates from as late as 1867. But John Theodore Merz, *A History of European Thought in the Nineteenth Century* (Edinburgh: William Blackwood and Sons, 1896) vol. 1, p. 89, is probably right when he suggests that 'science' acquired its present meaning about the time of the formation of the British Association for the Advancement of Science (1831).

was there any distinction made which singled out the physical or natural sciences and attributed to them a special dignity. Those who devoted themselves to those fields indeed readily chose the designation of philosophy when they were concerned with the more general aspects of their problems,[3] and occasionally we even find 'natural philosophy' contrasted with 'moral science'.

During the first half of the nineteenth century a new attitude made its appearance. The term 'science' came more and more to be confined to the physical and biological disciplines which at the same time began to claim for themselves a special rigorousness and certainty which distinguished them from all others. Their success was such that they soon came to exercise an extraordinary fascination on those working in other fields, who rapidly began to imitate their teaching and vocabulary. Thus the tyranny commenced which the methods and technique of the Sciences[4] in the narrow sense of the term have ever since exercised over the other subjects. These became increasingly concerned to vindicate their equal status by showing that their methods were the same as those of their brilliantly successful sisters rather than by adapting their methods more and more to their own particular problems. And, although in the 120 years or so, during which this ambition to imitate Science in its methods rather than its spirit has now dominated social studies, it has contributed scarcely anything to our understanding of social phenomena, not only does it continue to confuse and discredit the work of the social disciplines, but demands for further attempts in this direction are still presented to us as the latest revolutionary innovations which, if adopted, will secure rapid undreamed of progress.

Let it be said at once, however, that those who were loudest in these demands were rarely themselves men who had noticeably enriched our knowledge of the Sciences. From Francis Bacon, the lord chancellor, who will forever remain the prototype of the 'demagogue of science', as he has justly been called, to Auguste Comte and the 'physicalists' of our own day, the claims for the exclusive virtues of the specific methods employed by the natural sciences were mostly advanced by men whose right to speak on behalf of the scientists was not above suspicion, and who indeed in many cases had shown in the Sciences themselves as much bigoted prejudice as in their attitude to other subjects.[5] Just as Francis Bacon opposed Copernican

---

[3] E.g., John Dalton's *New System of Chemical Philosophy* (Manchester: S. Russell for R. Bickerstaff, London, 1808); Jean Lamarck's *Philosophie zoologique* (Paris: Dentu, 1809); or Antoine-François de Fourcroy's *Philosophie chimique* (Paris: Levrault, Schoell et cie, 1806).

[4] We shall use the term Science with a capital letter when we wish to emphasise that we use it in the modern narrow meaning.

[5] [English statesman and philosopher Francis Bacon (1561–1626) advocated in his *Novum Organum* (1620) an experimental and inductive approach for the sciences, and Auguste Comte (1798–1857), who coined the term 'sociology', propounded a positivist approach to the study of social phenomena. For Hayek's views on Bacon see "Francis Bacon: Progenitor of Scientism (1561–1626)", chapter 5 of *The Trend of Economic Thinking*; and on Comte see this volume, chapters 13

astronomy,[6] and as Comte taught that any too minute investigation of the phenomena by such instruments as the microscope was harmful and should be suppressed by the spiritual power of the positive society, because it tended to upset the laws of positive science, so this dogmatic attitude has so often misled men of this type in their own field that there should have been little reason to pay too much deference to their views about problems still more distant from the fields from which they derived their inspiration.

There is yet another qualification which the reader ought to keep in mind throughout the following discussion. The methods which scientists or men fascinated by the natural sciences have so often tried to force upon the social sciences were not always necessarily those which the scientists in fact followed in their own field, but rather those which they believed that they employed. This is not necessarily the same thing. The scientist reflecting and theorising about his procedure is not always a reliable guide. The views about the character of the method of Science have undergone various fashions during the last few generations, while we must assume that the methods actually followed have remained essentially the same. But since it was what scientists believed that they did, and even the views which they had held some time before, which have influenced the social sciences, the following comments on the methods of the natural sciences also do not necessarily claim to be a true account of what the scientists in fact do, but an account of the views on the nature of scientific method which were dominant in recent times.[7]

The history of this influence, the channels through which it operated, and the direction in which it affected social developments, will occupy us throughout the series of historical studies to which the present essay is designed to serve as an introduction.[8] Before we trace the historical course of this influence and its effects, we shall here attempt to describe its general characteristics and the nature of the problems to which the unwarranted and unfortunate extensions of the habits of thought of the physical and biological sciences have given rise. There are certain typical elements of this attitude which we

---

and 15–17. Otto Neurath (1882–1945), the social science representative of the Vienna Circle of logical positivists, was perhaps the most prominent advocate of physicalism, the doctrine that factual scientific knowledge is formulated in statements about observable physical objects and activities. Hayek criticises the doctrine, along with behaviourism in psychology, in chapter 5 below.—Ed.]

[6] See Morris R. Cohen, "The Myth about Bacon and the Inductive Method", *Scientific Monthly*, vol. 23, December 1926, p. 505 [pp. 504–5].

[7] [This entire paragraph was added in the 1952 version. It reflects Hayek's acceptance of Karl Popper's criticism that the procedures *actually followed* in the natural sciences are different from those that scientistically inclined writers ascribed to them. For more on this, see the editor's introduction, this volume, pp. 36–37.—Ed.]

[8] [The "historical studies" are contained in "The Counter-Revolution of Science" and "Comte and Hegel", parts 2 and 3 of this volume.—Ed.]

shall meet again and again and whose *prima facie* plausibility makes it necessary to examine them with some care. While in the particular historical instances it is not always possible to show how these characteristic views are connected with or derived from the habits of thought of the scientists, this is easier in a systematic survey.

It need scarcely be emphasised that nothing we shall have to say is aimed against the methods of Science in their proper sphere or is intended to throw the slightest doubt on their value. But to preclude any misunderstanding on this point we shall, wherever we are concerned, not with the general spirit of disinterested inquiry but with slavish imitation of the method and language of Science, speak of 'scientism' or the 'scientistic' prejudice. Although these terms are not completely unknown in English,[9] they are actually borrowed from the French, where in recent years they have come to be generally used in very much the same sense in which they will be used here.[10] It should be noted that, in the sense in which we shall use these terms, they describe, of course, an attitude which is decidedly unscientific in the true sense of the word, since it involves a mechanical and uncritical application of habits of thought to fields different from those in which they have been formed. The scientistic as distinguished from the scientific view is not an unprejudiced but a very prejudiced approach which, before it has considered its subject, claims to know what is the most appropriate way of investigating it.[11]

It would be convenient if a similar term were available to describe the characteristic mental attitude of the engineer which, although in many respects closely related to scientism, is yet distinct from it but which we intend to consider here in connection with the latter. No single word of equal expressiveness suggests itself, however, and we shall have to be content to describe this second element so characteristic of nineteenth- and twentieth-century thought as the 'engineering type of mind'.

[9] Murray's *New English Dictionary* knows both 'scientism' and 'scientistic', the former as the "habit and mode of expression of a man of science", the latter as "characteristic of, or having the attributes of, a scientist (used depreciatively)". The terms 'naturalistic' and 'mechanistic', which have often been used in a similar sense, are less appropriate because they tend to suggest the wrong kind of contrast.

[10] See, e.g., Jean Fiolle, *Scientisme et science* (Paris: Mercure de France, 1936), and André Lalande, *Vocabulaire technique et critique de la philosophie*, 4th ed. (Paris: F. Alcan, 1932), vol. 2, p. 740.

[11] Perhaps the following passage by a distinguished physicist may help to show how much the scientists themselves suffer from the same attitude which has given their influence on other disciplines such a baneful character: "It is difficult to conceive of anything more scientifically bigoted than to postulate that all possible experience conforms to the same type as that with which we are already familiar, and therefore to demand that explanation use only elements familiar in everyday experience. Such an attitude bespeaks an unimaginativeness, a mental obtuseness and obstinacy, which might be expected to have exhausted their pragmatic justification at a lower plane of mental activity". See Percy W. Bridgman, *The Logic of Modern Physics* (New York: Macmillan, 1928), p. 46 [pp. 46–47].

TWO

THE PROBLEM AND THE METHOD
OF THE NATURAL SCIENCES

Before we can understand the reasons for the trespasses of scientism we must try to understand the struggle which Science itself had to wage against concepts and ideas which were as injurious to its progress as the scientistic prejudice now threatens to become to the progress of the social studies. Although we live now in an atmosphere where the concepts and habits of thoughts of everyday life are to a high degree influenced by the ways of thinking of Science, we must not forget that the Sciences had in their beginning to fight their way in a world where most concepts had been formed from our relations to other men and in interpreting their actions. It is only natural that the momentum gained in that struggle should carry Science beyond the mark and create a situation where the danger is now the opposite one of the pre-dominance of scientism impeding the progress of the understanding of society.[1] But even if the pendulum has now definitely swung in the opposite direction, only confusion could result if we failed to recognise the factors which have created this attitude and which justify it in its proper sphere.

There were three main obstacles to the advance of modern Science against which it has struggled ever since its birth during the Renaissance; and much of the history of its progress could be written in terms of its gradual overcoming of these difficulties. The first, although not the most important, was that for various reasons scholars had grown used to devoting most of their effort to analysing other people's opinions: this was so not only because in the disciplines most developed at that time, like theology and law, this was the actual object, but even more because, during the decline of Science in the Middle

[1] On the significance of this 'law of inertia' in the scientific sphere and its effects on the social disciplines, see Hugo Münsterberg, *Grundzüge der Psychologie* (Leipzig: J. A. Barth, 1918), p. 137; Ernst Bernheim, *Lehrbuch der historischen Methode und Geschichtsphilosophie*, 5th ed. (Leipzig: Duncker and Humblot, 1908), p. 144; and Ludwig von Mises, *Nationalökonomie: Theorie des Handelns und Wirtschaftens* (Geneva: Editions Union, 1940), p. 24. The phenomenon that we tend to overstrain a new principle of explanation is, perhaps, more familiar with respect to particular scientific doctrines than with respect to Science as such. Gravitation and evolution, relativity and psychoanalysis, all have for certain periods been strained far beyond their capacity. That for Science as a whole the phenomenon has lasted even longer and had still more far-reaching effects is not surprising in the light of this experience.

Ages, there seemed to be no better way of arriving at the truth about nature than to study the work of the great men of the past. More important was the second fact, the belief that the 'ideas' of the things possessed some transcendental reality, and that by analysing ideas we could learn something or everything about the attributes of the real things. The third and perhaps most important fact was that man had begun everywhere to interpret the events in the external world after his own image, as animated by a mind like his own, and that the natural sciences therefore met everywhere explanations by analogy with the working of the human mind, with 'anthropomorphic' or 'animistic' theories which searched for a purposive design and were satisfied if they had found in it the proof of the operation of a designing mind.

Against all this the persistent effort of modern Science has been to get down to 'objective facts', to cease studying what men thought about nature or regarding the given concepts as true images of the real world, and, above all, to discard all theories which pretended to explain phenomena by imputing to them a directing mind like our own. Instead, its main task became to revise and reconstruct the concepts formed from ordinary experience on the basis of a systematic testing of the phenomena, so as to be better able to recognise the particular as an instance of a general rule. In the course of this process not only the provisional classification which the commonly used concepts provided, but also the first distinctions between the different perceptions which our senses convey to us, had to give way to a completely new and different way in which we learned to order or classify the events of the external world.

The tendency to abandon all anthropomorphic elements in the discussion of the external world has in its most extreme development even led to the belief that the demand for 'explanation' itself is based on an anthropomorphic interpretation of events and that all Science ought to aim at is a complete description of nature.[2] There is, as we shall see, that element of truth in the first part of this contention that we can understand and explain human action in a way we cannot with physical phenomena, and that consequently the term *explain* tends to remain charged with a meaning not applicable to physical phenomena.[3] The actions of other men were probably the first experiences which

---

[2] This view was, I believe, first explicitly formulated by the German physicist Gustav Kirchhoff in his *Vorlesungen über die mathematische Physik; Mechanik* (Leipzig: B. G. Teubner, 1876), p. 1, and later made widely known through the philosophy of Ernst Mach. [Ernst Mach's work on physics, psychology, and the philosophy of science was greatly influential in Vienna when Hayek was a student, as he recounts in his essay "Ernst Mach (1838–1916) and the Social Sciences in Vienna", chapter 7 of *The Fortunes of Liberalism.*—Ed.]

[3] The word *explain* is only one of many important instances where the natural sciences were forced to use concepts originally formed to describe human phenomena. *Law* and *cause*, *function* and *order*, *organism* and *organisation* are others of similar importance where Science has more or less succeeded in freeing them from their anthropomorphic connotations, while in other instances, particularly, as we shall see, in the case of *purpose*, though it cannot entirely dispense

made man ask the question why, and it took him a long time to learn, and he has not yet fully learned,[4] that with events other than human actions he could not expect the same kind of 'explanation' as he can hope to obtain in the case of human behaviour.

That the ordinary concepts of the kind of things that surround us do not provide an adequate classification which enables us to state general rules about their behaviour in different circumstances, and that in order to do so we have to replace them by a different classification of events is familiar. It may, however, still sound surprising that what is true of these provisional abstractions should also be true of the very sense qualities which most of us are inclined to regard as the ultimate reality. But although it is less familiar that science breaks up and replaces the system of classification which our sense qualities represent, yet this is precisely what Science does. It begins with the realisation that things which appear to us the same do not always behave in the same manner, and that things which appear different to us sometimes prove in all other respects to behave in the same way; and it proceeds from this experience to substitute for the classification of events which our senses provide a new one which groups together not what appears alike but what proves to behave in the same manner in similar circumstances.

While the naïve mind tends to assume that external events which our senses register in the same or in a different manner must be similar or different in more respects than merely in the way in which they affect our senses, the systematic testing of Science shows that this is frequently not true. It constantly shows that the 'facts' are different from 'appearances'. We learn to regard as alike or unlike not simply what by itself looks, feels, smells, etc., alike or unlike, but what regularly appears in the same spatial and temporal context. And we learn that the same constellation of simultaneous sense perceptions may prove to proceed from different 'facts', or that different combinations of sense qualities may stand for the same 'fact'. A white powder with a certain weight and 'feel' and without taste or smell may prove to be any one of a number of different things according as it appears in different circumstances or after different combinations of other phenomena, or as it produces different results if combined in certain ways with other things. The systematic testing of behaviour in different circumstances will thus often show that things which to our senses appear different behave in the same or at least a very similar manner. We not only may find that, for example, a blue thing which we see in a certain light or after eating a certain drug is the same thing as the green thing

---

with them, it has not yet succeeded in doing so and is therefore with some justification afraid of using these terms.

[4] See T. Percy Nunn, "Anthropomorphism and Physics" [1926], *Proceedings of the British Academy*, vol. 13 [8] (London: H. Milford, 1928), pp. 13–45.

which we see in different circumstances, or that what appears to have an elliptical shape may prove to be identical with what at a different angle appears to be circular, but also may find that phenomena which appear as different as ice and water are 'really' the same 'thing'.

This process of reclassifying 'objects' which our senses have already classified in one way, of substituting for the 'secondary' qualities in which our senses arrange external stimuli a new classification based on consciously established relations between classes of events is, perhaps, the most characteristic aspect of the procedure of the natural sciences. The whole history of modern Science proves to be a process of progressive emancipation from our innate classification of the external stimuli till in the end they completely disappear so that "physical science has now reached a state of development that renders it impossible to express observable occurrences in language appropriate to what is perceived by our senses. The only appropriate language is that of mathematics",[5] that is, the discipline developed to describe complexes of relationships between elements which have no attributes except these relations. While at first the new elements into which the physical world was 'analysed' were still endowed with 'qualities', that is, conceived as in principle visible or touchable, neither electrons nor waves, neither the atomic structure nor electromagnetic fields can be adequately represented by mechanical models.

The new world which man thus creates in his mind, and which consists entirely of entities which cannot be perceived by our senses, is yet in a definite way related to the world of our senses. It serves, indeed, to explain the world of our senses. The world of Science might in fact be described as no more than a set of rules which enables us to trace the connections between different complexes of sense perceptions. But the point is that the attempts to establish such uniform rules which the perceptible phenomena obey have been unsuccessful so long as we accepted as natural units, given entities, such constant complexes of sense qualities as we can simultaneously perceive. In their place new entities, 'constructs', are created which can be defined only in terms of sense perceptions obtained of the 'same' thing in different circumstances and at different times—a procedure which implies the postulate that the thing has in some sense remained the same although all its perceptible attributes may have changed.

In other words, although the theories of physical science at the stage which has now been reached can no longer be stated in terms of sense qualities, their significance is due to the fact that we possess rules, a 'key', which enables us to translate them into statements about perceptible phenomena. One might

---

[5] L. Susan Stebbing, *Thinking to Some Purpose* (Harmondsworth, Middlesex: Penguin Books, 1939), p. 107 [111]. See also Bertrand Russell, *The Scientific Outlook* (London: G. Allen and Unwin, 1931), p. 85.

compare the relation of modern physical theory to the world of our senses to that between the different ways in which one might 'know' a dead language existing only in inscriptions in peculiar characters. The combinations of different characters of which these inscriptions are composed and which are the only form in which the language occurs correspond to the different combinations of sense qualities. As we come to know the language we gradually learn that different combinations of these characters may mean the same thing and that in different contexts the same group of characters may mean different things.[6] As we learn to recognise these new entities we penetrate into a new world where the units are different from the letters and obey in their relations definite laws not recognisable in the sequence of the individual letters. We can describe the laws of these new units, the laws of grammar, and all that can be expressed by combining the words according to these laws, without ever referring to the individual letters or the principle on which they are combined to make up the signs for whole words. It would be possible, for example, to know all about the grammar of Chinese or Greek and the meaning of all the words in these languages without knowing Chinese or Greek characters (or the sounds of the Chinese or Greek words). Yet if Chinese or Greek occurred only written in their respective characters, all this knowledge would be of as little use as knowledge of the laws of nature in terms of abstract entities or constructs without knowledge of the rules by which these can be translated into statements about phenomena perceptible by our senses.

As in our description of the structure of the language there is no need for a description of the way in which the different units are made up from various combinations of letters (or sounds), so in our theoretical description of nature the different sense qualities through which we perceive nature disappear. They are no longer treated as part of the object and come to be regarded merely as ways in which we spontaneously perceive or classify external stimuli.[7]

The problem how man has come to classify external stimuli in the particular way which we know as sense qualities does not concern us here.[8] There

---

[6] The comparison becomes more adequate if we conceive that only small groups of characters, say words, appear to us simultaneously, while the groups as such appear to us only in a definite time sequence, as the words (or phrases) actually do when we read.

[7] The old puzzle over the miracle that qualities which are supposed to attach to the things are transmitted to the brain in the form of indistinguishable nervous processes differing only in the organ which they affect, and then in the brain retranslated into the original qualities, ceases to exist. We have no evidence for the assumption that the things in the external world in their relations to each other differ or are similar in the way our senses suggest to us. In fact we have in many instances evidence to the contrary.

[8] It may just be mentioned that this classification is probably based on a pre-conscious learning of those relationships in the external world which are of special relevance for the existence of the human organism in the kind of environment in which it developed, and that it is closely connected with the infinite number of 'conditioned reflexes' which the human species had to

are only two connected points which must be briefly mentioned now and to which we must return later. One is that, once we have learned that the things in the external world show uniformity in their behaviour towards each other only if we group them in a way different from that in which they appear to our senses, the question why they appear to us in that particular way, and especially why they appear in the same[9] way to different people, becomes a genuine problem calling for an answer. The second is that the fact that different men do perceive different things in a similar manner which does not correspond to any known relation between these things in the external world, must be regarded as a significant datum of experience which must be the starting point in any discussion of human behaviour.

We are not interested here in the methods of the Sciences for their own sake and we cannot follow up this topic further. The point which we mainly wanted to stress was that what men know or think about the external world or about themselves, their concepts and even the subjective qualities of their sense perceptions are to Science never ultimate reality, data to be accepted. Its concern is not what men think about the world and how they consequently behave, but what they ought to think. The concepts which men actually employ, the way in which they see nature, is to the scientists necessarily a provisional affair and his task is to change this picture, to change the concepts in use so as to be able to make more definite and more certain our statements about the new classes of events.

There is one consequence of all this which in view of what follows requires a few more words. It is the special significance which numerical statements and quantitative measurements have in the natural sciences. There is a widespread impression that the main importance of this quantitative nature of most natural sciences is their greater precision. This is not so. It is not merely adding precision to a procedure which would be possible also without the mathematical form of expression—it is of the essence of this process of breaking up our immediate sense data and of substituting for a description in terms of sense qualities one in terms of elements which possess no attributes but these relations to each other. It is a necessary part of the general effort of

---

acquire in the course of its evolution. The classification of the stimuli in our central nervous system is probably highly 'pragmatic' in the sense that it is not based on all observable relations between the external things, but stresses those relations between the external world (in the narrower sense) and our body which in the course of evolution have proved significant for the survival of the species. The human brain will, for example, classify external stimuli largely by their association with stimuli emanating from the reflex action of parts of the human body caused by the same external stimulus without the intervention of the brain.

[9] That different people classify external stimuli in the 'same' way does not mean that individual sense qualities are the same for different people (which would be a meaningless statement), but that the systems of sense qualities of different people have a common structure (are homeomorphic systems of relations).

getting away from the picture of nature which man has now, of substituting for the classification of events which our senses provide another based on the relations established by systematic testing and experimenting.

To return to our more general conclusion: the world in which Science is interested is not that of our given concepts or even sensations. Its aim is to produce a new organisation of all our experience of the external world, and in doing so it has not only to remodel our concepts but also to get away from the sense qualities and to replace them by a different classification of events. The picture which man has actually formed of the world and which guides him well enough in his daily life, his perceptions and concepts, are for Science not an object of study but an imperfect instrument to be improved. Nor is Science as such interested in the relation of man to things, in the way in which man's existing view of the world leads him to act. It *is* rather such a relation, or better a continuous process of changing these relationships. When the scientist stresses that he studies objective facts he means that he tries to study things independently of what men think or do about them. The views people hold about the external world are to him always a stage to be overcome.

But what are the consequences of the fact that people perceive the world and each other through sensations and concepts which are organised in a mental structure common to all of them? What can we say about the whole network of activities in which men are guided by the kind of knowledge they have and a great part of which at any time is common to most of them? While Science is all the time busy revising the picture of the external world that man possesses, and while to it this picture is always provisional, the fact that man has a definite picture, and that the picture of all beings whom we recognise as thinking men and whom we can understand is to some extent alike, is no less a reality of great consequence and the cause of certain events. Until Science had literally completed its work and not left the slightest unexplained residue in man's intellectual processes, the facts of our mind must remain not only data to be explained but also data on which the explanation of human action guided by those mental phenomena must be based. Here a new set of problems arises with which the scientist does not directly deal. Nor is it obvious that the particular methods to which he has become used would be appropriate for these problems. The question is here not how far man's picture of the external world fits the facts, but how by his actions, determined by the views and concepts he possesses, man builds up another world of which the individual becomes a part. And by 'the views and concepts people hold' we do not mean merely their knowledge of external nature. We mean all they know and believe about themselves, about other people, and about the external world, in short everything which determines their actions, including science itself.

This is the field to which the social studies or the 'moral sciences' address themselves.

THREE

THE SUBJECTIVE CHARACTER OF THE DATA OF THE SOCIAL SCIENCES

Before we proceed to consider the effect of scientism on the study of society it will be expedient briefly to survey the peculiar object and the methods of the social studies. They deal not with the relations between things, but with the relations between men and things or the relations between man and man. They are concerned with man's actions, and their aim is to explain the unintended or undesigned results of the actions of many men.

Not all the disciplines of knowledge which are concerned with the life of men in groups, however, raise problems which differ in any important respect from those of the natural sciences. The spread of contagious diseases is evidently a problem closely connected with the life of man in society and yet its study has none of the special characteristics of the social sciences in the narrower sense of the term. Similarly the study of heredity, or the study of nutrition, or the investigation of changes in the number or age composition of populations, does not differ significantly from similar studies of animals.[1] And the same applies to certain branches of anthropology, or ethnology, insofar as they are concerned with physical attributes of men. There are, in other words, natural sciences of man which do not necessarily raise problems with which we cannot cope with the methods of the natural sciences. Wherever we are concerned with unconscious reflexes or processes in the human body there is no obstacle to treating and investigating them 'mechanically' as caused by objectively observable external events. They take place without the knowledge of the man concerned and without his having power to modify them; and the conditions under which they are produced can be established by external observation without recourse to the assumption that the person observed classifies the external stimuli in any way differently from that in which they can be defined in purely physical terms.

The social sciences in the narrower sense, that is, those which used to be described as the moral sciences,[2] are concerned with man's conscious or

---

[1] Most of the problems of this latter group will, however, raise problems of the kind characteristic of the social sciences proper when we attempt to explain them.

[2] Sometimes the German term *Geisteswissenschaften* is now used in English to describe the social sciences in the specific narrow sense with which we are here concerned. But this German term

reflected action, actions where a person can be said to choose between various courses open to him, and here the situation is essentially different. The external stimulus which may be said to cause or occasion such actions can of course also be defined in purely physical terms. But if we tried to do so for the purposes of explaining human action, we would confine ourselves to less than we know about the situation. It is not because we have found two things to behave alike in relation to other things, but because they appear alike to us, that we expect them to appear alike to other people. We know that people will react in the same way to external stimuli which according to all objective tests are different, and perhaps also that they will react in a completely different manner to a physically identical stimulus if it affects their bodies in different circumstances or at a different point. We know, in other words, that in his conscious decisions man classifies external stimuli in a way which we know solely from our own subjective experience of this kind of classification. We take it for granted that other men treat various things as alike or unlike just as we do, although no objective test, no knowledge of the relations of these things to other parts of the external world justifies this. Our procedure is based on the experience that other people as a rule (though not always—for example, not if they are colour-blind or mad) classify their sense impressions as we do.

But we not only know this. It would be impossible to explain or understand human action without making use of this knowledge. People do behave in the same manner towards things, not because these things are identical in a physical sense, but because they have learned to classify them as belonging to the same group, because they can put them to the same use or expect from them what to the people concerned is an equivalent effect. In fact, most of the objects of social or human action are not 'objective facts' in the special narrow sense in which this term is used by the Sciences and contrasted to 'opinions', and they cannot at all be defined in physical terms. So far as human actions are concerned the things *are* what the acting people think they are.

This is best shown by an example for which we can choose almost any object of human action. Take the concept of a 'tool' or 'instrument', or of any particular tool such as a hammer or a barometer. It is easily seen that these concepts cannot be interpreted to refer to 'objective facts', that is, to

---

was introduced by the translator of J. S. Mill's *Logic* to render the latter's moral sciences, and so there seems to be little case for using this translation instead of the original English term. [Hayek refers to John Stuart Mill, *System of Logic Ratiocinative and Inductive, Being a Connected View of the Principles of Evidence and the Methods of Scientific Investigation* [1843], ed. J. M. Robson, comprising vols. 7 (1973) and 8 (1974) of *Collected Works of John Stuart Mill*. The first German translation of Mill's *Logic* was *System der deductiven und inductiven Logik: Eine Darlegung der Principien wissenschaftlicher Forschung, inbesondere der Naturforschung*, translated by Jacob Schiel (Braunsweig: Vieweg, 1862–63).—Ed.]

things irrespective of what people think about them. Careful logical analysis of these concepts will show that they all express relationships between several (at least three) terms, of which one is the acting or thinking person, the second some desired or imagined effect, and the third a thing in the ordinary sense. If the reader will attempt a definition he will soon find that he cannot give one without using some term such as 'suitable for' or 'intended for' or some other expression referring to the use for which it is designed by somebody.[3] And a definition which is to comprise all instances of the class will not contain any reference to its substance, or shape, or other physical attribute. An ordinary hammer and a steam-hammer, or an aneroid barometer and a mercury barometer, have nothing in common except the purpose[4] for which men think they can be used.

[3] It has often been suggested that for this reason economics and the other theoretical sciences of society should be described as 'teleological' sciences. This term is, however, misleading as it is apt to suggest that not only the actions of individual men but also the social structures which they produce are deliberately designed by somebody for a purpose. It leads thus either to an 'explanation' of social phenomena in terms of ends fixed by some superior power or to the opposite and no less fatal mistake of regarding all social phenomena as the product of conscious human design, to a 'pragmatic' interpretation which is a bar to all real understanding of these phenomena. Some authors, particularly O. Spann, have used the term *teleological* to justify the most abstruse metaphysical speculations. Others, like K. Engliš, have used it in an unobjectionable manner and sharply distinguished between teleological and normative sciences. See particularly the illuminating discussions of the problem in Karel Engliš, *Teleologische Theorie der Staatswirtschaft* (Brünn: R. M. Rohrer, 1933). But the term remains nevertheless misleading. If a name is needed, the term *praxeological* sciences, deriving from A. Espinas, adopted by T. Kotarbinski and E. Slutsky, and now clearly defined and extensively used by Ludwig von Mises, *Nationalökonomie*, would appear to be the most appropriate. [Austrian sociologist and economist Othmar Spann (1878–1950), prophet of 'intuitive universalism', was a critic of democracy, individualism, socialism, and liberalism, and for a time was Hayek's teacher at the University of Vienna. For more on Spann, see Caldwell, *Hayek's Challenge*, pp. 138–39. For more on Czech economist Karel Engliš's (1880–1961) teleological approach to the study of economics, see Jaroslav G. Polach's introduction to Engliš's book *An Essay on Economic Systems: A Teleological Approach*, translated by Ivo Moravčík (Boulder, CO: East Europe Monographs, 1986). French scholar Alfred Victor Espinas (1844–1922), who appears to have been the first to use the term *praxeology* in his article "Les origines de la technologie", *Revue philosophique*, vol. 30, August 1890, pp. 114–15, argued that social science should be based on organicism and evolutionism. Polish philosopher Tadeusz Kotarbinski (1886–1981) wrote on the philosophy of action utilising praxeological categories; both he and Oskar Lange thought that the use of such categories could improve the workings of a socialist economy. Russian economist Eugen Slutsky (1880–1948), best remembered among economists for identifying the income and substitution effects of a price change in his Slutsky equation, also made contributions in statistics and probability theory. Austrian economist Ludwig von Mises (1881–1973) was Hayek's mentor and friend; besides using the term in his 1940 book, he identified praxeology as constituting 'the science of human action' in part 1 of his book, *Human Action: A Treatise on Economics* (New Haven: Yale University Press, 1949; 3rd revised edition, Chicago: Henry Regnery, 1966).—Ed.]

[4] While the great majority of the objects or events which determine human action, and which from that angle have to be defined not by their physical characteristics but by the human atti-

It must not be objected that these are merely instances of abstractions to arrive at generic terms just as those used in the physical sciences. The point is that they are abstractions from *all* the physical attributes of the things in question and that their definitions must run entirely in terms of mental attitudes of men towards the things. The significant difference between the two views of the things stands out clearly if we think, for example, of the problem of the archaeologist trying to determine whether what looks like a stone implement is in truth an 'artefact', made by man, or merely a chance product of nature. There is no way of deciding this but by trying to understand the working of the mind of pre-historic man, of attempting to understand how he would have made such an implement. If we are not more aware that this is what we actually do in such cases and that we necessarily rely on our own knowledge of the working of a human mind, this is so mainly because of the impossibility of conceiving of an observer who does not possess a human mind and interprets what he sees in terms of the working of his own mind.

We can do no better when describing this difference between the approach of the natural and that of the social sciences than to call the former 'objective' and the latter 'subjective'. Yet these terms are ambiguous and might prove misleading without further explanation. While for the natural scientist the contrast between objective facts and subjective opinions is a simple one, the distinction cannot as readily be applied to the object of the social sciences. The reason for this is that the object or the 'facts' of the social sciences are also opinions—not opinions of the student of the social phenomena, of course, but opinions of those whose actions produce the object of the social scientist. In one sense his facts are thus as little 'subjective' as those of the natural sciences, because they are independent of the particular observer; what he studies is not determined by his fancy or imagination but is in the same manner given to the observation by different people. But in another sense in which we distinguish facts from opinions, the facts of the social sciences are merely opinions, views held by the people whose actions we study. They differ from the facts of the physical sciences in being beliefs or opinions held by particular people, beliefs which as such are our data, irrespective of whether they are true or false, and which, moreover, we cannot directly observe in the minds of the people but which we can recognise from what they do and say merely because we have ourselves a mind similar to theirs.

---

tudes towards them, are means for an end, this does not mean that the purposive or 'teleological' nature of their definition is the essential point. The human purposes for which different things serve are the most important, but still only one, kind of human attitudes which will form the basis of such classification. A ghost or a bad or good omen belongs no less to the class of events determining human action which have no physical counterpart, although such cannot possibly be regarded as an instrument of human action.

In the sense in which we here use the contrast between the subjectivist approach of the social sciences and the objectivist approach of the natural sciences it says little more than what is commonly expressed by saying that the former deal in the first instance with the phenomena of individual minds, or mental phenomena, and not directly with material phenomena. They deal with phenomena which can be understood only because the object of our study has a mind of a structure similar to our own. That this is so is no less an empirical fact than our knowledge of the external world. It is shown not merely by the possibility of communicating with other people—we act on this knowledge every time we speak or write; it is confirmed by the very results of our study of the external world. So long as it was naïvely assumed that all the sense qualities (or their relations) which different men had in common were properties of the external world, it could be argued that our knowledge of other minds is no more than our common knowledge of the external world. But once we have learned that our senses make things appear to us alike or different which prove to be alike or different in none of their relations between themselves, but only in the way in which they affect our senses, this fact that men classify external stimuli in a particular way becomes a significant fact of experience. While qualities disappear from our scientific picture of the external world they must remain part of our scientific picture of the human mind. In fact, the elimination of qualities from our picture of the external world does not mean that these qualities do not 'exist', but that when we study qualities we study not the physical world but the mind of man.

In some connections, for instance when we distinguish between the 'objective' properties of things which manifest themselves in their relations to each other, and the properties merely attributed to them by men, it might be preferable to contrast 'objective' with 'attributed', instead of using the ambiguous term *subjective*. The word *attributed* is, however, only of limited usefulness. The main reasons why it is expedient to retain the terms *subjective* and *objective* for the contrast with which we are concerned, although they inevitably carry with them some misleading connotations, are that most of the other available terms, such as *mental* and *material*, carry with them an even worse burden of metaphysical associations, and that at least in economics[5] the term *subjective* has long been used precisely in the sense in which we use it here. What is more important is that the term *subjective* stresses another important fact to which we shall yet have to refer: that the knowledge and beliefs of different people, while possessing that common structure which makes communication possible, will yet be different and often conflicting in many respects. If we could assume that all the knowledge and beliefs of different people were identical, or if we were concerned with a single mind, it would not matter whether we

---

[5] I believe also in the discussions on psychological methods.

described it as an 'objective' fact or as a subjective phenomenon. But the concrete knowledge which guides the action of any group of people never exists as a consistent and coherent body. It only exists in the dispersed, incomplete, and inconsistent form in which it appears in many individual minds, and the dispersion and imperfection of all knowledge are two of the basic facts from which the social sciences have to start. What philosophers and logicians often contemptuously dismiss as a 'mere' imperfection of the human mind becomes in the social sciences a basic fact of crucial importance. We shall later see how the opposite 'absolutist' view, as if knowledge, and particularly the concrete knowledge of particular circumstances, were given 'objectively', that is, as if it were the same for all people, is a source of constant errors in the social sciences.

The 'tool' or 'instrument' which we have before used as an illustration of the objects of human action can be matched by similar instances from any other branch of social study. A 'word' or a 'sentence', a 'crime' or a 'punishment',[6] is of course not an objective fact in the sense that it can be defined without referring to our knowledge of people's conscious intentions with regard to it. And the same is quite generally true wherever we have to explain human behaviour towards things; these things must then not be defined in terms of what we might find out about them by the objective methods of science, but in terms of what the person acting thinks about them. A medicine or a cosmetic, for example, for the purposes of social study, is not what cures an ailment or improves a person's looks, but what people think will have that effect. Any knowledge which we may happen to possess about the true nature of the material thing, but which the people whose action we want to explain do not possess, is as little relevant to the explanation of their actions as our private disbelief in the efficacy of a magic charm is to understanding the behaviour of the savage who believes in it. If in investigating our contemporary society the 'laws of nature', which we have to use as a datum because they affect people's actions, are approximately the same as those which figure in the works of the natural scientists, this is for our purposes an accident which must not deceive us about the different character of these laws in the two fields. What is relevant in the study of society is not whether these laws of nature are true in any objective sense, but solely whether they are believed and acted upon by the people. If the current 'scientific' knowledge of the society which we study included the belief that the soil will bear not fruit till

[6] It is sheer illusion when some sociologists believe that they can make 'crime' an objective fact by defining it as those acts for which a person is punished. This only pushes the subjective element a step further back, but does not eliminate it. Punishment is still a subjective thing which cannot be defined in objective terms. If, for example, we see that every time a person commits a certain act he is made to wear a chain around his neck, this does not tell us whether it is a reward or a punishment.

certain rites or incantations are performed, this would be quite as important for us as any law of nature which we now believe to be correct. And all the 'physical laws of production' which we meet, for example, in economics, are not physical laws in the sense of the physical sciences, but people's beliefs about what they can do.

What is true about the relations of men to things is, of course, even more true of the relations between men, which for the purposes of social study cannot be defined in the objective terms of the physical sciences but only in terms of human beliefs. Even such a seemingly purely biological relationship as that between parent and child is in social study not defined in physical terms and cannot be so defined for their purposes: it makes no difference with regard to people's actions whether their belief that a particular child is their natural offspring is mistaken or not.

All this stands out most clearly in that among the social sciences whose theory has been most highly developed, economics. And it is probably no exaggeration to say that every important advance in economic theory during the last hundred years was a further step in the consistent application of subjectivism.[7] That the objects of economic activity cannot be defined in objective terms but only with reference to a human purpose goes without saying. Neither a 'commodity' or an 'economic good', nor 'food' or 'money', can be defined in physical terms but only in terms of views people hold about things. Economic theory has nothing to say about the little round disks of metal as which an objective or materialist view might try to define money. It has nothing to say about iron or steel, timber or oil, or wheat or eggs as such. The history of any particular commodity indeed shows that as human knowledge changes the same material thing may represent quite different economic categories. Nor could we distinguish in physical terms whether two men barter or exchange or whether they are playing some game or performing some religious ritual. Unless we can understand what the acting people mean by their

[7] This is a development which has probably been carried out most consistently by Ludwig von Mises, and I believe that most peculiarities of his views which at first strike many readers as strange and unacceptable trace to the fact that in the consistent development of the subjectivist approach he has for a long time moved ahead of his contemporaries. Probably all the characteristic features of his theories—from his theory of money (so much ahead of the time in 1912) to what he calls his *a priorism*—his views about mathematical economics in general and the measurement of economic phenomena in particular, and his criticism of planning all follow directly (although, perhaps, not all with the same necessity) from this central position. See particularly his *Grundprobleme der Nationalökonomie* (Jena: G. Fischer, 1933) and *Human Action*. [In mentioning Mises's 'theory of money' Hayek refers to Ludwig von Mises, *Theorie des Geldes und der Umlaufsmittel* (Munich: Duncker and Humblot, 1912; 2nd ed., 1924), 2nd edition translated by H. E. Batson as *The Theory of Money and Credit* (London: Cape, 1934; reprinted, Indianapolis, IN: LibertyClassics, 1981). Mises's *Grundprobleme* is also now available in English as *Epistemological Problems of Economics*, translated by George Reisman (Princeton, NJ: Van Nostrand, 1960).—Ed.]

actions any attempt to explain them, that is, to subsume them under rules which connect similar situations with similar actions, is bound to fail.[8]

This essentially subjective character of all economic theory, which it has developed much more clearly than most other branches of the social sciences,[9] but which I believe it has in common with all the social sciences in the narrower sense, is best shown by a closer consideration of one of its simplest theorems, for example, the 'law of rent'. In its original form this was a proposition about changes in the value of a thing defined in physical terms, namely, land. It stated, in effect,[10] that changes in the value of the commodities in the production of which land was required would cause much greater changes in the value of land than in the value of the other factors whose co-operation was required. In this form it is an empirical generalisation which tells us neither why nor under what conditions it will be true. In modern economics its place is taken by two distinct propositions of different character which together lead to the same conclusion. One is part of pure economic theory and asserts that whenever in the production of one commodity different (scarce) factors are

[8] This was seen very clearly by some of the early economists, but later obscured by the attempts to make economics 'objective' in the sense of the natural sciences. Ferdinando Galiani, for example, in his *Della Moneta* (1751) emphasised that "those things are equal which afford equal satisfaction to the one with respect to whom they are said to be equivalent. Anyone who seeks equality elsewhere, following other principles, and expects to find it in weight, or similarity of appearance, will show little understanding of the facts of human life. A sheet of paper is often the equivalent of money, from which it differs both in weight and appearance; on the other hand, two moneys of equal weight and quality, and similar in appearance, are often not equal" (in *Early Economic Thought: Selections from Economic Literature Prior to Adam Smith*, ed. Arthur Eli Monroe (Cambridge, MA: Harvard University Press, 1930), p. 303 [pp. 303–4]). [Italian economist and civil servant Ferdinando Galiani (1728–87) was only 22 when he published *Della Moneta*, or *Money*. In it he developed, among other things, a subjective approach to the theory of value. —Ed.]

[9] Except probably linguistics, for which it may indeed be claimed with some justification that it "is of strategic importance for the methodology of the social sciences" (Edward Sapir, *Selected Writings in Language, Culture, and Personality*, ed. David G. Mandelbaum (Berkeley: University of California Press, 1949), p. 166). Sapir, whose writings were unknown to me when I wrote this essay, stresses many of the points here emphasised. See, for instance, ibid., p. 46: "No entity in human experience can be adequately defined as the mechanical sum or product of its physical properties", and "all significant entities in experience are thus revised from the physically given by passing through the filter of the functionally or relatedly meaningful".

[10] In the extreme Ricardian form the statement is, of course, that a change in the value of the product will affect *only* the value of the land and leave the value of the co-operating labour altogether unaffected. In this form (connected with Ricardo's 'objective' theory of value) the proposition can be regarded as a limiting case of the more general proposition stated in the text. [Hayek refers to the theory of rent and labour theory of value articulated by the English economist David Ricardo (1772–1823) in his *On the Principles of Political Economy and Taxation* [3rd ed., 1821], reprinted as vol. 1 (1951) of *The Works and Correspondence of David Ricardo*, ed. Piero Sraffa with the collaboration of M. H. Dobb (Cambridge: For the Royal Economic Society by Cambridge University Press, 1951–73).—Ed.]

required in proportions which can be varied, and of which one can be used only for this purpose (or only for comparatively few) while the others are of a more general usefulness, a change in the value of the product will affect the value of the former more than that of the latter. The second proposition is the empirical statement that land is as a rule in the position of the first kind of factor, that is, that people know of many more uses of their labour than they will know for a particular piece of land. The first of these propositions, like all propositions of pure economic theory, is a statement about the implications of certain human attitudes towards things and as such necessarily true irrespective of time and place. The second is an assertion that the conditions postulated in the first proposition prevail at a given time and with respect to a particular piece of land, because the people dealing with it hold certain beliefs about its usefulness and the usefulness of other things required in order to cultivate it. As an empirical generalisation it can of course be disproved and frequently will be disproved. If, for example, a piece of land is used to produce some special fruit the cultivation of which requires a certain rare skill, the effect of a fall in the demand for the fruit may fall exclusively on the wages of the men with the special skill, while the value of the land may remain practically unaffected. In such a situation it would be labour to which the 'law of rent' applies. But when we ask why, or how can we find out whether the law of rent will apply in any particular case, no information about the physical attributes of the land, the labour, or the product can give us the answer. It depends on the subjective factors stated in the theoretical law of rent; and only insofar as we can find out what the knowledge and beliefs of the people concerned are in the relevant respects shall we be in a position to predict in what manner a change in the price of the product will affect the prices of the factors. What is true of the theory of rent is true of the theory of price generally: it has nothing to say about the behaviour of the price of iron or wool, of things of such and such physical properties, but only about things about which people have certain beliefs and which they want to use in a certain manner. And our explanation of a particular price phenomenon can therefore also never be affected by any additional knowledge which we (the observers) acquire about the good concerned, but only by additional knowledge about what the people dealing with it think about it.

We cannot here enter into a similar discussion of the more complex phenomena with which economic theory is concerned and where in recent years progress has been particularly closely connected with the advance of subjectivism. We can only point to the new problems which these developments make appear more and more central, such as the problem of the compatibility of intentions and expectations of different people, of the division of knowledge between them, and the process by which the relevant knowledge is acquired and expectations formed.[11] We are not here concerned, however, with the specific problems of economics, but with the common character of all disciplines which deal with the results of conscious human action. The points which we want to stress are that in all such attempts we must start from what men think and mean to do: from the fact that the individuals which compose society are guided in their actions by a classification of things or events according to a system of sense qualities and of concepts which has a common structure and which we know because we, too, are men; and that the concrete knowledge which different individuals possess will differ in important respects. Not only man's action towards external objects but also all the relations between men and all the social institutions can be understood only by what men think about them. Society as we know it is, as it were, built up from the concepts and ideas held by the people; and social phenomena can be recognised by us and have meaning to us only as they are reflected in the minds of men.

The structure of men's minds, the common principle on which they classify external events, provides us with the knowledge of the recurrent elements of which different social structures are built up and in terms of which we can alone describe and explain them.[12] While concepts or ideas can, of course, exist only in individual minds, and while, in particular, it is only in individual minds that different ideas can act upon another, it is not the whole of the individual minds in all their complexity, but the individual concepts, the views people have formed of each other and of the things, which form the true elements of the social structure. If the social structure can remain the same although different individuals succeed each other at particular points, this is not because the individuals which succeed each other are completely identical, but because they succeed each other in particular relations, in particular attitudes they take towards other people and as the objects of particular views held by other people about them. The individuals are merely the *foci* in the network of relationships and it is the various attitudes of the individuals towards each other (or their similar or different attitudes towards physical objects) which form the recurrent, recognisable and familiar elements of the

[11] For some further discussion of these problems, see the author's article "Economics and Knowledge", *Economica*, n.s., vol. 4, February 1937, reprinted in *Individualism and Economic Order*.

[12] See Charles V. Langlois and Charles Seignobos, *Introduction to the Study of History*, translated by George Godfrey Berry (London: Duckworth, 1898), p. 218: "Actions and words all have this characteristic, that each was the action or word of an individual; the imagination can only represent to itself *individual* acts, copied from those which are brought before us by direct physical observation. As these are the actions of men living in a society, most of them are performed simultaneously by several individuals, or are directed to some common end. These are collective acts; but in the imagination as in direct observation, they always reduce to a sum of individual actions. The 'social fact', as recognised by certain sociologists, is a philosophical construction, not an historical fact".

structure. If one policeman succeeds another at a particular post, this does not mean that the new man will in all respects be identical with his predecessor, but merely that he succeeds him in certain attitudes towards his fellow man and as the object of certain attitudes of his fellow men which are relevant to his function as policeman. But this is sufficient to preserve a constant structural element which can be separated and studied in isolation.

While we can recognise these elements of human relationships only because they are known to us from the working of our own minds, this does not mean that the significance of their combination in a particular pattern relating different individuals must be immediately obvious to us. It is only by the systematic and patient following up of the implications of many people holding certain views that we can understand, and often even only learn to see, the unintended and often uncomprehended results of the separate and yet interrelated actions of men in society. That in this effort to reconstruct these different patterns of social relations we must relate the individual's action not the objective qualities of the persons and things towards which he acts, but that our data must be man and the physical world as they appear to the men whose actions we try to explain, follows from the fact that only what people know or believe can enter as a motive into their conscious action.

FOUR

THE INDIVIDUALIST AND 'COMPOSITIVE' METHOD OF THE SOCIAL SCIENCES

At this point it becomes necessary briefly to interrupt the main argument in order to safeguard ourselves against a misconception which might arise from what has just been said. The stress which we have laid on the fact that in the social sciences our data or 'facts' are themselves ideas or concepts must, of course, not be understood to mean that *all* the concepts with which we have to deal in the social sciences are of this character. There would be no room for any scientific work if this were so; and the social sciences no less than the natural sciences aim at revising the popular concepts which men have formed about the objects of their study, and at replacing them by more appropriate ones. The special difficulties of the social sciences, and much confusion about their character, derive precisely from the fact that in them ideas appear in two capacities, as it were, as part of their object and as ideas about that object. While in the natural sciences the contrast between the object of our study and our explanation of it coincides with the distinction between ideas and objective facts, in the social sciences it is necessary to draw a distinction between those ideas which are *constitutive* of the phenomena we want to explain and the ideas which either we ourselves or the very people whose actions we have to explain may have formed *about* these phenomena and which are not the cause of, but theories about, the social structures.

This special difficulty of the social sciences is a result, not merely of the fact that we have to distinguish between the views held by the people which are the object of our study and our views about them, but also of the fact that the people who are our object themselves not only are motivated by ideas but also form ideas about the undesigned results of their actions—popular theories about the various social structures or formations which we share with them and which our study has to revise and improve. The danger of substituting 'concepts' (or 'theories') for the 'facts' is by no means absent in the social sciences and failure to avoid it has exercised as detrimental an effect here as in the natural sciences;[1] but it appears on a different plane and is very inad-

---

[1] See the excellent discussions of the effects of conceptual realism (*Begriffsrealismus*) on economics in Walter Eucken, *The Foundations of Economics: History and Theory in the Analysis of Economic Reality*, translated by T. W. Hutchison (London: W. Hodge, 1950), pp. 51 et seq.

equately expressed by the contrast between ideas and facts. The real contrast is between ideas which by being held by the people become the causes of a social phenomenon and the ideas which people form about that phenomenon. That these two classes of ideas are distinct (although in different contexts the distinction may have to be drawn differently)[2] can easily be shown. The changes in the opinions which people hold about a particular commodity and which we recognise as the cause of a change in the price of that commodity stand clearly in a different class from the ideas which the same people may have formed about the causes of the change in price or about the 'nature of value' in general. Similarly, the beliefs and opinions which lead a number of people regularly to repeat certain acts, for example, to produce, sell, or buy certain quantities of commodities, are entirely different from the ideas they may have formed about the whole of the 'society', or the 'economic system', to which they belong and which the aggregate of all their actions constitutes. The first kind of opinions and beliefs is a condition of the existence of the 'wholes' which would not exist without them; they are, as we have said, 'constitutive', essential for the existence of the phenomenon which the people refer to as 'society' or the 'economic system', but which will exist irrespectively of the concepts which the people have formed about these wholes.

It is very important that we should carefully distinguish between the motivating or constitutive opinions on the one hand and the speculative or explanatory views which people have formed about the wholes; confusion between the two is a source of constant danger. Is it the ideas which the popular mind has formed about such collectives as society or the economic system, capitalism or imperialism, and other such collective entities, which the social scientist must regard as no more than provisional theories, popular abstractions, and which he must not mistake for facts? That he consistently refrains from treating these pseudo-entities as facts, and that he systematically starts from the concepts which guide individuals in their actions and not from the results of their theorising about their actions, is the characteristic feature of that methodological individualism which is closely connected with the subjectivism of the social sciences. The scientist approach, on the other hand, because it is afraid of starting from the subjective concepts determining indi-

[2] In some contexts concepts which by another social science are treated as mere theories to be revised and improved upon may have to be treated as data. One could, for example, conceive of a 'science of politics' showing what kind of political action follows from the people holding certain views on the nature of society and for which these views would have to be treated as data. But while in man's actions towards social phenomena, that is, in explaining his political actions, we have to take his views about the constitution of society as given, we can on a different level of analysis investigate their truth or untruth. The fact that a particular society may believe that its institutions have been created by divine intervention we would have to accept as a fact in explaining the politics of that society; but it need not prevent us from showing that this view is probably false.

vidual actions, is, as we shall presently see, regularly led into the very mistake it attempts to avoid, namely of treating as facts those collectives which are no more than popular generalisations. Trying to avoid using as data the concepts held by individuals where they are clearly recognisable and explicitly introduced as what they are, people brought up in scientistic views frequently and naïvely accept the speculative concepts of popular usage as definite facts of the kind they are familiar with.

We shall have to discuss the nature of this collectivist prejudice inherent in the scientistic approach more fully in a later section.

A few more remarks must be added about the specific theoretical method which corresponds to the systematic subjectivism and individualism of the social sciences. From the fact that it is the concepts and views held by individuals which are directly known to us and which form the elements from which we must build up, as it were, the more complex phenomena, follows another important difference between the method of the social disciplines and the natural sciences. While in the former it is the attitudes of individuals which are the familiar elements and by the combination of which we try to reproduce the complex phenomena, the results of individual actions, which are much less known—a procedure which often leads to the *discovery* of principles of structural coherence of the complex phenomena which had not been (and perhaps could not be) established by direct observation—the physical sciences necessarily begin with the complex phenomena of nature and work backwards to infer the elements from which they are composed. The place where the human individual stands in the order of things brings it about that in one direction what he perceives are the comparatively complex phenomena which he analyses, while in the other direction what are given to him are elements from which those more complex phenomena are composed that he cannot observe as wholes.[3] While the method of the natural sciences is in this

---

[3] See Lionel Robbins, *An Essay on the Nature and Significance of Economic Science*, 2nd ed. (London: Macmillan, 1935), p. 105: "In economics . . . the ultimate constituents of our fundamental generalisations are known to us by immediate acquaintance. In the natural sciences they are known only inferentially". Perhaps the following quotation from an earlier essay of my own, in *Collectivist Economic Planning* (London: Routledge and Sons, 1935 [reprinted, Clifton, NJ: Kelley, 1975]), p. 11, may help further to explain the statement in the text: "The position of man, midway between natural and social phenomena—of the one of which he is an effect and of the other a cause—brings it about that the essential basic facts which we need for the explanation of social phenomena are part of common experience, part of the stuff of our thinking. In the social sciences it is the elements of the complex phenomena which are known to us beyond the possibility of dispute. In the natural sciences they can only be at best surmised". [Hayek's essay, titled "The Nature and History of the Problem" and which introduced the other essays in the edited volume, is reprinted as chapter 1 of *Socialism and War*, vol. 10 (1997) of *The Collected Works of F. A. Hayek.*—Ed.] See also Menger, *Untersuchungen über die Methode der Socialwissenschaften*, p. 157 [pp. 157–58], note 51: "Die letzten Elemente, auf welche die exacte theoretische Interpretation der Naturphänomene zurückgehen muß, sind 'Atome' und 'Kräfte'. Beide

sense, analytic, the method of the social sciences is better described as compositive[4] or synthetic. It is the so-called wholes, the groups of elements which are structurally connected, which we learn to single out from the totality of

---

sind unempirischer Natur. Wir vermögen uns 'Atome' überhaupt nicht, und die Naturkräfte nur unter einem Bilde vorzustellen, und verstehen wir in Wahrheit unter den letzteren lediglich die uns unbekannten Ursachen realer Bewegungen. Hieraus ergeben sich für die exacte Interpretation der Naturphänomene in letzter Linie ganz außerordentliche Schwierigkeiten. Anders in den exacten Socialwissenschaften. Hier sind die menschlichen *Individuen* und ihre *Bestrebungen*, die letzten Elemente unserer Analyse, empirischer Natur und die exacten theoretischen Socialwissenschaften somit in großem Vortheil gegenüber den exacten Naturwissenschaften. Die 'Grenzen des Naturerkennens' und die hieraus für das theoretische Verständniss der Naturphänomene sich ergebenden Schwierigkeiten bestehen in Wahrheit nicht für die exacte Forschung auf dem Gebiete der Socialerscheinungen. Wenn A. Comte die 'Gesellschaften' als reale Organismen und zwar als Organismen complicirterer Art, denn die natürlichen, auffaßt und ihre theoretische Interpretation als das unvergleichlich complicirtere und schwierigere wissenschaftliche Problem bezeichnet, so befindet er sich somit in einem schweren Irrthume. Seine Theorie wäre nur gegenüber Socialforschern richtig, welche den, mit Rücksicht auf den heutigen Zustand der theoretischen Naturwissenschaften, geradezu wahnwitzigen Gedanken fassen würden, die Gesellschaftsphänomene nicht in specifisch socialwissenschaftlich-, sondern in naturwissenschaftlich-atomistischer Weise interpretiren zu wollen". [In Menger, *Investigations into the Method of the Social Sciences*, p. 142, note 51, this passage is rendered as follows: "The ultimate elements to which the exact theoretical interpretation of natural phenomena must be reduced are 'atoms' and 'forces'. Neither is of empirical nature. We cannot imagine 'atoms' at all, and natural forces only by a representation, and by these we really understand merely unknown causes of real motions. From this there arise ultimately quite extraordinary difficulties for the exact interpretation of natural phenomena. It is otherwise in the exact social sciences. Here the human *individuals* and their *efforts*, the final elements of our analysis, are of empirical nature, and thus the exact theoretical social sciences have a great advantage over the exact natural sciences. The 'limits of knowledge of nature' and the difficulties resulting from this for the theoretical understanding of natural phenomena do not really exist for exact research in the realm of social phenomena. When A. Comte conceives of 'societies' as real organisms and to be sure as organisms of a more complicated nature than the natural ones and designates their theoretical interpretation as the incomparably more complicated and more difficult scientific problem, he exposes himself forthwith to a serious error. His theory would be correct only as against sociologists who might get the idea, which is really insane in the light of the present state of the theoretical natural sciences, of wanting to interpret social phenomena not in a specifically sociological way, but in the atomistic way of the natural sciences".—Ed.]

[4] I have borrowed the term 'compositive' from a manuscript note of Carl Menger, who, in his personal annotated copy of Schmoller's review of his *Methode der Socialwissenschaften* ("Zur Methodologie der Staats- und Sozial-Wissenschaften", *Jahrbuch für Gesetzgebung, Verwaltung und Volkswirtschaft im Deutschen Reich*, vol. 7, no. 3, 1883, p. 42 [242]), wrote it above the word 'deductive' used by Schmoller. Since writing this I have noticed that Ernst Cassirer in his *Philosophie der Aufklärung* (Tübingen: Mohr, 1932), pp. 12, 25, 341 uses the term 'compositive' in order to point out rightly that the procedure of the natural sciences pre-supposes the successive use of the 'resolutive' and the 'compositive' technique. This is useful and links up with the point that, since the elements are directly known to us in the social sciences, we can start here with the compositive procedure. [Gustav Schmoller (1838–1917) was the leader of the so-called younger German historical school of economics. His review prompted Menger to write a scathing reply, *Die Irrthümer*

observed phenomena only as a result to our systematic fitting together of the elements with familiar properties, and which we build up or reconstruct from the known properties of the elements.

It is important to observe that in all this the various types of individual beliefs or attitudes are not themselves the object of our explanation, but merely the elements from which we build up the structure of possible relationships between individuals. Insofar as we analyse individual thought in the social sciences the purpose is not to explain that thought but merely to distinguish the possible types of elements with which we shall have to reckon in the construction of different patterns of social relationships. It is a mistake, to which careless expressions by social scientists often give countenance, to believe that their aim is to *explain* conscious action. This, if it can be done at all, is a different task, the task of psychology. For the social sciences the types of conscious action are data[5] and all they have to do with regard to these data is to arrange them in such orderly fashion that they can be effectively used for their task.[6] The problems which they try to answer arise only insofar as the conscious actions of many men produce undesigned results, insofar as regularities are observed which are not the result of anybody's design. If social phenomena showed no order except insofar as they were consciously designed, there would indeed be no room for theoretical sciences of society and there would be, as is often argued, only problems of psychology. It is only insofar as some sort of order arises as a result of individual action but without being designed by any individual that a problem is raised which demands a theoretical explanation. But although people dominated by the scientistic prejudice are often inclined to deny the existence of any such order (and thereby the existence of an object for theoretical sciences of society), few if any would be prepared to do so consistently: that at least language shows a definite order which is not the result of any conscious design can scarcely be questioned.

The reason for the difficulty which the natural scientist experiences in

---

des Historismus in der deutschen Nationalökonomie (Vienna: Hölder, 1884), which initiated the *Methodenstreit*, or battle over methods, between the German and Austrian schools. For more on the conflict, see Caldwell, *Hayek's Challenge*, chapters 3 and 4. For a translation of Ernst Cassirer's book, see *The Philosophy of the Enlightenment* (Princeton: Princeton University Press, 1951).—Ed.]

[5] As Robbins, *Essay on the Nature and Significance*, p. 86, rightly says, economists in particular regard "the things which psychology studies as the data of their own deductions".

[6] That this task absorbs a great part of the economist's energies should not deceive us about the fact that by itself this 'pure logic of choice' (or 'economic calculus') does not explain any facts, or at least does no more so by itself than does mathematics. For the precise relationship between the pure theory of the economic calculus and its use in the explanation of social phenomena, I again refer to my article "Economics and Knowledge". It should perhaps be added that while economic theory might be very useful to the director of a completely planned system in helping him to see what he ought to do to achieve his ends, it would not help us to explain his actions—except insofar as he was actually guided by it.

admitting the existence of such an order in social phenomena is that these orders cannot be stated in physical terms, that if we define the elements in physical terms no such order is visible, and that the units which show an orderly arrangement do not (or at least need not) have any physical properties in common (except that men react to them in the 'same' way—although the 'sameness' of different people's reaction will again, as a rule, not be definable in physical terms). It is an order in which things behave in the same way because they mean the same thing to man. If, instead of regarding as alike and unlike what appears so to the acting man, we were to take for our units only what Science shows to be alike or unlike, we should probably find no recognisable order whatever in social phenomena—at least not till the natural sciences had completed their task of analysing all natural phenomena into their ultimate constituents and psychology had also fully achieved the reverse task of explaining in all detail how the ultimate units of physical science come to appear to man just as they do, that is, how that apparatus of classification operates which our senses constitute.

It is only in the very simplest instances that it can be shown briefly and without any technical apparatus how the independent actions of individuals will produce an order which is no part of their intentions; and in those instances the explanation is usually so obvious that we never stop to examine the type of argument which leads us to it. The way in which footpaths are formed in a wild broken country is such an instance. At first everyone will seek for himself what seems to him the best path. But the fact that such a path has been used once is likely to make it easier to traverse and therefore more likely to be used again; and thus gradually more and more clearly defined tracks arise and come to be used to the exclusion of other possible ways. Human movements through the region come to conform to a definite pattern which, although the result of deliberate decisions of many people, has yet not been consciously designed by anyone. This explanation of how this happens is an elementary 'theory' applicable to hundreds of particular historical instances; and it is not the observation of the actual growth of any particular track, and still less of many, from which this explanation derives its cogency, but from our general knowledge of how we and other people behave in the kind of situation in which the successive people find themselves who have to seek their way and who by the cumulative effect of their action create the path. It is the elements of the complex of events which are familiar to us from everyday experience, but it is only by a deliberate effort of directed thought that we come to see the necessary effects of the combination of such actions by many people. We 'understand' the way in which the result we observe can be produced, although we may never be in a position to watch the whole process or to predict its precise course and result.

It makes no difference for our present purpose whether the process extends over a long period of time, as it does in such cases as the evolution of money or the formation of language, or whether it is a process which is constantly repeated anew, as in the case of the formation of prices or the direction of production under competition. The former instances raise theoretical (that is, generic) problems (as distinguished from the specifically historical problems in the precise sense which we shall have to define later) which are fundamentally similar to the problems raised by such recurring phenomena as the determination of prices. Although in the study of any particular instance of the evolution of an 'institution' like money or language the theoretical problem will frequently be so overlaid by the consideration of the particular circumstances involved (the properly historical task), this does not alter the fact that any explanation of a historical process involves assumptions about the kind of circumstances that can produce certain kinds of effects—assumptions which, where we have to deal with results which were not directly willed by somebody, can only be stated in the form of a generic scheme, in other words a theory.

The physicist who wishes to understand the problems of the social sciences with the help of an analogy from his own field would have to imagine a world in which he knew by direct observation the inside of the atoms and had neither the possibility of making experiments with lumps of matter nor the opportunity to observe more than the interactions of a comparatively few atoms during a limited period. From his knowledge of the different kinds of atoms he could build up models of all the various ways in which they could combine into larger units and make these models more and more closely reproduce all the features of the few instances in which he was able to observe more complex phenomena. But the laws of the macrocosm which he could derive from his knowledge of the microcosm would always remain 'deductive'; they would, because of his limited knowledge of the data of the complex situation, scarcely ever enable him to predict the precise outcome of a particular situation; and he could never confirm them by controlled experiment—although they might be disproved by the observation of events which according to his theory are impossible.

In a sense some problems of theoretical astronomy are more similar to those of the social sciences than those of any of the experimental sciences. Yet there remain important differences. While the astronomer aims at knowing all the elements of which his universe is composed, the student of social phenomena cannot hope to know more than the types of elements from which his universe is made up. He will scarcely ever know even of all the elements of which it consists and he will certainly never know all the relevant properties of each of them. The inevitable imperfection of the human mind becomes here not only a basic datum about the object of explanation but, since it applies no less to the observer, also a limitation on what he can hope to accomplish in his attempt to explain the observed facts. The number of separate variables which in any particular social phenomenon will determine the result of a given change will as a rule be far too large for any human mind to master and manipulate them effectively.[7] In consequence our knowledge of the principle by which these phenomena are produced will rarely if ever enable us to predict the precise result of any concrete situation. While we can explain the principle on which certain phenomena are produced and can from this knowledge exclude the possibility of certain results, for example, of certain events occurring together, our knowledge will in a sense be only negative; that is, it will merely enable us to preclude certain results but not enable us to narrow the range of possibilities sufficiently so that only one remains.

The distinction between an explanation merely of the principle on which a phenomenon is produced and an explanation which enables us to predict the precise result is of great importance for the understanding of the theoretical methods of the social sciences. It arises, I believe, also elsewhere, for example, in biology and certainly in psychology. It is, however, somewhat unfamiliar and I know no place where it is adequately explained. The best illustration in the field of the social sciences is probably the general theory of prices as represented, for example, by the Walrasian or Paretian systems of equations.[8] These systems show merely the principle of coherence between the prices of the various types of commodities of which the system is composed; but without knowledge of the numerical values of all the constants which occur in it and which we never do know, this does not enable us to predict the precise

---

[7] Cf. M. R. Cohen, *Reason and Nature* (New York: Harcourt, Brace and Co., 1931), p. 356: "If, then, social phenomena depend upon more factors than we readily manipulate, even the doctrine of universal determinism will not guarantee an attainable expression of laws governing the specific phenomena of social life. Social phenomena, though determined, might not to a finite mind in limited time display any laws at all".

[8] [Hayek refers here to the general equilibrium approach associated with Léon Walras (1834–1910), a founder of the Lausanne School (and who, with Carl Menger in Austria and William Stanley Jevons in England, was a co-founder of the marginal revolution), and with Walras's greatest disciple, the Italian economist and sociologist Vilfredo Pareto (1848–1923). Hayek's opinion of the system of equations approach of the Lausanne School may best be described as ambivalent. While he and Robbins were instrumental in introducing the writings of Walras and Pareto to British economists in the 1930s, and endorsed the approach for stressing the interdependence of consumption, production and distribution decisions, Hayek always emphasised (as in the note that follows) that one could not provide numerical estimates for the variables in the system so as to arrive at accurate predictions of economic activity. Market socialists used the Paretian analysis to argue that a planned economic system and a free market system are structurally equivalent, the only difference being that socialist managers made decisions in one, and entrepreneurs in the other, thereby disputing Ludwig von Mises's claim that rational decision making under socialism is impossible. For more on the debate, see the "Editor's Introduction" and chapters 1–3 of Hayek, *Socialism and War*.—Ed.]

results which any particular change will have.[9] Apart from this particular case, a set of equations which shows merely the form of a system of relationships but does not give the values of the constants contained in it, is perhaps the best general illustration of an explanation merely of the principle on which any phenomenon is produced.

This must suffice as a positive description of the characteristic problems of the social sciences. It will become clearer as we contrast in the following sections the specific procedure of the social sciences with the most characteristic aspects of the attempts to treat their object after the fashion of the natural sciences.

---

[9] Pareto himself has clearly seen this. After stating the nature of the factors determining the prices in his system of equations, he adds (*Manuel d'économie politique*, translated by Alfred Bonnet, 2nd ed. (Paris: Marcel Giard, 1927), pp. 233–34): "It may be mentioned here that this determination has by no means the purpose of arriving at a numerical calculation of prices. Let us make the most favourable assumptions for such a calculation; let us assume that we have triumphed over all the difficulties of finding the data of the problem and that we know the *ophélimités* of all the different commodities for each individual, and all the conditions of production of all the commodities, etc. This is already an absurd hypothesis to make. Yet it is not sufficient to make the solution of the problem possible. We have seen that in the case of 100 persons and 700 commodities there will be 70,699 conditions (actually a great number of circumstances which we have so far neglected will still increase that number); we shall, therefore, have to solve a system of 70,699 equations. This exceeds practically the power of algebraic analysis, and this is even more true if one contemplates the fabulous number of equations which one obtains for a population of forty million and several thousand commodities. In this case the rôles would be changed: It would be not mathematics which would assist political economy, but political economy which would assist mathematics. In other words, if one really could know all these equations, the only means to solve them which is available to human powers is to observe the practical solution given by the market". Cf. also Augustin Cournot, *Researches into the Mathematical Principles of the Theory of Wealth* [1838], translated by Nathaniel T. Bacon (New York: Macmillan, 1927 [reprinted, New York: Kelley, 1971]), p. 127, where he says that if in our equations we took the entire economic system into consideration, "this would surpass the powers of mathematical analysis and of our practical methods of calculation, even if the values of all the constants could be assigned to them numerically". [The 1927 French edition of Pareto's *Manuel* served as the basis both for Hayek's own translation into English of the passage above, and for the following English translation of the book: Vilfredo Pareto, *Manual of Political Economy*, Ann S. Schwier and Alfred N. Page, eds, translated by Ann S. Schwier (New York: Kelley, 1971). The passage Hayek translated appears on p. 171.—Ed.]

FIVE

THE OBJECTIVISM OF THE
SCIENTISTIC APPROACH

The great differences between the characteristic methods of the physical sciences and those of the social sciences explain why the natural scientist who turns to the work of the professional students of social phenomena so often feels that he has got among a company of people who habitually commit all the mortal sins which he is most careful to avoid, and that a science of society conforming to his standards does not yet exist. From this to the attempt to create a new science of society which satisfies his conception of Science is but a step. During the last four generations attempts of this kind have been constantly made; and though they have never produced the results which had been expected, and though they did not even succeed in creating that continuous tradition which is the symptom of a healthy discipline, they are repeated almost every month by someone who hopes thereby to revolutionise social thought. Yet, though these efforts are mostly disconnected, they regularly show certain characteristic features which we must now consider. These methodological features can be conveniently treated under the headings of 'objectivism', 'collectivism', and 'historicism', corresponding to the 'subjectivism', the 'individualism', and the theoretical character of the developed disciplines of social study.

The attitude which, for want of a better term, we shall call the 'objectivism' of the scientistic approach to the study of man and society, has found its most characteristic expression in the various attempts to dispense with our subjective knowledge of the working of the human mind, attempts which in various forms have affected almost all branches of social study. From Auguste Comte's denial of the possibility of introspection, through various attempts to create an 'objective psychology', down to the behaviourism of J. B. Watson and the 'physicalism' of O. Neurath, a long series of authors have attempted to do without the knowledge derived from 'introspection'.[1] But, as can be eas-

---

[1] [Hayek discusses Comte's views on psychology and introspection in chapter 16, section 3. The American psychologist John Broadus Watson (1878–1958) was a founder of behaviourism, which he promoted as a natural science approach to psychology. For Watson, truly scientific psychology avoids all reference to introspection or to states of consciousness and only studies 'objectively verifiable' (i.e., observable) behaviour. See his *Psychology from the Standpoint of a Behaviorist*,

ily shown, these attempts to avoid the use of knowledge which we possess are bound to break down.

A behaviourist or physicalist, to be consistent, ought not to begin by observing the reactions of people to what our senses tell us are similar objects; he ought to confine himself to studying the reactions to stimuli which are identical in a strictly physical sense. He ought, for example, not to study the reactions of persons who are shown a red circle or made to hear a certain tune, but solely the effects of a light wave of a certain frequency on a particular point of the retina of the human eye, etc., etc. No behaviourist, however, seriously contemplates doing so. They all take it naïvely for granted that what appears alike to us will also appear alike to other people. Though they have no business to do so, they make constant use of the classification of external stimuli by our senses and our mind as alike or unlike, a classification which we know only from our personal experience of it and which is not based on any objective tests showing that these facts also behave similarly in relation to each other. This applies as much to what we commonly regard as simple sense qualities, such as colour, the pitch of sound, smell, etc., as to our perception of configurations (*Gestalten*) by which we classify physically very different things as specimens of a particular 'shape', for example, as a circle or a certain tune. To the behaviourist or physicalist the fact that we recognise these things as similar is no problem.

This naïve attitude, however, is in no way justified by what the development of physical science itself teaches us. As we have seen before,[2] one of the main results of this development is that things that to us appear alike may not be alike in any objective sense, that is, may have no other properties in common. Once we have to recognise, however, that things differ in their effects on our senses not necessarily in the same way in which they differ in their behaviour towards each other, we are no longer entitled to take it for granted that what to us appears alike or different will also appear so to others. That this is so as a rule is an important empirical fact which, on the one hand, demands explanation (a task for psychology) and which, on the other hand, must be accepted as a basic datum in our study of people's conduct. That different objects mean the same thing to different people, and that different people mean the same thing by different acts, remain important facts though physical science may show that these objects or acts possess no other common properties.

It is true, of course, that we know nothing about other people's minds except through sense perceptions, that is, the observation of physical facts. But this does not mean that we know nothing but physical facts. Of what kind

---

3rd ed. (Philadelphia: J. B. Lippincott, 1929), esp. pp. 1–4. Otto Neurath and his doctrine of physicalism were first mentioned in chapter 1, note 5.—Ed.]

[2] See above, pp. 83 et seq.

the facts are with which we have to deal in any discipline is not determined by all the properties possessed by the concrete objects to which the discipline applies, but only by those properties by which we classify them for the purposes of the discipline in question. To take an example from the physical sciences: all levers or pendulums of which we can conceive have chemical and optical properties; but when we talk about levers or pendulums we do not talk about chemical or optical facts. What make a number of individual phenomena facts of one kind are the attributes which we select in order to treat them as members of one class. And though all social phenomena with which we can possibly be concerned will possess physical attributes, this does not mean that they must be physical facts for our purpose.

The significant point about the objects of human activity with which we are concerned in the social sciences, and about these human activities themselves, is that in interpreting human activities we spontaneously and unconsciously class together as instances of the same object or the same act any one of a large number of physical facts which may have no physical property in common. We know that other people like ourselves regard any one of a large number of physically different things, a, b, c, d, . . . etc., as belonging to the same class; and we know this because other people, like ourselves, react to any one of these things by any one of the movements α, β, γ, δ, . . . , which again may have no physical property in common. Yet this knowledge on which we constantly act, which must necessarily precede, and is pre-supposed by, any communication with other men, is not conscious knowledge in the sense that we are in a position exhaustively to enumerate all the different physical phenomena which we unhesitatingly recognise as members of the class: we do not know which of many possible combinations of physical properties we shall recognise as a certain word, or as a 'friendly face' or a 'threatening gesture'. Probably in no single instance has experimental research yet succeeded in precisely determining the range of different phenomena which we unhesitatingly treat as meaning the same thing to us as well as to other people; yet we constantly and successfully act on the assumption that we do classify these things in the same manner as other people do. We are not in a position—and may never be in the position—to substitute objects defined in physical terms for the mental categories we employ in talking about other people's actions.[3] Whenever we do so the physical facts to which we refer are significant not as physical facts, that is, not as members of a class all of which have certain

[3] The attempts often made to evade this difficulty by an *illustrative* enumeration of some of the physical attributes by which we recognise the object as belonging to one of these mental categories are just begging the question. To describe a man's anger in terms of showing certain physical symptoms helps us very little unless we can exhaustively enumerate all the symptoms by which we ever recognise, and which always when they are present mean, that the man who shows them is angry. Only if we could do this would it be legitimate to say that in using this term we mean no more than *certain* physical phenomena.

physical properties in common, but as members of a class of what may be physically completely different things but which 'mean' the same thing to us.

It becomes necessary here to state explicitly a consideration which is implied in the whole of our argument on this point and which, though it seems to follow from the modern conception of the character of physical research, is yet still somewhat unfamiliar. It is that not only those mental entities, such as 'concepts' or 'ideas', which are commonly recognised as 'abstractions', but *all* mental phenomena, sense perceptions and images as well as the more abstract 'concepts' and 'ideas', must be regarded as acts of classification performed by the brain.[4] This is, of course, merely another way of saying that the qualities which we perceive are not properties of the objects but ways in which we (individually or as a race) have learned to group or classify external stimuli. To perceive is to assign to a familiar category (or categories): we could not perceive anything completely different from everything else we have ever perceived before.[5] This does not mean, however, that everything which we actually class together must possess common properties additional to the fact

[4] This must also serve as a justification for what may have seemed the very loose way in which we have throughout, in illustrative enumerations of mental entities, indiscriminately lumped together such concepts as sensation, perceptions, concepts, and ideas. These different types of mental entities all have in common that they are classifications of possible external stimuli (or complexes of such stimuli). This contention will perhaps appear less strange now than would have been the case fifty years ago, since in the configurations or *Gestalt* qualities we have become familiar with something that is intermediate between the old 'elementary' sense qualities and concepts. It may be added that on this view there would, however, seem to be no justification for the unwarranted ontological conclusions which many members of the *Gestalt* school draw from their interesting observations; there is no reason to assume that the 'wholes' which we perceive are properties of the external world and not merely ways in which our mind classifies complexes of stimuli; like other abstractions, the relations between the parts thus singled out may be significant or not.

Perhaps it should also be mentioned here that there is no reason to regard values as the only purely mental categories which do therefore not appear in our picture of the physical world. Although values must necessarily occupy a central place wherever we are concerned with purposive action, they are certainly not the only kind of purely mental categories which we shall have to employ in interpreting human activities: the distinction between true and false provides at least one other instance of such purely mental categories which is of great importance in this connection. On the connected point that it is not necessarily value considerations which will guide us in selecting the aspects of social life which we study, see chapter 7, note 10, below. [The idea that all mental phenomena are acts of classification by the brain is a central theme in Hayek's book *The Sensory Order: An Inquiry into the Foundations of Theoretical Psychology* (Chicago: University of Chicago Press, 1952). Hayek also discusses the findings of the *Gestalt* school in the book; for more on this, see Nicolò De Vecchi, "The Place of *Gestalt* Psychology in the Making of Hayek's Thought", *History of Political Economy*, vol. 35, Spring 2003, pp. 135–62.—Ed.]

[5] [In the original article in *Economica*, Hayek placed a note here that read, "Although the second time we are exposed to a new stimulus we may already 'recognise' it as identical with what happened to us in circumstances which its recurrence calls to our mind, we should still not have been 'conscious' of it on the first occasion when it had not yet acquired a place in the structure of our mind".—Ed.]

that we react in the same way to these things. It is a common but dangerous error to believe that things which our senses or our mind treat as members of the same class must have something else in common beyond being
registered in the same manner by our mind. Although there will usually exist
some objective justification why we regard certain things as similar, this need
not always be the case. But while in our study of nature classifications which
are not based on any similarity in the behaviour of the objects towards each
other must be treated as 'deceptions' of which we must free ourselves, they
are of positive significance in our attempts to understand human action. The
important difference between the position of these mental categories in the
two spheres is that when we study the working of external nature our sensations and thoughts are not links in the chain of observed events—they are
merely about them; but in the mechanism of society they form an essential
link, the forces here at work operate through these mental entities which are
directly known to us: while the things in the external world do not behave
alike or differently because they appear alike to us, we do behave in a similar
or different manner because the things appear alike or different to us.

The behaviourist or physicalist who in studying human behaviour wished
really to avoid using the categories which we find ready in our mind, and who
wanted to confine himself strictly to the study of man's reactions to objects
defined in physical terms, would consistently have to refuse to say anything
about human actions till he had experimentally established how our senses
and our mind group external stimuli as alike or unlike. He would have to
begin by asking which physical objects appear alike to us and which do not
(and how it comes about that they do) before he could seriously undertake to
study human behaviour towards these things.

It is important to observe that our contention is not that such an attempt to
explain the principle of how our mind or our brain transforms physical facts
into mental entities is impossible. Once we recognise this as a process of classification there is no reason why we should not learn to understand the principle on which it operates. Classification is, after all, a mechanical process,
that is, a process which could be performed by a machine which 'sorts out'
and groups objects according to certain properties.[6] Our argument is, rather,
in the first instance, that for the task of the social sciences such an explanation of the formation of mental entities and their relations to the physical facts
which they represent is unnecessary, and that such an explanation would help
us in no way in our task; and, second, that such an explanation, although conceivable, is not only not available at present and not likely to be available for
a long time yet, but also unlikely to be ever more than an 'explanation of the

---

[6] Which, as we have already seen, does not, of course, mean that it will always treat only elements which have common properties as members of the same class.

principle'[7] on which this apparatus of classification works. It would seem that any apparatus of classification would always have to possess a degree of complexity greater than any one of the different things which it classifies; and if this is correct it would follow that it is impossible that our brain should ever be able to produce a complete explanation (as distinguished from a mere explanation of the principle) of the particular ways in which it itself classifies external stimuli. We shall later have to consider the significance of the related paradox that to 'explain' our own knowledge would require that we should know more than we actually do, which is, of course, a self-contradictory statement.

But let us assume for the moment that we had succeeded in fully reducing all mental phenomena to physical processes. Assume that we knew the mechanism by which our central nervous system groups anyone of the (elementary or complex) stimuli, a, b, c, ... or l, m, n, ... or r, s, t, ... into definite classes determined by the fact that to any member of one class we shall react by any one of the members of the corresponding classes or reactions α, β, γ, ... or v, ξ, o, ... or φ, χ, ψ, ... This assumption implies both that this system is not merely familiar to us as the way in which our own mind acts, but that we explicitly know all the relations by which it is determined, and that we also know the mechanism by which the classification is actually effected. We should then be able strictly to correlate the mental entities with definite groups of physical facts. We should thus have 'unified' science, but we should be in no better position with respect to the specific task of the social sciences than we are now. We should still have to use the old categories, though we should be able to explain their formation and though we should know the physical facts 'behind' them. Although we should know that a different arrangement of the facts of nature is more appropriate for explaining external events, in interpreting human actions we should still have to use the classification in which these facts actually appear in the minds of the acting people. Thus, quite apart from the fact that we should probably have to wait forever till we were able to substitute physical facts for the mental entities, even if this were achieved we should be no better equipped for the task we have to solve in the social sciences.

The idea, implied in Comte's hierarchy of the sciences[8] and in many similar arguments, that the social sciences must in some sense be 'based' on the physical sciences, that they can only hope for success after the physical sciences have advanced far enough to enable us to treat social phenomena in physical terms, in 'physical language', is, therefore, entirely erroneous. The problem of explaining mental processes by physical ones is entirely distinct from the problems of the social sciences, it is a problem for physiological psy-

---

[7] See pp. 105–6, herein.
[8] Cf. the comment on this by Carl Menger, in the passage quoted in chapter 4, note 3, herein.

chology. But whether it is solved or not, for the social sciences the given mental entities must provide the starting point, whether their formation has been explained or not.

We cannot discuss here all the other forms in which the characteristic 'objectivism' of the scientistic approach has made itself felt and led to error in the social sciences. We shall, in the course of our historical survey, find this tendency to look for the 'real' attributes of the objects of human activity which lie behind men's views about them, represented in a great many different ways. Only a brief survey can be attempted here.

Nearly as important as the various forms of behaviourism, and closely connected with them, is the common tendency in the study of social phenomena to attempt to disregard all the 'merely' qualitative phenomena and to concentrate, on the model of the natural sciences, on the quantitative aspects, on what is measurable. We have seen before[9] how in the natural sciences this tendency is a necessary consequence of their specific task of replacing the picture of the world in terms of sense qualities by one in which the units are defined exclusively by their explicit relations. The success of this method in that field has brought it about that it is now generally regarded as the hallmark of all genuinely scientific procedure. Yet its *raison d'être*, the need to replace the classification of events which our senses and our mind provide by a more appropriate one, is absent where we try to understand human beings, and where this understanding is made possible by the fact that we have a mind like theirs, and that from the mental categories we have in common with them we can reconstruct the social complexes which are our concern. The blind transfer of the striving for quantitative measurements[10] to a field in which the specific conditions are not present which give it its basic importance in the natural sciences, is the result of an entirely unfounded prejudice. It is probably responsible for the worst aberrations and absurdities produced by scientism in the social sciences. It not only leads frequently to the selection for study of the most irrelevant aspects of the phenomena because they happen to be measurable, but also to 'measurements' and assignments of numerical values which are absolutely meaningless. What a distinguished philosopher recently wrote about psychology is at least equally true of the social sciences, namely, that it

---

[9] See herein, pp. 86–87.

[10] It should, perhaps, be emphasised that there is no necessary connection between the use of mathematics in the social sciences and the attempts to measure social phenomena—as particularly people who are acquainted only with elementary mathematics are apt to believe. Mathematics may be—and in economics probably is—absolutely indispensable to describe certain types of complex structural relationships, though there may be no chance of ever knowing the numerical values of the concrete magnitudes (misleadingly called 'constants') that appear in the formulae describing these structures.

is only too easy "to rush off to measure something without considering what it is that we are measuring, or what the measurement means. In this respect some recent 'measurements' are of the same logical type as Plato's determination that a just ruler is 729 times as happy as an unjust one".[11]

Closely connected with the tendency to treat the objects of human activity in terms of their 'real' attributes instead of as what they appear to the acting people is the propensity to conceive of the student of society as endowed with a kind of super-mind, with some sort of absolute knowledge, which makes it unnecessary for him to start from what is known by the people whose actions he studies. Among the most characteristic manifestations of this tendency are the various forms of social 'energetics' which, from the earlier attempts of Ernest Solvay, Wilhelm Ostwald, and F. Soddy down to our own day,[12] have constantly reappeared among scientists and engineers when they turned to the problems of social organisation. The idea underlying these theories is that, as science is supposed to teach that everything can be ultimately reduced to quantities of energy, man should in his plans treat the various things not according to the concrete usefulness they possess for the purposes for which he knows how to use them, but as the interchangeable units of abstract energy which they 'really' are.

Another, hardly less crude and even more widespread, example of this tendency is the conception of the 'objective' possibilities of production, of the quantity of social output which the physical facts are supposed to make possible, an idea which frequently finds expression in quantitative estimates of the supposed 'productive capacity' of society as a whole. These estimates regularly refer, not to what men can produce by means of any stated organisa-

---

[11] Cohen, *Reason and Nature*, p. 305.

[12] Cf. Lancelot Hogben, *Lancelot Hogben's Dangerous Thoughts* (London: G. Allen and Unwin, 1939), p. 99: "Plenty is the excess of free energy over the collective calorie debt of human effort applied to securing the needs which all human beings share". [Hogben italicized the entire sentence that Hayek quotes. The energetics movement, which saw in the concept of energy "an all-encompassing principle to reform the method and content of science" (Philip Mirowski, *More Heat Than Light: Economics as Social Physics, Physics as Nature's Economics* (Cambridge: Cambridge University Press, 1989), p. 53), emerged in the latter half of the nineteenth century, and some of its enthusiasts sought to apply the principles to the study of social phenomena as well. Belgian chemist, politician, and author Ernest Solvay (1838–1922) contributed to the social energetics movement in his *Questions d'énergétique sociale: Notes et publications* (1894–1910). He also helped found the Solvay School of Commerce at the Free University of Brussels, where students would study to become 'commercial engineers'. German chemist and Nobel laureate Wilhelm Ostwald (1853–1932) identified the progress of civilisation as moving hand in hand with mankind's control over energy. Among his non-scientific writings was a biography of Auguste Comte: *Auguste Comte: Der Mann und sein Werk* (1914). After World War I the British radiochemist and Nobel laureate Frederick Soddy (1877–1956) began writing about how scientific principles could be employed to solve economic and social problems in such books as *Wealth, Virtual Wealth, and Debt* (1926) and *Money versus Man* (1933).—Ed.]

tion, but to what in some undefined objective sense 'could' be produced from the available resources. Most of these assertions have no ascertainable meaning whatever. They do not mean that x or y or any particular organisation of people could achieve these things. What they amount to is that *if* all the knowledge dispersed among many people could be mastered by a single mind, and *if* this mastermind could make all the people act at all times as he wished, certain results could be achieved; but these results could, of course, not be known to anybody except to such a mastermind. It need hardly be pointed out that an assertion about a 'possibility' which is dependent on such conditions has no relation to reality. There is no such thing as the productive capacity of society in the abstract—apart from particular forms of organisation. The only fact which we can regard as given is that there are particular people who have certain concrete knowledge about the way in which particular things can be used for particular purposes. This knowledge never exists as an integrated whole or in one mind, and the only knowledge that can in any sense be said to exist is these separate and often inconsistent and even conflicting views of different people.

Of very similar nature are the frequent statements about the objective needs of the people, where *objective* is merely a name for somebody's views about what the people ought to want. We shall have to consider further manifestations of this objectivism towards the end of this part when we turn from the consideration of scientism proper to the effects of the characteristic outlook of the engineer, whose conceptions of 'efficiency' have been one of the most powerful forces through which this attitude has affected current views on social problems.

SIX

THE COLLECTIVISM OF THE
SCIENTISTIC APPROACH

Closely connected with the objectivism of the scientistic approach is its methodological collectivism, its tendency to treat wholes like society or the economy, capitalism (as a given historical 'phase') or a particular industry or class or country as definitely given objects about which we can discover laws by observing their behaviour as wholes. While the specific subjectivist approach of the social sciences starts, as we have seen, from our knowledge of the inside of these social complexes, the knowledge of the individual attitudes which form the elements of their structure, the objectivism of the natural sciences tries to view them from the outside;[1] it treats social phenomena not as something of which the human mind is a part and the principles of whose organisation we can reconstruct from the familiar parts, but as if they were objects directly perceived by us as wholes.

There are several reasons why this tendency should so frequently show itself with natural scientists. They are used to seek first for empirical regularities in the relatively complex phenomena that are immediately given to observation, and only after they have found such regularities to try and explain them as the product of a combination of other, often purely hypothetical, elements (constructs) which are assumed to behave according to simpler and more general rules. They are therefore inclined to seek in the social field, too, first for empirical regularities in the behaviour of the complexes before they feel that there is need for a theoretical explanation. This tendency is further strengthened by the experience that there are few regularities in the behaviour of individuals which can be established in a strictly objective manner; and they turn therefore to the wholes in the hope that they will show such regularities. Finally, there is the rather vague idea that since 'social phenomena' are to be the object of study, the obvious procedure is to start from the direct observation of these 'social phenomena', where the existence in popular usage of

---

[1] The description of this contrast as one between the view from the inside and the view from the outside, though, of course, metaphorical, is less misleading than such metaphors usually are and is perhaps the best short way to indicate the nature of the contrast. It brings out that what of social complexes are directly known to us are only the parts, and that the whole is never directly perceived but always reconstructed by an effort of our imagination.

such terms as *society* or *economy* is naïvely taken as evidence that there must be definite 'objects' corresponding to them. The fact that people all talk about 'the nation' or 'capitalism' leads to the belief that the first step in the study of these phenomena must be to go and see what they are like, just as we should if we heard about a particular stone or a particular animal.[2]

The error involved in this collectivist approach is that it mistakes for facts what are no more than provisional theories, models constructed by the popular mind to explain the connection between some of the individual phenomena which we observe. The paradoxical aspect of it, however, is, as we have seen before,[3] that those who by the scientistic prejudice are led to approach social phenomena in this manner are induced, by their very anxiety to avoid all merely subjective elements and to confine themselves to 'objective facts', to commit the mistake they are most anxious to avoid, namely, that of treating as facts what are no more than vague popular theories. They thus become, when they least suspect it, the victims of the fallacy of 'conceptual realism' (made familiar by A. N. Whitehead as the 'fallacy of misplaced concreteness').[4]

The naïve realism which uncritically assumes that where there are commonly used concepts there must also be definite 'given' things which they describe is so deeply embedded in current thought about social phenomena that it requires a deliberate effort of will to free ourselves from it. While most people will readily admit that in this field there may exist special difficulties in recognising definite wholes because we have never many specimens of a kind before us and therefore cannot readily distinguish their constant from their merely accidental attributes, few are aware that there is a much more fundamental obstacle: that the wholes as such are never given to our observation but are without exception constructions of our mind. They are not 'given facts', objective data of a similar kind which we spontaneously recognise as similar by their common physical attributes. They cannot be perceived at all apart from a mental scheme that shows the connection between some of the many individual facts which we can observe. Where we have to deal with such social wholes we cannot (as we do in the natural sciences) start from the observation of a number of instances which we recognise spontaneously by their common sense attributes as instances of 'societies' or 'economies', 'capitalism' or

[2] It would, of course, be false to believe that the first instinct of the student of social phenomena is any less to 'go and see'. It is not ignorance of the obvious but long experience which has taught him that to look directly for the wholes, which popular language suggests to exist, leads nowhere. It has, indeed, rightly become one of the first maxims which the student of social phenomena learns (or ought to learn), namely, never to speak of 'society' or a 'country' as acting or behaving in a certain manner, but always and exclusively to think of individuals as acting.

[3] See herein, pp. 100–101.

[4] [English-born mathematician and philosopher of science Alfred North Whitehead (1861–1947) discussed this error in his *Science and the Modern World* (New York: Macmillan, 1925), pp. 51–55.—Ed.]

'nations', 'language' or 'legal systems', and where only after we have collected a sufficient number of instances we begin to seek for common laws which they obey. Social wholes are not given to us as what we may call 'natural units' which we recognise as similar with our senses, as we do with flowers or butterflies, minerals or light rays, or even forests or ant heaps. They are not given to us as similar things before we even begin to ask whether what looks alike to us also behaves in the same manner. The terms for collectives which we all readily use do not designate definite things in the sense of stable collections of sense attributes which we recognise as alike by inspection; they refer to certain structures of relationships between some of the many things which we can observe within given spatial and temporal limits and which we select because we think that we can discern connections between them—connections which may or may not exist in fact.

What we group together as instances of the same collective or whole are different complexes of individual events, by themselves perhaps quite dissimilar, but believed by us to be related to each other in a similar manner; they are selections of certain elements of a complex picture on the basis of a theory about their coherence. They do not stand for definite things or classes of things (if we understand the term *thing* in any material or concrete sense) but for a pattern or order in which different things may be related to each other—an order which is not a spatial or temporal order but can be defined only in terms of relations which are intelligible human attitudes. This order or pattern is as little perceptible as a physical fact as these relations themselves; and it can be studied only by following up the implications of the particular combination of relationships. In other words, the wholes about which we speak exist only if, and to the extent to which, the theory is correct which we have formed about the connection of the parts which they imply, and which we can explicitly state only in the form of a model built from those relationships.[5]

The social sciences, thus, do not deal with 'given' wholes but their task is to *constitute* these wholes by constructing models from the familiar elements—models which reproduce the structure of relationships between some of the many phenomena which we always simultaneously observe in real life. This is no less true of the popular concepts of social wholes which are represented by the terms current in ordinary language; they too refer to mental models, but instead of a precise description they convey merely vague and indistinct suggestions of the way in which certain phenomena are connected. Sometimes the wholes constituted by the theoretical social sciences will roughly correspond with the wholes to which the popular concepts refer, because popular usage has succeeded in approximately separating the significant from the acci-

[5] See Felix Kaufmann, "Soziale Kollektiva", *Zeitschrift für Nationalökonomie*, 1930, vol. 1, pp. 294–308.

dental; sometimes the wholes constituted by theory may refer to entirely new structural connections of which we did not know before systematic study commenced and for which ordinary language has not even a name. If we take current concepts like those of 'market' or of 'capital', the popular meaning of these words corresponds at least in some measure to the similar concepts which we have to form for theoretical purposes, although even in these instances the popular meaning is far too vague to allow the use of these terms without first giving them a more precise meaning. If they can be retained in theoretical work at all it is, however, because in these instances even the popular concepts have long ceased to describe particular concrete things, definable in physical terms, and have come to cover a great variety of different things which are classed together solely because of a recognised similarity in the structure of the relationships between men and things. A 'market', for example, has long ceased to mean only the periodical meeting of men at a fixed place to which they bring their products to sell them from temporary wooden stalls. It now covers any arrangements for regular contacts between potential buyers and sellers of any thing that can be sold, whether by personal contact, by telephone or telegraph, by advertising, etc., etc.[6]

When, however, we speak of the behaviour of, for example, the price system as a whole and discuss the complex of connected changes which will correspond in certain conditions to a fall in the rate of interest, we are not concerned with a whole that obtrudes itself on popular notice or that is ever definitely given; we can only reconstruct it by following up the reactions of many individuals to the initial change and its immediate effects. That in this case certain changes 'belong together'—that among the large number of other changes which in any concrete situation will always occur simultaneously with them and which will often swamp those which form part of the complex in which we are interested, a few form a more closely interrelated complex— we do not know from observing that these particular changes regularly occur together. That would indeed be impossible because what in different circumstances would have to be regarded as the same set of changes could not be determined by any of the physical attributes of the things but only by singling out certain relevant aspects in the attitudes of men towards the things; and this can be done only by the help of the models we have formed.

The mistake of treating as definite objects wholes that are no more than constructions, and that can have no properties except those which follow from the way in which we have constructed them from the elements, has probably appeared most frequently in the form of the various theories about a 'social'

---

[6] It should be noted that, though observation may assist us to understand what people mean by the terms they use, it can never tell us what 'market', 'capital', etc., really are; that is, what significant relations it would be useful to single out and combine into a model.

or 'collective' mind[7] and has in this connection raised all sorts of pseudo-problems. The same idea is frequently but imperfectly concealed under the attributes of personality or individuality which are ascribed to society. Whatever the name, these terms always mean that, instead of reconstructing the wholes from the relations between individual minds which we directly know, a vaguely apprehended whole is treated as something akin to the individual mind. It is in this form that in the social sciences an illegitimate use of anthropomorphic concepts has had as harmful an effect as the use of such concepts in the natural sciences. The remarkable thing here is, again, that it should so frequently be the empiricism of the positivists, the archenemies of any anthropomorphic concepts even where they are in place, which leads them to postulate such metaphysical entities and to treat humanity, as for instance Comte does, as one 'social being', a kind of super-person. But as there is no other possibility than either to compose the whole from the individual minds or to postulate a super-mind in the image of the individual mind, and as positivists reject the first of these alternatives, they are necessarily driven to the second. We have here the root of that curious alliance between nineteenth-century positivism and Hegelianism which will occupy us in a later study.[8]

The collectivist approach to social phenomena has not often been so emphatically proclaimed as when the founder of sociology, Auguste Comte, asserted with respect to them that, as in biology, "the whole of the object is here certainly much better known and more immediately accessible"[9] than the constituent parts. This view has exercised a lasting influence on that scientistic study of society which he attempted to create. Yet the particular similarity between the objects of biology and those of sociology, which fitted so well in Comte's hierarchy of the sciences, does not in fact exist. In biology we do indeed first recognise as things of one kind natural units, stable combinations of sense properties, of which we find many instances which we spontaneously recognise as alike. We can, therefore, begin by asking why these definite sets of attributes regularly occur together. But where we have to deal with social wholes or structures it is not the observation of the regular coexistence of certain physical facts which teaches us that they belong together or form a whole. We do not first observe that the parts always occur together and afterward ask

[7] On this whole problem, see Morris Ginsberg, *The Psychology of Society* (London: Methuen and Co., Ltd., 1921), chapter 4. What is said in the text does not, of course, preclude the possibility that our study of the way in which individual minds interact may reveal to us a structure which operates in some respects similarly to the individual mind. And it may be that the term 'collective mind' will prove the best term available to describe such structure—though it is most unlikely that the advantages of the use of this term will ever outweigh its disadvantages. But even if this were the case, the employment of this term should not mislead us into thinking that it describes any observable object that can be directly studied.

[8] [See chapter 17 below.—Ed.]

[9] Auguste Comte, *Cours de philosophie positive*, 4th ed. (Paris: J.-B. Baillière, 1877), vol. 4, p. 258.

what holds them together; but it is only because we know the ties that hold them together that we can select a few elements from the immensely complicated world around us as parts of a connected whole.

We shall presently see that Comte and many others regard social phenomena as given wholes in yet another, different, sense, contending that concrete social phenomena can be understood *only* by considering the totality of everything that can be found within certain spatio-temporal boundaries, and that any attempt to select parts or aspects as systematically connected is bound to fail. In this form the argument amounts to a denial of the possibility of a theory of social phenomena as developed, for example, by economics, and leads directly to what has been misnamed the 'historical method' with which, indeed, methodological collectivism is closely connected. We shall have to discuss this view below under the heading of 'historicism'.

The endeavour to grasp social phenomena as wholes finds its most characteristic expression in the desire to gain a distant and comprehensive view in the hope that thus regularities will reveal themselves which remain obscure at closer range. Whether it is the conception of an observer from a distant planet, which has always been a favourite with positivists from Condorcet to Mach,[10] or whether it is the survey of long stretches of time through which it is hoped that constant configurations or regularities will reveal themselves, it is always the same endeavour to get away from our inside knowledge of human affairs and to gain a view of the kind which, it is supposed, would be commanded by somebody who was not himself a man but stood to men in the same relation as that in which we stand to the external world.

This distant and comprehensive view of human events at which the scientistic approach aims is now often described as the 'macroscopic view'. It would probably be better called the 'telescopic view' (meaning simply the distant view—unless it be the view through the inverted telescope) since its aim is deliberately to ignore what we can see only from the inside. In the 'macrocosm' which this approach attempts to see, and in the 'macrodynamic' theo-

---

[10] Cf. Ernst Mach, *Erkenntnis und Irrtum*, 3rd ed. (Leipzig: J. A. Barth, 1917), p. 28, where, however, he points out correctly, "Könnten wir die Menschen aus größerer Entfernung, aus der Vogelperspektiv, vom Monde aus beobachten, so würden die feineren Einzelheiten mit den von individuellen Erlebnissen herrührenden Einflüssen für uns verschwinden, und wir würden nichts wahrnehmen, als Menschen, die mit großer Regelmäßigkeit wachsen, sich nähren, sich fortpflanzen". [This may be translated as follows: "If it were possible to observe human beings from a great distance, with a bird's eye view, or from the moon, then all the particularities that result from the influence of individual experiences would vanish, and we would only perceive human beings that mature, nourish themselves, and propagate with great regularity". Both Henri, Comte de Saint-Simon, and Auguste Comte viewed the French Enlightenment philosopher, mathematician, *encyclopédiste*, and reformer Jean-Antoine-Nicolas de Caritat, Marquis de Condorcet (1743–94) as an important precursor. For a more detailed discussion by Hayek of the rôle played by Condorcet in the development of scientism, see chapter 11.—Ed.]

ries which it endeavours to produce, the elements would not be individual human beings but collectives, constant configurations which, it is presumed, could be defined and described in strictly objective terms.

In most instances this belief that the total view will enable us to distinguish wholes by objective criteria, however, proves to be just an illusion. This becomes evident as soon as we seriously try to imagine of what the macrocosm would consist if we were really to dispense with our knowledge of what things *mean* to the acting men, and if we merely observed the actions of men as we observe an ant heap or a beehive. In the picture such a study could produce there could not appear such things as means or tools, commodities or money, crimes or punishments, or words or sentences; it could contain only physical objects defined either in terms of the sense attributes they present to the observer or even in purely relational terms. And since the human behaviour towards the physical objects would show practically no regularities discernible to such an observer, since men would in a great many instances not appear to react alike to things which would to the observer seem to be the same, nor differently to what appeared to him to be different, he could not hope to achieve an explanation of their actions unless he had first succeeded in reconstructing in full detail the way in which men's senses and men's minds pictured the external world to them. The famous observer from Mars, in other words, before he could understand even as much of human affairs as the ordinary man does, would have to reconstruct from our behaviour those immediate data of our mind which to us form the starting point of any interpretation of human action.

If we are not more aware of the difficulties which would be encountered by an observer not possessed of a human mind, this is so because we never seriously imagine the possibility that any being with which we are familiar might command sense perceptions or knowledge denied to us. Rightly or wrongly we tend to assume that the other minds which we encounter can differ from ours only by being inferior, so that everything which they perceive or know can also be perceived or be known to us. The only way in which we can form an approximate idea of what our position would be if we had to deal with an organism as complicated as ours but organised on a different principle, so that we should not be able to reproduce its working on the analogy of our own mind, is to conceive that we had to study the behaviour of people with a knowledge vastly superior to our own. If, for example, we had developed our modern scientific technique while still confined to a part of our planet, and then had made contact with other parts inhabited by a race which had advanced knowledge much further, we clearly could not hope to understand many of their actions by merely observing what they did and without directly learning from them their knowledge. It would not be from observing them in action that we should acquire their knowledge, but it would be through being taught their knowledge that we should learn to understand their actions.

There is yet another argument which we must briefly consider which supports the tendency to look at social phenomena 'from the outside', and which is easily confused with the methodological collectivism of which we have spoken though it is really distinct from it. Are not social phenomena, it may be asked, from their definition mass phenomena, and is it not obvious, therefore, that we can hope to discover regularities in them only if we investigate them by the method developed for the study of mass phenomena, that is, statistics? Now this is certainly true of the study of certain phenomena, such as those which form the object of vital statistics and which, as has been mentioned before, are sometimes also described as social phenomena, although they are essentially distinct from those with which we are here concerned.

Nothing is more instructive than to compare the nature of these statistical wholes, to which the same word *collective* is sometimes also applied, with that of the wholes or collectives with which we have to deal in the theoretical social sciences. The statistical study is concerned with the attributes of individuals, though not with attributes of particular individuals, but with attributes of which we know only that they are possessed by a certain quantitatively determined proportion of all the individuals in our 'collective' or 'population'. In order that any collection of individuals should form a true statistical collective it is even necessary that the attributes of the individuals whose frequency distribution we study should not be systematically connected or, at least, that in our selection of the individuals which form the 'collective' we are not guided by any knowledge of such a connection. The collectives of statistics, on which we study the regularities produced by the 'law of large numbers', are thus emphatically not wholes in the sense in which we describe social structures as wholes. This is best seen from the fact that the properties of the collectives which statistics studies must remain unaffected if from the total of elements we select at random a certain part. Far from dealing with structures of relationships, statistics deliberately and systematically disregard the relationships between the individual elements. It is, to repeat, concerned with the properties of the *elements* of the collective, though not with the properties of particular elements, but with the frequency with which elements with certain properties occur among the total. And, what is more, it assumes that these properties are *not* systematically connected with the different ways in which the elements are related to each other.

The consequence of this is that in the statistical study of social phenomena the structures with which the theoretical social sciences are concerned actually disappear. Statistics may supply us with very interesting and important information about what is the raw material from which we have to reproduce these structures, but it can tell us nothing about these structures themselves. In some fields this is immediately obvious as soon as it is stated. That the statistics of words can tell us nothing about the structure of a language will hardly be denied. But although the contrary is sometimes suggested, the same holds no less true of other systematically connected wholes such as, for example, the price system. No statistical information about the elements can explain to us the properties of the connected wholes. Statistics could produce knowledge of the properties of the wholes only if they informed us about statistical collectives the elements of which were wholes, that is, if we had statistical information about the properties of many languages, many price systems, etc. But, quite apart from the practical limitations imposed on us by the limited number of instances which are known to us, there is an even more serious obstacle to the statistical study of these wholes: the fact, which we have already discussed, that these wholes and their properties are not given to our observation but can only be formed or composed by us from their parts.

What we have said applies, however, by no means to all that goes by the name of statistics in the social sciences. Much that is thus described is not statistics in the strict modern sense of the term; it does not deal with mass phenomena at all, but is called statistics only in the older, wider sense of the word in which it is used for any descriptive information about the state or society. Though the term will today be used only where the descriptive data are of a quantitative nature, this should not lead us to confuse it with the science of statistics in the narrower sense. Most of the economic statistics which we ordinarily meet, such as trade statistics, figures about price changes, and most 'time series', or statistics of the 'national income', are not data to which the technique appropriate to the investigation of mass phenomena can be applied. They are just 'measurements' and frequently measurements of the type already discussed at the end of chapter 5 above. If they refer to significant phenomena they may be very interesting as information about the conditions existing at a particular moment. But unlike statistics proper, which may indeed help us to discover important regularities in the social world (though regularities of an entirely different order from those with which the theoretical sciences of society deal), there is no reason to expect that these measurements will ever reveal anything to us which is of significance beyond the particular place and time at which they have been made. That they cannot produce generalisations does, of course, not mean that they may not be useful, even very useful; they will often provide us with the data to which our theoretical generalisations must be applied to be of any practical use. They are an instance of the historical information about a particular situation the significance of which we must further consider in the next chapters.

SEVEN

THE HISTORICISM OF THE SCIENTISTIC APPROACH

To see the 'historicism'[1] to which we must now turn described as a product of the scientistic approach may cause surprise since it is usually represented as the opposite of the treatment of social phenomena on the model of the natural sciences. But the view for which this term is properly used (and which must not be confused with the true method of historical study) proves on closer consideration to be a result of the same prejudices as the other typical scientistic misconceptions of social phenomena. If the suggestion that historicism is a form rather than the opposite of scientism has still somewhat the appearance of a paradox, this is so because the term is used in two different, and in some respects opposite, and yet frequently confused senses: for the older view which justly contrasted the specific task of the historian with that of the scientist and which denied the possibility of a theoretical science of history, and for the later view which, on the contrary, affirms that history is the only road which can lead to a theoretical science of social phenomena. However great is the contrast between these two views sometimes called 'historicism', if we take them in their extreme forms, they have yet enough in common to have made possible a gradual and almost unperceived transition from the historical method of the historian to the scientistic historicism which attempts to make history a 'science' and the only science of social phenomena.

The older historical school, whose growth has recently been so well described by the German historian Meinecke, though under the misleading name of *Historismus*,[2] arose mainly in opposition to certain generalising and 'prag-

---

[1] [In the original essay in *Economica*, Hayek used the term 'historism' instead of 'historicism' throughout this section. Between then and 1952, Karl Popper published in *Economica* his essay, "The Poverty of Historicism", and Hayek subsequently adopted his friend's terminology. As is evident in the next note, Hayek used the term 'historicism' exclusively to refer to the 'scientistic' method advocated by younger historical school economists, and not to the methods propounded by the older historical school economists.

This may have been the source for some problems with the original translation into German of the essay, one that was published in 1959 and done by Hayek's second wife, who used the original 'historism' rather than 'historicism'.—Ed.]

[2] Friedrich Meinecke, *Die Entstehung des Historismus* (Munich: R. Oldenbourg, 1936). The term 'historicism', applied to the older historical school discussed by Meinecke, is inappropriate and

matic' tendencies of some, particularly French, eighteenth-century views.[3] Its emphasis was on the singular or unique (*individuell*) character of all historical phenomena which could be understood only genetically as the joint result of many forces working through long stretches of time. Its strong opposition to the 'pragmatic' interpretation, which regards social institutions as the product of conscious design, implies in fact the use of a 'compositive' theory which explains how such institutions can arise as the unintended result of the separate actions of many individuals. It is significant that among the fathers of this view Edmund Burke is one of the most important and Adam Smith occupies an honourable place.

Yet, although this historical method implies theory, that is, an understanding of the principles of structural coherence of the social wholes, the historians who employed it not only did not systematically develop such theories and were hardly aware that they used them; but their just dislike of any generalisation about historical developments also tended to give their teaching an anti-theoretical bias which, although originally aimed only against the wrong kind

---

misleading since it was introduced by Carl Menger (see Menger, *Untersuchungen über die Methode der Socialwissenschaften*, pp. 216–20—with reference to Gervinus and Roscher—and *Die Irrthümer des Historismus*) to describe the distinguishing features of the younger historical school in economics represented by Schmoller and his associates. Nothing else shows more clearly the difference between this younger historical school and the earlier movement from which it inherited the name than that it was Schmoller who accused Menger of being an adherent of the 'Burke-Savigny school' and not the other way around (cf. Schmoller, "Zur Methodologie der Staats- und Sozialwissenschaften", p. 250). [Hayek here criticises the German intellectual and political historian Friedrich Meinecke (1862–1954) for lumping together members of the older German historical school, which included such figures as Wilhelm Roscher (1817–94), Bruno Hildebrand (1812–78), and Karl Knies (1821–98), with members of the younger school like Gustav Schmoller, against whom Menger fought the *Methodenstreit*, or battle over methods. Friedrich Karl von Savigny (1779–1861) was a leader of the German historical school of law, which was contemporaneous with the older historical school of economics and whose doctrines were presumably compatible with it. That Schmoller would associate his rival Menger with Savigny makes clear the doctrinal distance between the older and younger historical schools. Savigny's legal theories bear some resemblance to Hayek's: for example, Savigny compared the evolution of law to that of language and customs and cautioned against arbitrarily changing law by legislation. For more on the various historical schools and the *Methodenstreit* see Caldwell, *Hayek's Challenge*, chapters 2–4.—Ed.]

[3] [Historicism was in part a reaction against the generalising views of the Enlightenment. Among the ideas opposed were that there exists a discoverable natural order in society comparable to that which exists in the natural world, that knowledge of the natural order could allow humans to restructure a society along more reasonable lines, that human nature was everywhere the same, and that all this meant that a universally applicable science of the social was possible. Especially to the German mind, Enlightenment thought was associated with France—the Scottish enlightenment philosopher Adam Smith was, for example, at first considered by German scholars simply to be a Scottish physiocrat. For more on this, see Caldwell, *Hayek's Challenge*, chapter 2, and citations therein.—Ed.]

of theory, yet created the impression that the main difference between the methods appropriate to the study of natural and to that of social phenomena was the same as that between theory and history. This opposition to theory of the largest body of students of social phenomena made it appear as if the difference between the theoretical and the historical treatment was a necessary consequence of the differences between the objects of the natural and social sciences; and the belief that the search for general rules must be confined to the study of natural phenomena, while in the study of the social world the historical method must rule, became the foundation on which later historicism grew up. But while historicism retained the claim for the pre-eminence of historical research in this field, it almost reversed the attitude to history of the older historical school, and under the influence of the scientistic currents of the age came to represent history as the empirical study of society from which ultimately generalisation would emerge. History was to be the source from which a new science of society would spring, a science which should at the same time be historical and yet produce what theoretical knowledge we could hope to gain about society.

We are here not concerned with the actual steps in that process of transition from the older historical school to the historicism of the younger. It may just be noticed that historicism in the sense in which the term is used here, was created not by historians but by students of the specialised social sciences, particularly economists, who hoped thereby to gain an empirical road to the theory of their subject. But to trace this development in detail and to show how the men responsible for it were actually guided by the scientistic views of their generation must be left to the later historical account.[4]

The first point we must briefly consider is the nature of the distinction between the historical and the theoretical treatment of any subject which in fact makes it a contradiction in terms to demand that history should become a theoretical science or that theory should ever be 'historical'. If we understand that distinction, it will become clear that it has no necessary connec-

---

[4] Although in its German origins the connection of historicism with positivism is perhaps less conspicuous than is the case with its English followers such as Ingram or Ashley, it was no less present and is overlooked only because historicism is erroneously connected with the historical method of the older historians, instead of with the views of Roscher, Hildebrand, and particularly Schmoller and his circle. [Irish economist John Kells Ingram (1823–1907) was a fervent admirer of Auguste Comte and favoured replacing the deductive method of classical political economy with empirical generalisations drawn from history. A fierce critic of Ricardian economics, the English economic historian Sir William J. Ashley (1860–1927) held that the truth of economic theories was relative to time and place. Ashley was a major figure in the establishment of economic history in Britain, an opponent of free trade and an advocate of social legislation. For more on the English historical school, see Gerard Koot, *English Historical Economics 1870–1926: The Rise of Economic History and Neomercantilism* (Cambridge: Cambridge University Press, 1987).—Ed.]

tion with the difference of the concrete objects with which the two methods of approach deal, and that for the understanding of any concrete phenomenon, be it in nature or in society, both kinds of knowledge are equally required.

That human history deals with events or situations which are unique or singular when we consider all aspects which are relevant for the answer of a particular question which we may ask about them, is, of course, not peculiar to human history. It is equally true of any attempt to explain a concrete phenomenon if we only take into account a sufficient number of aspects—or, to put it differently, so long as we do not deliberately select only such aspects of reality as fall within the sphere of any one of the systems of connected propositions which we regard as distinct theoretical sciences. If I watch and record the process by which a plot in my garden that I leave untouched for months is gradually covered with weeds, I am describing a process which in all its details is no less unique than any event in human history. If I want to explain any particular configuration of different plants which may appear at any stage of that process, I can do so only by giving an account of all the relevant influences which have affected different parts of my plot at different times. I shall have to consider what I can find out about the differences of the soil in different parts of the plot, about differences in the radiation of the sun, of moisture, of the air currents, etc., etc.; and in order to explain the effects of all these factors I shall have to use, apart from the knowledge of all these particular facts, various parts of the theory of physics, of chemistry, biology, meteorology, and so on. The result of all this will be the explanation of a particular phenomenon, but not a theoretical science of how garden plots are covered with weeds.

In an instance like this the particular sequence of events, their causes and consequences, will probably not be of sufficient general interest to make it worth while to produce a written account of them or to develop their study into a distinct discipline. But there are large fields of natural knowledge, represented by recognised disciplines, which in their methodological character are no different from this. In geography, for example, and at least in a large part of geology and astronomy, we are mainly concerned with particular situations, either of the earth or of the universe; we aim at explaining a unique situation by showing how it has been produced by the operation of many forces subject to the general laws studied by the theoretical sciences. In the specific sense of a body of general rules in which the term *science* is often used,[5] these disciplines are not sciences, that is, they are not theoretical sciences but endeavours to apply the laws found by the theoretical sciences to the explanation of particular 'historical' situations.

---

[5] It will be noted that this, still restricted, use of the term 'science' (in the sense in which the Germans speak of *Gesetzeswissenschaft*) is wider than the even narrower sense in which its meaning is confined to the theoretical sciences of nature.

The distinction between the search for generic principles and the explanation of concrete phenomena has thus no necessary connection with the distinction between the study of nature and the study of society. In both fields we need generalisations in order to explain concrete and unique events. Whenever we attempt to explain or understand a particular phenomenon we can do so only by recognising it or its parts as members of certain classes of phenomena, and the explanation of the particular phenomenon pre-supposes the existence of general rules.

There are very good reasons, however, for a marked difference in emphasis, reasons why, generally speaking, in the natural sciences the search for general laws has the pride of place, with their application to particular events usually little discussed and of small general interest, while with social phenomena the explanation of the particular and unique situation is as important as, and often of much greater interest than, any generalisation. In most natural sciences the particular situation or event is generally one of a very large number of similar events, which as particular events are only of local and temporary interest and scarcely worth public discussion (except as evidence of the truth of the general rule). The important thing for them is the general law applicable to all the recurrent events of a particular kind. In the social field, on the other hand, a particular or unique event is often of such general interest and at the same time so complex and so difficult to see in all its important aspects, that its explanation and discussion constitute a major task requiring the whole energy of a specialist. We study here particular events because they have contributed to create the particular environment in which we live or because they are part of that environment. The creation and dissolution of the Roman Empire or the Crusades, the French Revolution or the growth of modern industry—these are unique complexes of events which have helped to produce the particular circumstances in which we live and whose explanation is therefore of great interest.

It is necessary, however, to consider briefly the logical nature of these singular or unique objects of study. Probably the majority of the numerous disputes and confusions which have arisen in this connection are due to the vagueness of the common notion of what can constitute *one* object of thought—and particularly to the misconception that the totality (that is, all possible aspects) of a particular situation can ever constitute one single object of thought. We can touch here only on a very few of the logical problems which this belief raises.

The first point which we must remember is that, strictly speaking, *all* thought must be to some degree abstract. We have seen before that all perception of reality, including the simplest sensations, involves a classification of the object according to some property or properties. The same complex of phenomena which we may be able to discover within given temporal and spatial limits may in this sense be considered under many different aspects; and the principles according to which we classify or group the events may differ from each other not merely in one but in several different ways. The various theoretical sciences deal only with those aspects of the phenomena which can be fitted into a single body of connected propositions. It is necessary to emphasise that this is no less true of the theoretical sciences of nature than of the theoretical sciences of society, since an alleged tendency of the natural sciences to deal with the 'whole' or the totality of the real things is often quoted by writers inclined to historicism as a justification for doing the same in the social field.[6] Any discipline of knowledge, whether theoretical or historical, however, can deal only with certain selected aspects of the real world; and in the theoretical sciences the principle of selection is the possibility of subsuming these aspects under a logically connected body of rules. The same thing may be for one science a pendulum, for another a lump of brass, and for a third a convex mirror. We have already seen that the fact that a pendulum possesses chemical and optical properties does not mean that in studying laws of pendulums we must study them by the methods of chemistry and optics—though when we apply these laws to a particular pendulum we may well have to take into account certain laws of chemistry or optics. Similarly, as has been pointed out, the fact that all social phenomena have physical properties does not mean that we must study them by the methods of the physical sciences.[7]

The selection of the aspects of a complex of phenomena which can be

[6] Cf., e.g., E. F. M. Durbin, "Methods of Research—A Plea for Co-operation in the Social Sciences", *Economic Journal*, vol. 48, June 1938, p. 191, in which the writer argues that in the social sciences, "unlike the natural sciences, our subdivisions are largely (though not entirely) *abstractions from* reality rather than *sections* of reality", and asserts of the natural sciences that "in all these cases the objects of study are real and independent objects and groups. They are not aspects of something complex. They are real things". How this can be really asserted, for example, of crystallography (one of Durbin's examples), is difficult to comprehend. This argument has been extremely popular with the members of the German historical school in economics, though, it should be added, Durbin is probably entirely unaware how closely his whole attitude resembles that of the *Kathedersozialisten* of that school. [British economist and Labour politician Evan Durbin (1906–48) taught a course on democratic socialist planning at the LSE in the 1930s that competed with Hayek's course criticising collectivist economic planning. Unlike Durbin, the younger German historical school economists were conservative imperialists, but their program included many social reforms—better to strengthen the Empire—and because they had the ear of Chancellor Bismarck, they were successful in implementing them. *Kathedersozialisten*, or 'socialists of the chair', was a term of derision coined by the liberal journalist Heinrich Oppenheim that alluded to the reformist proclivities of the German historical school economists. In his inaugural lecture at the LSE, "The Trend of Economic Thinking" [1933], reprinted in *The Trend of Economic Thinking*, Hayek noted the similarities between the views of the German historical school economists and British socialists of the 1930s.—Ed.]

[7] [In the original article in *Economica*, Hayek placed a note here that read, "It is significant that all of H. Rickert's well-known work on the differences between the *Naturwissenschaften* and *Kulturwissenschaften* is based on the assertion that since all phenomena which we can observe are

explained by means of a connected body of rules is, however, not the only method of selection or abstraction which the scientist will have to use. Where investigation is directed, not at establishing rules of general applicability, but at answering a particular question raised by the events in the world about him, he will have to select those features that are relevant to the particular question. The important point, however, is that he still must select a limited number from the infinite variety of phenomena which he can find at the given time and place. We may, in such cases, sometimes speak as if he considered the 'whole' situation as he found it. But what we mean is not the inexhaustible totality of everything that can be observed within certain spatio-temporal limits, but certain features thought to be relevant to the question asked. If I ask why the weeds in my garden have grown in this particular pattern, no single theoretical science will provide the answer. This, however, does not mean that to answer it we must know everything that can be known about the space-time interval in which the phenomenon occurred. While the question we ask designates the phenomena to be explained, it is only by means of the laws of the theoretical sciences that we are able to select the other phenomena which are relevant for its explanation. The object of scientific study is never the totality of all the phenomena observable at a given time and place, but always only certain selected aspects: and according to the question we ask the same spatio-temporal situation may contain any number of different objects of study. The human mind indeed can never grasp a 'whole' in the sense of all the different aspects of a real situation.

The application of these considerations to the phenomena of human history leads to very important consequences. It means nothing less than that a historical process or period is never a single definite object of thought but becomes such only by the question we ask about it; and that, according to the question we ask, what we are accustomed to regard as a single historical event can become any number of different objects of thought.

It is confusion on this point which is mainly responsible for the doctrine now so much in vogue that all historical knowledge is necessarily relative, determined by our 'standpoint' and bound to change with the lapse of time.[8] This view is a natural consequence of the belief that the commonly used names for historical periods or complexes of events, such as 'the Napoleonic Wars', or 'France during the Revolution', or 'the Commonwealth period', stand for definitely given objects, unique individuals[9] which are given to us in

---

physical phenomena, all generalising (theoretical) science must be physical science". Rickert is mentioned again in note 10 of this chapter.—Ed.]

[8] For a good survey of the modern theories of historical relativism, see Maurice Mandelbaum, *The Problem of Historical Knowledge: An Answer to Relativism* (New York: Liveright Publishing Corp., 1938).

[9] See note 12 in this chapter.

the same manner as the natural units in which biological specimens or planets present themselves. Those names of historical phenomena define in fact little more than a period and a place and there is scarcely a limit to the number of different questions which we can ask about events which occurred during the period and within the region to which they refer. It is only the question that we ask, however, which will define our object; and there are, of course, many reasons why at different times people will ask different questions about the same period.[10] But this does not mean that history will at different times and on the basis of the same information give different answers to the same question. Only this, however, would entitle us to assert that historical knowledge is relative. The kernel of truth in the assertion about the relativity of historical knowledge is that historians will at different times be interested in different objects, but not that they will necessarily hold different views about the same object.

We must dwell a little longer on the nature of the wholes which the historian studies, though much of what we have to say is merely an application of what has been said before about the wholes which some authors regard as objects of theoretical generalisations. What we said then is just as true of the wholes which the historian studies. They are never given to him as wholes, but always reconstructed by him from their elements which alone can be directly perceived. Whether he speaks about the government that existed or the trade that was carried on, the army that moved, or the knowledge that was preserved or disseminated, he is never referring to a constant collection of physical attributes that can be directly observed, but always to a system of relationships between some of the observed elements which can be merely inferred. Words like *government, trade, army*, and *knowledge* stand not for single observable things but for structures of relationships which can be described only by a schematic representation or 'theory' of the persistent system of relationships between

[10] It is not possible here to pursue further the interesting question of the reasons which make the historian ask particular questions and which make him ask at different times different questions about the same period. We ought, however, perhaps briefly to refer to one view which has exercised wide influence, since it claims application not only to history but to all *Kulturwissenschaften*. It is Rickert's contention that the social sciences, to which, according to him, the historical method is alone appropriate, select their object exclusively with reference to certain values with respect to which they are important. Unless by 'value consideration' (*Wertbezogenheit*) any kind of practical interest in a problem is meant so that this concept would include the reasons which make us, say, study the geology of Cumberland, this is certainly not necessarily the case. If, merely to indulge my taste in detective work, I try to find out why in the year x Mr. N was elected mayor of Cambridge, this is no less historical work though no known value may have been affected by the fact that Mr. N rather than somebody else was elected. It is not the reason why we are interested in a problem, but the character of the problem that makes it a historical problem. [Hayek refers to the German philosopher Heinrich Rickert (1863–1936), a founder of the Baden School of neo-Kantianism, who wrote about the appropriate methodology for an objective science of culture.—Ed.]

the ever-changing elements.[11] These 'wholes', in other words, do not exist for us apart from the theory by which we constitute them, apart from the mental technique by which we can reconstruct the connections between the observed elements and follow up the implications of this particular combination.

The place of theory in historical knowledge is thus in forming or constituting the wholes to which history refers; it is prior to these wholes which do not become visible except by following up the system of relations which connects the parts. The generalisations of theory, however, do not refer, and cannot refer, as has been mistakenly believed by the older historians (who for that reason opposed theory), to the concrete wholes, the particular constellations of the elements, with which history is concerned. The models of wholes, of structural connections, which theory provides ready-made for the historian to use (though even these are not the given elements about which theory generalises but the results of theoretical activity), are not identical with the wholes which the historian considers. The models provided by any one theoretical science of society consist necessarily of elements of one kind, elements which are selected because their connection can be explained by a coherent body of principles and not because they help to answer a particular question about concrete phenomena. For the latter purpose the historian will regularly have to use generalisations belonging to different theoretical spheres. His work, thus, as is true of all attempts to explain particular phenomena, pre-supposes theory; it is, as is all thinking about concrete phenomena, an application of generic concepts to the explanation of particular phenomena.

If the dependence of the historical study of social phenomena on theory is not always recognised, this is mainly due to the very simple nature of the majority of theoretical schemes which the historian will employ and which brings it about that there will be no dispute about the conclusions reached by their help, and little awareness that he has used theoretical reasoning at all. But this does not alter the fact that in their methodological character and validity the concepts of social phenomena which the historian has to employ are essentially of the same kind as the more elaborate models produced by the systematic social sciences. All the unique objects of history which he studies are in fact either constant patterns of relations, or repeatable processes in which the elements are of a generic character. When the historian speaks of a state or a battle, a town or a market, these words cover coherent structures of individual phenomena which we can comprehend only by understanding the intentions of the acting individuals. If the historian speaks of a certain system, say the feudal system, persisting over a period of time, he means that a

---

[11] It does not alter the essential fact that the theorising will usually already have been done for the historian by his source, who in reporting the 'facts' will use such terms as *state* and *town*, which cannot be defined by physical characteristics but which refer to a complex of relationships which, made explicit, is a 'theory' of the subject.

certain pattern of relationships continued, a certain type of actions was regularly repeated, structures whose connection he can understand only by mental reproduction of the individual attitudes of which they were made up. The unique wholes which the historian studies, in short, are not given to him as individuals,[12] as natural units of which he can find out by observation what features belong to them, but constructions made by the kind of technique that is systematically developed by the theoretical sciences of society. Whether he endeavours to give a genetic account of how a particular institution arose, or a descriptive account of how it functioned, he cannot do so except by a combination of generic considerations applying to the elements from which the unique situation is composed. Though in this work of reconstruction he cannot use any elements except those he empirically finds, not observation but only the 'theoretical' work of reconstruction can tell him which among those that he can find are part of a connected whole.

Theoretical and historical labours are thus logically distinct but complementary activities. If their task is rightly understood, there can be no conflict between them. And though they have distinct tasks, neither is of much use without the other. But this does not alter the fact that neither can theory be historical nor history theoretical. Though the general is of interest only because it explains the particular, and though the particular can be explained only in generic terms, the particular can never be the general and the general never the particular. The unfortunate misunderstandings that have arisen between historians and theorists largely trace to the name 'historical school', which has been usurped by the mongrel view better described as historicism and which is indeed neither history nor theory.

The naïve view which regards the complexes which history studies as given wholes naturally leads to the belief that their observation can reveal 'laws' of the development of these wholes. This belief is one of the most characteristic features of that scientistic history which under the name of historicism was trying to find an empirical basis for a theory of history or (using

---

[12] The confusion that reigns in this field has evidently been assisted by a purely verbal confusion apt to arise in German, in which most of the discussions of this problem have been conducted. In German the singular or unique is called the *Individuelle*, which almost inevitably calls forth a misleading association with the term for the individual (*Individuum*). Now, *individual* is the term which we employ to describe those natural units which in the physical world our senses enable us to single out from the environment as connected wholes. Individuals in this sense, whether human individuals or animals or plants, or stones, mountains, or stars, are constant collections of sense attributes which, either because the whole complex can move together in space relatively to its environment, or for cognate reasons, our senses spontaneously single out as connected wholes. But this is precisely what the objects of history are *not*. Though singular (*individuelle*), as the individual is, they are not definite individuals in the sense in which this term is applied to natural objects. They are not given to us as wholes but only found to be wholes.

the term *philosophy* in its old sense of 'theory') a 'philosophy of history', and to establish necessary successions of definite 'stages' or 'phases', 'systems' or 'styles', following each other in historical development. This view on the one hand endeavours to find laws where in the nature of the case they cannot be found, in the succession of the unique and singular historical phenomena, and on the other hand denies the possibility of the kind of theory which alone can help us to understand unique wholes, the theory which shows the different ways in which the familiar elements can be combined to produce the unique combinations we find in the real world. The empiricist prejudice thus led to an inversion of the only procedure by which we can comprehend historical wholes, their reconstruction from the parts; it induced scholars to treat as if they were objective facts vague conceptions of wholes which were merely intuitively comprehended; and it finally produced the view that the elements, which are the only things that we can directly comprehend and from which we must reconstruct the wholes, on the contrary, could be understood only from the whole, which had to be known before we could understand the elements.

The belief that human history, which is the result of the interaction of innumerable human minds, must yet be subject to simple laws accessible to human minds is now so widely held that few people are at all aware what an astonishing claim it really implies. Instead of working patiently at the humble task of rebuilding from the directly known elements the complex and unique structures which we find in the world, and of tracing from the changes in the relations between the elements the changes in the wholes, the authors of these pseudo-theories of history pretend to be able to arrive by a kind of mental shortcut at a direct insight into the laws of succession of the immediately apprehended wholes. However doubtful their status, these theories of development have achieved a hold on public imagination much greater than any of the results of genuine systematic study. 'Philosophies' or 'theories'[13] of history (or 'historical theories') have indeed become the characteristic feature, the 'darling vice'[14] of the nineteenth century. From Hegel and Comte, and particularly Marx, down to Sombart and Spengler, these spurious theories came to be regarded as representative results of social science; and through the belief that one kind of 'system' must as a matter of historical necessity be superseded by a new and different system, they have even exercised a pro-

---

[13] There is, of course, also a legitimate sense in which we may speak of historical theories, where 'theory' is used as a synonym for 'factual hypothesis'. In this sense the unconfirmed explanation of a particular event is often called a historical theory, but such a theory is of course something altogether different from the theories which pretend to state laws which historical developments obey.

[14] Léon Brunschvicg, in *Philosophy and History, Essays Presented to E. Cassirer*, Raymond Klibansky and H. J. Paton, eds (Oxford: Clarendon Press, 1936), p. 30.

found influence on social evolution.[15] This they achieved mainly because they looked like the kind of laws which the natural sciences produced; and in an age when these sciences set the standard by which all intellectual effort was measured, the claim of these theories of history to be able to predict future developments was regarded as evidence of their pre-eminently scientific character. Though merely one among many characteristic nineteenth-century products of this kind, Marxism more than any of the others has become the vehicle through which this result of scientism has gained so wide an influence that many of the opponents of Marxism equally with its adherents are thinking in its terms.

Apart from setting up a new ideal this development had, however, also the negative effect of discrediting the existing theory on which past understanding of social phenomena had been based. Since it was supposed that we could directly observe the changes in the whole of society or of any particular changed social phenomenon, and that everything within the whole must necessarily change with it, it was concluded that there could be no timeless generalisations about the elements from which these wholes were built up, no universal theories about the ways in which they might be combined into wholes. All social theory, it was said, was necessarily historical, *zeitgebunden*, true only of particular historical phases or systems.

All concepts of individual phenomena, according to this strict historicism, are to be regarded as merely historical categories, valid only in a particular historical context. A price in the twelfth century or a monopoly in the Egypt of 400 BC, it is argued, is not the same 'thing' as a price or a monopoly today, and any attempt to explain that price or the policy of that monopolist by the same theory which we would use to explain a price or a monopoly of today is therefore vain and bound to fail. This argument is based on a complete misapprehension of the function of theory. Of course, if we ask why a particular price was charged at a particular date, or why a monopolist then acted in a particular manner, this is a historical question which cannot be fully answered by any one theoretical discipline; to answer it we must take into account the particular circumstances of time and place. But this does not mean that we must not, in selecting the factors relevant to the explanation of the particular

---

[15] [Historian of the development of capitalism Werner Sombart (1863–1941) was perhaps the last of the historical school economists. In *The Road to Serfdom*, in a chapter titled "The Socialist Roots of Naziism", Hayek argued that Sombart's movement from left-wing socialism towards anti-capitalism of the fascist variety exemplified a natural tendency. See Hayek, *The Road to Serfdom: Text and Documents*, chapter 12, pp. 183–84. German philosopher of history Oswald Spengler (1880–1936), another critic of liberal parliamentary democracy, foretold the inevitable decay of European culture, which would be replaced by a new age of Caesarism (analogous to the replacement of Greek culture by Roman) in his book *The Decline of the West*, translated by Charles Francis Atkinson, 2 vols. (New York: A. A. Knopf, 1926–28).—Ed.]

price, etc., use precisely the same theoretical reasoning as we would with regard to a price of today.

What this contention overlooks is that price and monopoly are not names for definite 'things', fixed collections of physical attributes which we recognise by some of these attributes as members of the same class and whose further attributes we ascertain by observation; rather, they are objects which can be defined only in terms of certain relations between human beings and which cannot possess any attributes except those which follow from the relations by which they are defined. They can be recognised by us as prices or monopolies only because, and insofar as, we can recognise these individual attitudes, and from these as elements compose the structural pattern which we call a price or monopoly. Of course, the 'whole' situation, or even the 'whole' of the men who act, will greatly differ from place to place and from time to time. But it is solely our capacity to recognise the familiar elements from which the unique situation is made up which enables us to attach any meaning to the phenomena. Either we cannot thus recognise the meaning of the individual actions—they are nothing but physical facts to us, the handing over of certain material things, etc.—or we must place them in the mental categories familiar to us but not definable in physical terms. If the first contention were true this would mean that we could not know the facts of the past at all, because in that case we could not understand the documents from which we derive all knowledge of them.[16]

Consistently pursued historicism necessarily leads to the view that the human mind is itself variable and that not only are most or all manifestations of the human mind unintelligible to us apart from their historical setting, but that from our knowledge of how the whole situations succeed each other we can learn to recognise the laws according to which the human mind changes, and that it is the knowledge of these laws which alone puts us in a position to understand any particular manifestation of the human mind. Historicism, because of its refusal to recognise a compositive theory of universal applicability, unable to see how different configurations of the same elements may produce altogether different complexes, and unable, for the same reason, to comprehend how the wholes can ever be anything but what the human mind consciously designed, was bound to seek the cause of the changes in the social structures in changes of the human mind itself—changes which it claims to understand and explain from changes in the directly apprehended wholes. From the extreme assertion of some sociologists that logic itself is variable, and the belief in the 'pre-logical' character of the thinking of primitive people, to the more sophisticated contentions of the modern 'sociology of knowledge',

---

[16] Cf. Langlois and Seignobos, *Introduction to the Study of History*, p. 222 [220]: "If former humanity did not resemble humanity of today, documents would be unintelligible".

this approach has become one of the most characteristic features of modern sociology.[17] It has raised the old question of the 'constancy of the human mind' in a more radical form than has ever been done before.

This phrase is, of course, so vague that any dispute about it without giving it further precision is futile. That not only any human individual in its historically given complexity, but also certain types pre-dominant in particular ages or localities, differ in significant respects from other individuals or types is, of course, beyond dispute. But this does not alter the fact that in order that we should be able to recognise or understand them at all as human beings or minds, there must be certain invariable features present. We cannot recognise 'mind' in the abstract. When we speak of mind what we mean is that certain phenomena can be successfully interpreted on the analogy of our own mind, that the use of the familiar categories of our own thinking provides a satisfactory working explanation of what we observe. But this means that to recognise something as mind is to recognise it as something similar to our own mind, and that the possibility of recognising mind is limited to what is similar to our own mind. To speak of a mind with a structure fundamentally different from our own, or to claim that we can observe changes in the basic structure of the human mind is not only to claim what is impossible: it is a meaningless statement. Whether the human mind is in this sense constant can never become a problem—because to recognise mind cannot mean anything but to recognise something as operating in the same way as our own thinking.

To recognise the existence of a mind always implies that we add something to what we perceive with our senses, that we interpret the phenomena in the light of our own mind, or find that they fit into the ready pattern of our own thinking. This kind of interpretation of human actions may not be always successful, and, what is even more embarrassing, we may never be absolutely certain that it is correct in any particular case; all we know is that it works in the overwhelming number of cases. Yet it is the only basis on which we ever understand what we call other people's intentions, or the meaning of their actions; and certainly the only basis of all our historical knowledge since this is all derived from the understanding of signs or documents. As we pass from men of our own kind to different types of beings we may, of course, find that what we can thus understand becomes less and less. And we cannot exclude the possibility that one day we may find beings who, though perhaps physically

---

[17] [The sociology of knowledge originates in the writings of the German phenomenologist Max Scheler (1874–1928) and the Hungarian-born sociologist Karl Mannheim (1883–1947). It asserts generally that all knowledge is conditioned by the social setting in which we find ourselves. Thus in *Ideology and Utopia* (1936) Mannheim analysed the fictions that are embraced by those who wish to retain a given social order (ideologies), and those held by those who wish radically to transform that order (utopias). Both ideologies and utopias are distortions of reality. —Ed.]

resembling men, behave in a way which is entirely unintelligible to us. With regard to them we should indeed be reduced to the 'objective' study which the behaviourists want us to adopt towards men in general. But there would be no sense in ascribing to these beings a mind different from our own. We should know nothing of them which we could call mind, we should indeed know nothing about them but physical facts. Any interpretation of their actions in terms of such categories as intention or purpose or will, would be meaningless. A mind about which we can intelligibly speak must be like our own.

The whole idea of the variability of the human mind is a direct result of the erroneous belief that mind is an object which we observe as we observe physical facts. The sole difference between mind and physical objects, however, which entitles us to speak of mind at all, is precisely that wherever we speak of mind we interpret what we observe in terms of categories which we know only because they are the categories in which our own mind operates. There is nothing paradoxical in the claim that all mind must run in terms of certain universal categories of thought, because where we speak of mind this means that we can successfully interpret what we observe by arranging it in these categories. And anything which can be comprehended through our understanding of other minds, anything which we recognise as specifically human, must be comprehensible in terms of these categories.

Through the theory of the variability of the human mind, to which the consistent development of historicism leads, it cuts, in effect, the ground under its own feet: it is led to the self-contradictory position of generalising about facts which, if the theory were true, could not be known. If the human mind were really variable so that, as the extreme adherents of historicism assert, we could not directly understand what people of other ages meant by a particular statement, history would be inaccessible to us. The wholes from which we are supposed to understand the elements would never become visible to us. And even if we disregard this fundamental difficulty created by the impossibility of understanding the documents from which we derive all historical knowledge, without first understanding the individual actions and intentions the historian could never combine them into wholes and never explicitly state what these wholes are. He would, as indeed is true of so many of the adherents of historicism, be reduced to talking about wholes which are intuitively comprehended, to making uncertain and vague generalisations about styles or systems whose character could not be precisely defined.

It follows indeed from the nature of the evidence on which all our historical knowledge is based that history can never carry us beyond the stage where we can understand the working of the minds of the acting people because they are similar to our own. Where we cease to understand, where we can no longer recognise categories of thought similar to those in terms of which we think, history ceases to be human history. And precisely at that point, and only at that point, do the general theories of the social sciences cease to be valid. Since history and social theory are based on the same knowledge of the working of the human mind, the same capacity to understand other people, their range and scope are necessarily co-terminous. Particular propositions of social theory may have no application at certain times, because the combination of elements to which they refer do not occur.[18] But they remain nevertheless true. There can be no different theories for different ages, though at some times certain parts and at others different parts of the same body of theory may be required to explain the observed facts, just as, for example, generalisations about the effect of very low temperatures on vegetation may be irrelevant in the tropics but still true. Any true theoretical statement of the social sciences will cease to be valid only where history ceases to be human history. If we conceive of somebody observing and recording the doings of another race, unintelligible to him and to us, his records would in a sense be history, such as, for example, the history of an ant heap. Such history would have to be written in purely objective, physical terms. It would be the sort of history which corresponds to the positivist ideal, such as the proverbial observer from another planet might write of the human race. But such history could not help us to understand any of the events recorded by it in the sense in which we understand human history.

When we speak of man we necessarily imply the presence of certain familiar mental categories. It is not the lumps of flesh of a certain shape which we mean, nor any units performing definite functions which we could define in physical terms. The completely insane, none of whose actions we can understand, is not a man to us—he could not figure in human history except as the object of other people's acting and thinking. When we speak of man we refer to one whose actions we can understand. As old Democritus said: "ἄνθρωπός ἐστιν ὃ πάντες ἴδμεν".[19]

---

[18] Cf. Walter Eucken, *Die Grundlagen der Nationalökonomie* (Jena: G. Fischer, 1940), pp. 203–5. [For the same discussion in translation, see Eucken, *Foundations of Economics*, pp. 234–36.—Ed.]

[19] "Man is what is known to all". Cf. Herman Diehls [Diels], *Die fragmente der Vorsokratiker: Griechisch und deutsch*, 4th ed. (Berlin: Weidmann, 1922), "Democritus", vol. 2, p. 94 [pp. 93–94], note 165. I owe the reference to Democritus in this connection to Professor Alexander Rüstow. [For a translation of Diels' book, see *The Older Sophists: A Complete Translation by Several Hands of Die Fragmente der Vorsokratiker* (Columbia: University of South Carolina Press, 1972). The pre-Socratic Greek philosopher Democritus (c. 430 BC) is remembered today mainly for his early formulation of the atomic hypothesis.—Ed.]

EIGHT

'PURPOSIVE' SOCIAL FORMATIONS

In the concluding portions of this essay we have to consider certain practical attitudes which spring from the theoretical views already discussed. Their most characteristic common feature is a direct result of the inability, caused by the lack of a compositive theory of social phenomena, to grasp how the independent action of many men can produce coherent wholes, persistent structures of relationships which serve important human purposes without having been designed for that end. This produces a 'pragmatic'[1] interpretation of social institutions which treats all social structures which serve human purposes as the result of deliberate design and which denies the possibility of an orderly or purposeful arrangement in anything which is not thus constructed.

This view receives strong support from the fear of employing any anthropomorphic conceptions, a fear so characteristic of the scientistic attitude. This fear has produced an almost complete ban on the use of the concept of 'purpose' in the discussion of spontaneous social growths, and it often drives positivists into an error similar to that they wish to avoid: having learned that it is erroneous to regard everything that behaves in an apparently purposive manner as created by a designing mind, they are led to believe that no result of the action of many men can show order or serve a useful purpose unless it is the result of deliberate design. They are thus driven back to a view which is essentially the same as that which, till the eighteenth century, made man think of language or the family as having been 'invented' or the state as having been created by an explicit social contract, and in opposition to which the compositive theories of social structures were developed.

As the terms of ordinary language are somewhat misleading, it is necessary to move with great care in any discussion of the 'purposive' character of spontaneous social formations. The risk of being lured into an illegitimate anthropomorphic use of the term *purpose* is as great as that of denying that the term *purpose* in this connection designates something of importance. In its strict original meaning *purpose* indeed pre-supposes an acting person deliber-

---

[1] On this concept of the 'pragmatic' interpretation of social institutions as for the whole of this section, see Menger, *Untersuchungen*, Book 2 [3], chapter 2; this is still the most comprehensive and most careful survey known to me of the problems here discussed.

ately aiming at a result. The same, however, as we have seen before,[2] is true of other concepts like 'law' or 'organisation', which we have nevertheless been forced, by the lack of other suitable terms, to adopt for scientific use in a non-anthropomorphic sense. In the same way we may find the term *purpose* indispensable in a carefully defined sense.

The character of the problem may usefully be described first in the words of an eminent contemporary philosopher who, though elsewhere, in the strict positivist manner, he declares that "the concept of purpose must be entirely excluded from the scientific treatment of the phenomena of life", yet admits the existence of "a general principle which proves frequently valid in psychology and biology and also elsewhere: namely that the result of unconscious or instinctive processes is frequently exactly the same as would have arisen from rational calculation".[3] This states one aspect of the problem very clearly: namely, that a result which, if it were deliberately aimed at, could be achieved only in a limited number of ways, may actually be achieved by one of those methods, although nobody has consciously aimed at it. But it still leaves open the question why the particular result which is brought about in this manner should be regarded as distinguished above others and therefore deserves to be described as the 'purpose'.

If we survey the different fields in which we are constantly tempted to describe phenomena as 'purposive' though they are not directed by a conscious mind, it becomes rapidly clear that the 'end' or 'purpose' they are said to serve is always the preservation of a 'whole', of a persistent structure of relationships, whose existence we have come to take for granted before we understood the nature of the mechanism which holds the parts together. The most familiar instances of such wholes are the biological organisms. Here the conception of the function of an organ as an essential condition for the persistence of the whole has proved to be of the greatest heuristic value. It is easily seen how paralysing an effect on research it would have had if the scientific prejudice had effectively banned the use of all teleological concepts in biology and, for example, prevented the discoverer of a new organ from immediately asking what purpose or function it serves.[4]

Though in the social sphere we meet with phenomena which in this respect

---

[2] See herein, chapter 2, note 3.

[3] See Moritz Schlick, *Fragen der Ethik* (Vienna: J. Springer, 1930), p. 72. [For an English translation, see Moritz Schlick, *Problems of Ethics*, translated by David Rynin (New York: Prentice Hall, 1939). The passage quoted is found on p. 98, in a chapter entitled "What Is the Meaning of 'Moral'?".—Ed.]

[4] On the use of teleological concepts in biology, compare the careful discussion in Joseph H. Woodger, *Biological Principles: A Critical Study* (London: K. Paul, Trench, Trubner and Co., 1929), particularly "The Antithesis between Teleology and Causation", pp. 429–51; also the earlier discussion in the same work (p. 291) on the "scientific habit of thought" causing the "scandal" of biologists not taking organisation seriously and "in their haste to become physicists, neglecting their business".

raise analogous problems, it is, of course, dangerous to describe them for that reason as organisms. The limited analogy provides as such no answer to the common problem, and the loan of an alien term tends to obscure the equally important differences. We need not labour further the now familiar fact that the social wholes, unlike the biological organisms, are not given to us as natural units, fixed complexes which ordinary experience shows us to belong together, but are recognisable only by a process of mental reconstruction; or that the parts of the social whole, unlike those of a true organism, can exist away from their particular place in the whole and are to a large extent mobile and exchangeable. Yet, though we must avoid overworking the analogy, certain general considerations apply in both cases. As in the biological organisms we often observe in spontaneous social formations that the parts move as if their purpose were the preservation of the wholes. We find again and again that *if* it were somebody's deliberate aim to preserve the structure of those wholes, and *if* he had knowledge and the power to do so, he would have to do it by causing precisely those movements which in fact are taking place without any such conscious direction.

In the social sphere these spontaneous movements which preserve a certain structural connection between the parts are, moreover, connected in a special way with our individual purposes: the social wholes which are thus maintained are the condition for the achievement of many of the things at which we as individuals aim, the environment which makes it possible even to conceive of most of our individual desires and which gives us the power to achieve them.

There is nothing more mysterious in the fact that, for example, money and the price system enable man to achieve things which he desires, although they were not designed for that purpose, and hardly could have been consciously designed before that growth of civilisation which they made possible, than that, unless man had tumbled upon these devices, he would not have achieved the powers he has gained. The facts to which we refer when we speak of purposive forces being at work here, are the same as those which create the persistent social structures which we have come to take for granted and which form the conditions of our existence. The spontaneously grown institutions are 'useful' because they were the conditions on which the further development of man was based—which gave him the powers which he used. If, in the form in which Adam Smith put it, the phrase that man in society "constantly promotes ends which are no part of his intention" has become the constant source of irritation of the scientistically minded, it describes nevertheless the central problem of the social sciences.[5] As it was put a hundred years after Smith by Carl Menger, who did more than any other writer to carry

[5] [Hayek refers to Adam Smith's famous line about the invisible hand: "by directing that industry in such a manner as its produce may be of the greatest value, he intends only his own gain, and he is in this, as in many other cases, led by an invisible hand to promote an end which was no part of his intention". See Smith, *The Wealth of Nations*, Book 4, chapter 2, p. 456.—Ed.]

beyond Smith the elucidation of the meaning of this phrase, the question "how it is possible that institutions which serve the common welfare and are most important for its advancement can arise without a common will aiming at their creation" is still "the significant, perhaps the most significant, problem of the social sciences".[6]

That the nature and even the existence of this problem are still so little recognised[7] is closely connected with a common confusion about what we mean when we say that human institutions are made by man. Though in a sense man-made, that is, entirely the result of human actions, they may yet not be designed, not be the intended product of these actions. The term *institution* itself is rather misleading in this respect, as it suggests something deliberately instituted. It would probably be better if this term were confined to particular contrivances, like particular laws and organisations, which have been created for a specific purpose, and if a more neutral term like *formations* (in a sense similar to that in which the geologists use it, and corresponding to the German *Gebilde*) could be used for those phenomena, which, like money or language, have not been so created.

From the belief that nothing which has not been consciously designed can be useful or even essential to the achievement of human purposes, it is an easy transition to the belief that since all institutions have been made by man, we must have complete power to refashion them in any way we desire.[8] But,

---

[6] Menger, *Untersuchungen*, p. 163: "Hier ist es, wo uns das merkwürdige, vielleicht das merkwürdigste Problem der Socialwissenschaften entgegentritt: *Wieso vermögen dem Gemeinwohl dienende und für dessen Entwicklung höchst bedeutsame Institutionen ohne einen auf ihre Begründung gerichteten* **Gemeinwillen** *zu entstehen?*" [See Menger, *Investigations*, p. 146: "It is here that we meet a noteworthy, perhaps the most noteworthy, problem of the social sciences: *How can it be that institutions which meet the common welfare and are extremely significant for its development come into being without a* **common will** *directed towards establishing them?*"—Ed.] If for the ambiguous and somewhat question-begging 'social welfare' we substitute in this statement 'institutions that are necessary conditions for the achievement of man's conscious purposes', it is hardly saying too much that the way in which such 'purposive wholes' are formed and preserved is *the* specific problem of social theory, just as the existence and persistence of organisms are the problem of biology.

[7] How much intellectual progress has been obstructed here by political passions is readily seen when we compare the discussion of the problem in the economic and political sciences with, say, the study of language, wherein what is still disputed in the former, is a commonplace which nobody dreams of questioning.

[8] Menger, *Untersuchungen*, p. 208, speaks in this connection rightly of "a pragmatism which, against the wishes of its representatives, leads inevitably to socialism". [See Menger, *Investigations*, p. 177, as well as this volume, "Individualism: True and False", note 9, where Hayek also makes reference to this passage.—Ed.] Today this view is most frequently found in the writings of the American 'institutionalists', of which the following, from Professor Walton H. Hamilton, "Institution", in *Encyclopedia of the Social Sciences* (New York: Macmillan, 1932), vol. 8, pp. 87–89 [87, 89], is a good example: "The tangled thing called capitalism was never created by design or cut to a blueprint; but now that it is here, contemporary schoolmen have intellectualised it into a purposive and self-regulating instrument of general welfare". From this it is of course only a few steps to the demand that "order and direction be imposed upon an unruly society".

though this conclusion at first sounds like a self-evident commonplace, it is, in fact, a complete *non sequitur*, based on the equivocal use of the term *institution*. It would be valid only if all the 'purposive' formations were the result of design. But phenomena like language or the market, money or morals, are not real artefacts, products of deliberate creation.[9] Not only have they not been designed by any mind, but they are also preserved by, and depend for their functioning on, the actions of people who are not guided by the desire to keep them in existence. And, as they are not due to design but rest on individual actions which we do not now control, we at least cannot take it for granted that we can improve upon, or even equal, their performance by any organisation which relies on the deliberate control of the movements of its parts. Insofar as we learn to understand the spontaneous forces, we may hope to use them and modify their operations by proper adjustment of the institutions which form part of the larger process. But there is all the difference between thus utilising and influencing spontaneous processes and an attempt to replace them by an organisation which relies on conscious control.

We flatter ourselves undeservedly if we represent human civilisation as entirely the product of conscious reason or as the product of human design, or when we assume that it is necessarily in our power deliberately to re-create or to maintain what we have built without knowing what we were doing. Though our civilisation is the result of a cumulation of individual knowledge, it is not by the explicit or conscious combination of all this knowledge in any individual brain, but by its embodiment in symbols which we use without understanding them, in habits and institutions, tools and concepts,[10] that man in society

---

[The American institutionalists were critics of the classical and neoclassical deductive approach to economic theory, which they considered too simple to explain complex modern economies, as well as of the laissez faire policies usually associated with classical economics. A central figure in the inter-war institutionalist movement and an advocate of the public control of business, American economist and lawyer Walton Hale Hamilton (1881–1958) is generally credited with coining the term 'the institutional approach' in a paper presented at a meeting of the American Economic Association in 1918; see Walton H. Hamilton, "The Institutional Approach to Economic Theory", *American Economic Review Papers and Proceedings*, vol. 9, March 1919, pp. 309–18. For more on Hayek's views of institutionalism, see the editor's introduction, this volume, pp. 19–24.—Ed.]

[9] A typical example of the treatment of social institutions as if they were true artefacts, in a characteristic scientistic setting, is provided by Joseph Mayer, *Social Science Principles in the Light of Scientific Method with Particular Application to Modern Economic Thought* (Durham, N. C.: Duke University Press, 1941), p. 20; here society is explicitly "designated. . . . as an 'artificial creation', much as an automobile or steel mill is, that is to say, made by the artifice of man".

[10] The best illustration, perhaps, of how we constantly make use of the experience or knowledge acquired by others is the way in which, by learning to speak, we learn to classify things in a certain manner without acquiring the actual experiences which have led successive generations to evolve this system of classification. There is a great deal of knowledge which we never consciously know implicit in the knowledge of which we are aware, knowledge which yet constantly serves us in our actions, though we can hardly be said to 'possess' it.

is constantly able to profit from a body of knowledge neither he nor any other man completely possesses. Many of the greatest things man has achieved are the result not of consciously directed thought, and still less the product of a deliberately co-ordinated effort of many individuals, but of a process in which the individual plays a part which he can never fully understand. They are greater than any individual precisely because they result from the combination of knowledge more extensive than a single mind can master.

It has been unfortunate that those who have recognised this so often draw the conclusion that the problems it raises are purely historical problems, and thereby deprive themselves of the means of effectively refuting the views they try to combat. In fact, as we have seen,[11] much of the older 'historical school' was essentially a reaction against the type of erroneous rationalism we are discussing. If it failed it was because it treated the problem of explaining these phenomena as entirely one of the accidents of time and place and refused systematically to elaborate the logical process by which alone we can provide an explanation. We need not return here to this point already discussed.[12] Though the explanation of the way in which the parts of the social whole depend upon each other will often take the form of a genetic account, this will be at most 'schematic history' which the true historian will rightly refuse to recognise as real history. It will deal, not with the particular circumstances of an individual process, but only with those steps which are essential to produce a particular result, with a process which, at least in principle, may be repeated elsewhere or at different times. As is true of all explanations, it must run in generic terms, it will deal with what is sometimes called the 'logic of events', neglect much that is important in the unique historical instance, and be concerned with a dependence of the parts of the phenomenon upon each other which is not even necessarily the same as the chronological order in which they appeared. In short, it is not history, but compositive social theory.

One curious aspect of this problem which is rarely appreciated is that it is only by the individualist or compositive method that we can give a definite meaning to the much abused phrases about the social processes and formations being in any sense 'more' than 'merely the sum' of their parts, and that we are enabled to understand how structures of inter-personal relationships emerge, which make it possible for the joint efforts of individuals to achieve desirable results which no individual could have planned or foreseen. The collectivist, on the other hand, who refuses to account for the wholes by systematically following up the interactions of individual efforts, and who claims to be able directly to comprehend social wholes as such, is never able to define the

---

[11] See herein, chapter 7.

[12] See herein, pp. 131–35. See also Menger, *Untersuchungen*, pp. 165 et seq. [See Menger, *Investigations*, pp. 147 et. seq.—Ed.]

precise character of these wholes or their mode of operation, and is regularly driven to conceive of these wholes on the model of an individual mind.

Even more significant of the inherent weakness of the collectivist theories is the extraordinary paradox that from the assertion that society is in some sense more than merely the aggregate of all individuals their adherents regularly pass by a sort of intellectual somersault to the thesis that in order that the coherence of this larger entity be safeguarded it must be subjected to conscious control, that is, to the control of what in the last resort must be an individual mind. It thus comes about that in practice it is regularly the theoretical collectivist who extols individual reason and demands that all forces of society be made subject to the direction of a single mastermind, while it is the individualist who recognises the limitations of the powers of individual reason and consequently advocates freedom as a means for the fullest development of the powers of the inter-individual process.

NINE

'CONSCIOUS' DIRECTION AND
THE GROWTH OF REASON

The universal demand for 'conscious' control or direction of social processes is one of the most characteristic features of our generation. It expresses perhaps more clearly than any of its other clichés the peculiar spirit of the age. That anything is not consciously directed as a whole is regarded as itself a blemish, a proof of its irrationality and of the need completely to replace it by a deliberately designed mechanism. Yet few of the people who use the term *conscious* so freely seem to be aware of precisely what it means; most people seem to forget that *conscious* and *deliberate* are terms which have meaning only when applied to individuals, and that the demand for conscious control is therefore equivalent to the demand for control by a single mind.

This belief that processes which are consciously directed are necessarily superior to any spontaneous process is an unfounded superstition. It would be truer to say, as A. N. Whitehead has argued in another connection, that on the contrary "civilisation advances by extending the number of important operations we can perform without thinking about them".[1] If it is true that the spontaneous interplay of social forces sometimes solves problems no individual mind could consciously solve, or perhaps even perceives, and if they thereby create an ordered structure which increases the power of the individuals without having been designed by any one of them, they are superior to conscious action. Indeed, any social processes which deserve to be called 'social' in distinction from the action of individuals are almost *ex definitione* not conscious. Insofar as such processes are capable of producing a useful order which could not have been produced by conscious direction, any attempt to make them subject to such direction would necessarily mean that we restrict what social activity can achieve to the inferior capacity of the individual mind.[2]

---

[1] Alfred North Whitehead, *An Introduction to Mathematics*, Home University Library of Modern Knowledge, no. 15 (London: Williams and Norgate, 1911), p. 61.

[2] It cannot be objected to this that what is meant by conscious control is control not by a single mind but by a concerted and 'co-ordinated' effort of all, or all the best minds, instead of by their fortuitous interplay. This phrase about the deliberate co-ordination merely shifts the task of the individual mind to another stage but leaves the ultimate responsibility still with the co-ordinating mind. Committees and other devices for facilitating communications are excellent means to

The full significance of this demand for universal conscious control will be seen most clearly if we consider it first in its most ambitious manifestation, even though this is as yet merely a vague aspiration and important mainly as a symptom: this is the application of the demand for conscious control to the growth of the human mind itself. This audacious idea is the most extreme result to which man has yet been led by the success of reason in the conquest of external nature. It has become a characteristic feature of contemporary thought and appears in what on a first view seem to be altogether different and even opposite systems of ideas. Whether it is the late L. T. Hobhouse who holds up to us "the ideal of collective humanity, self-determining in its progress, as the supreme object of human activity and the final standard by which the laws of conduct should be judged",[3] or Dr. Joseph Needham who argues that "the more control consciousness has over human affairs, the more truly human, and hence super-human, man will become",[4] whether it is the strict followers of Hegel who adumbrate the master's view of Reason becoming conscious of itself and taking control of its fate, or Dr. Karl Mannheim who thinks that "man's thought has become more spontaneous and absolute than it ever was, since it now perceives the possibility of determining itself",[5] the

---

assist the individual in learning as much as possible; but they do not extend the capacity of the individual mind. The knowledge that can be consciously co-ordinated in this manner is still limited to what the individual mind can effectively absorb and digest. As every person with experience of committee work knows, its fertility is limited to what the best mind among the members can master; if the results of the discussion are not ultimately turned into a coherent whole by an individual mind, they are likely to be inferior to what would have been produced unaided by a single mind.

[3] L. T. Hobhouse, *Democracy and Reaction* (London: T. F. Unwin,1904), p. 108. [English sociologist, journalist, and political activist Leonard Trelawny Hobhouse (1864–1929) was an advocate of the 'new' liberalism that emerged in the early twentieth century. As Richard Cockett, *Thinking the Unthinkable: Think-Tanks and the Economic Counter-Revolution, 1931–1983* (London: Harper Collins, 1994), p. 15, put it, it was "under the guidance of mentors J. A. Hobson and L. T. Hobhouse" that the Liberal Party "adopted Bismarck's social insurance system and applied it to Britain during Asquith's Liberal administrations of 1908–15". In such books as *Mind in Evolution* (1901) and *Morals in Evolution* (1906) Hobhouse argued that progress in human thought and moral conduct were the result not of biology but of self-conscious human direction and control.—Ed.]

[4] Joseph Needham, *Integrative Levels: A Revaluation of the Idea of Progress*, Herbert Spencer Lecture (Oxford: Clarendon Press, 1937), p. 47. [A British biochemist, Joseph Needham (1900–95) became famous as an historian of the development of Chinese science. In the 1930s he was one of the 'men of science' (natural scientists who advocated the planning of science and of society) against whom Hayek fought. For more on this, see the editor's introduction, this volume, pp. 27–28.—Ed.]

[5] Karl Mannheim, *Man and Society in an Age of Reconstruction* (London: K. Paul, Trench, Trubner and Co., 1940), p. 213. [We have already met Karl Mannheim (see chapter 7, note 17) as one of the founders of the sociology of knowledge. Mannheim fled Frankfurt after the Nazis came to power, securing a position at the LSE. In *Man and Society* he argued that only through exten-

basic attitude is the same. Though, according as these doctrines spring from Hegelian or positivist views, those who hold them form distinct groups that mutually regard themselves as completely different from and greatly superior to the other, the common idea that the human mind is, as it were, to pull itself up by its own bootstraps, springs from the same general approach: the belief that by studying human Reason from the outside and as a whole we can grasp the laws of its motion in a more complete and comprehensive manner than by its patient exploration from the inside, by actually following up the processes in which individual minds interact.

This pretension to be able to increase the powers of the human mind by consciously controlling its growth is thus based on the same theoretical view which claims to be able fully to explain this growth, a claim which implies the possession of a kind of super-mind on the part of those who make it; and it is no accident that those who hold these theoretical views should also wish to see the growth of mind thus directed.

It is important to understand the precise sense in which the claim to be able to 'explain' existing knowledge and beliefs must be interpreted in order to justify the aspirations based on it. For this purpose it would not be sufficient if we possessed an adequate theory which explained the *principles* on which the processes operate to which the growth of mind is due. Such knowledge of the mere principles (either a theory of knowledge or a theory of the social processes involved) will assist in creating conditions favourable to that growth, but could never provide a justification for the claim that it should be deliberately directed. This claim pre-supposes that we are able to arrive at a substantive explanation of why we hold the particular views we hold, of how our actual knowledge is determined by specific conditions. It is this which the 'sociology of knowledge' and the various other derivatives of the 'materialist interpretation of history' undertake when, for example, they 'explain' the Kantian philosophy as the product of the material interests of the German bourgeoisie in the late eighteenth century, or whatever other similar theses they present.

We cannot enter here into a discussion of the reasons why even with respect to views now regarded as errors, and which on the basis of our better present knowledge we may in a sense be able to explain, that method does not really provide an explanation. The crucial point is that to attempt this with respect to our present knowledge involves a contradiction: if we knew how our present knowledge is conditioned or determined, it would no longer be our pres-

sive planning of society could the western democracies avoid the fate of the communist Soviet Union or fascist Europe. Planning was inevitable; the only choice was between good planning and the sort that would be imposed by totalitarian regimes of the left or right. Hayek modified Mannheim's original passage, which, referring to an individual in a planned society, read, "his thought has become more spontaneous and absolute than it ever was before, since he now perceives the possibility of determining himself".—Ed.]

ent knowledge. To assert that we can explain our own knowledge is to assert that we know more than we do know, a statement which is nonsense in the strict meaning of that term.[6] There may, perhaps, be sense in the statement that to a greatly superior mind our present knowledge would appear as 'relative', or as conditioned in a certain manner by assignable circumstances. But the only conclusion *we* should be entitled to draw from this would be one opposite to that of the 'bootstrap theory of mental evolution': it would be that on the basis of our present knowledge we are not in a position successfully to direct its growth. To draw any other conclusion than this, to derive from the thesis that human beliefs are determined by circumstances the claim that somebody should be given power to determine these beliefs, involves the claim that those who are to assume that power possess some sort of supermind. Those who hold these views have indeed regularly some special theory which exempts their own views from the same sort of explanation and which credits them, as a specially favoured class, or simply as the 'free-floating intelligentsia', with the possession of absolute knowledge.[7]

While in a sense this movement represents thus a sort of super-rationalism, a demand for the direction of everything by a super-mind, it prepares at the same time the ground for a thorough irrationalism. If truth is no longer discovered by observation, reasoning, and argument, but by uncovering hidden causes which, unknown to the thinker, have determined his conclusions, if whether a statement is true or false is no longer decided by logical argument and empirical tests, but by examining the social position of the person who made it, when in consequence it becomes the membership of a class or race which secures or prevents the achievement of truth, and when in the end it is claimed that the sure instinct of a particular class or a people is always right, reason has been finally driven out.[8] This is no more than the natural result of a doctrine which starts out with the claim that it can intuitively recognise wholes in a manner superior to the rational reconstruction attempted by compositive social theory.

If it is true, moreover, as in their different ways both individualists and collectivists contend, that social processes can achieve things which it is beyond the power of the individual mind to achieve and plan, and that it is from those

---

[6] See herein, pp. 138–41.

[7] [In chapter 3 of his *Ideology and Utopia*, which is titled "The Prospects of Scientific Politics", Karl Mannheim gives a key rôle to the intelligentsia, that "unanchored, *relatively* classless stratum", in developing a true science of politics. The term 'free-floating intelligentsia' is thus often associated with Mannheim, though Mannheim nowhere claims that this free-floating intelligentsia would possess absolute knowledge.—Ed.]

[8] Interesting illustrations of the length to which these absurdities have been carried will be found in Ernst Grünwald, *Das Problem der Soziologie des Wissens* (Vienna: Wilhelm Braumüller, 1934), a posthumously published sketch of a very young scholar which still constitutes the most comprehensive survey of the literature of the subject.

social processes that the individual mind derives what power it possesses, the attempt to impose conscious control on these processes must have even more fatal consequences. The presumptuous aspiration that 'reason' should direct its own growth could in practice only have the effect that it would set limits to its own growth, that it would confine itself to the results which the directing individual mind can already foresee. Though this aspiration is a direct outcome of a certain brand of rationalism, it is, of course, the result of a misunderstood or misapplied rationalism which fails to recognise the extent to which individual reason is a product of inter-individual relationships. Indeed, the demand that everything, including the growth of the human mind, should be consciously controlled is itself a sign of the inadequate understanding of the general character of the forces which constitute the life of the human mind and of human society. It is the extreme stage of these self-destructive forces of our modern 'scientific' civilisation, of that abuse of reason whose development and consequences will be the central theme of the following historical studies.

It is because the growth of the human mind presents in its most general form the common problem of all the social sciences that it is here that minds most sharply divide, and that two fundamentally different and irreconcilable attitudes manifest themselves: on the one hand the essential humility of individualism, which endeavours to understand as well as possible the principles by which the efforts of individual men have in fact been combined to produce our civilisation, and which from this understanding hopes to derive the power to create conditions favourable to further growth; and, on the other hand, the hubris of collectivism, which aims at conscious direction of all forces of society.

The individualist approach, in awareness of the constitutional limitations of the individual mind,[9] attempts to show how man in society is able, by the use of various resultants of the social process, to increase his powers with the help of the knowledge implicit in them and of which he is never aware; it makes us understand that the only 'reason' which can in any sense be regarded as superior to individual reason does not exist apart from the inter-individual process in which, by means of impersonal media, the knowledge of successive generations and of millions of people living simultaneously is combined and mutually adjusted, and that this process is the only form in which the totality of human knowledge ever exists.

The collectivist method, on the other hand, not satisfied with the partial knowledge of this process from the inside, which is all the individual can gain, bases its demands for conscious control on the assumption that it can comprehend this process as a whole and make use of all knowledge in a system-

[9] See herein, pp. 93 and 105–6.

atically integrated form. It leads thus directly to political collectivism; though, logically, methodological collectivism and political collectivism are distinct, it is not difficult to see how the former leads to the latter and how, indeed, without methodological collectivism political collectivism would be deprived of its intellectual basis: without the pretension that conscious individual reason can grasp all the aims and all the knowledge of 'society' or 'humanity', the belief that these aims are best achieved by conscious central direction loses its foundation. Consistently pursued it must lead to a system in which all members of society become merely instruments of the single directing mind and in which all the spontaneous social forces to which the growth of the mind is due are destroyed.[10]

It may indeed prove to be far the most difficult and not the least important task for human reason rationally to comprehend its own limitations. It is essential for the growth of reason that as individuals we should bow to forces and obey principles which we cannot hope fully to understand, yet on which the advance and even the preservation of civilisation depend.[11] Historically this has been achieved by the influence of the various religious creeds and by traditions and superstitions which made man submit to those forces by an appeal to his emotions rather than to his reason. The most dangerous stage in the growth of civilisation may well be that in which man has come to regard all these beliefs as superstitions and refuses to accept or to submit to anything which he does not rationally understand. The rationalist whose reason is not sufficient to teach him those limitations of the powers of conscious reason, and who despises all the institutions and customs which have not been consciously designed, would thus become the destroyer of the civilisation built upon them. This may well prove a hurdle which man will repeatedly reach, only to be thrown back into barbarism.

It would lead too far here to refer more than briefly to another field in which this same characteristic tendency of our age shows itself: that of morals. Here it is against the observance of any general and formal rules whose *rationale* is not explicitly demonstrated that the same kind of objections are raised. But the demand that every action should be judged after full consideration of all its consequences and not by any general rules is due to a failure to see that the submission to general rules, couched in terms of immediately ascertainable circumstances, is the only way in which for man with his limited knowledge

---

[10] It is, perhaps, not so obvious as to make it unnecessary to mention that the fashionable disparagement of any activity which, in science or the arts, is carried on 'for its own sake', and the demand for a 'conscious social purpose' in everything, are expressions of the same general tendency and are based on the same illusions of complete knowledge as those discussed in the text.

[11] Additional aspects of the big problems here just touched upon are discussed in my *The Road to Serfdom*, especially chapters 6, 14.

freedom can be combined with the essential minimum degree of order. Common acceptance of formal rules is indeed the only alternative to direction by a single will man has yet discovered. The general acceptance of such a body of rules is no less important because they have not been rationally constructed. It is at least doubtful whether it would be possible in this way to construct a new moral code that would have any chance of acceptance. But so long as we have not succeeded in doing so, any general refusal to accept existing moral rules merely because their expediency has not been rationally demonstrated (as distinguished from the case when the critic believes he has discovered a better moral rule in a particular instance and is willing to brave public disapproval in testing it) is to destroy one of the roots of our civilisation.[12]

---

[12] It is characteristic of the spirit of the time, and of positivism in particular, when Auguste Comte speaks in vol. 1 (1851) of *Système de politique positive* (Paris: L. Mathias, 1851–54) p. 356, of "la supériorité nécessaire de la morale démontrée sur la morale révélée" [the necessary superiority of demonstrated over revealed moral standards.—Ed.], characteristic especially in its implied assumption that a rationally constructed moral system is the only alternative to one revealed by a higher being.

TEN

ENGINEERS AND PLANNERS

The ideal of conscious control of social phenomena has made its greatest influence felt in the economic field.[1] The present popularity of 'economic planning' is directly traceable to the prevalence of the scientistic ideas we have
been discussing. As in this field the scientistic ideals manifest themselves in the
particular forms which they take in the hands of the applied scientist and especially the engineer, it will be convenient to combine the discussion of this
influence with some examination of the characteristic ideals of the engineers.
We shall see that the influence on current views about problems of social organisation of this technological approach, or the engineering point of view, is
much greater than is generally realised. Most of the schemes for a complete
remodelling of society, from the earlier utopias to modern socialism, bear indeed the distinct mark of this influence. In recent years this desire to apply
engineering technique to the solution of social problems has become very
explicit;[2] 'political engineering' and 'social engineering' have become fashionable catchwords which are quite as characteristic of the outlook of the present

[1] For those who wish to pursue the matters discussed in the previous chapter, a few references
to several relevant works may be added which have appeared since this was first published. In
addition to the *Selected Writings of Edward Sapir*, especially pp. 46ff., 104, 162, 166, 546ff., and
553, already mentioned earlier, the reader will with advantage consult Gilbert Ryle, "Knowing
How and Knowing That", *Proceedings of the Aristotelian Society*, vol. 46, 1945, pp. 1–16, and the corresponding passages in the same author's *The Concept of Mind* (London: Hutchison's University
Library, 1949); Karl R. Popper, *The Open Society and Its Enemies* (London: G. Routledge and Sons,
1945); and Michael Polanyi, *The Logic of Liberty* (London: Routledge and Kegan Paul, 1951).

[2] Again, one of the best illustrations of this tendency is provided by K. Mannheim, *Man and
Society in an Age of Reconstruction*, especially pp. 240–44, wherein he explains that "functionalism
made its first appearance in the field of the natural sciences, and could be described as the technical point of view. It has only recently been transferred to the social sphere. . . . Once this technical approach was transferred from natural science to human affairs, it was bound to bring
about profound changes in man himself. . . . The functional approach no longer regards ideas
and moral standards as absolute values, but as products of the social process which can, if necessary, be changed by scientific guidance combined with political practice. . . . The extension of
the doctrine of technical supremacy which I have advocated in this book is in my opinion inevitable. . . . Progress in the technique of organisation is nothing but the application of technical
conceptions to the forms of human co-operation. A human being, regarded as part of the social

generation as its predilection for 'conscious' control; in Russia even the artists appear to pride themselves on the name of 'engineers of the soul', bestowed upon them by Stalin.[3] These phrases suggest a confusion about the fundamental differences between the task of the engineer and that of social organisations on a larger scale which make it desirable to consider their character somewhat more fully.

We must confine ourselves here to a few salient features of the specific problems which the professional experience of the engineer constantly brings up and which determine his outlook. The first is that his characteristic tasks are usually in themselves complete: he will be concerned with a single end, control all the efforts directed towards this end, and dispose for this purpose over a definitely given supply of resources. It is as a result of this that the most characteristic feature of his procedure becomes possible, namely that, at least in principle, all the parts of the complex of operations are pre-formed in the engineer's mind before they start, that all the 'data' on which the work is based have explicitly entered his preliminary calculations and been condensed into the blueprint that governs the execution of the whole scheme.[4] The engineer,

---

machine, is to a certain extent stabilised in his reactions by training and education, and all his newly acquired activities are co-ordinated according to a definite principle of efficiency within an organised framework".

[3] [In the Soviet Union under Lenin and Stalin, 'socialist realism' in art was mandated: the function of art was to aid in the revolutionary transformation of society and of mankind by representing and glorifying the proletariat as it built a new socialist world. For their rôle in helping to create the New Soviet Man, artists were termed 'engineers of the soul'. Hayek makes a similar reference in his discussions of Saint-Simonian theories of art in chapter 13, p. 207.—Ed.]

[4] The best description of this feature of the engineering approach by an engineer which I have been able to find occurs in a speech of the great German optical engineer Ernst Abbe: "Wie der Architekt ein Bauwerk, bevor eine Hand zur Ausführung sich rührt, schon im Geist vollendet hat, nur unter Beihilfe von Zeichenstift und Feder zur Fixierung seiner Idee, so muß auch das komplizierte Gebilde von Glas und Metall sich aufbauen lassen rein verstandesmäßig, in allen Elementen bis ins Letzte vorausbestimmt, in rein geistiger Arbeit, durch theoretische Ermittlung der Wirkung aller Teile, bevor diese Teile noch körperlich ausgeführt sind. Der arbeitenden Hand darf dabei keine andere Funktion mehr verbleiben als die genaue Verwirklichung der durch die Rechnung bestimmten Formen und Abmessungen aller Konstruktionselemente, und der praktischen Erfahrung keine andere Aufgabe als die Beherrschung der Methoden und Hilfsmittel, die für letzteres, die körperliche Verwirklichung, geeignet sind", quoted in Franz Schnabel, *Deutsche Geschichte im neunzehnten Jahrhundert* (Freiburg: Herder and Co., 1934), vol. 3, p. 222, a work which is a mine of information on this as on all other matters of the intellectual history of Germany in the nineteenth century. [The passage might be translated as follows, "Before the builder ever lifts a finger, the architect has already completed the building in his mind, with only the help of a pen to fix his ideas. In the same way, a complex object made of glass and metal must be built only by the mind, with all its elements pre-determined by purely abstract thought, through a theoretical determination of the function of all the parts, before these parts ever take physical shape. The hand that executes this plan has no purpose other than the exact realisation of the forms and measurements that have been determined by the mind, and practical experi-

in other words, has complete control of the particular little world with which he is concerned, surveys it in all its relevant aspects and has to deal only with 'known quantities'.[5] So far as the solution of his engineering problem is concerned, he is not taking part in a social process in which others may take independent decisions, but lives in a separate world of his own. The application of the technique which he has mastered, of the generic rules he has been taught, indeed pre-supposes such complete knowledge of the objective facts; those rules refer to objective properties of the things and can be applied only after all the particular circumstances of time and place have been assembled and brought under the control of a single brain. His technique, in other words, refers to typical situations defined in terms of objective facts, not to the problem of how to find out what resources are available or what is the relative importance of different needs. He has been trained in objective possibilities, irrespective of the particular conditions of time and place, in the knowledge of those properties of things which remain the same everywhere and at all times and which they possess irrespective of a particular human situation.

It is important, however, to observe that the engineer's view of his job as complete in itself is, in some measure, a delusion. He is in a position in a competitive society to treat it as such because he can regard that assistance from society at large on which he counts as one of his data, as given to him without having to bother about it. That he can buy at given prices the materials and the services of the men he needs, that if he pays his men they will be able to procure their food and other necessities, he will usually take for granted. It is through basing his plans on the data offered to him by the market that they are fitted in to the larger complex of social activities; and it is because he need not concern himself how the market provides him with what he needs that he can treat his job as self-contained. So long as market prices do not change unexpectedly he uses them as a guide in his calculations without much reflection about their significance. But, though he is compelled to take them into account, they are not properties of things of the same kind as those which he understands. They are not objective attributes of things but reflections of a particular human situation at a given time and place. And as his knowledge does not explain why those changes in prices occur which often interfere with

---

ence has no purpose other than to provide those methods and tools that are suited to the physical realisation of the plan".—Ed.]

[5] It would take too long here to explain in any detail why, whatever delegation or division of labour is possible in preparing an engineering blueprint, it is very limited and differs in essential respects from the division of knowledge on which the impersonal social processes rest. It must suffice to point out that not only must the precise nature of the result be fixed which anyone who has to draw up part of an engineering plan must achieve, but also, to make such delegation possible, it must be known that the result can be achieved at no more than a certain maximum cost.

his plans, any such interference appears to him due to irrational (that is, not consciously directed) forces, and he resents the necessity of paying attention to magnitudes which appear meaningless to him. Hence the characteristic and ever-recurrent demand for the substitution of *in natura*[6] calculation for the 'artificial' calculation in terms of price or value, that is, of a calculation which takes explicit account of the objective properties of things.

The engineer's ideal which he feels the 'irrational' economic forces prevent him from achieving, based on his study of the objective properties of the things, is usually some purely technical optimum of universal validity. He rarely sees that his preference for these particular methods is merely a result of the type of problem he has most frequently to solve, and justified only in particular social positions. Since the most common problem the builder of machines meets is to extract from given resources the maximum of power, with the machinery to be used as the variable under his control, this maximum utilisation of power is set up as an absolute ideal, a value in itself.[7] But there is,

[6] The most persistent advocate of such *in natura* calculation is, significantly, Dr. Otto Neurath, the protagonist of modern 'physicalism' and 'objectivism'. [For more on Neurath, see chapter 1, note 5.—Ed.]

[7] Cf. the characteristic passage in Bernhard Bavinck [Bavink], *The Anatomy of Modern Science*, translated by H. Stafford Hatfield, from the 4th German ed. (London: George Bell and Sons, 1932), p. 564: "When our technology is still at work on the problem of transforming heat into work in a manner better than that possible with our present-day steam and other heat engines . . . this is not directly done in order to cheapen the production of energy, but first of all because it is an end in itself to increase the thermal efficiency of a heat engine as much as possible. If the problem set is to transform heat into work, then this must be done in such a way that the greatest possible fraction of the heat is so transformed. . . . The ideal of the designer of such machines is therefore the efficiency of the so-called Carnot cycle, the ideal process which delivers the greatest theoretical efficiency".

It is easy to see why this approach, together with the desire to achieve a calculation *in natura*, leads engineers so frequently to the construction of systems of 'energetics' that it has been said, with much justice, that "das Charakteristikum der Weltanschauung des Ingenieurs ist die energetische Weltanschauung", in Ludwig Brinkmann, *Der Ingenieur* (Frankfurt: Rütten and Loening, 1908), p. 16. [Hayek's quotation may be rendered, "Characteristic of the worldview of engineers is the energetics worldview", but what Brinkmann actually wrote was, "Das Charakteristikum des Ingenieurs ist die energetische Weltauffassung".—Ed.] We have already referred (pp. 115–16) to this characteristic manifestation of scientistic 'objectivism', and there is no space here to return to it in greater detail. But it deserves to be recorded how widespread and typical this view is and how great the influence it has exercised. E. Solvay, G. Ratzenhofer, W. Ostwald, P. Geddes, F. Soddy, H. G. Wells, the 'Technocrats', and L. Hogben are only a few of the influential authors in whose works energetics play a more or less prominent rôle. There are several studies of this movement in French and German, e.g., Emile Nyssens, *Essai de philosophie precise: L'énergétisme, système d'énergétique intégrale* (Brussels: H. Lamertin, 1908); Georges Barnich, *Essai de politique positive basée sur l'énergétique sociale de Solvay avec tableau de synthèse sociale* (Brussels: Bothy, 1918); Wilhelm von Schnehen, *Energetische Weltanschauung? Eine kritische Studie* (Leipzig: Theo. Thomas, 1907); Abraham Dochmann, *F. W. Ostwalds Energetik* (Bern: Inaugural Dissertation, 1908); and the best, Max Weber, "'Energetische' Kulturtheorien" (1909), reprinted in *Gesa-*

of course, no special merit economising one of the many factors which limit the possible achievement, at the expense of others. The engineer's 'technical optimum' proves frequently to be simply that method which it would be desir-

---

mmelte Aufsätze zur Wissenschaftslehre (Tübingen: J. C. B. Mohr, 1922), pp. 376–402, but none of them is adequate and none, to my knowledge, is in English.

The section from the work of Bavink from which a passage has been quoted above condenses the gist of the enormous literature, mostly German, on the 'philosophy of technology' which has had a wide circulation and of which the best known is Eberhard Zschimmer, *Philosophie der Technik: Einführung in die technische Ideenwelt*, 3rd ed. (Stuttgart: F. Enke, 1933). (Similar ideas pervade the well-known American works of Lewis Mumford.) This German literature is very instructive as a psychological study, though otherwise about the dreariest mixture of pretentious platitudes and revolting nonsense this author has ever perused. Its common feature is the enmity towards all economic considerations, the attempted vindication of purely technological ideals, and the glorification of the organisation of the whole of society on the principle on which a single factory is run. (On the last point, see particularly Friedrich Dessauer, *Philosophie der Technik: Das Problem der Realisierung* (Bonn: F. Cohen, 1927), p. 129.)

[Hayek discussed the energetics movement as an example of the objectivism of the scientistic approach in chapter 5 and mentioned there such luminaries of the movement as Ernest Solvay, Wilhelm Ostwald, and Frederick Soddy. For more on the energetics and Technocracy movements, see Philip Mirowski, "Energy and Energetics in Economic Theory: A Review Essay", *Journal of Economic Issues*, vol. 22, September 1988, pp. 811–830. The Austrian sociologist and military jurist Gustav Ratzenhofer (1840–1942) saw social conflict among ethnic groups as originating in basic biological, chemical, and physical drives and processes, but held out the hope that the new field of sociology might guide the species to improved social relations. The Scottish biologist and botanist Patrick Geddes (1854–1932), considered one of the founders of the urban planning profession, argued for urban renewal that would balance economic and community concerns, emphasise environmental quality, and aim towards sustainable development. He applied his principles in the revitalisation of Edinburgh's 'Old Town'. Geddes greatly influenced the prolific American student of architecture, city planning, and sociology Lewis Mumford (1895–1990), who, in *Technics and Civilization* (New York: Harcourt, Brace, and Co., 1934) traced the impact of 'the machine' on human civilisation. Echoing the claims of technocracy, Mumford argued in his final chapter that, because machines allow a massive increase in our ability to convert energy to productive purposes, we should abandon capitalism for a new social and economic system, basic (but non-Marxist) communism. Among the imperatives under the coming system of social energetics are to "Increase Conversion!", "Normalise Consumption!", and "Socialise Creation!" (pp. 373–435). Best remembered today for science fiction novels like *The Time Machine* (1895), *The Invisible Man* (1897), and *The War of the Worlds* (1898), Herbert George Wells (1866–1946) was an advocate of national planning as early as 1912 and, in such works as *Anticipations* (1902) and *The Shape of Things to Come* (1933), an advocate and practitioner of the scientific prediction of the future. Wells was also a frequent critic of the social and class structures of Victorian and Edwardian England and known in the inter-war period for his writings on social reform; for example, some of the ideas from his 1939 newspaper piece "Declaration of the Rights of Man" were incorporated into the Universal Declaration of Human Rights adopted by the U.N. General Assembly in December 1948. In addition to his scientific work the English physiologist Lancelot Hogben (1895–1975) was also the author of popular books on science like *Science for the Citizen: A Self-Educator Based on the Social Background of Scientific Discovery* (1938). Hogben taught mainly at Birmingham but held a chair in social biology at the LSE in the early 1930s.—Ed.]

able to adopt if the supply of capital were unlimited, or the rate of interest were zero, which would indeed be a position in which we would aim at the highest possible rate of transformation of current input into current output. But to treat this as an immediate goal is to forget that such a state can be reached only by diverting for a long time resources which are wanted to serve current needs to the production of equipment. In other words, the engineer's ideal is based on the disregard of the most fundamental economic fact which determines our position here and now, the scarcity of capital.

The rate of interest is, of course, only one, though the least understood and therefore the most disliked, of those prices which act as impersonal guides to which the engineer must submit if his plans are to fit into the pattern of activity of society as a whole, and against the restraint of which he chafes because they represent forces whose *rationale* he does not understand. It is one of those symbols in which the whole complex of human knowledge and wants is automatically (though by no means faultlessly) recorded, and to which the individual must pay attention if he wants to keep in step with the rest of the system. If, instead of using this information in the abridged form in which it is conveyed to him through the price system, he were to try in every instance to go back to the objective facts and take them consciously into consideration, this would be to dispense with the method which makes it possible for him to confine himself to the immediate circumstances and to substitute for it a method which requires that all this knowledge be collected in one centre and explicitly and consciously embodied in a unitary plan. The application of engineering technique to the whole of society requires indeed that the director possess the same complete knowledge of the whole society that the engineer possesses of his limited world. Central economic planning is nothing but such an application of engineering principles to the whole of society based on the assumption that such a complete concentration of all relevant knowledge is possible.[8]

Before we proceed to consider the significance of this conception of a rational organisation of society, it will be useful to supplement the sketch of the typical outlook of the engineer by an even briefer sketch of the functions of the merchant or trader. This will not only further elucidate the nature of the problem of the utilisation of knowledge dispersed among many people, but also help to explain the dislike which not only the engineer but our whole generation shows for all commercial activities, and the general preference that is

---

[8] That this is fully recognised by its advocates is shown by the popularity among all socialists from Saint-Simon to Marx and Lenin, of the phrase that the whole of society should be run in precisely the same manner as a single factory is now being run. Cf. Vladimir Ilyich Lenin, *State and Revolution*, Little Lenin Library (New York: International Publishers, 1933), vol. 14, p. 78: "The whole of society will have become a single office and a single factory with equality of work and equality of pay"; and for Saint-Simon and Marx, p. 192, note 23, herein.

now accorded to 'production' as compared with that accorded to activities which, somewhat misleadingly, are referred to as 'distribution'.

Compared with the work of the engineer that of the merchant is in a sense much more 'social', that is, interwoven with the free activities of other people. He contributes a step towards the achievement now of one end, now of another, and hardly ever is concerned with the complete process that serves a final need. What concerns him is not the achievement of a particular final result of the complete process in which he takes part, but the best use of the particular means of which he knows. His special knowledge is almost entirely knowledge of particular circumstances of time or place, or, perhaps, a technique of ascertaining those circumstances in a given field. But though this knowledge is not of a kind which can be formulated in generic propositions, or acquired once and for all, and though in an age of Science it is for that reason regarded as knowledge of an inferior kind, it is for all practical purposes no less important than scientific knowledge. And while it is perhaps conceivable that all theoretical knowledge might be combined in the heads of a few experts and thus made available to a single central authority, it is this knowledge of the particular, of the fleeting circumstances of the moment and of local conditions, which will never exist otherwise than dispersed among many people. The knowledge of when a particular material or machine can be used most effectively or where each can be obtained most quickly or cheaply is quite as important for the solution of a particular task as the knowledge of what is the best material or machine for the purpose. The former kind of knowledge has little to do with the permanent properties of classes of things which the engineer studies, but is knowledge of a particular human situation. And it is as the person whose task is to take account of these facts that the merchant will constantly come into conflict with the ideals of the engineer, with whose plans he interferes and whose dislike he thereby contracts.[9]

The problem of securing an efficient use of our resources is thus very largely one of how that knowledge of the particular circumstances of the moment can be most effectively utilised; and the task which faces the designer of a rational order of society is to find a method whereby this widely dispersed knowledge may best be drawn upon. It is begging the question to describe this task, as is usually done, as one of effectively using the 'available' resources to satisfy 'existing' needs. Neither the 'available' resources nor the 'existing' needs are objective facts in the sense of those with which the engineer deals in his limited field: they can never be directly known in all relevant detail to

---

[9] On these problems, see my essay "The Use of Knowledge in Society", *American Economic Review*, vol. 35, September 1945, reprinted in *Individualism and Economic Order*, pp. 77–91. [This article will be reprinted in a forthcoming volume of *The Collected Works of F. A. Hayek.*—Ed.]

a single planning body. Resources and needs exist for practical purposes only through somebody knowing about them, and there will always be infinitely more known to all the people together than can be known to the most competent authority.[10] A successful solution can therefore not be based on the authority dealing directly with the objective facts, but must be based on a method of utilising the knowledge dispersed among all members of society, knowledge of which in any particular instance the central authority will usually know neither who possesses it nor whether it exists at all. It can therefore not be utilised by consciously integrating it into a coherent whole, but only through some mechanism which will delegate the particular decisions to those who possess it, and for that purpose supply them with such information about the general situation as will enable them to make the best use of the particular circumstances of which only they know.

This is precisely the function which the various 'markets' perform. Though every party in them will know only a small sector of all the possible sources of supply, or of the uses, of a commodity, yet, directly or indirectly, the parties are so interconnected that the prices register the relevant net results of all changes affecting demand or supply.[11] It is as such an instrument for communicating to all those interested in a particular commodity the relevant information in an abridged and condensed form that markets and prices must be seen if we are to understand their function. They help to utilise the knowledge of many people without the need of first collecting it in a single body, and thereby make possible that combination of decentralisation of decisions and mutual adjustment of these decisions which we find in a competitive system.

In aiming at a result which must be based not on a single body of integrated knowledge or of connected reasoning which the designer possesses, but on the separate knowledge of many people, the task of social organisation differs fundamentally from that of organising given material resources. The fact that no single mind can know more than a fraction of what is known to all individual minds sets limits to the extent to which conscious direction can improve upon the results of unconscious social processes. Man has not deliberately designed this process and has begun to understand it only long after it had grown up. But that something which not only does not rely on deliberate control for its working, but has not even been deliberately designed, should bring about desirable results, which we might not be able to bring about otherwise, is a conclusion the natural scientist seems to find difficult to accept.

[10] It is important to remember in this connection that the statistical aggregates, upon which, it is often suggested, the central authority could rely in its decisions, are always arrived at by a deliberate disregard of the peculiar circumstances of time and place.

[11] See in this connection the suggestive discussion of the problem in Karl Friedrich Mayer [Maier], *Goldwanderungen* (Jena: G. Fischer, 1935), pp. 66–68, and also my article "Economics and Knowledge".

It is because the moral sciences tend to show us such limits to our conscious control, while the progress of the natural sciences constantly extends the range of conscious control, that the natural scientist finds himself so frequently in revolt against the teaching of the moral sciences. Economics, in particular, after being condemned for employing methods different from those of the natural scientist, stands doubly condemned because it claims to show limits to the technique by which the natural scientists continuously extend our conquest and mastery of nature.

It is this conflict with a strong human instinct, greatly strengthened in the person of the scientist and engineer, that makes the teaching of the moral sciences so very unwelcome. As Bertrand Russell has well described the position, "The pleasure of planned construction is one of the most powerful motives in men who combine intelligence with energy; whatever can be constructed according to a plan, such man will endeavour to construct . . . the desire to create is not in itself idealistic since it is a form of the love of power, and while the power to create exists there will be men desirous of using this power even if unaided nature would produce a better result than any that can be brought about by deliberate intention".[12] This statement occurs, however, at the beginning of a chapter, significantly headed "Artificially Created Societies", in which Russell himself seems to support these tendencies by arguing that "no society can be regarded as fully scientific unless it has been created deliberately with a certain structure in order to fulfill certain purposes".[13] As this statement will be understood by most readers, it expresses concisely that scientistic philosophy which through its popularisers has done more to create the present trend towards socialism than all the conflicts between economic interests which, though they raise a problem, do not necessarily indicate a particular solution. Of the majority of the intellectual leaders of the socialist movement, at least, it is probably true to say that they are socialists because socialism appears to them, as A. Bebel, the leader of the German social democratic movement, defined it sixty years ago, as "science applied in clear awareness and with full insight to all fields of human activity".[14] The proof that the

---

[12] Bertrand Russell, *The Scientific Outlook* (London: G. Allen and Unwin, 1931), p. 211 [pp. 211–12].

[13] Ibid, p. 209. The passage quoted could be interpreted in an unobjectionable sense if the phrase 'certain purposes' is taken to mean not particular pre-determined results but the capacity to provide what the individuals at any time wish—that is, if what is planned is machinery which can serve many ends and need not in turn be 'consciously' directed towards a particular end.

[14] August Bebel, *Die Frau und der Sozialismus*, 13th ed. (Stuttgart: J. H. W. Dietz, 1892), p. 376: "Der Sozialismus ist die mit klarem Bewußtsein und mit voller Erkenntnis auf alle Gebiete menschlicher Tätigkeit angewandte Wissenschaft". See also Enrico Ferri, *Socialism and Positive Science: Darwin, Spencer, Marx*, translated by Edith C. Harvey, 2nd ed. (London: Independent Labour Party, 1905). The first clearly to see this connection seems to have been Marin Ferraz, *Etude sur la philosophie en France au XIXe siècle: Le socialisme, le naturalisme et le positivisme* (Paris: Didier,

program of socialism actually derives from this kind of scientistic philosophy must be reserved for the detailed historical studies. At present our concern is mainly to show to what extent sheer intellectual error in this field may profoundly affect all prospects of humanity.

What the people who are so unwilling to renounce any of the powers of conscious control seem to be unable to comprehend is that this renunciation of conscious power, power which must always be power by men over other men, is for society as a whole only an apparent resignation, a self-denial individuals are called upon to exercise in order to increase the powers of the race, to release the knowledge and energies of the countless individuals that could never be utilised in a society consciously directed from the top. The great misfortune of our generation is that the direction which by the amazing progress of the natural sciences has been given to its interests is not one which assists us in comprehending the larger process of which as individuals we form merely a part or in appreciating how we constantly contribute to a common effort without either directing it or submitting to orders of others. To see this requires a kind of intellectual effort different in character from that necessary for the control of material things, an effort in which the traditional education in the 'humanities' gave at least some practice, but for which the now pre-dominant types of education seem less and less to prepare. The more our technical civilisation advances and the more, therefore, the study of things as distinct from the study of men and their ideas qualifies for the more important and influential positions, the more significant becomes the gulf that separates two different types of mind: the one represented by the man whose supreme ambition is to turn the world round him into an enormous machine, every part of which, on his pressing a button, moves according to his design; and the other represented by the man whose main interest is the growth of the human mind in all its aspects, who in the study of history or literature, the arts or the law, has learned to see the individual as part of a process in which his contribution is not directed but spontaneous, and where he assists in the creation of something greater than he or any other single mind can ever plan for. It is this awareness of being part of a social process, and of the manner in which individual efforts interact, which the education solely in the Sciences or in technology seems so lamentably to fail to convey. It is not surprising that many of the more active minds among those so trained sooner or later react violently against the deficiencies of their education and develop a passion for imposing on society the order which they are unable to detect by the means with which they are familiar.

1877). [The socialist theoretician and politician Ferdinand August Bebel (1840–1913) was one of the founders of the German Social Democratic Party. For an English translation of his book, see *Women under Socialism*, translated by Daniel De Leon (New York: New York Labor News, 1904; reprinted, New York: Schocken, 1971).—Ed.]

In conclusion it is, perhaps, desirable to remind the reader once more that all we have said here is directed solely against a misuse of Science, not against the scientist in the special field where he is competent, but against the application of his mental habits in fields where he is not competent. There is no conflict between our conclusions and those of legitimate science. The main lesson at which we have arrived is indeed the same as that which one of the acutest students of scientific method has drawn from a survey of all fields of knowledge: it is that "the great lesson of humility which science teaches us, that we can never be omnipotent or omniscient, is the same as the lesson of all great religions: man is not and never will be the god before whom he must bow down".[15]

[15] Morris Cohen, *Reason and Nature*, p. 449. It is significant that one of the leading members of the movement with which we are concerned, the German philosopher Ludwig Feuerbach, explicitly chose the opposite principle, *homo homini Deus*, as his guiding maxim. [The phrase from Feuerbach may be translated, "Man's God is man". In his 1841 book *The Essence of Christianity*, the German philosopher Ludwig Feuerbach (1804–72) argued that men create the idea of God by projecting their highest aspirations for mankind onto an imaginary being. He concluded that reverence for God should be transferred to reverence for, and concern for the well-being of, humanity. Feuerbach turned on its head Hegel's idealist argument that all history was the product of God contemplating himself. He is often viewed as providing a 'bridge' from Hegel's idealism to Marx's materialism.—Ed.]

PART II

THE COUNTER-REVOLUTION OF SCIENCE

The age preferred the reign of intellect to the reign of liberty.

—Lord Acton

[An initial version of "The Counter-Revolution of Science" was published in *Economica*, n.s., vol. 8, 1941, pp. 9–39, 119–50, and 281–320. A slightly revised version, which serves as the basis of this edition, was published in F. A. Hayek, *The Counter-Revolution of Science: Studies on the Abuse of Reason* (Glencoe, IL: Free Press, 1952; reprinted, Indianapolis, IN: Liberty Fund, 1979), pp. 183–363. Most of the differences between the 1941 and 1952 versions involve either Hayek changing phrasing to make a passage more clear, or the addition of new citations of pieces that appeared between 1941 and 1952. Any significant differences between the two versions are noted.—Ed.]
[Lord Acton, "Sir Erskine May's *Democracy in Europe*", in *History of Freedom and Other Essays*, p. 85. See *Essays in the History of Liberty*, p. 73.—Ed.]

ELEVEN

THE SOURCE OF THE SCIENTISTIC
HUBRIS: *L'ECOLE POLYTECHNIQUE*

I

Never will man penetrate deeper into error than when he is continuing on a road which has led him to great success. And never can pride in the achievements of the natural sciences and confidence in the omnipotence of their methods have been more justified than at the turn of the eighteenth and nineteenth centuries, and nowhere more so than at Paris, where almost all the great scientists of the age congregated. If it is true, therefore, that the new attitude of man towards social affairs in the nineteenth century was due to the new mental habits acquired in the intellectual and material conquest of nature, we should expect it to appear where modern science celebrated its greatest triumphs. In this we shall not be disappointed. Both the two great intellectual forces which in the course of the nineteenth century transformed social thought—modern socialism and that species of modern positivism, which we prefer to call scientism—spring directly from this body of professional scientists and engineers which grew up in Paris, and more particularly from the new institution which embodied the new spirit as no other, the *Ecole polytechnique*.

It is well known that the French Enlightenment was characterised by a general enthusiasm for the natural sciences as never was known before. Voltaire is the father of that cult of Newton which later was to be carried to ridiculous heights by Saint-Simon.[1] And the new passion soon began to bear great fruits. At first the interest concentrated on the subjects connected with Newton's great name. In Clairault and d'Alembert, with Euler, the greatest mathematicians of the period, Newton soon found worthy successors who in turn

---

[1] [Voltaire was in England at the time of Newton's death and was much impressed by his burial in Westminster Abbey, remarking that the English treated their scientists like kings. Voltaire's lifelong friend and mistress Emilie, Marquise du Châtelet-Laumont, translated Newton's *Principia Mathematica* into French, and Voltaire helped to popularise Newton's scientific thought with the publication in 1738 of his *Eléments de la philosophie de Newton.*—Ed.]

were followed by Lagrange and Laplace, no less giants.[2] And with Lavoisier, not only the founder of modern chemistry but also a great physiologist, and, to a lesser degree, with Buffon in biological science, France began to take the lead in all important fields of natural knowledge.[3]

The great *Encyclopédie* was a gigantic attempt to unify and popularise the achievements of the new science, and d'Alembert's "Discours préliminaire" (1754) to the great work, in which he attempted to trace the rise, progress, and affinities of the various sciences, may be regarded as the Introduction not only to the work but to a whole period. This great mathematician and physicist did much to prepare the way for the revolution in mechanics by which towards the end of the century his pupil Lagrange finally freed it from all metaphysical concepts and restated the whole subject without any reference to ultimate causes or hidden forces, merely describing the laws by which the effects were connected.[4] No other single step in any science expresses more clearly the ten-

---

[2] [Alexis-Claude Clairault (1713–65) was noted for his work in mathematics, mechanics, and celestial mechanics; his essay *Théorie de la lune* (1752) built directly on Newton's work. The prolific Swiss mathematician and physicist Leonhard Euler (1707–83) is remembered for his contributions to number theory, differential and integral calculus, and other areas, as well as to astronomy and hydromechanics. In his book *Mechanica* (1736–37) he presented a mathematical analysis of Newtonian dynamics. Joseph Louis Lagrange (1736–1813), an Italian, and Pierre Simon, Marquis de Laplace (1749–1827), a Frenchman, also contributed to mathematics, physics, and celestial mechanics. For more on the rôle of French scientists in furthering the development of the mathematical foundations of the Newtonian system, see Keith M. Baker, *Condorcet: From Natural Philosophy to Social Mathematics* (Chicago: University of Chicago Press, 1975), pp. 7–9.—Ed.]

[3] [The French chemist Antoine-Laurent Lavoisier (1743–94) composed the first modern textbook in chemistry; in addition to identifying a number of basic elements, he also challenged the phlogiston theory and stated the law of the conservation of matter. He also wrote on economics, and his political activities cost him his life in the French revolution. George-Louis Leclerc, Comte de Buffon (1707–88) was author of *Histoire naturelle* (1747–88), a massive encyclopedia of the natural world. He is also remembered for challenging church doctrine by insisting that geological time far surpassed that posited in the Bible.—Ed.]

[4] D'Alembert was fully aware of the significance of the tendency he was supporting and anticipated later positivism to the extent of expressly condemning everything that did not aim at the development of *positive* truths and even suggesting that "all occupations with purely speculative subjects should be excluded from a healthy state as profitless pursuits". Yet he did not include in this the moral sciences and even, with his master Locke, regarded them as *a priori* sciences comparable with mathematics and of equal certainty with it. On all this, see Georg Misch, "Zur Entstehung des französischen Positivismus", *Archiv für Philosophie*, part 1, *Archiv für Geschichte der Philosophie*, vol. 14, 1901, pp. 1–40 and 156–209, esp. pp. 7, 31, and 158; Max Schinz, *Die Anfänge des französischen Positivismus*, vol. 1 of *Geschichte der französischen Philosophie seit der Revolution* (Strassburg: K. J. Trübner, 1914), pp. 58, 67–69, 71, 96, and 149; and Henri Gouhier, *La jeunesse d'Auguste Comte et la formation du positivisme*, vol. 2, *Saint-Simon jusqu'à la restauration* (Paris: Librarie Philosophique J. Vrin, 1936), introduction.

dency of the scientific movement of the age or had greater influence or symbolic significance.[5]

Yet while this step was still gradually preparing in the field where it was to take its most conspicuous form, the general tendency which it expressed was already recognised and described by d'Alembert's contemporary Turgot. In the amazing and masterly discourses which as a young man of twenty-three he delivered at the opening and the closing of the session of the Sorbonne in 1750, and in the sketch of a *Discourse on Universal History* of the same period, he outlined how the advance of our knowledge of nature was accompanied throughout by a gradual emancipation from those anthropomorphic concepts which first led man to interpret natural phenomena after his own image as animated by a mind like his own.[6] This idea, which was later to become the leading theme of positivism and was ultimately misapplied to the science of man himself, was soon afterward widely popularised by Président C. de Brosses under the name of fetishism,[7] the name under which it remained known till it was much later replaced by the expressions 'anthropomorphism' and 'animism'. But Turgot went even further and, completely anticipating Comte on this point, described how this process of emancipation passed through three stages where, after supposing that natural phenomena were produced by intelligent beings, invisible but resembling ourselves, they began to be explained by abstract expressions such as essences and faculties, till at last "by observing reciprocal mechanical action of bodies hypotheses were formed which could be developed by mathematics and verified by experience".[8]

It has often been pointed out[9] that most of the leading ideas of French positivism had already been formulated by d'Alembert and Turgot and their friends and pupils Lagrange and Condorcet. For most of what is valid and

[5] Cf. Ernst Mach, *Die Mechanik in ihrer Entwicklung: Historisch-kritisch Dargestellt*, 3rd ed. (Leipzig: F. A. Brockhaus, 1897), p. 449.

[6] [For more on Turgot, see chapter 1, note 1. A translation of his essay on universal history may be found in *Turgot on Progress, Sociology, and Economics*, ed. and translated by Ronald Meek (Cambridge: Cambridge University Press, 1973), pp. 61–118. In his editor's introduction Meek provides a useful discussion of the essay, as well as of Turgot's Sorbonne period.—Ed.].

[7] In his famous work *Du culte des dieux fétiches* (Paris: n.p., 1760). [Charles de Brosses (1709–77), known as Président de Brosses, is remembered for his writings on geography, the Roman republic, the origins of language, and primitive culture. In its original meaning, a fetish is an object of nature thought by members of primitive cultures to be inhabited by a spirit or to possess preternatural powers.—Ed.]

[8] *Œuvres de Turgot*, ed. Eugène Daire (Paris: Guillaumin, 1844), vol. 2, p. 656. Compare also ibid., p. 601. [Hayek's first citation is to a passage in Turgot's *Discours sur l'histoire universelle*, and the second to a section of his 1750 address "Discours en Sorbonne".—Ed]

[9] See particularly the detailed analysis by Misch and the books by Schinz and Gouhier cited in note 4 of this chapter, and also Michel Uta, *La théorie du savoir dans la philosophie d'Auguste Comte* (Paris: Alcan, 1928).

valuable in that doctrine this is unquestionably true, although their positivism differed from that of Hume by a strong tinge of French rationalism. And, as there will be no opportunity to go into this aspect more fully, it should perhaps be specially stressed at this stage that throughout the development of French positivism this rationalist element, probably due to the influence of Descartes, continued to play an important rôle.[10]

[10] To avoid giving a wrong impression it should perhaps also be stressed at this point that the liberalism of the French Revolution was of course based not yet on the understanding of the market mechanism provided by Adam Smith and the utilitarians, but on the law of nature and the rationalistic-pragmatic interpretation of social phenomena which is essentially pre-Smithian and of which Rousseau's social contract is the prototype. One might indeed trace much of the contrast, which with Saint-Simon and Comte became an open opposition to classical econom- ics, back to the differences which existed, say, between Montesquieu and Hume, Quesnay and Smith, or Condorcet and Bentham. Those French economists who like Condillac and J. B. Say followed essentially the same trend as Smith never had an influence on French political thought comparable to that of Smith in England. The result of this was that the transition from the older rationalist views of society, which regarded it as a conscious creation of man, to the newer view which wanted to re-create it on scientific principles, took place in France without passing through a stage in which the working of the spontaneous forces of society was generally under- stood. The revolutionary cult of Reason was symptomatic of the general acceptance of the pragmatic conception of social institutions—the very opposite of the view of Smith. And in a sense it would be as true to say that it was the same veneration of Reason as the universal cre- ator which led to the triumphs of science that led to the new attitude to social problems as it is to say that it was the influence of the new habits of thought created by the triumphs of science and technology. If socialism is not a direct child of the French Revolution, it springs at least from that rationalism which distinguished most of the French political thinkers of the period from the contemporary English liberalism of Hume and Smith and (to a lesser degree) Bentham and the philosophical radicals. On all this, see now the first essay in my *Individualism and Economic Order* (Chicago: University Press, 1948).

[One can see in the text and in this long note Hayek's first articulation of the differences between French and British enlightenment thinkers that he would explore in more detail in "Individualism: True and False", a paper published in 1945, that is, a few years after "Counter- Revolution", and which appeared as the first essay of his 1948 collection *Individualism and Eco- nomic Order*. Hayek added the reference to his 1945 essay to the 1952 reprinting of "Counter- Revolution"; the essay now appears as the introduction to the present volume. Most of the political thinkers mentioned in this note are discussed there, with three exceptions. The French philosopher and economist Etienne Bonnet de Condillac, l'Abbé de Mureau (1714–80) argued that freedom of trade stimulates production and increases national wealth in his *Le Commerce et le gouvernement* (1776), where he also outlined a theory of value based on the scarcity of goods rela- tive to subjective needs. The French economist Jean-Baptiste Say (1767–1832), author of *Traité d'économie politique*, published in five editions between 1803 and 1826, is often identified as the great French expositor of Adam Smith. Say disagreed, however, with Smith's cost of production theory of value, arguing that utility was the ultimate foundation, and he gave more of a rôle to the 'wise legislator' than did Smith. For more on this, as well as on Say's activities in the repub- lican movement and his relations with proponents of *idéologie*, a movement discussed by Hayek later in this chapter, see Evelyn L. Forget, *The Social Economics of Jean-Baptiste Say: Markets and Vir- tue* (London: Routledge, 1999). Finally, the Marquis de Condorcet, first noted in chapter 6, note 10, and discussed by Hayek in the next few paragraphs, was convinced that the social sciences

It must be pointed out, however, that these great French thinkers of the eighteenth century showed scarcely any trace yet of that illegitimate extension to the phenomena of society of scientistic methods of thought which later became so characteristic of that school—excepting perhaps certain ideas of Turgot about the philosophy of history and still more so some of Condorcet's last suggestions. But none of them had any doubt about the legitimacy of the abstract and theoretical method in the study of social phenomena, and they were all staunch individualists. It is particularly interesting to observe that Turgot, and the same is true of David Hume, was at the same time one of the founders of positivism and of abstract economic theory, against which positivism was later to be employed. But in some respects most of these men unwittingly started trains of thought which produced views on social matters very different from their own.

This is particularly true of Condorcet. A mathematician like d'Alembert and Lagrange, he definitely turned to the theory as well as to the practice of politics. And although to the last he understood that "meditation alone may lead us to general truths in the science of man",[11] he was not merely anxious to supplement this by extensive observation but occasionally expressed himself as if the method of the natural sciences were the only legitimate one in the treatment of the problems of society. It was particularly his desire to apply his beloved mathematics, especially the newly developed calculus of probability, to his second sphere of interest, which led him to stress more and more the study of those social phenomena which would be objectively observed and measured.[12] As early as 1783, in the oration at his reception into the academy, he gave expression to what was to become a favourite idea of positivist sociology, that of an observer to whom physical and social phenomena would appear in the same light, because, "a stranger to our race, he would study human society as we study those of the beavers and bees".[13] And although

---

were amenable to mathematical analysis. In his last work, the *Esquisse* (*Sketch of an Historical Picture of the Progress of the Human Mind*), he argued that human history follows general laws, that its future could therefore be predicted, and that our history has been one of steady progress and improvement. Condorcet appeared to believe that there were no ultimate obstacles to reaching perfection; Thomas Robert Malthus's pessimistic *An Essay on the Principle of Population* (1798) was written in part as a response to Condorcet's optimistic vision.—Ed.]

[11] See Marquis de Condorcet, *Esquisse d'un tableau historique des progrès de l'esprit humain* [1795], ed. Oliver H. Prior (Paris: Boivin et cie, 1933), p. 11. [Sans doute, la méditation seule peut, par d'heureuses combinaisons, nous conduire aux vérités générales de la science de l'homme. In his translation, Hayek left out the phrase, "by fortunate combinations".—Ed.]

[12] Cf. his *Tableau général de la science qui a pour objet l'application du calcul aux sciences politiques et morales*, in François Arago and Arthur-Condorcet O'Connor, eds. *Œuvres de Condorcet* (Paris: Firmin Didot frères, 1847–49), vol. 1, pp. 539–73.

[13] Ibid., p. 392. [On its title page it states that the *discours* was delivered on 21 February 1782, not 1783.—Ed.]

he admits that this is an unattainable ideal because "the observer is himself a part of human society", he repeatedly exhorts the scholars "to introduce into the moral sciences the philosophy and the method of the natural sciences".[14]

The most seminal of his suggestions, however, occurs in his *Sketch of a Historical Picture of the Progress of the Human Mind*, the famous testament of the eighteenth century, as it has been called, in which the unbounded optimism of the age found its last and greatest expression. Tracing human progress in a great outline through all history, he conceives of a science which might foresee the future progress of the human race, accelerate and direct it.[15] But to establish laws which will enable us to predict the future, history must cease to be a history of individuals and must become a history of the masses, must at the same time cease to be a record of individual facts but must become based on systematic observation.[16] Why should the attempt to base on the results of the history of the human race a picture of its future destiny be regarded as chimerical? "The only foundation for the knowledge of the natural sciences is the idea that the general laws, known or unknown, which regulate the phenomena of the universe, are necessary and constant; and why should that principle be less true for the intellectual and moral faculties of man than for the other actions of nature?"[17] The idea of natural laws of historical development and the collectivist view of history were born, not merely as bold suggestions, it is true, but to remain with us in a continuous tradition to the present day.[18]

---

[14] Marquis de Condorcet, *Rapport et projet de décret sur l'organization générale de l'instruction publique*, ed. Gabriel Compayré [1792] (Paris: Hachette, 1883), p. 120.

[15] Condorcet, *Esquisse*, p. 11.

[16] Ibid., p. 200.

[17] Ibid., p. 203. The famous passage in which this sentence occurs figures, characteristically, as the motto of book 6, "On the Logic of the Moral Sciences", of J. S. Mill's *Logic*. [Le seul fondement de croyance dans les sciences naturelles, est cette idée, que les lois générales, connues ou ignorées, qui règlent les phénomènes de l'univers, sont nécessaires et constantes; et par quelle raison ce principe serait-il moins vrai pour le développement des facultés intellectuelles et morales de l'homme, que pour les autres opérations de la nature? See Mill, *System of Logic*, p. 832.—Ed.]

[18] It is worthy of mention that the man who was so largely responsible for the creation of what in the late nineteenth century came to be regarded as 'historical sense', that is, of the *Entwicklungsgedanke* with all its metaphysical associations, was the same man who was capable of celebrating in a discourse the deliberate destruction of papers relating to the history of the noble families of France. "Today Reason burns the innumerable volumes which attest the vanity of a caste. Other vestiges remain in public and private libraries. They must be involved in a common destruction". [Condorcet made the statement in a speech before the Legislative Assembly on June 19, 1792. The speech appeared the next day in the journal *Gazette nationale, ou le Moniteur universel*. See *Réimpression de l'ancien Moniteur: Seule histoire authentique et inaltérée de la Révolution française depuis la réunion des Etats-Généraux jusqu'au Consulat (mai 1789–novembre 1799)* (Paris: Plon, 1862), vol. 12, p. 702.—Ed.]

II

Condorcet himself became a victim of the Revolution. But his work guided to a large extent that same Revolution, particularly its educational reforms, and it was only as a result of these that towards the beginning of the new century the great institutionalised and centralised organisation of science arose which created one of the most glorious periods of scientific advance, became not only the birthplace of that scientism which is more particularly our concern, but was probably also largely responsible for the relative decline of the position of French science in the course of the century from indubitably the first place in the world to one not only behind Germany but also behind other nations. As is so often the case with similar movements, it was only on the second or third generation that the mischief was done by the pupils of the great men who exaggerated the ideas of their masters and misapplied them beyond their proper limits.

In three respects the direct consequences of the Revolution are of special interest to us. In the first place, the very collapse of the existing institutions called for immediate application of all the knowledge which appeared as the concrete manifestation of that Reason which was the goddess of the Revolution. As one of the new scientific journals which sprang up at the end of the Terror expressed it: "The Revolution has razed everything to the ground. Government, morals, habits, everything has to be rebuilt. What a magnificent site for the architects! What a grand opportunity of making use of all the fine and excellent ideas that had remained speculative, of employing so many materials that could not be used before, of rejecting so many others that had been obstructions for centuries and which one had been forced to use".[19]

The second consequence of the Revolution which we must briefly consider is the complete destruction of the old and the creation of an entirely new educational system which had profound effects on the outlook and general views of the whole next generation. The third is more particularly the foundation of the *Ecole polytechnique*.

The Revolution had swept away the old system of colleges and universities, which system was based largely on classical education, and after some short-lived experiments the Revolution replaced them in 1795 with the new *écoles centrales*, which became the sole centres of secondary education.[20] In conformity with the ruling spirit and by an over-violent reaction against the older schools, the teaching in the new institutions was for some years confined almost exclu-

---

[19] *Décade philosophique*, 1794, vol. 1, in Gouhier, *La jeunesse d'Auguste Comte*, vol. 2, p. 31.

[20] See Ernest Allain, *L'œuvre scolaire de la révolution, 1789–1802: Etudes critiques et documents inédits* (Paris: Firmin-Didot, 1891); Célestin Hippeau, *L'instruction publique en France pendant la révolution* (Paris: Didier, 1883); and François Picavet, *Les idéologues, essai sur l'histoire des idées et des théories scientifiques, philosophiques, religieuses, etc., en France depuis 1789* (Paris: F. Alcan, 1891), pp. 56–61.

sively to the scientific subjects. Not only the ancient languages were reduced to a minimum and in practice almost entirely neglected, even the instruction in literature, grammar, and history was very inferior, and moral and religious instruction, of course, completely absent.[21] Although after some years a new reform endeavoured to make good some of the gravest deficiencies,[22] the interruption for a series of years of the instruction in those subjects was sufficient to change the whole intellectual atmosphere. Saint-Simon described this change in 1812 or 1813: "Such is the difference in this respect between the state of . . . even thirty years ago and that of today that while in those not distant days, if one wanted to know whether a person had received a distinguished education, one asked: 'Does he know his Greek and Latin authors well?' Today one asks: 'Is he good at mathematics? Is he familiar with the achievements of physics, of chemistry, of natural history, in short, of the positive sciences and those of observation?'"[23]

Thus a whole generation grew up to whom that great storehouse of social wisdom, the only form indeed in which an understanding of the social processes achieved by the greatest minds is transmitted, the great literature of all ages, was a closed book. For the first time in history that new type appeared which as the product of the German *Realschule* and of similar institutions was to become so important and influential in the later nineteenth and the twentieth century: the technical specialist who was regarded as educated because he had passed through difficult schools but who had little or no knowledge of society, its life, growth, problems, and values, which only the study of history, literature, and languages can give.

III

Not only in secondary education but still more so in higher education the Revolutionary Convention had created a new type of institution which was to become permanently established and a model imitated by the whole world: the *Ecole polytechnique*. The wars of the Revolution and the help which some of the scientists had been able to render in the production of essential supplies[24] had led to a new appreciation of the need of trained engineers, in the first instance for military purposes. But industrial advance also created a new interest in machines. Scientific and technological progress created a widespread enthusi-

---

[21] See Allain, *L'œuvre scolaire de la révolution*, pp. 117–20.

[22] After 1803 the ancient languages were at least partly restored in Napoleon's *lycées*.

[23] Henri de Saint-Simon, "Mémoire sur la science de l'homme" [1813], in *Œuvres de Saint-Simon et d'Enfantin* (Paris: E. Dentu, 1877–78), vol. 40, p. 16.

[24] Particularly of saltpetre for the production of gunpowder.

asm for technological studies, which expressed itself in the foundation of such societies as the *Association philotechnique* and the *Société polytechnique*.[25] Higher technical education had till then been confined to specialised schools such as the *Ecole des Ponts et Chaussés* and the various military schools. It was at one of the latter that Gaspard Monge,[26] the founder of descriptive geometry, minister of marine during the Revolution, and later friend of Napoleon, taught. He sponsored the idea of a single great school in which all classes of engineers should receive their training in the subjects they had in common.[27] He communicated that idea to Lazare Carnot, the 'organiser of victory', his old pupil and himself no mean physicist and engineer.[28] These two men impressed their stamp on the new institution which was created in 1794. The new *Ecole polytechnique* was (against the advice of Laplace)[29] to be devoted mainly to the applied sciences—in contrast to the *Ecole normale*, created at the same time and devoted to theory—and remained so during the first ten or twenty years of its existence. The whole teaching centred, to a much higher degree than is still true of similar institutions, around Monge's subject, descriptive geometry, or the art of blueprint making, as we may call it to show its special significance

[25] See Antoine Pressard, *Histoire de l'association philotechnique* (Paris: Hachette, 1889 [1898]), and Gouhier, *La jeunesse d'Auguste Comte*, vol. 2, p. 54.

[26] [French mathematician Gaspard Monge (1746–1818) served as the Minister of the Navy from 1792–93.—Ed.]

[27] On the foundation and history of the *Ecole polytechnique*, see Ambroise Fourcy, *Histoire de l'Ecole polytechnique* (Paris: Chez l'auteur, 1828); Gaston Pinet, *Histoire de l'Ecole polytechnique* (Paris: Baudry et cie, 1887); Carl Gustav Jakob Jacobi, "Über die Pariser polytechnische Schule (Ein Vortrag, gehalten am 22. Mai 1835 in einer öffentlichen Sitzung der physikalisch-ökonomischen Gesellschaft zu Königsberg)", in *Gesammelte Werke* (Berlin: G. Reimer, 1891), vol. 6 [7], p. 355 [pp. 355–70]; Franz Schnabel, *Die Anfänge des technischen Hochschulwesens* (Stuttgart: C. F. Müller, 1925); and Felix Klein, *Vorlesungen über die Entwicklung der Mathematik im 19 Jahrhundert* (Berlin: J. Springer, 1926), vol. 1, pp. 63–89.

[28] Carnot [Lazare-Nicolas-Marguérite Carnot (1753–1823)] had in 1783 published *Essays on Machines in General* in the second edition of *Principes fondamentaux de l'équilibre du mouvement* (Paris: Chez Deterville, 1803) in which he not only expounded Lagrange's new view of mechanics but developed the idea of the 'ideal machine' which takes nothing away from the force that puts it into motion. His work did much to prepare the way for that of his son, Sadi Carnot [(1796–1832)], 'the founder of the science of energy'. His younger son, Hippolyte [(1801–88)], was the leading member of the Saint-Simonian group and actual writer of the *Doctrine de Saint-Simon*, which we shall meet later. Lazare Carnot, the father, had been a lifelong admirer and protector of Saint-Simon himself. As Arago reports of Lazare Carnot, he "always discoursed with (Arago) on the political organisation of society precisely in the same manner as he speaks in his work of a machine". See François Arago, *Biographies of Distinguished Scientific Men*, translated by W. H. Smyth, Baden Powell, and others (London: Longman, Brown, Green, Longmans, and Roberts, 1857), vol. 2, pp. 300–4, and Eugen Dühring, *Kritische Geschichte der allgemeinen Principien der Mechanik*, 3rd ed. (Leipzig: Fues, 1887), pp. 258–61.

[29] Louis de Launay, *Un grand Français: Monge, fondateur de l'Ecole polytechnique* (Paris: Editions Pierre Roger, 1933), p. 130.

for engineers.[30] First organised on essentially civilian lines, the school was later given a purely military organisation by Napoleon who also, however much he favoured it otherwise, resisted any attempt to liberalise its curriculum, and conceded even the provision of a course in so harmless a subject as literature only with reluctance.[31]

Yet in spite of the limitations as to the subjects taught, and the even more serious limitations of the previous education of the students in its early years, the *Ecole* commanded from the very beginning a teaching staff probably more illustrious than any other institution in Europe has had before or since. Lagrange was among its first professors, and although Laplace was not a regular teacher there, he was connected with the school in many ways, including the office of chairman of its council. Monge, Fourier, Prony, and Poinsot were among the first generation of teachers of mathematical and physical subjects;[32] Berthollet,[33] who continued the work of Lavoisier, and several others hardly less distinguished,[34] taught chemistry. The second generation, which began to take over early in the new century, included such names as Poisson, Ampère, Gay-Lussac, Thénard, Arago, Cauchy, Fresnel, Malus, to mention only the best known—and incidentally, nearly all ex-students of the *Ecole*.[35] The institution had existed for only a few years when it became

---

[30] Cf. Auguste Comte, "Philosophical Considerations on the Sciences and Men of Science", in *Early Essays on Social Philosophy* [1825], translated by Henry Dix Hutton, New Universal Library (London: G. Routledge and Sons, and New York: Dutton, 1911), p. 272, in which he says that he knows "but one conception capable of giving a precise idea of [the characteristic doctrines fitted to constitute the special existence of the class of engineers—FAH], that of the illustrious Monge, in his *Géométrie descriptive*, where he gives a general theory of the arts of construction".

[31] Jacobi, "Über die Pariser polytechnische Schule", p. 370.

[32] [Gaspard de Prony (1755–1839) was an engineer with the *Ecole des Ponts et Chaussés*; Louis Poinsot (1777–1859) is remembered for his contributions to mathematics and mechanics. —Ed.]

[33] [Chemist Claude Louis, Comte Berthollet (1748–1822) is noted for his analyses of ammonia and chlorine, and for his collaboration with Lavoisier in establishing chemical nomenclature. —Ed.]

[34] Fourcroy, Vauquelin, Chaptal. [Antoine François, Comte de Fourcroy (1755–1809) made contributions in chemistry, medicine, and, as director general of education under Napoleon, to scientific education in primary and secondary schools. French chemist Nicolas Louis Vauquelin (1763–1829) is remembered for his analyses, with Fourcroy, of vegetable and animal substances. Applied chemist and science populariser Jean Antoine Chaptal (1756–1822) contributed to the scientific modernisation of industry and agriculture. The addition of sugar to unfermented wine in order to increase its final alcohol level is named chaptalisation after him.—Ed.]

[35] [Siméon-Denis Poisson (1781–1840), in addition to identifying the Poisson distribution, worked on a variety of problems in mathematics, mechanics, static electricity, and magnetism. André-Marie Ampère (1775–1836) was a mathematician, chemist, and physicist, and is noted for his work in electrodynamics. Chemist and physicist Joseph Louis Gay-Lussac (1778–1850) is remembered for his work on the properties of gases; the chemist Louis Jacques Thenard (1777–1857) was one of Gay-Lussac's collaborators. François Arago (1786–1853) was a mathemati-

famous all over Europe, and the first interval of peace in 1801–2 brought Volta, Count Rumford, and Alexander von Humboldt[36] on pilgrimage to the new temple of science.

IV

This is not the place to speak at length of the conquests of nature associated with these names. We are only concerned with the general spirit of exuberance which they engendered, with the feeling which they created that there were no limits to the powers of the human mind and to the extent to which man could hope to harness and control all the forces which so far had threatened and intimidated him. Nothing perhaps expresses more clearly this spirit than Laplace's bold idea of a world formula which he expressed in a famous passage of his *Essai philosophique sur les probabilités*: "A mind that in a given instance knew all the forces by which nature is animated and the position of all the bodies of which it is composed, if it were vast enough to include all these data within his analysis, could embrace in one single formula the movements of the largest bodies of the universe and of the smallest atoms; nothing would be uncertain for him; the future and the past would be equally before his eyes".[37] This idea, which exercised so profound a fascination[38] on generations of scientistically minded people, is, as is now becoming apparent, not only a conception which describes an unattainable ideal, but in fact a quite

---

cian, physicist and astronomer, and author of *Biographies of Distinguished Scientific Men*. Augustin-Louis Cauchy (1789–1857), who made numerous contributions to mathematics, also contributed to physics and celestial mechanics. Augustin Jean Fresnel (1788–1827) and Etienne Louis Malus (1775–1812) both made contributions in optics.—Ed.]

[36] In March 1808, shortly after he had arrived in Paris (nominally on a diplomatic mission), Alexander von Humboldt wrote to a friend: "Je passe ma vie à l'Ecole Polytechnique et aux Tuileries. Je travaille à l'Ecole, j'y couche; j'y suis tous les nuits, tous les matins. J'habite la même chambre avec Gay-Lussac", in Karl Christian Bruhns, *Alexander von Humboldt: Eine wissenschaftliche biographie* (Leipzig: F. A. Brockhaus, 1872), vol. 2, p. 6. [Alexander, Baron von Humboldt (1769–1859) was a German natural historian, geologist, and botanist. The passages from his sometimes ungrammatical letter to a friend translate as follows: "I spend my life at the Ecole Polytechnique and at the Tuileries; I work at the Ecole, I sleep there; I am there every night, every morning. I live in the same room with Gay-Lussac". The Italian physicist Alessandro Volta (1745–1827), after whom 'volt' in electricity is named, invented the first battery and also contributed to meteorology. American-born physicist Benjamin Thompson, Count Rumford (1753–1814) is also credited with a number of practical inventions, among them the double broiler, thermal underwear, and the Rumford fireplace.—Ed.]

[37] Pierre-Simon, Marquis de Laplace, *Essai philosophique sur les probabilités* [1814], in *Les maitres de la pensée scientifique* (Paris: Gauthier-Villars, 1921), p. 3.

[38] See, for instance, the reference to it in Abel Transon, *De la religion saint-simonienne: Aux élèves de l'Ecole polytechnique* (Paris: A. Mesnier, 1830), p. 27. See also herein, chapter 12, note 20.

illegitimate deduction from the principles by which we establish laws for particular physical events. It is now itself regarded by modern positivists as a "metaphysical fiction".[39]

It has been well described how the whole of the teaching at the *Ecole polytechnique* was penetrated with the positivist spirit of Lagrange and all the courses and the textbooks used were modelled on his example.[40] Perhaps even more important, however, for the general outlook of the polytechnicians was the definite practical bent inherent in all its teaching, the fact that all the sciences were taught mainly in their practical applications and that all the pupils looked forward to using their knowledge as military or civil engineers. The very type of the engineer with his characteristic outlook, ambitions, and limitations was here created. That synthetic spirit which would not recognise sense in anything that had not been deliberately constructed, that love of organisation that springs from the twin sources of military and engineering practices,[41] the aesthetic predilection for everything that had been consciously constructed over anything that had 'just grown', was a strong new element which was added to—and in the course of time even began to replace—the revolutionary ardour of the young polytechnicians. The peculiar characteris-

---

[39] See Otto Neurath, *Empirische Soziologie* (Vienna: J Springer, 1931), p. 129. On the postulate of universal determinism which is really involved, see particularly Karl Popper, *Logik der Forschung* (Vienna: J. Springer, 1935), p. 183; Philipp Frank, *Das Kausalgesetz und seine Grenzen* (Vienna: J. Springer, 1932); and Richard von Mises, *Probability, Statistics and Truth*, translated by J. Neyman, D. Sholl, and E. Rabinowitsch (London: W. Hodge, 1939), pp. 284–94. Equally characteristic of the positivist spirit and no less influential in spreading it is the famous anecdote about Laplace's answer to Napoleon when asked why in his *Mécanique céleste* the name of God did not appear: "Je n'ai pas besoin de cette hypothèse". [I have no need of that hypothesis. Hayek refers to Laplace's *Traité de mécanique céleste* (Paris: J. B. M. Duprat, 1798–1825). The sentence in the text "It is now itself regarded by modern positivists as a 'metaphysical fiction'" to which this note is attached was different in the original 1941 version in *Economica*, where it read, "It has been shown by modern logical analysis to be itself a piece of 'metaphysical speculation'". The reference to Neurath's work is also a later addition. Both Popper and Neurath's books are now translated; see Karl Popper, *The Logic of Scientific Discovery* (New York: Basic Books, 1959), pp. 247–48; Otto Neurath, "Empirical Sociology", which comprises chapter 10 of *Empiricism and Sociology*, Maria Neurath and Robert S. Cohen, eds (Dordrecht, Holland: D. Reidel, 1973), p. 404.—Ed.]

[40] Dühring, *Kritische Geschichte*, pp. 569 et seq.

[41] Honoré de Balzac, after remarking in one of his novels (*Autre étude de femme*) how different periods had enriched the French language by certain characteristic words (*organiser*, for example), adds that it is "un mot de l'empire qui contient Napoléon tout entier". [Balzac's phrase translates as, "a word of the Empire in which the whole of Napoleon is summed up". Hayek refers to a passage from Honoré de Balzac's (1799–1850) novelette, "Autre étude de femme" ("Another Study of Woman"), one of six collected in his *Scènes de la vie privée* (Paris: Calmann Levy, 1884). This constituted just one part of Balzac's multivolume *La comédie humaine*, in which he laid bare the customs, manners, and habits of the French bourgeoisie in the periods of the Restoration and the July monarchy (1815–48). He was one of the earliest 'social realists', artists who focused on the moral failings of modern society.—Ed.]

tics of this new type who, as it has been said, "prided themselves on having more precise and more satisfactory solutions than anyone else for all political, religious, and social questions",[42] and who "ventured to create a religion as one learns at the *Ecole* to build a bridge or a road"[43] were early noticed, and their propensity to become socialists has often been pointed out.[44] Here we must confine ourselves to point out that it was in this atmosphere that Saint-Simon conceived some of the earliest and most fantastic plans for the reorganisation of society, and that it was at the *Ecole polytechnique* where, during the first twenty years of its existence, Auguste Comte, Prosper Enfantin, Victor Considérant, and some hundreds of later Saint-Simonians and Fourierists received their training, followed by a succession of social reformers throughout the century down to Georges Sorel.[45]

But, whatever the tendencies among the pupils of the institution, it must again be pointed out that the great scientists who built the fame of the *Ecole polytechnique* were not guilty of illegitimate extensions of their technique and habits of thought to fields which were not their own. They little concerned themselves with problems of man and society.[46] This was the province of another group of men, in their time no less influential and admired, but whose efforts to continue the eighteenth-century traditions in the social sciences were

---

[42] Emile Keller, *Le Général de la Moricière: Sa vie militaire, politique et religiuese* (Paris: Librarie Militaire de J. Dumaine, 1874), quoted in Pinet, *Histoire de l'Ecole polytechnique*, p. 136.

[43] Albert Thibaudet, quoted in Gouhier, *La jeunesse d'Auguste Comte*, vol. 1, *Sous le signe de la liberté*, p. 146.

[44] See Arago, *Biographies of Distinguished Scientific Men*, vol. 3, p. 109, and Frédéric Bastiat, *Baccalauréat et socialisme* (Paris: Guillaumin, 1850).

[45] See Gaston Pinet, *Ecrivains et penseurs polytechniciens* (Paris: P. Ollendorff, 1898).

[Barthélemy Prosper Enfantin (1796–1864) was a leader of the Saint-Simonian movement after Saint-Simon's death in 1825. His rôle in systematising Saint-Simonian thought, and in turning it into a religion, is detailed by Hayek in chapter 14. The French social reformer Charles Fourier (1772–1837) would reorganise society via the voluntary association of individuals into self-sufficient communities called *phalanstères*, where each person's rôle would be determined by their personal characteristics, or 'passions'. His writings inspired the formation of many Fourierist communes, among them Brook Farm in Massachusetts. A follower of Fourier, Victor Considérant (1808–93) wrote extensively on political and economic issues. As the leader of the movement after its founder's death, he helped to popularise Fourierist ideas in France, and later established a Fourierist commune, *La Réunion*, in Texas. A retired engineer when he first began writing, the French political philosopher Georges Sorel (1847–1922) was the father of syndicalism, which saw the trade union as the means for overthrowing the capitalist state. In his *Réflexions sur la violence* (1908) Sorel emphasised the necessity of a well-conceived 'myth' to move workers to act, and saw the general strike as the principal tool for action.—Ed.]

[46] See, however, the essays of Lavoisier and Lagrange in Eugène Daire and Gustave de Molinari, *Mélanges d'économie politique*, 2 vols. (Paris: Guillaumin, 1847–48), vol. 1, pp. 575–607. [Lavoisier's essay, titled *De la richesse territoriale du royaume de France*, is found on pp. 575–607. Lagrange's contribution, *Essai d'arithmétique politique, sur les premiers besoins de l'intérieur de la république*, appears on pp. 608–14.—Ed.]

in the end to be swamped by the tide of scientism and silenced by political persecution. It was the misfortune of the *idéologues*, as they called themselves, that their very name should be perverted into a catchword describing the very opposite from what they stood for, and that their ideas should fall into the hands of the young engineers who distorted and changed them beyond recognition.

V

It is a curious fact that the French scholars of the time of which we are speaking should have been divided into two "distinct societies which had only one single trait in common, the celebrity of their names".[47] The first were the professors and examiners at the *Ecole polytechnique* which we already know and those at the *Collège de France*. The second was the group of physiologists, biologists, and psychologists, mostly connected with the *Ecole de médecine* and known as the ideologues.

Not all of the great biologists of which France could boast at the time belonged to this second group. At the *Collège de France*, Cuvier, the founder of comparative anatomy and probably the most famous of them, stood close to the pure scientists.[48] The advances of the biological sciences as expounded by him contributed perhaps as much as anything else to create the belief in the omnipotence of the methods of pure science. More and more problems that had seemed to evade the powers of exact treatment were shown to be conquerable by the same methods.[49] The two other biologists whose names are now even better known than his, Lamarck and Geoffry St. Hilaire, remained at the periphery of the ideologist group and did not concern themselves much

---

[47] See Arago, *Biographies of Distinguished Scientific Men*, vol. 2, p. 34, wherein he points out that Ampère (a physiologist by training) was one of the few connecting links between the two groups.

[48] [Georges Cuvier (1769–1832) was also a founder of vertebrate paleontology; in his studies he helped establish the then contentious idea that certain species had become extinct.—Ed.]

[49] On Cuvier's influence, see the account in Merz, *A History of European Thought*, vol. 1, pp. 136 et seq., wherein the following characteristic passage is quoted (p. 154) from Cuvier's Rapport *historique sur le progrès des sciences naturelles depuis 1789* (Paris: De l'Imprimerie impériale, 1810), p. 389: "Experiments alone, experiments that are precise, made with weights, measures, and calculation, by comparison of all substances employed and all substances obtained: this today is the only legitimate way of reasoning and demonstration. Thus, though the natural sciences escape the application of the calculus, they glory in being subject to the mathematical spirit, and by the wise course they have invariably adopted, they do not expose themselves to the risk of taking a backwards step". See also Lord Acton, "The Study of History", *Lectures on Modern History*, pp. 22; 338, note 82. [See Acton, *Essays in the Study and Writing of History*, pp. 541–42. The reference to Acton's "Study of History" was added to the 1952 version.—Ed.]

with the study of man as a thinking being.[50] But Cabanis and Main de Biran, with their friends Destutt de Tracy and Degérando, made the latter the central problem of their labours.[51]

Ideology,[52] in the sense in which the term was used by that group, meant simply the analysis of human ideas and of human action, including the relation between man's physical and mental constitution.[53] The inspiration of the group came mainly from Condillac and the field of their studies was outlined by Cabanis, one of the founders of physiological psychology, in his *Rapports du physique et du moral de l'homme* (1802).[54] And although there was much talk among them about applying the methods of natural science to man, this meant no more than that they proposed to study man without prejudices and without nebulous speculations about his end and destiny. But this prevented neither Cabanis nor his friends from devoting a large part of their life work to that analysis of human ideas which gave ideology its name. Nor did it occur to them to doubt the legitimacy of introspection. If the second head of the group, Destutt de Tracy, proposed to regard the whole of ideology as part of zoology,[55] this did not preclude his confining himself entirely to that part of it

[50] [The French natural scientist Jean-Baptiste de Monet, Chevalier de Lamarck (1744–1829), who made contributions in botany, systematic invertebrate biology, and geological history, is remembered today for Lamarckism, the theory that acquired traits can be inherited. The French naturalist Etienne Geoffroy Saint-Hilaire (1772–1844) established the principle of the 'unity of composition', the idea that all animals share in common a single structural plan, which became a major tenet of comparative anatomy.—Ed.]

[51] [The physiologist Pierre Jean Georges Cabanis (1757–1808) argued for biological bases for psychological functions. Thus, just as the stomach receives food and digests it, producing nourishment, the brain receives sense impressions and produces thought. Antoine Louis Claude, Comte Destutt de Tracy (1754–1836), author of *Eléments d'idéologie* (1801–15) was, with Cabanis, a leader of the group of *idéologues*. Joseph Marie de Gérando (1772–1842) wrote on the influence of signs on idea formation; he also introduced reforms in French elementary education. The French philosopher François-Pierre-Gonthier Maine de Biran (1766–1824) contributed an essay on habit formation and a treatise on the analysis of thought.—Ed.]

[52] Antoine Claire, Comte Thibaudeau, *Bonaparte and the Consulate* [1843] translated by G. K. Fortescue (New York: Macmillan, 1908), p. 153, points out that, although the terms *idéologues* and *idéologie*, commonly ascribed to Napoleon, were introduced as technical terms by Destutt de Tracy in the first volume of his *Eléments d'idéologie* (1801), at least the word *idéologie* was known in French as early as 1684.

[53] On the whole ideological school, see the comprehensive exposition in François Picavet, *Les Idéologues*, and, published since this essay first appeared, Emile Cailliet, *La tradition littéraire des idéologues* (Philadelphia: American Philosophical Society, 1943). The expression was indeed used in very much the same wide sense as their German contemporaries used the term *anthropology*. On the German parallel to the *idéologues*, see Felix Günther, "Die Wissenschaft vom Menschen, ein Beitrag zum deutschen Geistesleben im Zeitalter des Rationalismus", ed. Karl Lamprecht, vol. 5, book 1 of *Geschichtliche Untersuchungen* (Gotha: F. A. Perthes, 1907), pp. 59–67.

[54] [Pierre Jean Georges Cabanis, *Rapports du physique et du moral de l'homme* (Paris: Crapart, Caille et Ravier, 1802)—Ed.]

[55] Picavet, *Les Idéologues*, p. 337.

which he called *idéologie rationnelle*, in contrast to the *idéologie physiologique*, and which consisted of logic, grammar, and economics.[56]

It cannot be denied that in all this, out of their enthusiasm for the pure sciences, they used many misleading expressions which were grossly misunderstood by Saint-Simon and Comte. Cabanis in particular stressed repeatedly that physics must be the basis of the moral sciences;[57] but with him too this meant no more than that account must be taken of the physiological bases of mental activities, and he always recognised the three separate parts of the "science de l'homme": physiology, analysis of ideas, and morals.[58] But, insofar as the problems of society are concerned, while Cabanis' work remained mainly programmatic in character, Destutt de Tracy made very important contributions. We need mention here only one: his analysis of value and its relation to utility, where, proceeding from the foundations laid by Condillac, he went very far in providing what classical English political economy lacked and what might have saved it from the impasse into which it got—a correct theory of value. Destutt de Tracy (and Louis Say, who later continued his work) may indeed be said to have anticipated by more than half a century what was to become one of the most important advances of social theory, the subjective (or marginal utility) theory of value.[59]

It is true that others outside their circle went much further in the application of the technique of the natural sciences to social phenomena, particularly the *Société des observateurs de l'homme*, which, largely under Cuvier's influence, went some way in confining social study to a mere recording of observations reminiscent of similar organisations of our own day.[60] But on the whole there can be no doubt that the ideologues preserved the best tradition of the eighteenth-century *philosophes*. And while their colleagues at the *Ecole polytechnique* became the admirers and friends of Napoleon and received from him all possible sup-

---

[56] Ibid., p. 314.

[57] Ibid., p. 250. See also pp. 131–35, wherein Cabanis's predecessor in these efforts, Volney, is discussed. In 1793, Volney had published *Catéchisme du citoyen Français*, later to become *La loi naturelle, ou, Principes physiques de la morale*, in which he unsuccessfully attempted to make morals into a physical science. [Hayek refers to Constantin François de Chasseboeuf, Comte de Volney (1757–1820), who wrote on geography, linguistics, and sociology, and to his works *La loi naturelle, ou, Catéchisme du citoyen Français* (Paris: n.p., 1789) and *La loi naturelle, ou, Principes physiques de la morale*, found in *Les Ruines, ou, Méditation sur les révolutions des empires*, 10th ed. (Paris: Bossange frères, 1821).—Ed.]

[58] Picavet, *Les Idéologues*, p. 226.

[59] On Destutt de Tracy, see Henry Michel, *L'Idée de l'état*, 2nd ed. (Paris: Hachette, 1896), pp. 282–86; on Louis Say, see Albert Schatz, *L'Individualisme économique et social*, pp. 153 et seq. [Louis Auguste Say (1774–1840), brother of Jean-Baptiste, wrote several books on economic subjects. In his *Principales causes de la richesse ou de la misère des peuples et des particuliers* (1818) he criticised the ideas of his brother and of other writers, among them Adam Smith.—Ed.]

[60] Picavet, *Les Idéologues*, p. 82.

port, the ideologues remained staunch defenders of individual freedom and consequently incurred the wrath of the despot.

VI

It was Napoleon who gave currency to the word *ideologue* in its new sense by using it as a favourite expression of contempt for all those who ventured to defend freedom against him.[61] And he did not content himself with abuse. The man who understood better than any of his imitators that "in the long run the sword is always beaten by the spirit" did not hesitate to carry his "repugnance for all discussion and the teaching of political matters"[62] into practice. The economist J. B. Say, a member of the ideologist group and for some years editor of its journal, the *Décade philosophique*, was one of the first to feel the strong

[61] See the passage from Napoleon's reply to the Council of State at its session of December 20, 1812, quoted by Vilfredo Pareto, *The Mind and Society*, translated by Andrew Bongiorno and Arthur Livingston (New York: Harcourt Brace and Co., 1935), vol. 3, p. 1244 [pp. 1244–45], from the *Moniteur universel* (Paris), December 21, 1812: "All the misfortunes that our beautiful France has been experiencing have to be ascribed to 'ideology', to that cloudy metaphysics which goes ingeniously seeking first causes and would ground the legislation of the peoples upon them instead of adapting laws to what we know of the human heart and to the lessons of history. Such errors could only lead to a regime by men of blood, and they have in fact done so. Who cajoled the people by thrusting upon it a sovereignty it was unable to exercise? Who destroyed the sacredness of the laws and respect for the laws by basing them not on the sacred principles of justice, on the nature of things and the nature of civic justice, but simply on the will of an assembly made up of individuals who are strangers to any knowledge of law whether civil, criminal, administrative, political, or military? When a man is called upon to reorganise a state, he must follow principles that are forever in conflict. . . . The advantages and disadvantages of different systems of legislation have to be sought in history". See also Hippolyte Taine, *Les origines de la France contemporaine* (Paris: Hachette, 1876), vol. 2, pp. 214–33. [Taine's discussion of Napoleon's suppression of the moral and political sciences actually occurs in Book 6, chapter 2, parts 4 and 5 of *Le régime moderne*, which may be found in volume 11 of *Les origines de la France contemporaine*. For a translation see *The Modern Regime*, translated by John Durand, vol. 2 (New York: Henry Holt, 1894), pp. 192–207.—Ed.] Not because of its historical correctness, which may be questioned, but to show how all this appeared to the next generation, the following characteristic statement by a leading Saint-Simonian may be quoted: "Après 1793, *l'Académie des sciences* prend le sceptre; les *mathématiciens* et *physiciens* remplacent les *littérateurs*: Monge, Fourcroy, Laplace . . . règnent dans le royaume de l'intelligence. . . . En même temps, Napoléon, membre de l'Institut, classe de *mécanique*, étouffe au berceau les enfants légitimes de la philosophie du XVIIIe siècle". [After 1793 the Academy of Sciences takes the sceptre; mathematicians and physicists replace literary scholars: Monge, Fourcroy, Laplace . . . reign in the kingdom of the intellect. . . . At the same time, Napoleon, a member of the institute, class of mechanics, stifled in the cradle the legitimate children of the philosophers of the eighteenth century.—Ed.] From Prosper Enfantin, *Colonisation de l'Algérie* (Paris: P. Bertrand, 1843), pp. 521–22.

[62] See Antoine Claire, Comte Thibaudeau, *Histoire de la France et de Napoléon Bonaparte de 1799 à 1815*, vol. 3, *Le consulat et l'empire*, vol. 3 (Paris: Renouard, 1834), p. 396.

hand. When he refused to change a chapter in his *Traité d'économie politique* to suit the wishes of the dictator, the second edition was prohibited and the author removed from the *tribunat*.[63] In 1806 Destutt de Tracy had to appeal to President Jefferson to secure the publication of at least an English translation of his *Commentaire sur l'esprit des lois* which he was not allowed to publish in his own country.[64] A little earlier (1803) the whole of the second class of the *Institut*, that of the moral and political science, had been suppressed.[65] In consequence, these subjects remained excluded from the great *Tableau de l'état et des progrès des sciences et des arts depuis 1789* which the three classes of the *Institut* had been ordered to furnish in 1802. This was symbolic of the whole position of these subjects under the empire. The teaching of them was prevented and the whole younger generation grew up in ignorance of the achievements of the past. The door was thus opened to a new start unencumbered by the accumulated results of earlier study. Social problems were to be approached from a new angle. The methods, which since d'Alembert had so successfully been used in physics, whose character had now become explicit, and which more recently had been equally successful in chemistry and biology, were now to be applied to the science of man. With what results we shall gradually see.

[63] See Jean-Baptiste Say, *Traité d'économie politique*, 2nd ed. (Paris: Antoine-Augustin Renouard, 1814), Avertissement. [Taine, *The Modern Regime*, p. 197, note 3, translates Say's words in his Avertissement as follows: "The press was no longer free. Every exact presentation of things received the censure of a government founded on a lie".—Ed.]

[64] See Gilbert Chinard, *Jefferson et les idéologues d'après sa correspondence inédite avec Destutt de Tracy, Cabanis, J.-B. Say et Auguste Comte* (Baltimore: Johns Hopkins Press, 1925).

[65] See Merz, *History of European Thought*, p. 149.

TWELVE

THE "ACCOUCHEUR D'IDÉES": HENRI DE SAINT-SIMON

I

Early training and experience can hardly be said to have qualified the count Henri de Saint-Simon for the rôle of a scientific reformer. But it must be admitted that when in 1798, at the age of thirty-eight,[1] he took up his abode opposite the *Ecole polytechnique*, henceforth to interpret to the world the significance of scientific progress for the study of society, he was already a man of rich and varied experience; but scientific study had scarcely been included. The facts of his earlier life, only quite recently brought to light,[2] are considerably less elevating than the numerous anecdotes which he himself and his pupils have transmitted to us and which until lately formed almost our sole information about his youth. The legends tell us that he descended from Charlemagne, that d'Alembert supervised his education, and that his valet had orders to wake the ambitious young man daily with the words: *Levez-vous, Monsieur le Comte, vous avez des grandes choses à faire.*[3] All this is not altogether impossible. It is certain, however, that for the first twenty years of his adult life he lived the life of an adventurer, as many sons of aristocratic families must have done during the period, but on a scale and with an intensity that could have been equalled by few of his contemporaries.

Almost as soon as he obtained a commission in the French army he followed Lafayette to America and when, after four years, fighting ceased, he bade farewell to his profession. Even before this we find him dreaming of piercing the Isthmus of Panama. A little later he offered his services in Holland for an expedition against the British Indies and was also concerned more concretely with projects for building canals in Spain. The Revolution found

---

[1] The date, hence the age, is not quite certain.

[2] See *Gouhier, La jeunesse d'Auguste Comte*, vol. 2, which for the first forty-five years of Saint-Simon's life supersedes all earlier biographies, including the best of them: Georges Weill, *Saint-Simon et son œuvre: Un précurseur du socialisme* (Paris: Perrin, 1894); Maxime Leroy, *La vie véritable du comte Henri de Saint-Simon, 1760–1825* (Paris: B. Grasset, 1925); and Georges Dumas, *Psychologie de deux messies positivistes, Saint-Simon et Auguste Comte* (Paris: F. Alcan, 1905).

[3] [Rise up, Monsieur le Comte, you have great things to do.—Ed.]

him back in Paris, as the *citoyen Bonhomme*, forswearing his title and acting the extreme *Sansculotte*. But soon more profitable ventures offered themselves. In the sale of the church lands we find him as one of the most active intermediaries, speculating with borrowed money on a colossal scale, one of the great profiteers of inflation, who did not scorn any business that came his way, such as an attempted sale of the lead from the roofs of Notre Dame. It is not surprising to find him in prison during the Terror. It was during the time he spent there that according to his own account he decided on the career of a philosopher. But, released, he once more preferred financial to metaphysical speculation. So long as the source of his funds (a Saxon diplomatist[4]) continued to provide him with sufficient capital, he tried his hand at all sorts of commercial ventures, such as organising a stage coach service, selling wine retail, manufacturing textiles and even 'republican' playing cards in which the obnoxious kings and queens were replaced by *le génie* and *la liberté*. His plans were even more ambitious. He seems to have begun the construction of some large industrial plant and he at least contemplated a combined commercial and banking enterprise that "should be unique in the world". He also acted as spokesman for French financial interests at the Anglo-French discussions at Lille in 1797.[5]

All these activities, however, came to a sudden end when in 1798 his partner returned to Paris and asked to be shown the accounts. Saint-Simon certainly knew what high living meant, and his house, run by the former *maître d'hôtel* of the Duc de Choiseul, and his kitchen, presided over by an equally reputed *chef*, were famous. But that all the costs of this should have gone down as expenses on the joint account rather upset the good Saxon count. He withdrew his funds, and Saint-Simon, still in possession of a fortune, substantial but no longer adequate to support further grandiose ventures, found it advisable to withdraw from commercial activity and henceforth to seek glory in the intellectual sphere.

We need not doubt that in the mind of the disappointed *faiseur* vague plans for the reorganisation of society were already forming; and it is not surprising that he should soon find that all his experiences had not provided him with the knowledge which would enable him to elaborate these ideas. He therefore

---

[4] [Hayek refers to the Prussian diplomat and Saint-Simon's business partner, Sigismund Ehrenreich, the Count of Redern (1761–1841).—Ed.]

[5] [In August 1797 Saint-Simon was the spokesman for a group of private French financiers who, eager to see the war with England come to an end, held conversations with British government representatives at Lille. His portrayal of the low intelligence and personal foibles of, as well as lapses in judgement by, the leaders of the Directorate led Pitt to comment that Saint-Simon had "the merit of furnishing one of the most interesting and certainly the most entertaining dialogues that ever made part of a negotiation", quoted in Frank E. Manuel, *The New World of Henri Saint-Simon* (Cambridge, MA: Harvard University Press, 1956), p. 52.—Ed.]

decided "to employ his money to acquire scientific knowledge".[6] It was at this time that he spent three years in close contact with the teachers and students of the *Ecole polytechnique* as a kind of Maecenas-pupil, feasting the professors and assisting the students, one of whom, the great mathematician Poisson, he entirely supported for years and treated as his adopted son.[7]

The method of study which Saint-Simon chose for himself was not of the ordinary. Feeling that his brain was no longer elastic enough to pursue a systematic course, he preferred to learn what he could in the more pleasant form of dinner-table conversation. He asked the scholars from whose knowledge he hoped to profit to his house, and appears even to have married for the sole purpose of keeping a house where he could properly entertain the great savants. Lagrange, Monge, Berthollet, and, probably after 1801, when he felt he had completed his education in the mechanical sciences and moved to the neighbourhood of the *Ecole de médecine*, Gall, Cabanis, and Bichat are reported to have partaken of his hospitality.[8] Yet this method of study seems to have proved to be of questionable value. At any rate in later life our hero complained to a friend that his "scholars and artists ate much but talked little. After dinner I went to sit in an easy chair in a corner of the salon and fell asleep. Fortunately Madame de Saint-Simon did the *honneurs* with much grace and *esprit*".[9]

Whether it was merely that he became aware that this had been a bad investment and decided to cut the losses, or whether it was that another mar-

[6] "J'ai employé mon argent à acquérir de la science; grande chère, bon vin, beaucoup d'empressement vis-à-vis des professeurs auxquels ma bourse était ouverte, me procuraient toutes les facilités que je pouvais désirer" [I used my money to acquire scientific knowledge; high living, good wine, a lot of professors to whom my purse was open—and all the facilities that I could long for, were thus granted to me.—Ed.], in Leroy, *Vie du Saint-Simon*, p. 210.

[7] [Gaius Cilnius Maecenas (?-8 BC), Roman statesman and advisor to Augustus, and later in life a patron to Horace, Vergil, and Propertius, his name is synonymous with a patron of letters.—Ed.]

[8] [Franz Joseph Gall (1758–1828) was the founder of phrenology, a 'science' based on the belief that intelligence, aptitudes, and personality are wholly determined by brain size and shape, and that this may be inferred by the careful expert examination of the skull. French anatomist Marie-François-Xavier Bichat (1771–1802) was a pioneer in the areas of histology (the study of tissue structure, accomplished by the examination of thin slices of tissue) and pathology (the study of the nature, causes, and development of disease).—Ed.]

[9] Léon Halévy, "Souvenirs de Saint-Simon", *La France littéraire*, March 1832, partially reproduced in Georges Brunet, 'Saint-Simon et Léon Halévy", *Revue d'histoire économique et sociale*, 13th année, 1925, p. 168. [Hayek's translation is a bit loose; Saint-Simon actually said that he would listen while sitting in the easy chair, but most of the time he only heard platitudes, and hence fell asleep! The original reads, " . . . mes savans et mes artistes mangeaient beaucoup et parlaient peu. Après le dîner, j'allais m'asseoir dans une bergère, dans un coin de salon, et j'écoutais. Malheureusement, les trois quarts du temps, je n'entendais que des fadaises, et je m'endormais. Heureusement que Mme. de Saint-Simon faisait avec beaucoup de grâce et d'esprit les honneurs de mon salon".—Ed.]

riage appeared to him a more attractive method of instruction, not only the dinners but also the marriage came to an end soon after he had moved to the new place. He explained to his wife that "the first man of the world ought to be married to the first woman" and that, therefore, with much regret he had to ask her to be released. Was it an accident that the divorce was effected in the month after Madame de Staël had become a widow, the Madame de Staël who, in a book that had fired Saint-Simon's imagination, had only just celebrated the "positive sciences" and emphasised that the "science of politics was yet to be created"?[10] It is alleged that as soon as he was free he hurried to Le Coppet on the Lake of Geneva and proposed in the following words: "Madame, you are the most extraordinary woman on earth and I am the most extraordinary man; together we shall undoubtedly produce a still more extraordinary child". Legend adds that he also proposed that they should celebrate their nuptials in a balloon. About the terms in which the refusal was couched the versions vary.

II

The visit to Switzerland was also the occasion of Saint-Simon's first publication. In 1803 there appeared in Geneva the *Lettres d'un habitant de Genève à ses contemporains*,[11] a little tract in which the Voltairean cult of Newton was revived in a fantastically exaggerated form. It begins by proposing that a subscrip-

---

[10] Madame de Staël, *De la littérature considérée dans ses rapports avec les institutions sociales* [1800], passages quoted from "Discours préliminaire" 3rd ed. (Paris: Maradan, 1818), vol. 1, p. 58, and vol. 2, part 2, p. 215. [Because of her opposition to Napoleon, the formidable Anne-Louise-Germaine Necker, Baroness de Staël-Holstein (1766–1817), was forced to spend much of her life in exile; her salon in Coppet, Switzerland, attracted many leading intellectuals of Europe. —Ed.]

[11] See *Œuvres de Saint-Simon et d'Enfantin* (Paris: E. Dentu, 1865–78) (henceforth cited as OSSE), vol. 15, pp. 7–60, and the new edition reprinted from the original, Henri, Comte de Saint-Simon, *Lettres d'un habitant de Genève à ses contemporaines* (1803), edited with an introduction by Alfred Pereire (Paris: F. Alcan, 1925). Nearly all the important passages from Saint-Simon's works are conveniently brought together in *L'œuvre d'Henri de Saint-Simon, Textes choisis avec une introduction par C. Bouglé, Notice bibliographique de Alfred Pereire* (Paris: F. Alcan, 1925). In the references below, the first refers to the *Œuvres*, the second (in parentheses) to the separate edition of the *Lettres* of 1925. For the complicated history of the various editions and manuscripts of this work, see Gouhier, *La jeunesse d'Auguste Comte*, pp. 224 et seq. [Because many readers might not have access to the full collected works version of Saint-Simon and Enfantin (*OSSE*), Hayek here alerts the reader to Pereire's (perhaps more widely available) 1925 editions of Saint-Simon's first major work, *Lettres d'un habitant de Genève*, and of a selection of his works, *L'œuvre d'Henri de Saint-Simon: Textes choisis*. Hayek's procedure of citing the more recent edition of *Lettres* in parentheses is repeated below. As always, [bracketed] page numbers indicate the actual pages where a cite may be found, in those cases where Hayek's citation is inaccurate.—Ed.]

tion should be opened before the tomb of Newton to finance the project of a great "Council of Newton" for which each subscriber is to have the right of nominating three mathematicians, three physicists, three chemists, three physiologists, three *littérateurs*, three painters, and three musicians.[12] The twenty-one scholars and artists thus elected by the whole of mankind, and presided over by the mathematician who received the largest number of votes,[13] should become in their collective capacity the representatives of God on earth,[14] who would deprive the pope, the cardinals, the bishops, and the priests of their office because they do not understand the divine science which God has entrusted to them and which some day will again turn earth into paradise.[15] In the divisions and sections into which the supreme Council of Newton will divide the world, similar local Councils of Newton will be created which will have to organise worship, research, and instruction in and around the temples of Newton which will be built everywhere.[16]

Why this new "social organisation", as Saint-Simon calls it for the first time in an unpublished manuscript of the same period?[17] Because we are still governed by people who do not understand the general laws that rule the universe. "It is necessary that the physiologists chase from their company the philosophers, moralists, and metaphysicians just as the astronomers have chased out the astrologers and the chemists have chased out the alchemists".[18] The physiologists are competent in the first instance because "we are organised bodies; and it is by regarding our social relationships as physiological phenomena that I have conceived the project which I present to you".[19]

But the physiologists themselves are not yet quite scientific enough. They have yet to discover how their science can reach the perfection of astronomy by basing itself on the single law to which God has subjected the universe, the law of universal gravitation.[20] It will be the task of the Council of Newton

[12] *OSSE*, vol. 15, p. 11 (3).

[13] Ibid., p. 51 (55).

[14] Ibid., p. 49 (53).

[15] Ibid., p. 48 (52).

[16] Ibid., pp. 50–53 (54–58).

[17] In *Lettres*, ed. A. Pereire, pp. xv, 93.

[18] *OSSE*, vol. 15, p. 39 [pp. 39–40] (39).

[19] Ibid., p. 40 (40).

[20] Ibid., pp. 39–40, 55 (39,61). The passage in which Saint-Simon praises the significance of that universal law is a curious anticipation of Laplace's famous world formula (ibid., p. 59 (67)): "Faites la supposition que vous avez acquis connaissance de la manière dont la matière s'est trouvée répartie à une époque quelconque, et que vous avez fait le plan de l'Univers, en désignant par des nombres la quantité de matière qui se trouvait contenue dans chacune des ses parties, il sera clair à vos yeux qu'en faisant sur ce plan application de la loi de la pesanteur universelle, vous pourriez prédire (aussi exactement que l'état des connaissances mathématiques vous le permettrait tous les changements successifs qui arriveraient dans l'Univers". Although Laplace published his formula only in 1814, we must, no doubt, assume that the idea would have been familiar from his

by exercising its spiritual power to make people understand this law. Its tasks, however, go far beyond that. It will not only have to vindicate the rights of the men of genius, the scientists, the artists, and all the people with liberal views;[21] it will also have to reconcile the second class of people, the proprietors, and the third, the people without property, to whom Saint-Simon addresses himself specially as his friends and whom he exhorts to accept this proposal which is the only way to prevent that "struggle which, from the nature of things, necessarily always exists between" the two classes.[22]

All this is revealed to Saint-Simon by the Lord himself, who announces to His prophet that He has placed Newton at His side and entrusted him with the enlightenment of the inhabitants of all planets. The instruction culminates in the famous passage from which much of later Saint-Simonian doctrine springs: "All men will work; they will regard themselves as labourers attached to one workshop whose efforts will be directed to guide human intelligence according to my divine foresight. The supreme Council of Newton will direct their works".[23] Saint-Simon has no qualms about the means that will be

---

lectures delivered in 1796, to which he later added the introduction containing the famous phrase. [Saint-Simon's statement may be translated as, "Suppose that you have acquired the knowledge of the repartition of Matter at any period of Time, and that you scheduled the whole Universe, designating by numbers the quantity of matter contained in each of its components, then it will be obvious to you that, applying to your scheme the law of universal gravity, you would be able to predict—so far as the development of mathematical science would permit—all of the successive changes likely to take place in the universe". Hayek compares this to Laplace's 'world formula,' which appeared in his *Essai philosophique sur les probabilités* (Paris: Courcier, 1814). In the English translation, *A Philosophical Essay on Probabilities*, translated by Frederick Wilson Truscott and Frederick Lincoln Emory (New York: Dover, 1951), p. 4, Laplace's formula is rendered as follows: "Given for one instant an intelligence which could comprehend all the forces by which nature is animated and the respective situation of the beings who compose it—an intelligence sufficiently vast to submit these data to analysis—it would embrace in the same formula the movements of the greatest bodies in the universe and those of the lightest atom; for it, nothing would be uncertain and the future, as the past, would be present to its eyes".—Ed.]

[21] Ibid., p. 26 (23).

[22] Ibid., p. 28 (25).

[23] Ibid., p. 55 (61). Cf. p. 57 [pp. 57–58] (65): "L'obligation est imposée à chacun de donner constamment à ses forces personnelles une direction utile à l'humanité; les bras du pauvre continueront à nourrir le riche, mais le riche reçoit le commandement de faire travailler sa cervelle, et si sa cervelle n'est pas propre au travail, il sera bien obligé de faire travailler ses bras; car Newton ne laissera sûrement pas sur cette planète (une des plus voisines du soleil) des ouvriers volontairement inutiles dans l'atelier".[Every one of us is duty-bound constantly to use all of his powers in ways that are useful for mankind; the hands of the poor will ever provide food for the rich; but the rich are commanded to work their brain, and if their brains are not able to work, they will have to work with their hands; because Newton will certainly not allow on this planet—one of the nearest to the Sun—workers who remain idle in the workshop.—Ed.] The idea of the organisation of society on the example of the workshop, which appears here for the first time in literature, has, of course, since played an important rôle in all socialist literature. See par-

employed to enforce the instructions of his central planning body: "Anybody who does not obey the orders will be treated by the others as a quadruped".[24]

In condensing we had to try and bring some order into the incoherent and rambling jumble of ideas which this first pamphlet of Saint-Simon represents. It is the outpouring of a megalomaniac visionary who sprouts half-digested ideas, who all the time is trying to attract the attention of the world to his unappreciated genius and to the necessity of financing his works, and who does not forget to provide for himself as the founder of the new religion great power and the chairmanship of all the councils for life.[25]

III

Soon after the publication of this first work, Saint-Simon found that his funds were entirely exhausted and the next few years he spent in increasing misery, importuning his old friends and associates with demands for money and, it appears, not stopping short of blackmail. Even his appeals to now powerful friends of the past, such as the Comte de Ségur, Napoleon's *grand maître de cérémonies*[26], procured him in the end no more than the miserable and humiliating position of copyist in a pawn-broking institution. After six months of this, weakened and ill, he met his former valet, who took him into his house. For four years (1806–10) until his death that devoted servant provided for all the needs of his ex-master and even defrayed the cost of printing Saint-Simon's next work.

It seems that during this period Saint-Simon read more extensively than ever before; at least the *Introduction aux travaux scientifiques du 19ᵐᵉ siècle*[27] shows a wide although still very superficial and ill-digested knowledge of the scien-

---

ticularly Georges Sorel, "Le syndicalisme révolutionnaire", in *Mouvement socialiste*, November 1 and 15, 1905, pp. 265–80. Cf. also Karl Marx, *Das Kapital*, 10th ed., vol. 1, chapter 12, section 4, pp. 319–24. [There is no discussion of organising society on the example of the workshop in chapter 12, section 4 of volume 1 of *Das Kapital*. Hayek may have been referring to chapter 14, section 4, where Marx compares the division of labour within a society to that which occurs within a workshop.—Ed.]

[24] *Lettres*, ed. A. Pereire, p. 54. The passage has been discreetly suppressed by his pupils who edited *Œuvres*. [The suppressed passage reads, "Tout homme qui n'obéira pas à ce commandement sera considéré et traité par les autres comme un quadrupède".—Ed.]

[25] *OSSE*, vol. 15, p. 54 (59) [55 (60)].

[26] [Hayek refers to the French diplomat and historian Louis-Philippe, Comte de Ségur (1753–1830).—Ed.]

[27] Henri, Comte de Saint-Simon, *Introduction aux travaux scientifiques du dix-neuvième siècle*, 2 vols. (Paris: J.-L. Scherff, 1807–8). The *Introduction* has not been included in *OSSE* and must be consulted in *Œuvres choisies de C.-H. de Saint-Simon* (Brussels: Fr. van Meenen, 1859), vol. 1, pp. 43–264.

tific literature of the period. The main theme is still the same, but the methods proposed have somewhat changed. Before science can organise society, science itself must be organised.[28] The Council of Newton therefore now becomes the editorial committee of a great new *Encyclopædia* which is to systematise and unify all knowledge: "We must examine and co-ordinate it all from the point of view of physicism".[29] This physicism is not merely a new general scientific method; it is to be a new religion, even if at first only for the educated classes.[30] It is to be the third great stage in the evolution of religion from polytheism through "deism"[31] to physicism. But although the growth of physicism has now been under way for eleven hundred years,[32] the victory is not yet complete. The reason is that the work of the past, particularly that of the French Encyclopedists, was merely critical and destructive.[33] It is for the great Emperor Napoleon, "the scientific chief of humanity as he is its political chief", "the most positive man of the age", to organise the scientific system in a new encyclopedia worthy of his name.[34] Under his direction the "physicist clergy" in the *atelier scientifique* will create a work that will organise physicism and found, on reasoning and observation, the principles which forever will serve as guides to humanity.[35] The greatest man after the emperor, and that is "undoubtedly the man who admires him most profoundly", offers himself for the task as his "scientific lieutenant, as a second Descartes, under whose leadership the works of the new school will be prodigious".[36]

[28] *Œuvres choisies*, vol. 1 ("mon portefeuille"): "Trouver une synthèse scientifique qui codifie les dogmes du nouveau pouvoir et serve de base à une réorganisation de l'Europe". [Saint-Simon's aspiration might be rendered, "To find a scientific synthesis that would codify the dogmas of the new power and serve as a basis for a reorganisation of Europe". I could not locate this sentence in *Mon portefeuille*, which comprises the last section of *Introduction aux travaux scientifiques* and which consists of a series of 25 brief essays and observations, found on pp. 157—260 of *Œuvres choisies*.—Ed.]

[29] Ibid., p. 219. See also pp. 195, 214–15, 223–24 [the last entry should be 243–44].

[30] Ibid., p. 214: "Je crois à la nécessité d'une religion pour le maintien de l'ordre social; je crois que le déisme est usé, je crois que le physicisme n'est point assez solidement établi pour pouvoir servir de base à une religion. Je crois que la force des choses veut qu'il y ait deux doctrines distinctes: le Physicisme pour les gens instruits, et le Déisme pour la classe ignorante". [I believe in the necessity of religion to maintain the social order; I believe that the time for deism has passed, I believe that physicism is in no way solidly enough established to serve as the basis of a religion. I believe that the state of affairs requires that there be two distinct doctrines: Physicism for educated people, and Deism for the ignorant.—Ed.]

[31] Saint-Simon uses *deism* and *theism* indiscriminately for *monotheism*.

[32] Ibid., p. 195.

[33] Ibid., p. 146.

[34] Ibid., p. 61.

[35] Ibid., pp. 243–44.

[36] Ibid., pp. 231, 236. Descartes has now become the hero because our perpetual time-server has become violently nationalistic, deplores the English pre-dominance which is still defiling French science, and wants to give the initiative to the French. The work pretends to be an answer to Napoleon's question to the *Académie* on the progress of French sciences since 1789.

It need hardly be said that this work is no more systematic than the first. After a vain attempt at coherent exposition it soon becomes admittedly a collection of disjointed notes from Saint-Simon's *portefeuille*. He abandoned the ambitious plan outlined at the beginning, as he himself explains in the sketch of his autobiography, because of lack of funds, or as he admits elsewhere, because he was not yet ripe for the task.[37] Yet, with all its defects, the work is a remarkable document. It combines, for the first time, nearly all the characteristics of the modern scientistic organiser. The enthusiasm for physicism (it is now called physicalism) and the use of "physical language",[38] the attempt to "unify science" and to make it the basis of morals, the contempt for all "theological", that is anthropomorphic, reasoning,[39] the desire to organise the work of others, particularly by editing a great encyclopedia, and the wish to plan life in general on scientific lines are all present. One can sometimes believe that one is reading a contemporary work of an H. G. Wells, a Lewis Mumford, or an Otto Neurath.[40] Nor is the complaint missing about the intellectual crisis, the moral chaos, which must be overcome by the imposition of a new scientific creed. The book is indeed, more than the *Lettres d'un habitant de Genève*, the first and most important document of that "counter-revolution of science", as their fellow reactionary Bonald called the movement,[41] which later found more open expression in Saint-Simon's avowed desire to 'terminate the revolution' by conscious reorganisation of society. It is the beginning of both modern positivism and modern socialism, which, thus, both began as definitely reactionary and authoritarian movements.

The *Introduction*, addressed to his fellow scientists, was not published but merely printed in a small number of copies for distribution among the members of the *Institut*. But although the great scientists to whom he sent it took no notice, he continued to appeal to them for assistance in a number of smaller tracts of a similar character. We can pass over the various minor writings of the next few years, which were mainly concerned with the project of an ency-

---

[37] *OSSE*, vol. 15, pp. 71, 77.

[38] *Œuvres choisies*, p. 112.

[39] Ibid., p. 217: "L'idée de Dieu n'est pas autre chose que l'idée de l'intelligence humaine généralisée" [The idea of God is none other than the idea of human intelligence generalised. —Ed.].

[40] [For more on Neurath, see chapter 1, note 5, and for more on Wells and Mumford, see chapter 10, note 7. The creation of an encyclopedia of unified science was a central project of Neurath and other members of the Vienna Circle of logical positivists.—Ed.]

[41] See Werner Sombart, *Sozialismus und soziale Bewegung*, 7th ed. (Jena: G. Fischer, 1919), p. 54. [Conservative philosopher and politician Louis-Gabriel-Ambroise, Vicomte de Bonald (1754–1840) was one of the chief theoreticians of reaction against the French Revolution. In his writings Bonald emphasised the need for absolute monarchy, the supremacy of religion over reason, and the value of tradition. Note that if positivism and scientism constitute the 'counter-revolution of science', then Hayek, in attempting to distinguish 'real science' from 'scientism', might be viewed as playing the rôle of a *counter*-counter-revolutionary.—Ed.]

clopedia; during this time we find, gradually added to the megalomania of the prophet, the characteristic persecution mania of the *verkannte Genie* which expressed itself in violent abuse of the formerly so-admired Laplace, whom he suspected of being responsible for his neglect.[42]

IV

There are no further important developments in Saint-Simon's writings till 1813. Once more plunged into abject poverty by the death of his faithful valet, he starved and in the end fell dangerously ill. He was rescued by an old acquaintance, a *notaire*, who negotiated a settlement with his family under which, in return for giving up all expectations of future inheritance, he received a small annual pension. Once again settled in tolerable comfort, his work entered a new phase. Finally disillusioned in his hope of obtaining the collaboration of the physicists, he turned away from the *brutiers, infinitésimaux, algébristes et arithméticiens*,[43] whom he no longer conceded the right to regard themselves as the scientific advance guard of humanity, and taking up the second strand of thought from his first work, he turned again to the biologists.

In his *Mémoire sur la science de l'homme* (part of which, however, still bears the separate title *Travail sur la gravitation universelle*), his problem is again how physiology, of which the science of man is a part, can be treated by the methods adopted by the physical sciences[44] and thus follow those sciences in the progress from the "conjectural" to the "positive" stage.[45] With the science of man, as part and summit of physiology, morals and politics must also become positive sciences,[46] and thus "the passage from the idea of many particular laws regulating the phenomena of the diverse branches of physics to the idea of a single and unique law regulating them all" must become completed.[47] When this is achieved and all the particular sciences have become positive, the general science, that is, philosophy, will also become positive.[48] It will then

---

[42] *OSSE*, vol. 15, pp. 42, 53–56. [I could not locate the criticism of Laplace in the materials printed in the *OSSE*. However, as G. Dumas reports in "L'Etat mental de Saint-Simon", *Revue philosophique de la France and de l'étranger*, vol. 53, January 1902, p. 84, which may have been Hayek's source for the anecdote, Saint-Simon attacked Laplace in a fragment in his 1810 piece *Histoire de l'homme*, blaming him for having ruined Saint-Simon's reputation over the course of the previous ten years. The phrase *verkannte Genie* translates as 'misunderstood genius'.—Ed.]

[43] [primitives, infinitesimals, algebraists, and mathematicians—Ed], *OSSE*, vol. 40, p. 39.

[44] Ibid., p. 17.

[45] Ibid., pp. 25, 186 [186–87].

[46] Ibid., p. 29.

[47] Ibid., pp. 161, 186. [It is not clear why p. 186 is also included; the quotation is found on p. 161.—Ed.]

[48] Ibid., p. 17.

at last be able to become the new spiritual power, which must remain separate from the temporal power, since this is a division incapable of improvement.[49] With this organisation of the "positive system" we shall have definitely
entered into the third great epoch of human history of which the first, or preliminary, was ended with Socrates while the second or conjectural has lasted
to the present.[50]

This development of ideas which we can observe enables us to predict
their future movement.[51] Since "the cause which acts strongest on society is
a change, a perfectioning of the ideas, the general beliefs",[52] we can do even
more, we can develop a theory of history, a general history of mankind, which
will deal not merely with the past and present but also with the future. Such
an abridged history of the past, future, and present of the human mind Saint-
Simon proposed in the program for a third memoir on the science of man.
It is "the happiest idea which has ever presented itself to his mind" and he is
"enchanted by the conception",[53] but for the moment he develops it no further. As with most of his works before 1814, the idea remained a promise
of future things to come, a prospectus of work he would like to do, but the
Mémoire itself is still an unorganised mass full of irrelevant detail and bizarre
conceits from which one can extract the fertile ideas only because one knows
their later development.

V

All this changed suddenly with Saint-Simon's next work, the *Réorganisation de
la société européenne*,[54] published in 1814. From that date onwards there issued
under his name a stream of books and pamphlets in which ideas were systematically expounded and which sometimes were even well written. It is true
that after a new period of abject misery, during which he underwent a cure
in what looks suspiciously like a mental home, he was enabled to make a new
start. But the man of fifty-five was hardly likely to have suddenly acquired
the gift of lucid exposition. It is difficult to resist the belief that the change
had something to do with the fact that from that date onwards he was able to

---

[49] Ibid., pp. 247, 310.

[50] Ibid., p. 265.

[51] Ibid., p. 172.

[52] Ibid., p. 161.

[53] Ibid., p. 287.

[54] *De la réorganisation de la société européenne, ou, De la nécessité et des moyens de rassembler les peuples
de l'Europe en un seul corps politique, en conservant à chacun son indépendance nationale*, par H.-C. Saint-
Simon et A. Thierry, son élève (Paris: A. Egron, 1814), in *OSSE*, vol. 15, pp. 153–248; also in
a new edition by A. Pereire (Paris: les Presses Français, 1925). [To honour the influence of his
mentor Thierry occasionally referred to himself as the 'adopted son' of Saint-Simon.—Ed.]

secure the help of young collaborators and that the influence of these young men went beyond matters of mere exposition.

The first of these young helpers, who even appeared on the title page of the *Réorganisation* as his coauthor and pupil, was the future historian Augustin Thierry, then nineteen years of age—the same Thierry who was later to become the leader of the new schools of historians that developed history as a history of the masses and of a struggle of class interests and, in this, profoundly influenced Karl Marx.[55]

The pamphlet on which he first collaborated with Saint-Simon is not of great interest to us, although it has achieved a certain celebrity for its advocacy of an Anglo-French federation, which, after the adherence of Germany, was to develop into a sort of European federation with a common parliament. The fall of the French empire and the negotiations going on at Vienna made Saint-Simon then apply his dominant idea of a reorganisation of society to the whole of Europe; but in the execution of the idea there was little of the old Saint-Simon, except for occasional flights of fancy of which the phrase "the golden age that is not behind us but in front of us and that will be realised by the perfection of the social order" has by its later use as a motto by the Saint-Simonians become widely known.[56]

The collaboration of Saint-Simon and Thierry lasted about two years. During the hundred days, they wrote first against Napoleon and then against the Allies. The great Carnot, always one of Saint-Simon's admirers and then temporarily returned to power, procured for Saint-Simon a sub-librarianship at the Arsenal, equally temporary.[57] After Waterloo he fell for a brief period back

---

[55] For a discussion of the significance of the work of Thierry, Mignet, and Guizot in this connection, see Georg Plechanow, "Über die Anfänge der Lehre vom Klassenkampf", *Die neue Zeit*, vol. 21, 1902, pp. 275–86, 292–305. See also Charles Seignobos, *La méthode historique appliqué aux sciences sociales*, 2nd ed. (Paris: F. Alcan,1909), p. 261: "C'est lui (Saint-Simon) qui a fourni à Augustin Thierry ses idées fondamentales". [This translates as, "It was he (Saint-Simon) who provided Augustin Thierry with his fundamental ideas". The three historians Hayek mentions, Saint-Simon's secretary Augustin Thierry (1795–1856), François Mignet (1796–1884), and François Guizot (1787–1874), were all associated with liberal movements that gained strength following the restoration of the French monarchy in 1814. Mignet, for example, sympathetically interpreted the French Revolution as contributing to the liberal cause. Guizot's views shifted from liberal to conservative following the July Revolution of 1830. In the 1840s he served as foreign minister, and his name was invoked (and linked with that of Metternich) by Marx and Engels in the first paragraph of the *Communist Manifesto* (1848).—Ed.]

[56] *OSSE*, vol. 15, p. 247 [pp. 247–48]. In the form of "L'âge d'or, qu'une aveugle tradition a placé jusqu'ici dans le passé, est devant nous" [The golden age that blind tradition has hitherto placed just in the past, lies before us.—Ed.], the phrase appears first in 1825 as the motto of Saint-Simon's *Opinions littéraires et philosophiques*, and later as the motto of the Saint-Simonian *Le Producteur*. [Hayek refers to Saint-Simon's *Opinions littéraires, philosophiques et industrielles* (Paris: Galerie de Bossange Père, 1825) and to the short-lived journal, *Le Producteur*, established by his disciples Olinde Rodrigues and Prosper Enfantin soon after his death.—Ed.]

[57] See Leroy, *Vie de Saint-Simon*, pp. 262, 277, and Hippolyte Carnot, "Sur le saint-simonisme", *Séances et travaux de l'académie des sciences morales et politiques*, 47th année, new series, vol. 28, 1887,

into poverty. But he had now young friends among the new generation of bankers and industrialists whose fortunes were rising, and it was to them that he attached himself. The enthusiasm for industry was henceforth to replace the enthusiasm for science; or, at least, as the old love was not quite forgotten, he found a new force worthy to exercise the temporal power at the side of science which was to wield the spiritual power. And he found that the praise of industry was better rewarded than the appeals to the scientists or the adulation of the emperor. Laffitte, governor of the Banque de France[58], was the first to help. He procured for Saint-Simon the considerable sum of 10,000 francs per month, to start a new journal to be called *L'Industrie littéraire et scientifique liguée avec l'industrie commerciale et manufacturière*.

Around the new editor a number of young men collected, and he began his career as the head of a school. At first the group consisted largely of artists, bankers, and industrialists—among them some very distinguished and influential men. There was even an economist among the contributors to the first volume of *L'Industrie*, St. Aubin, although one whom J. B. Say unkindly described as the "clown of political economy"[59]. He and Thierry appeared as the authors of the discussions of finance and politics which filled the first volume of *L'Industrie*. To the second volume, which appeared in 1817 under a slightly changed title,[60] Saint-Simon himself contributed some considerations on the relations between France and America.

This essay is on the whole in the spirit of the liberal group for whom Saint-Simon was then writing.[61] "The sole purpose towards which all our thoughts

---

p. 128, where Hippolyte Carnot reports the following characterisation of Saint-Simon by his father: "J'ai connu M. de Saint-Simon; c'est un singulier homme. Il a tort de se croire un savant, mais personne n'a des idées aussi neuves et aussi hardies" [I have met Monsieur de Saint-Simon; he is a singular man. He is wrong to believe that he is a scholar, but no one else has ideas as new and as bold as his.—Ed]. The only other scholars who seem ever to have given Saint-Simon any encouragement appear to be the astronomer Hallé and, characteristically, Cuvier. [Though Hayek identifies him as an astronomer, perhaps confusing him with Edmond Halley, Jean-Noël Hallé (1754–1822) was the first occupant of the chair of hygiene at the Ecole de Santé, an institution created in 1794.—Ed.]

[58] [Hayek refers to the French banker and politician Jacques Laffitte (1767–1844).—Ed.]

[59] [Camille Saint-Aubin (1758–1820) wrote on, among other things, banking, the public debt, and taxes. I could not locate where Say referred to him as "the clown of political economy", but that Say did so was reported in A. Augustin-Thierry, *Augustin Thierry (1795–1856): D'après sa correspondance et ses papiers de famille* (Paris: Plon-Nourrit et cie, 1922), p. 35. Hayek references this book in note 64 below, so it was probably his source.—Ed.]

[60] *L'Industrie, ou discussions politiques, morales et philosophiques, dans l'intérêt de tous les hommes livrés à des travaux utiles et indépendants*, in *OSSE*, vol. 18.

[61] For a comparison of Saint-Simon's views of this period with those of his liberal contemporaries, see Elie Halévy, *L'ère des tyrannies* (Paris: Gallimard, 1938), pp. 33–41. [See Elie Halévy, *The Era of Tyrannies*, translated by R. K. Webb (New York: New York University Press, 1966), pp. 24–35.—Ed.]

and all our efforts ought to be directed, the organisation of society most favourable to industry in the widest sense of the term", is still best achieved by a political power which does nothing except to see that "the workers are not disturbed" and which arranges everything in such a way that all workers, whose combined force forms the true society, are able to exchange directly, and in complete freedom, the products of their various labours.[62] But his attempt to base all politics on economic considerations as he understands them, that is, in fact, on technological considerations, began soon to lead him outside the views of his liberal friends. We need only quote two of the "most general and most important truths" to which his considerations lead: "First, the production of useful things is the only reasonable and positive end which politics can set itself and the principle *respect for production and the producers* is infinitely more fruitful than the principle *respect for property and the proprietors*", and "Seventh, as the whole of mankind has a common purpose and common interests each man ought to regard himself in his social relations as engaged in a company of workers". "Politics, therefore, to sum up in two words, is the science of production, that is, the science which has for its object the order of things most favourable to all sorts of production".[63] We are back at the ideas of the *Habitant de Genève*—and at the same time at the end of what can be regarded as the independent development of Saint-Simon's thought.

The beginning defection of liberalism soon cost Saint-Simon his first assistant. "I cannot conceive of association without government of someone" are reported to have been Saint-Simon's words in the final quarrel, to which Thierry replied that he "could not conceive of association without liberty".[64] Soon this desertion by his assistant was to be followed by a mass flight of his liberal friends. But this came only after a new assistant of great intellectual force began to push Saint-Simon further along the road which he had only indicated but had not the power to follow. In the summer of 1817 the young polytechnician Auguste Comte, the first and greatest of the host of engineers who were to recognise Saint-Simon as their master, joined him as secretary. Henceforth, to the death of Saint-Simon eight years later, the intellectual history of the two men is indissolubly fused. As we shall see in the next chapter, much of what is commonly regarded as Saint-Simonian doctrine, and what through the Saint-Simonians exercised a profound influence before Comte's public career as a philosopher began, traces to Auguste Comte.

---

[62] *OSSE*, vol. 18, p. 165 [pp. 165–66].

[63] Ibid., pp. 186, 188, 189. [The first quote appears on p. 186, and the next two on p. 188. It is not clear why p. 189 is also listed.—Ed.] See also vol. 19, p. 126.

[64] See A. Augustin-Thierry, *Augustin Thierry* (1795–1856): *D'après sa correspondance et ses papiers de famille*, p. 36.

THIRTEEN

SOCIAL PHYSICS:
SAINT-SIMON AND COMTE

I

More surprising than anything else in Saint-Simon's career is the great fascination that towards the end of his life he exercised on younger men, some of
them intellectually his superiors, who yet for years were satisfied to devil for
him, to recognise him as their leader, and to bring coherence and order into
the thoughts thrown out by him, and whose whole intellectual careers were
determined by his influence. Of none other is this more true than of Auguste
Comte, whatever in later life he may have said about "the unfortunate personal
influence that overshadowed my earliest efforts" or the "depraved juggler", as
whom he had come to regard Saint-Simon.[1]

It is a vain attempt to distinguish precisely what part of the work of the
period of seven years during which they collaborated is Saint-Simon's and
what is Comte's—particularly as it seems likely that in conversation Saint-
Simon was much more stimulating and inspiring than in his writings. Yet so
much confusion has been caused about the actual relationships by some historians constantly attributing to Saint-Simon thoughts which occur first in
works which appeared under his name but are known to have been written by
Comte, while others have tried to vindicate Comte's complete independence
of thought, that we must exercise some care about what in itself may not be a
matter of great consequence.

Auguste Comte was nineteen years of age when in August 1817 Saint-
Simon offered him the position of secretary. The young man had little more
than a year before been sent down from the *Ecole polytechnique*, after a brilliant
career and just before the final examination, as the ringleader in an insub-
ordination. Since then he had earned his living as a mathematical coach, at
the same time preparing himself for an appointment in America which did
not materialise, and had translated a textbook on geometry from the English.
During the same period he had steeped himself in the writings of Lagrange

---

[1] See Comte, *Early Essays on Social Philosophy*, p. 23; and *Système de politique positive* (Paris: L.
Mathias, 1851–54), vol. 3, p. 16 [p. xv].

and Monge, of Montesquieu and Condorcet, and more recently had taken some interest in political economy.

This seems to have been the qualification on which Saint-Simon, anxious to develop his 'science of production', engaged him to write the further parts of *L'Industrie*.[2] In any case, the new disciple was able to write in the three months or so during which he remained Saint-Simon's paid secretary the whole of the four parts of the third and the first and only part of the fourth volume of that publication.[3]

On the whole his contribution is merely a development of the doctrines of his new master which the disciple pushes somewhat further to their logical conclusions. The third volume is largely devoted to problems of the philosophy of history, the gradual transition from polytheism to the positive era, from the absolute monarchy through the transitory stage of the parliamentary liberal state to the new positive organisation, and, above all, from the old 'celestial' to the new terrestrial and positive morals.[4] Only now are we able to watch these transitions because we have learned to understand the laws to which they are subject.[5] All the institutions existing at any time, being an application of the ruling social philosophy, have their relative justification.[6] And anticipating one of the main features of his later philosophy, Comte sums up in the only sentence of this early work which he would later acknowledge: "There is nothing good and nothing bad absolutely speaking; everything is relative, this is the only absolute statement".[7]

No less alarming to Saint-Simon's supporters than the praise of 'terres-

---

[2] See Gouhier, *La jeunesse d'Auguste Comte*, vol. 1, chapter 6. As the third volume of this excellent work had not yet appeared at the time this essay was written, the following exposition relies for Comte's biography after 1817 largely on the same author's brief *La vie d'Auguste Comte* (Paris: Gallimard, 1931). [The 'third volume' to which Hayek refers is Henri Gouhier, *Auguste Comte et Saint-Simon*, vol. 3 of *La jeunesse d'Auguste Comte et la formation du positivism* (Paris: Librarie philosophique J. Vrin, 1941).—Ed.]

[3] Alfred Pereire, *Autour de Saint-Simon: Documents originaux* (Paris: H. Champion, 1912), p. 25.

[4] *Œuvres de Saint-Simon et d'Enfantin* (*OSSE*), vol. 19, pp. 37–38.

[5] Ibid., p. 27: "La grande supériorité de l'époque actuelle . . . consiste en ce qu'il nous est possible de savoir ce que nous faisons. . . . Ayant la conscience de notre état, nous avons celle de ce qu'il nous convient de faire". [The great superiority of the present epoch . . . consists in our having the possibility to know what we are doing . . . Being aware of our state, we are conscious of what is proper to do.—Ed.]

[6] Ibid., p. 23.

[7] *L'Industrie*, 1817, vol. 3, 2me cahier: "Il ne s'agit plus de disserter à perte de vue pour savoir quel est le meilleur des gouvernements: il n'y a rien de bon, il n'y a rien de mauvais, absolument parlant. Tout est relatif, voilà la seule chose absolue". [Hayek's reference is to the original publication of 1817, which is cited in Periere's *Autour de Saint-Simon*, pp. 24–25. The beginning of the passage that precedes the colon, which Hayek does not translate, might be rendered: "It is of no purpose any longer to argue endlessly and in vain over what is the best of governments" —Ed.]

trial morals' were the 'views on property and legislation' contained in volume four of *L'Industrie*. Although in general still mainly utilitarian (and consciously Benthamite)[8] in its insistence on the variability of the contents of property rights and the need to adapt them to the conditions of the time,[9] it strikes a new note in emphasising that, while parliamentary government is merely a form, it is the constitution of property which is the fundamental thing, and that it is therefore "this constitution which is the real basis of the social edifice"[10]—implying that with the revision of the law of property the whole social order can be changed.[11]

The third volume of *L'Industrie* was hardly completed when most of its liberal supporters withdrew from it after a public protest against the incursion of the journal into a field outside its professed program and against its advocacy of principles "which were destructive of all social order and incompatible with liberty".[12] Although Saint-Simon attempted a lame apology in the introduction of the fourth volume and promised to return to the original plan, the first issue of the new volume was also the last. The funds were exhausted and *L'Industrie*, and with it Comte's paid position, came to an end.

II

Comte continued, however, to collaborate with Saint-Simon in the various journalistic enterprises which the latter undertook during the next few years. His enthusiasm for his master was still undiminished. Saint-Simon is "the most excellent man he knows", the "most estimable and lovable of men", to whom he was sworn eternal friendship.[13] At the next attempt at a journalistic enter-

---

[8] *OSSE*, vol. 19, p. 13.

[9] Ibid., pp. 82–83, 89.

[10] Ibid., p. 83.

[11] Incidentally, and as a justification of this view, Comte develops for the first time the theory that the present constitution of property in France derives from the conquest of Gaul by the Franks. His statement (ibid., p. 87) that the successors of the victors are still the proprietors while the descendants of the vanquished are today the farmers provides the basic idea for the racial theories of history of Thierry and his school. It is on this that Saint-Simon, two years later, based his claim of priority vis-à-vis Guizot (see *OSSE*, vol. 21, p. 192).

[12] Pereire, *Autour de Saint-Simon*, pp. 25–28. [The quotation, which appears on p. 28, is from a letter to Saint-Simon from François Alexandre Frédéric, Duc de la Rochefoucauld-Liancourt (1747–1827). The Duke had headed the list of subscribers for earlier volumes of *L'industrie*, but in his letter he withdrew his support for the project.—Ed.]

[13] Auguste Comte, *Lettres d'Auguste Comte à M. Valat* (Paris: Dunod, 1870), pp. 51, 53. See also pp. 36–37 (letter dated April 17, 1818): "Je puis te dire que jamais je n'ai connu de jeune homme aussi ardent ni aussi généreux que lui: c'est un être original sous tous les rapports. . . . J'ai appris, par cette liaison de travail et d'amitié avec un des hommes qui voient le plus loin en politique philosophique, j'ai appris une foule de choses que j'aurais en vain cherchées dans les livres, et

prise, the *Politique*, Comte becomes a partner and shareholder with Saint-Simon.[14] It is just one of the numerous liberal journals which in these years sprung up and died like mushrooms; but even its strongly liberal views, the advocacy by Comte of economy and the freedom of the press, did not secure it a life of more than five months. But three months after its death, in September 1819, Saint-Simon, again with Comte's support, started another and more characteristic organ,[15] which contains perhaps the most remarkable of Saint-Simon's writings, the *Organisateur*, whose very name was a program. It was certainly the first of his publications which attracted wide attention inside and outside France and which made him generally known as a social reformer.

This is probably due more than anything else to the prosecution which he drew on himself by the celebrated "Parable" with which the new publication opens. In it Saint-Simon first shows that if France were suddenly deprived of the fifty chief scientists in each field, of the fifty chief engineers, artists, poets, industrialists, bankers, and artisans of various kinds, her very life and civilisation would be destroyed. He then contrasts this with the case of a similar misfortune befalling a corresponding number of persons of the aristocracy, of dignitaries of state, of courtiers, and of members of the high clergy, and points out how little difference this would really make to the prosperity of France.[16] But although the best known, the "Parable" is by no means the most interesting part of the *Organisateur*. To do justice to its title, he presents for the

---

mon esprit a fait plus de chemin depuis six mois que dure notre liaison qu'il n'en aurait fait en trois ans si j'avais été seul. Ainsi cette besogne m'a formé le jugement sur les sciences politiques, et, par contre-coup, elle a agrandi mes idées sur toutes les autres sciences, de sorte que je me trouve avoir acquis plus de philosophie dans la tête, un coup d'oeil plus juste, plus élevé". [I could tell you that I have never met a young man as ardent and generous as he: by all accounts he is an original. . . . Through collaboration and friendship with one of the men who see the furthest in matters of political philosophy, I have learned a multitude of things for which I would have searched in vain in books, and my soul has travelled farther during the six months that comprise our relationship than it would have done in three years had I been alone. Thus this work has formed my judgement about political science and, as a consequence, it has extended my ideas about all the other sciences, so that I find myself to have acquired more philosophy in my head, a more accurate insight and a lofty view.—Ed.] Maxime Leroy, in quoting this passage in *La vie véritable du comte Henri de Saint-Simon*, p. 293, inserts after the first sentence "Saint-Simon est un accoucheur d'idées". [Saint-Simon is a midwife of ideas (i.e., a maieutician).—Ed.] Although this sentence is probably not by Comte, we have taken the title of chapter twelve from it.

[14] Pereire, *Autour de Saint-Simon*, p. 60.

[15] The term *journal* and similar expressions in connection with Saint-Simon's works must not be taken too literally. They all appeared in irregular sequence, often out of numerical order, and in different formats and in various editions. This is true of the *Organisateur* even more than of his other works. [Hayek refers to the first edition of *L'Organisateur* (Paris: Chez Correard, 1819–20), which contained Saint-Simon's own writings. A second edition, begun in 1829 (after Saint-Simon's death) and published by his disciples Enfantin and Bazard, helped to spread what was by then being touted as the new Saint-Simonian religion more widely.—Ed.]

[16] *OSSE*, vol. 20, pp. 17–26.

first time in a series of letters a real plan for the reorganisation of society, or at least a plan for a reorganisation of the political system which would give all social activity the scientific direction which it needs.[17] While his starting point is now the English parliamentary system, which is the best system yet invented, his problem is how this system can be transformed into something resembling his Council of Newton of sixteen years before. The direction must be placed in the hands of the "industrialists",[18] that is, all those who do productive work. They are to be organised in three separate bodies. The first, the *chambre d'invention*,[19] is to consist of 200 engineers and 100 'artists' (poets, writers, painters, sculptors, architects, and musicians) and would have to draw up the plans for public undertakings. The *chambre d'examination*, consisting of 100 each of biologists, physicists, and mathematicians, would have to scrutinise and approve these plans. The *chambre d'exécution*, consisting entirely of the richest and most successful entrepreneurs, would watch over the execution of these works. Among the first tasks of the new parliament would be the reconstitution of the law of property, which "must be founded on a basis most favourable to production".[20]

The new system will come not only because its inherent advantages will be generally recognised, but, even more important, because it is the necessary outcome of the course which the advance of civilisation has taken during the last seven hundred years.[21] This proves that his plan is not a utopia[22] but the result of the scientific treatment of history, of a true history of the whole of civilisation, as Condorcet conceived it, which will enable us to continue on the pre-destined route with open eyes.[23]

As an "example of how industry ought to be conceived"[24] Saint-Simon then inserts two letters (the eighth and ninth) which, as we now know, were written by Comte, who later republished them under his own name.[25] The most

[17] Ibid., pp. 50–58.

[18] Ibid.

[19] The idea of the *chambre d'invention* is probably borrowed from Bacon's *New Atlantis*. [See, e.g., Francis Bacon, *The New Atlantis*, in *The Philosophical Works of Francis Bacon*, ed. John Robertson (London: G. Routledge and Sons, 1905), pp. 712–32. Bacon's fable recounts his shipwreck on the Isle of Bensalem, where he discovered a long-existing society that had flourished due to its systematic pursuit of the inductive and experimental sciences.—Ed.]

[20] *OSSE*, vol. 20, p. 59.

[21] Ibid., p. 63.

[22] Ibid., pp. 69–72.

[23] Ibid., p. 74.

[24] Ibid., p. 67 [76].

[25] In the appendix to the *Système de politique positive*, vol. 4, pp. 10–46, later reprinted under the title *Opuscules de philosophie sociale 1819–1828* (Paris: E. Leroux, 1883). An English translation of the latter by Henry Dix Hutton with an introduction by Frederic Harrison is available in Routledge's New Universal Library under the title *Early Essays on Social Philosophy*. Below, the parenthetical page references following those of the *OSSE* refer to this English edition. [Hayek first cited the *Early Essays* in chapter 11, note 30, and also in note 1 of the present chapter.—Ed.]

important parts of these are the brief passages elucidating Saint-Simon's suggestion that the rise of the new system is the necessary result of the law of progress: "At no period has the progress of society been regulated by a system conceived by a man of genius and adopted by the masses. This would, from the nature of things, be impossible, for the law of human progress guides and dominates all; men are only its instruments". Therefore, "all we can do is consciously to obey this law, which constitutes our true providence, ascertaining the course it marks out for us, instead of being blindly impelled by it. Here in truth lies the goal of the grand philosophic revolution for our own times".[26] For the rest, and although Comte's contribution still contains few ideas which cannot be found in Saint-Simon's earlier work, these are now presented with a terseness and force of which the latter was never capable. We find now even more stress placed on the need for the "scientific and positive capacity" to replace the old spiritual power,[27] the same exposition of the successive advances of science towards the positive stage till at last philosophy, morals, and politics also reach it and thereby make the new scientifically directed social system possible,[28] and the same impatience with the freedom of thought which is the denial of a spiritual power.[29] New is the special emphasis on the rôle of the new "class which occupies an intermediate position between the men of science, the artists, and the artisans, that of Engineers", which symbolises the new union between the spiritual and temporal capacities; a union which "prepares the way for this joint direction of society".[30] Under their direction the whole of society will be organised to "act upon nature" as it is now organised in its separate parts.[31] In this joint enterprise the people will no longer be subjects but associates or partners,[32] and for the first time we find the suggestion that there will then be need no longer of "government" but merely of "administration".[33]

To Comte's contribution Saint-Simon merely added at the end of the sec-

---

[26] *OSSE*, vol. 20, pp. 118–19 (56–57) [(57)].

[27] Ibid., p. 85 (35).

[28] Ibid., pp. 137–39 (68–71).

[29] Ibid., p. 106 (49) [(49–50)].

[30] Ibid., p. 142 (72). For Comte's considerations on the same subject a few years later, see also (272–74) [(271–73)]. The fear that his proposals might one day lead to a "despotism founded on science", Comte describes as "a ridiculous and absurd chimera, which could only arise in minds entirely foreign to positive ideas" (ibid., p. 158 (82)).

[31] Ibid., p. 161 [160] (85).

[32] Ibid., p. 150 (77).

[33] Ibid., pp. 144–45 (73) "Le peuple n'a plus besoin d'être gouverné, c'est-à-dire commandé. Il suffit, pour le maintien de l'ordre, que les affaires d'un intérêt commun soient administrées". [The translation in *Early Essays* reads, "the people do not require to be governed (that is to say, commanded). It is sufficient for the maintenance of order that the affairs of common interest should be regulated".—Ed.]

ond letter a characteristic appeal to the scientists and in particular to the artists, who, as the true 'engineers of the soul' as Lenin later described them, are
to use all the forces of imagination "to exercise on the common mass sufficient
action to determine them to follow irrevocably in the direction indicated and
to assist their natural leaders in that great co-operation"—a first indication of
the later Saint-Simonian theories about the social function of art.[34]

In the further description of the working of his new organisation, Saint-
Simon rises to an eloquence unknown to him before. "In the new political
order the social organisation will have for its sole and permanent purpose
the best possible use for the satisfaction of human needs of all the knowledge
acquired in the sciences, the fine arts, and industry"[35] and the increase of that
knowledge. He does not stop to describe in detail "the astonishing degree of
prosperity to which society can aspire with such an organisation".[36]

While, so far, men have applied to nature only their isolated forces and even
mutually counteracted their efforts in consequence of the division of mankind
into unequal parts of which the smaller has always used all its power to domi-
nate the other, men will cease to command each other and will organise to
apply to nature their combined efforts. All that is required is that in the place
of the vague ends which our social system now serves a positive social purpose
should be decided upon:

> In a society which is organised for the positive purpose of increasing its
> prosperity by means of science, art, and craftsmanship, the most important
> political act, that of determining the direction in which the community is to
> move, is no longer performed by men invested with social functions but by
> the body politic itself; . . . the aim and purpose of such an organisation are
> so clear and determined that there is no longer any room for arbitrariness
> of men or even of laws, because both can exist only in the vague, which is,
> so to speak, their natural, element. The actions of government that consist
> in commands will be reduced to nil or practically nil. All the questions that
> will have to be solved in such a political system, namely: By what enterprises
> can the community increase its present prosperity, making use of a given
> knowledge in science, in art, and in industry? By what measures can such
> knowledge be dispersed and brought to the furthest possible perfection? And
> finally by what means can these enterprises be carried out at a minimum
> cost and in minimum time?—all these questions, I contend, and all those to

[34] Ibid., p. 193 [166]. See also the passage in Saint-Simon's later *De l'organisation sociale*, *OSSE*,
vol. 39, p. 136 [pp. 136–37] and Comte's remarks on the same subject in his contribution to the
Catéchisme des industriels in *Early Essays*, p. 172. [For an earlier reference to 'engineers of the soul',
see chapter 10, note 3.—Ed.]

[35] *OSSE*, vol. 20, p. 194.[193]

[36] Ibid., pp. 194–95. [p. 194]

which they can give rise, are eminently positive and soluble. The decisions must be the result of scientific demonstrations totally independent of human will, and they will be subject to discussion by all those sufficiently educated to understand them. . . . Just as every question of social importance will necessarily be solved as well as the existing state of knowledge permits, so will all social functions necessarily be entrusted to those men who are most capable of exercising them in conformity with the general aims of the community. Under such an order we shall then see the disappearance of the three main disadvantages of the present political system, that is, arbitrariness, incapacity, and intrigue.[37]

How perfectly this describes the beautiful illusions that ever since Saint-Simon's times have seduced scientifically trained minds! And yet how obvious it is to us now, even in this first formulation, that it is a delusion; that the idea is based on an extension of the scientific and engineering technique far beyond the field to which they are appropriate. Saint-Simon is fully conscious of the significance of his ambitions; he knows that his way of treating the problem of social organisation "exactly in the same manner as one treats other scientific questions" is new.[38] And how well has he succeeded in his intention *d'imprimer au 19me siècle le caractère organisateur!*[39]

Yet at first he again fails with his appeals. It is the Bourbon king that he hopes will place himself at the head of the new movement and thereby not only meet all the dangers which threaten his house at the time, but also place France in the front of the march of civilisation. Beside the glory which the Bourbons can acquire by social reforms even the fame of Bonaparte will pale.[40] But the only response is the prosecution of Saint-Simon as a moral accomplice in the assassination of the Duc de Berry,[41] since in his "Parable" he had incited the people to do away with the nobility. Although in the end he was acquitted, the proceedings serving only to stimulate interest in the editor of the *Organisateur*, the journal did not survive this crisis. Saint-Simon's funds were once again exhausted, and after a new appeal to all those who felt in themselves the vocation to develop the philosophy of the nineteenth century and to subscribe as *fondateurs de la politique positive*, also failed, this enterprise too came to an end.

[37] Ibid., pp. 199–200 [197–200].

[38] Ibid., pp. 218, 226.

[39] Ibid., p. 220. [The latter part of Hayek's sentence may be translated, "to imprint on the nineteenth century its organizing feature".—Ed.]

[40] Ibid., pp. 236–37.

[41] Ibid., pp. 240–42. [Charles Ferdinand, Duc de Berry (1778–1820), the younger son of Charles, Comte de Artois (later Charles X of France), was assassinated by a saddler as he was leaving the opera in Paris.—Ed.]

III

Saint-Simon's next two major publications, although his most substantial works, are in the main only elaborations of the ideas sketched in the *Organisateur*. We can watch, however, how he moves more and more in the direction of that authoritarian socialism which was to take definite form only after his death in the hands of his pupils. In the exposition of his *Système industriel* (1821)—really more systematic than anything that had yet come from his pen—his main theme is the "measures finally to terminate the revolution".[42] He no longer attempts to conceal his dislike for the principles of liberty and for all those who by defending it stand in the way of the realisation of his plans. "The vague and metaphysical idea of liberty. . . impedes the action of the masses on the individual"[43] and is "contrary to the development of civilisation and to the organisation of a well-ordered system".[44] The theory of the rights of men[45] and the critical work of the lawyers and metaphysicians have served well enough to destroy the feudal and theological system and to prepare the industrial and scientific one. Saint-Simon sees more clearly than most socialists after him that the organisation of society for a common purpose,[46] which is fundamental to all socialist systems, is incompatible with individual freedom and requires the existence of a spiritual power which can "choose the direction to which the national forces are to be applied".[47] The existing "constitutional, representative, or parliamentary system" is a mongrel system that uselessly prolongs the existence of anti-scientific and anti-industrial tendencies[48] because it allows different ends to compete. The philosophy that studies the march of civilisation,[49] and the positive scientists[50] who are able to base scientific policy on co-ordinated series of historical facts,[51] are still to provide

---

[42] *OSSE*, vols. 21, 22. [Saint-Simon opened *Du système industriel* with a title page containing the words, "Considérations sur les mesures à prendre pour terminer la révolution" (p. 23).—Ed.]

[43] Ibid., vol. 21, p. 16. The phrasing of these passages is so clearly Comtian that there can be little doubt that they were written by Comte.

[44] *Du système industriel* (Paris: A. A. Reouard, 1821), pp. xiii–xiv.

[45] *OSSE*, vol. 21, p. 83. See also vol. 22, p. 179.

[46] Ibid., vol. 21, p. 14; vol. 22, p. 184.

[47] "Des Bourbons et des Stuarts" (1822), in *Œuvres choisies*, vol. 2, p. 447.

[48] *OSSE*, vol. 22, p. 248. See also p. 258, and vol. 21, pp. 14, 80, and vol. 37, p. 179 [89], where his disgust with the lack of organisation in England finds expression in the characteristic outburst that "cent volumes *in-folio*, du caractère le plus fin, ne suffiraient pas pour rendre compte de toutes les inconséquences organiques qui existent en Angleterre". [This may be translated, "One hundred folio volumes, with the thinnest characters, would not suffice to account for all the organic inconsistencies that exist in England". As noted in "Individualism: True and False", this volume, p. 67, note 30, "thinnest characters" refers to thin printed letters.—Ed.]

[49] Ibid., vol. 22, p. 188.

[50] Ibid., p. 148. [The phrase "positive scientists" does not appear on p. 148.—Ed.]

[51] Ibid., vol. 21, p. 20.

the spiritual power. Much more space, however, is now given to the organisation of the temporal power by the industrialists—a theme which is further developed in the *Catéchisme des industriels* (1823).[52]

To entrust the entrepreneurs with the task of preparing the national budget and therefore with the direction of the national administration is the best means of securing for the mass of the people the maximum of employment and the best livelihood.[53] The industrialists, by the nature of their various works, form a natural hierarchy and they ought to organise into one big corporation which will enable them to act in concert for the achievement of their political interests; in this hierarchy the bankers, who from their occupations know the relations between the different industries, are in the best position to co-ordinate the efforts of the different industries, and the biggest banking houses in Paris, by their central position, are called upon to exercise the central direction of the activities of all industrialists.[54] But while the direction of the work of all productive workers is to be in the hands of the entrepreneurs as their natural leaders, they are to use their powers in the interests of the poorest and most numerous classes;[55] the subsistence of the proletarians must be secured by the provision of work for the fit and by the support of the invalids.[56] In the one great factory which France will become, a new kind of freedom will exist: with the formula which Friedrich Engels was later to make famous, we are promised that under the new and definite organisation, which is the final destiny of mankind,[57] the governmental or military organisation will be replaced by the administrative or industrial.[58] The obstacles to

[52] Ibid., vols. 37–39.

[53] Ibid., vol. 22, p. 82 [pp. 82–83]. See also vol. 21, pp. 131–32.

[54] Ibid., vol. 21, p. 47.

[55] Ibid., p. 161.

[56] Ibid., p. 107.

[57] Ibid., vol. 22, pp. 80, 185.

[58] Ibid., vol. 37, p. 87. See also vol. 21, p. 151. The formula seems to have been originally Comte's (see above, pp. 205–6) and was later taken over by the Saint-Simonians. See particularly *Doctrine de Saint-Simon: Exposition, première année, 1829*, Célestin Bouglé and Elie Halévy, eds (Paris: M. Rivière, 1924), p. 162, in whose publications it occurs once in the form "Il s'agit pour lui [le travailleur—FAH] non seulement *d'administrer* des choses, mais de gouverner des hommes, œuvre difficile, immense, œuvre saint" (*Globe*, April 4, 1831). [An English translation now exists: see *The Doctrine of Saint-Simon: An Exposition, First Year, 1828–1829*, translated with notes and an introduction by Georg G. Iggers, 2nd ed. (New York: Schocken Books, 1972). The passage above is translated there as follows: "It is up to him [the worker] not only to administer things, but to rule over men—a difficult, immense, and holy task".—Ed.] Engels' use of the expression in the *Anti-Dühring: Herrn Eugen Dühring's Umwälzung der Wissenschaft*, 3rd ed. (Stuttgart: J. H. W. Diets, 1894), p. 302, runs in the original: "An die Stelle der Regierung über Personen tritt die Verwaltung von Sachen. Der Staat wird nicht 'abgeschafft', *er stirbt ab*". [This translates as, "The government of persons is replaced by the administration of things. . . . The state is not 'abolished',

this reorganisation are the nobles and the clergy, the lawyers and the metaphysicians, and the military and the proprietors who represent the two past eras. The bourgeois, who have made the revolution and destroyed the exclusive privilege of the nobility to exploit the wealth of the nation, have now merged into one class with the latter, and there are now only two classes left.[59] In the political struggle for the right to exploit, which has continued since the revolution, the industrialists, that is, all those who work, have not yet really taken part. But

the producers are not interested in whether they are pillaged by one class or another. It is clear that the struggle must in the end become one between the whole mass of the parasites and the whole mass of the producers till it is decided whether the latter will continue to be the prey of the former or whether they will obtain the supreme direction of a society of which they form already by far the largest part. This question must be decided as soon as it is put directly and plainly, considering the immense superiority of power of the producers over the non-producers.

The moment when this struggle must assume its true character has actually arrived. The party of the producers will not hesitate to show itself. And even among the men whom birth has placed in the class of parasites, those who excel by the width of their views and the greatness of their souls begin to feel that the only honourable rôle which they can play is to stimulate the producers to enter into political life, and to help them to obtain in the direction of the common affairs the preponderance they have already obtained in society.[60]

IV

To the *Catèchisme des industriels*, which was to spread these doctrines further, Auguste Comte contributed the third part, a substantial volume called a *Plan of the Scientific Operations Necessary for Reorganising Society*,[61] and two years later (1824) republished by its author under the even more ambitious title, *System of Positive Policy*—"a title premature indeed, but rightly indicating the scope" of

---

it withers away". The added ellipsis indicates that Hayek left out the phrase "und die Leitung von Produktionsprozeßen", that is, "and the direction of the processes of production", which ended the first sentence.—Ed.]

[59] *OSSE*, vol. 37, p. 8.

[60] Ibid., vol. 22, pp. 257–58 [258–59].

[61] Later included under the original title in the *Early Essays on Social Philosophy*, pp. 88–217.

his labours, as Comte said thirty years later.[62] It is the most significant single tract of the whole body of literature with which we are here concerned.[63]

In this first form the 'positive system' is little more than a brilliant restatement of Saint-Simon's doctrine.[64] Comte here carries still further his hatred of the dogma of the liberty of conscience, which is the great obstacle to reorganisation.[65] Just as in astronomy, physics, chemistry, and physiology there is no such thing as liberty of conscience,[66] so this transitory fact will disappear once politics has been elevated to the rank of a natural science and the true and final doctrine has been definitely established.[67] This new science of *social physics*, that is to say, the study of the collective development of the human race, is really a branch of physiology, or the study of man conceived in its entire extension. In other words, the history of civilisation is nothing but the indispensable result and complement of the natural history of man.[68] Politics is thus on the point of becoming a positive science in accordance with the law of the three stages, which is now pronounced in its final form: "Each branch of knowledge, in its development, is necessarily obliged to pass through three different theoretical states: the theological or fictitious state; the metaphysical or abstract state; lastly, the scientific or positive state", the definite state of all knowledge whatsoever.[69]

The object of social physics is to discover the natural and unavoidable laws of the progress of civilisation which are as necessary as that of gravitation.[70] By civilisation Comte means "the development of the human mind and its result, the increasing power of man over nature", the ways in which he has learned to act upon nature to modify it to his own advantage.[71] It is civilisation in this sense, that is, the state of science, fine arts, and industry, which deter-

---

[62] Ibid., Author's Preface, p. 24.

[63] [This sentence noting the importance of Comte's early essay was added to the 1952 version of Hayek's essay.—Ed.]

[64] Leaving it open as to how much of this 'Saint-Simonian' doctrine may not arise from Comte's earlier contributions.

[65] Ibid., pp. 96, 98 [96–99].

[66] Ibid., p. 97. This has now of course become orthodox Marxist doctrine. Cf. Vladimir Ilyich Lenin, *What Is to Be Done? Burning Questions of our Movement*. Little Lenin Library (New York: International Publishers, 1943), p. 14: "Those who are really convinced that they have advanced science, would demand, not freedom for the new views to continue side by side with the old, but the substitution of the old views by the new views".

[67] *Early Essays*, pp. 107, 130, 136.

[68] Ibid., pp. 200–1.

[69] Ibid., pp. 131–32. [The quotation appears on p. 131.—Ed.]

[70] Ibid., pp. 147–49, 157.

[71] Ibid., pp. 133, 144. [There is no reference to a definition of civilisation on p. 133, and Hayek does some paraphrasing with Comte's definition in his quotation from p. 144, which reads, "on the one hand, in the development of the human mind, on the other, in the result of this, namely, the increasing power of Man over Nature".—Ed.]

mines and regulates the course of social organisation.[72] Social physics, which, like all science, aims at prevision, enables us by observing the past to determine the social system which the progress of civilisation tends to realise in our own day.[73] The superiority of positive politics consists in the fact that it *discovers* what is made necessary by these natural laws while other systems *invent*.[74] All that remains for us to do is to help into life the positive system which the course of civilisation tends to produce, and we are certain to secure the best system now obtainable if we discover that which is most in harmony with the present state of civilisation.[75]

It will be noticed how close Comte's view on the philosophy of history, which is commonly regarded as the opposite of a 'materialist' interpretation, comes to that view—particularly if we remember the exact meaning which he gives to the term *civilisation*. In fact, what anticipation of the materialistic interpretation of history can be found in the Saint-Simonian writings— and we believe that they are the main source of that doctrine—can be traced directly to this and some of the earlier works of Comte.[76]

Although soon after the publication of the *Catéchisme des industriels* Comte was finally to break with Saint-Simon when the latter began to turn his doctrine into a religion, the next two works which Comte published shortly after Saint-Simon's death in the Saint-Simonian *Producteur*[77] still continue the common line of thought. The first of these is of interest mainly for the more careful analysis of the progress towards the positive method. He shows how man "necessarily begins by regarding all the bodies which attract his attention as

---

[72] Ibid., pp. 144, 149. [144–48]

[73] Ibid., pp. 180, 191.

[74] Ibid., p. 165. For a use of the same terms by Engels in his exposition of the materialist interpretation of history, compare his *Herrn Eugen Dühring's Umwältzung der Wissenschaft*, or *Herr Eugen Dühring's Revolution in Science*, translated by Emile Burns (New York: International Publishers, 1935), p. 300 [294], where he says that the means by which the existing abuses can be got rid of "are not to be *invented* by the mind, but *discovered* by means of the mind in the material facts of production".

[75] Ibid., pp. 154, 165, 167, 170.

[76] Although the influence of Saint-Simonian doctrine on the birth of the materialist interpretation of history has often been pointed out—see particularly Friedrich Muckle, *Henri de Saint-Simon: Die Persönlichkeit und ihr Werk* (Jena: G. Fischer, 1908), and Walter Sulzbach, *Die Anfänge der materialistischen Geschichtsauffassung* (Karlsruhe: G. Braun, 1911), these authors appear to have overlooked the fact that the crucial passages occur nearly always in works which are known to have been written by Comte.

[77] *Le Producteur*, vol. 1, 1825, pp. 289, 596; vol. 2, 1825, pp. 314, 348; and vol. 3, 1826, p. 450. These essays have been included by Comte in the collection of *Early Essays* in the appendix of the *Politique positive* and will be found in the English edition (pp. 217–75 [218–75] and 276–332) under the titles "Philosophical Considerations on the Sciences and Men of Science" and "Considerations on the Spiritual Power".

so many living beings, animated with a life resembling his own",[78] and it is interesting that at this stage Comte, who only a few years later was to deny the possibility of all introspection,[79] was still explaining this by the fact that "the personal action exerted by man on other beings is the only kind of which he comprehends the *modus operandi* through his consciousness of it".[80] But already he is on the way to denying the legitimacy of the disciplines which are based precisely on this knowledge. His attacks now aim not merely at the "revolting monstrosity", the anti-social dogma of the liberty of conscience,[81] and the anarchy of unregulated individualism generally,[82] but are already more specifically directed against the teachings of political economy.[83] Only by historical considerations can it be explained how that "strange phenomenon", the idea that a society ought not to be consciously organised, could ever have arisen.[84] But as "everything that develops itself spontaneously is necessarily legitimate during a certain period",[85] so the critical doctrine has had a relative justification during the past. But a perfect social order can be established only if we can in all cases "assign to every individual or nation that precise kind of activity for which they are respectively fitted".[86] But this pre-supposes a spiritual power, a moral code, of which again Comte cannot conceive except as deliberately constructed.[87] The necessary moral order can therefore be created only by a government of opinion which determines "the entire system of ideas and habits necessary for initiating individuals into the social order under which they must live".[88] The ideas, which, after he had allowed himself for twenty years to be deeply influenced by Comte, finally so revolted J. S. Mill that he described them as "the completest system of spiritual and temporal despotism, which ever yet emanated from a human brain, unless possibly that of Ignatius Loyola",[89] were present in Comte's thoughts from the beginning.

[78] *Early Essays*, p. 229 [220].

[79] In a review of François J. V. Broussais, *De l'irritation et de la folie* (Paris: Melle Delaunay, 1828), published in the same year and also included in the *Early Essays*. See particularly p. 339.

[80] *Early Essays*, p. 219.

[81] Ibid., pp. 281, 295.

[82] Ibid., p. 250 [pp. 250–51].

[83] Ibid., pp. 306, 320–24.

[84] Ibid., p. 282.

[85] Ibid., p. 281. The curious similarity of this statement to certain thoughts of Hegel, which will occupy us later, will not escape the reader. [Hayek discusses the similarities between Hegel and Comte in chapter 17.—Ed.]

[86] Ibid., p. 307.

[87] Ibid., pp. 319–20: "Every doctrine presupposes a founder".

[88] Ibid., p. 301 [pp. 300–1].

[89] J. S. Mill, *Autobiography* (1873), p. 213. [See *Collected Works of John Stuart Mill*, vol. 1, p. 221. Ignatius of Loyola (1491–1556) was the founder of the Society of Jesus, or the Jesuits, an order of the Catholic Church whose members were renowned for their strict discipline, missionary zeal, and absolute obedience to the Pope.—Ed.]

They are a necessary consequence of the whole system of thought which not only J. S. Mill but the whole world has taken over from Comte.

V

There is little more to say about the last phase of Saint-Simon's life. While the *Catéchisme des industriels* was in the process of publication, a new financial crisis in his affairs threatened him again with starvation, and early in 1823 the old man, now really discouraged, tried to blow out his brains. He recovered, however, from the self-inflicted wound with the loss of one eye, and soon assistance came from a new, enthusiastic, and this time wealthy pupil. The young banker and former instructor at the *Ecole polytechnique*, Olinde Rodrigues,[90] not only provided for Saint-Simon's necessities during the last two years of his life, but also became the centre of the little group which after his death developed into the *Ecole saint-simonien*. He was soon joined by the poet Léon Halévy, the physiologist Dr. Bailly, the lawyer Duveyrier, and others.[91] With them Saint-Simon prepared the *Opinions littéraires, philosophiques et industrielles* (1825) in which the banker, the poet, and the physiologist each elaborated the parts of the doctrine of the master for which they possessed special competence. Only a little later in the same year appeared the last work of Saint-Simon, marking the final phase of his work, the *Nouveau christianisme*.

Already for some time Saint-Simon had shown an increasing tendency away from the narrowly 'scientific' and towards a more mystical and religious form of his doctrine. This had indeed been the final cause of the estrangement between him and Comte, who, however, was to undergo a similar change towards the end of his own career. In Saint-Simon's case this development is partly a return to his first ideas.

Since the great schism at the time of the Reformation, he argues, none of the Christian churches represents true Christianity. They have all neglected the fundamental precept that men should behave as brothers towards each other. The main object of true Christianity must be "the speediest improvement of the moral and the physical existence of the poorest class"—a phrase which appears on almost every page of the brochure and which became the watchword of the Saint-Simonian group. Since the churches have made no

---

[90] [Benjamin-Olinde Rodrigues (1794–1850) was one of Saint-Simon's favourite disciples who, with Prosper Enfantin, began publication of *Le Producteur* soon after Saint-Simon's death in May 1825.—Ed.]

[91] [Hayek mentions Léon Halévy (1802–83), professor of literature at the *Ecole Polytechnique*, the medical doctor Etienne Marin Bailly (1796–1837), and the lawyer Charles Duveyrier (1803–66), all of whom contributed to Saint-Simon's *Opinions*. Duveyrier also contributed to *L'Organisateur* and *Le Globe*; Léon Halévy was the grandfather of Elie Halévy.—Ed.]

use of their opportunity to improve the lot of the poor by the teaching and encouragement of the arts and the organisation of industry, the Lord is now addressing the people and the princes through His new prophet. He undertakes to reconstruct theology, which from time to time needs to be renewed, just as physics, chemistry, and physiology must be periodically rewritten.[92] The new theology will pay more attention to the terrestrial interests of man. All that is required is an organisation of industry that will assure a great amount of work of the kind which will secure the quickest advance of human intelligence. "You can create such conditions; now that the extent of our planet is known, let the scholars, the artists, and the industrialists draw up a general plan of the works which must be carried out in order that the terrestrial possessions of the human race be put to the most productive use and made the most agreeable to inhabit in all respects".[93]

Saint-Simon survived the appearance of the *Nouveau christianisme* by only a few weeks. He died in May 1825 at the age of 65, calmly expecting his death while discussing future projects with the group of pupils that now surrounded him. The life that had been an example of the precepts he had laid down for all future sociologists, "passing through all classes of society, putting oneself personally in the greatest number of different social positions, and even creating for oneself and others relationships which have never existed before",[94] ended in peace, tolerable comfort, and even in possession of a considerable reputation.

The funeral reunited the older pupils like Thierry and Comte with the new ones. The old Saint-Simon had just seen the beginnings of the school that under his name was to spread far and wide a body of ideas derived from his work. It is due to them that he has become a figure of considerable importance in the history of social ideas. While he was certainly an *original*, he was scarcely an original or profound thinker. The ideas which he bequeathed to his pupils were unquestionably held by many people at the time. But by his persistence and enthusiasm he gained adherents for them among men who were capable of developing them and in whom he inspired sufficient enthusiasm to act as a body in spreading them. As one of his French biographers has said, his rôle was *de faire flamboyer les idées comme des réclames lumineuses*.[95] He has performed it to perfection.

---

[92] *OSSE*, vol. 23, p. 99 [108].

[93] Ibid., p. 152.

[94] Ibid., vol. 15, p. 82.

[95] Gouhier, *La jeunesse d'Auguste Comte*, vol. 2, p. 3. [Gouhier's phrase translates as "to launch ideas as blazing as illuminated advertising signs". Gouhier's book was published in 1936—today we might put it, "to launch ideas as bright as neon lights".—Ed.]

FOURTEEN

THE RELIGION OF THE ENGINEERS:
ENFANTIN AND THE SAINT-SIMONIANS

I

Less than a month after Saint-Simon's death his friends and disciples constituted themselves into a formal association in order to realise the project of
another journal which he had already discussed with them. *Producteur*, which
appeared in six volumes in 1825 and 1826, was edited by the group under the
leadership of Olinde Rodrigues, with the collaboration of Auguste Comte and
some others who were not strictly members. Soon another young engineer,
who had seen Saint-Simon only once when Rodrigues introduced him, was to
become the outstanding figure of the group and the editor of its journal.

Barthélemy-Prosper Enfantin was the son of a banker. He had entered the
Ecole polytechnique but had left it in 1814, two years before Comte, and, like
him, without completing the course. He had since entered business, spent some
years travelling and working in Germany and Russia, and had recently devoted
some time to the study of political economy and particularly to the works of
Jeremy Bentham. Although his education as an engineer had remained incomplete, or perhaps because of this, his belief in the unlimited powers of the
mathematical and technical sciences remained one of the most characteristic
features of his intellectual makeup. As he explained on one occasion, "When
I have found the words *probabilities, logarithm, asymptote,* I am happy, because I
have regained the road which leads me to formulas and forms".[1] An uncom-
monly handsome man according to the views of his contemporaries, he seems
to have possessed great personal charm, which made it possible for him gradually to swing the entire Saint-Simonian movement in the direction into which
his sentimental and mystical bent led him. But he also commanded considerable powers of intellect which enabled him to make important contributions
before Saint-Simonism passed from its philosophical to its religious phase.[2]

---

[1] *Livre nouveau, Résumé des conférences faites à Ménilmontant,* quoted in Pinet, *Ecrivains et penseurs polytechniciens,* p. 180.

[2] On Enfantin and the Saint-Simonians generally, see Sébastien Charléty, *Histoire du saint-
simonisme (1825–1864)* (Paris: Hachette, 1896; new ed., Paris: P. Hartmann, 1931), still the best

It has been said, with some truth, that Saint-Simonism was born after Saint-Simon's death.[3] However pregnant in suggestions Saint-Simon's writings were, he never achieved a coherent system. It is probably also true that the very obscurity of his writings was one of the greatest incentives for his disciples to develop his doctrines further. It also explains why the importance of the joint efforts of Saint-Simon and his pupils has rarely been properly appreciated. The natural tendency of those who have recognised it has been to ascribe too much to Saint-Simon himself. Others, who have been led by this to study Saint-Simon's own writings, have been bound to turn away disappointed. Although almost all ideas of the school can be found somewhere in the works that have appeared in Saint-Simon's name,[4] the real force which decisively influenced European thought was the Saint-Simonians and not Saint-Simon himself. And we must never forget that the greatest of the Saint-Simonians in their early years, and the medium through whom many of them had received the doctrine of the master,[5] was Auguste Comte, who, as we know, still contributed to the *Producteur*, although he was no longer a member of the group and soon broke off all relations with it.

---

exposition of the Saint-Simonian movement. It is rather surprising that *Enfantin* himself has not yet been made the subject of a monograph. Sébastian Charléty, *Enfantin* (Paris: Alcan, 1930), is merely a useful collection of texts with a brief introduction.

[3] Charléty, *Enfantin*, p. 2.

[4] See Henryk Grossman, "The Evolutionist Revolt Against Classical Economics. I: In France— Condorcet, Saint-Simon, Simonde de Sismondi", *Journal of Political Economy*, vol. 51, October 1943, p. 390, note 50, who contends that in this exposition I have overrated the originality of the Saint-Simonians at the expense of Saint-Simon himself. I am quite ready to agree that nearly all the elements of their system can be found in works that appeared during Saint-Simon's life and under his name (though partly written by Comte and probably others); but they are there so mixed up with other, and in part contradictory, ideas that I should rate the achievement of something like a coherent system by his disciples considerably higher than Dr. Grossman does.

[5] "Le travail de M. A. Comte . . . a servi à plusieurs d'entre nous d'introduction à la doctrine de Saint-Simon", in Bouglé and Halévy, *Doctrine de Saint-Simon*, p. 443. [Auguste Comte's work . . . served for several of us as an introduction to the doctrine of Saint-Simon.—Ed.] Comte (in a letter to Gustave d'Eichthal, December 11, 1829) claims even more influence on the Saint-Simonians: "Vous savez fort bien que je les ai vus naître, si je ne les ai formés (ce dont je serais du reste fort loin de me glorifier) . . . ; les prétendues pensées de ces messieurs ne sont autre chose qu'une dérivation ou plutôt une mauvaise transformation de conceptions que j'ai présentées et qu'ils ont gâtées en y mettant les conceptions hétérogènes dues à . . . Saint-Simon" [You know very well that, if I did not train their minds—and I should not dare and boast about it—at least I have known them from birth . . . the so-called 'thoughts' of these gentlemen are nothing but a derivation or rather a sheer distortion of conceptions that I expounded and that they corrupted with heterogeneous notions borrowed from . . . Saint-Simon.—Ed.] See Emile Littré, *Auguste Comte et la philosophie positive* (Paris: L. Hachette, 1863), pp. 173–74.

II

The new journal had for its express purpose "to develop and expand the principles of a philosophy of human nature based on the recognition that the destiny of our race is to exploit and modify external nature to its greatest advantage", and it believed that this could best be done by "incessantly extending association, one of the most powerful means at its command".[6] In order to attract the general public the programmatic articles were interspersed with others on technological or statistical subjects, which were often written by outsiders. But most of the journal was written by the little group of disciples. There can also be little doubt that, even during the year when the *Producteur* was the centre of their activities, Enfantin had already the largest share in the development of the doctrines of the school, although for some time his position was equalled or even overshadowed by the powerful personality of another new recruit, Saint-Amand Bazard.[7] Slightly older than Rodrigues or Enfantin, and, as a former member of the French Carbonari movement, an experienced revolutionary, he joined the collaborators of the *Producteur*, who already had attracted some old Babouvists and Carbonaris.[8] But although these, and Bazard in particular, played an important part in leading the Saint-Simonians towards more radical views, it is probable that the latter's doctrinal contributions are usually overrated and that his rôle is more appropriately

[6] *Le Producteur, journal de l'industrie, des sciences et des beaux-arts*, vol. 1, 1825, Introduction, p. 5. [The adjective *philosophique*, modifying *journal*, was added to the title starting with the third volume.—Ed.]

[7] On Bazard, see Willy Spühler, *Der Saint-Simonismus: Lehre und Leben von Saint-Amand Bazard (Zürcher Volkswirtschaftliche Forschungen, hg. v. M. Saitzew, no. 7)* (Zurich: Girsberger, 1926). [As Hayek will recount in section 5 to come, Saint-Amand Bazard (1791–1832) was, with Prosper Enfantin, one of the two fathers of the Saint-Simonian movement as it steadily moved towards becoming a church, or cult, in the later 1820s and early 1830s. Like many others, Bazard ultimately broke with Enfantin when the latter, in pressing for the emancipation of women, propounded a new ethics that distinguished between those of either sex with 'constant' and those with 'inconstant', or 'mobile', passional make-ups, which Bazard (and others) viewed as an invitation to promiscuity.—Ed.]

[8] [The Babouvists were absolute egalitarians who believed that all property should be held in common. Thinking they were carrying out the true intention of the French Revolution, they launched a failed coup (the 'Conspiracy of the Equals') in 1796. Subsequently most of the Babouvists were executed, but their ideas influenced many nineteenth century socialists and communists. The most famous Babouvists were François Noël Babeuf (1760–97), after whom the movement was named, and Filippo Michele Buonarroti (1761–1837). The Carbonari (charcoal-burners) was the name of a secret society that formed in Italy in the early nineteenth century. Devoted to the abolition of the restored absolute monarchies that were imposed upon Europe by the Holy Alliance, members disagreed about what should replace them, though many favoured republican forms of government. Their uprisings in Italy in 1820–21 led to the formation in France in 1821 of the Charbonnerie, of which Bazard was one of the founders.—Ed.]

described by a contemporary who said that "M. Enfantin found the ideas, M. Bazard formulated them".[9] Bazard's articles in the *Producteur*, apart from an even fiercer hatred of the liberty of conscience[10] than had been shown by Saint-Simon or even Comte, add little that is new. The same is true of most of the other contributors except Enfantin and, of course, Comte, although the elaboration of the Saint-Simonian doctrine of the social function of art by Léon Halévy must not be overlooked. He sees the time approaching when the "art of moving the masses" will be so perfectly developed that the painter, the musician, and the poet "will possess the power to please and to move with the same certainty as the mathematician solves a geometrical problem or the chemist analyses some substance. Then only will the moral side of society be firmly established".[11] The word *propaganda* was not yet used in this connection, but the art of the modern ministries of propaganda would have been fully appreciated and these institutions were even foreseen by the Saint-Simonians.

Important developments occur in the economic articles which Enfantin contributed to the *Producteur*. The growth of nearly all the new elements of the social doctrine of the Saint-Simonians, which we shall meet presently in their final form in the celebrated *Exposition*, can be traced in these articles. The general interest in the problems of industrial *organisation*, the enthusiasm for the new growth of joint-stock companies, the doctrine of general association, the increasing doubts about the usefulness of private property and of interest, the plans for the direction of all economic activity by the banks— all these ideas were gradually worked out and were more and more strongly

[9] See Louis Reybaud, *Etudes sur les réformateurs contemporians, ou socialistes modernes: Saint-Simon, Charles Fourier, Robert Owen* (Brussels: A. Wahlen [Paris: Guillaumin], 1841), p. 61: "M. Enfantin trouvait la pensée, M. Bazard la formulait". [I could not locate a Brussels edition of Reybaud's book. In the Paris edition, the quotation is found on p. 89 and reads, "M. Enfantin créait la pensée, M. Bazard trouvait la formule", that is, "Monsieur Enfantin created the ideas, Monsieur Bazard found the formulation".—Ed.] Cf. Charles Gide and Charles Rist, *Histoire des doctrines économiques*, 4th ed. (Paris: Recueil Sirey, 1922), p. 251.

[10] *Le Producteur*, pp. 399 et seq.; 1826, vol. 3, pp. 110, 526 et seq. Bazard's articles were the immediate occasion for one of Benjamin Constant's most eloquent essays in defence of liberty. [The Swiss-born cosmopolitan liberal Benjamin Constant (1767–1830), sometime companion of Madame de Staël, favoured a constitutional monarchy with a property-based, but fairly extensive, franchise. Hayek was probably referring to Constant's review essay "De M. Dunoyer et de quelques-uns de ses ouvrages", which was originally published on February 1, 1826, in the *Revue encyclopédique*, and then republished in slightly altered form in Benjamin Constant, *Mélanges de littérature et de politique* (Paris: Pichon et Didier, 1829), pp. 128–62. Dunoyer's work had been criticised in the pages of *Le Producteur* for its promotion of individualism, and at the end of his friendly review Constant rebukes the Saint-Simonians, accusing them of trying to create an "industrial papacy" (p. 157) in France.—Ed.]

[11] *Le Producteur*, vol. 1, p. 83. [In the original article in *Economica*, and in the 1952 version, this note and the one immediately preceding it were mistakenly reversed.—Ed.]

emphasised. We must here be content to quote two sentences particularly characteristic of his approach to the problems. One ridicules the idea that "a human society could exist without an intelligence which directs it".[12] The other describes the concepts which have so far formed the preoccupation of political economy, namely "value, price, and production, which do not contain any constructive idea for the composition or organisation of society", as "irrelevant details".[13]

III

The *Producteur*, which had appeared first weekly, and then monthly, came to an end in October 1826. While this meant the cessation for three years of all public activity of the group, there had already been created a common doctrine which could serve as the basis for intensive propaganda by word of mouth. It was at this time that they had their first great successes among the students of the *Ecole polytechnique*, to which they specially directed their efforts. As Enfantin later expressed it: "The *Ecole polytechnique* must be the channel through which our ideas will spread through society. It is the milk which we have sucked at our beloved school which must nourish the generations to come. It is there that we have learned the positive language and the methods of research and demonstration which today secure the advance of the political sciences".[14] The success of these efforts was such that within a few years the group consisted of some hundred engineers with only a sprinkling of doctors and a few artists and bankers, who were mostly left over from Saint-Simon's immediate disciples, or, like the brothers Pereire, the cousins of Rodrigues, or his friend Gustave d'Eichthal, were personally related to them.[15]

[12] *Le Producteur*, vol. 3, p. 74.

[13] Ibid., July 1826, vol. 4, p. 86 [388].

[14] *OSSE*, vol. 14, p. 86 [vol. 1, p. 165]. In a letter to Fournel of June 1832, quoted by Gaston Pinet, "L'Ecole polytechnique et les Saint-Simoniens", *La Revue de Paris*, May 15, 1894, p. 85, Enfantin describes the *Ecole polytechnique* as "la source précieuse, . . . où notre famille nouvelle, germe de l'humanité future, a puisé la vie. Or, le prolétaire et le savant aiment et respectent cette glorieuse Ecole". [the precious spring, . . . from where our new family, the seed of future humanity, drew life. Now, the proletarian and the intellectual love and respect this glorious School. —Ed.]

[15] [Emile Pereire (1800–75) and his brother Issac (1806–80) were French railroad builders and financiers who were introduced to Saint-Simonian ideas by their cousin Benjamin Olinde Rodrigues. Though like many others they eventually grew uncomfortable with Enfantin's religious mysticism, some of their later entrepreneurial projects were embodiments of Saint-Simon's ideal of the union of the bank and the factory. Their most famous project was the Crédit Mobilier, whose primary function was to grant long-term loans for industrial and commercial activities. The French publicist and Hellenist Gustave d'Eichthal (1804–82) became a disciple of Auguste Comte's in 1824, but later joined the Saint-Simonians. He was instrumental in spreading the

Among the first of the young engineers to join the movement were the two friends Abel Transon and Jules Lechevalier,[16] who through their knowledge of German philosophy helped to give the Saint-Simonian doctrines a certain Hegelian veneer which later proved so important in helping their success in Germany. A short time after followed Michel Chevalier, later famous as an economist, and Henri Fournel, who, to join the movement, resigned a position as director of the Creuzot works and later became Saint-Simon's biographer.[17] Hippolyte Carnot, although himself never a pupil of the *Ecole polytechnique*, since he had spent his youth with his father in exile, must also be counted with this group, not only as the son of Lazare, but still more as the brother of the polytechnician Sadi Carnot, the 'founder of the science of energy', discoverer of the 'Carnot cycle', the ideal of technical efficiency, with whom he lived in these years while the latter developed his famous theories and at the same time preserved a lively although never active interest in the political and social discussions of his friends.[18] At least by tradition and connections, if not by training, Hippolyte Carnot was as much an engineer as the others.

For a time the apartment of the Carnots was the place where Enfantin and Bazard taught an ever-increasing number of young enthusiasts.[19] But towards the end of 1828 they had outgrown that accommodation and it was decided

---

Saint-Simonian doctrine among the intelligentsia of other countries; e.g., after reading Thomas Carlyle's *Signs of the Times* (1829) he sent him a packet containing Saint-Simon's final book, *Le nouveau christianisme*, and copies of the Saint-Simonian periodical *L'Organisateur*. Hayek discusses d'Eichthal's relations with Carlyle and John Stuart Mill in chapter 15.—Ed.]

[16] See Charles Pellarin, *Une page de l'histoire du saint-simonisme et du fouriérisme: Notice sur Jules Lechevalier et Abel Transon* (Paris: Association ouvrière, 1877), which, however, deals largely with the part the two men played later in the Fourierist movement. Lechevalier, after studying German philosophy in France, actually spent a year (1829–30) in Berlin to attend Hegel's lectures. [Though both Abel Transon (1805–76) and Jules Lechevalier (ca. 1800–50) began as Saint-Simonians, they became Fourierists when they split with Enfantin.—Ed.]

[17] [The French economist Michel Chevalier (1806–79), as editor of *Le Globe*, was one of those tried and imprisoned with Enfantin in 1832 on the charge of corruption of public morals. Later a well-known and well-connected economist, Chevalier helped found the *Journal des économistes* and negotiated, with Richard Cobden, the 1860 Anglo-French commercial treaty, a great victory for free trade. Henri Fournel (1799–1876), director of the forges, foundries, and mines of the Creuzot works, gave much of his and his wife's fortunes to the Saint-Simonians. He was among those who travelled with Enfantin to Egypt, where he helped establish the plans for what would later become the Suez Canal. Hayek probably had in mind Fournel's 1833 book, *Bibliographie saint-simonienne*, but this would mean that Fournel was Saint-Simon's bibliographer, not his biographer.—Ed.]

[18] See Sadi Carnot, *Sadi Carnot: Biographie et manuscrit, publiés sous le haut patronage de l'Académie des sciences avec une introduction de M. Emile Picard* (Paris: Gauthier-Villars, 1927), pp. 17–20. See also Georges Mouret, *Sadi Carnot et la science de l'energie* (Paris: G. Carré, 1892). The *Réflexions sur la puissance motrice du feu* appeared in 1824, although its importance was recognised only much later. [Hayek refers to Sadi Carnot, *Réflexions sur la puissance motrice du feu* (Paris: Chez Bachelier, 1824). For more on the various members of the Carnot family, see chapter 11, note 28.—Ed.]

[19] See Hippolyte Carnot, "Sur le saint-simonisme", p. 132.

that a more formal oral exposition of their views should be given to a larger audience. It is probable that this was suggested by the success of a similar experiment by Comte, who in 1826 had begun to expound his *Positive Philosophy* to a distinguished audience, including, besides such scholars as Alexander von Humboldt and Poinsot, also Carnot, who had been sent there by Enfantin to receive his first instruction in Saint-Simonism.[20] Although Comte's attempt had soon been cut short by the mental affliction which interrupted his work for three years, it had attracted sufficient attention to invite imitation.[21]

The course of lectures which the Saint-Simonians arranged in 1829 and 1830, in the form in which it has come down to us as the two parts of the *Doctrine de Saint-Simon, Exposition*,[22] is by far the most important document produced by Saint-Simon or his pupils and one of the great landmarks in the history of socialism which deserves to be much better known than it is outside France. If it is not the Bible of socialism, as it has been called by a French scholar,[23] it deserves at least to be regarded as its Old Testament. And in some respects it did indeed carry socialist thought further than was done for nearly a hundred years after its publication.

IV

As befits one of the foundations of collectivist thought, the *Exposition* is the product of no single man. Although Bazard, as the most skilful speaker, delivered the majority of the lectures, their content was the result of discussion among the group. The published texts were actually written by Hippolyte Carnot from notes taken by him and others during the lectures, and it is presumably to him that the *Exposition* owes its elegance and power. An important supplement to it are the five lectures on the Saint-Simonian religion which Abel Transon delivered about the same time to the students of the *Ecole polytechnique*[24] and which are appended to some of the editions of the *Exposition*.

---

[20] Ibid., p. 129.

[21] [Comte's "mental affliction" was brought on by his discovery of his wife's affair with Antoine Cerclet, the editor of *Le Producteur*. Comte attempted suicide and was briefly institutionalised, then spent the next few years recovering.—Ed.]

[22] *Doctrine de Saint-Simon, Exposition, première année, 1829; deuxième année, 1829–1830*, 2 vols. (Paris: Au Bureau de l'Organisateur, 1830–31). An excellent edition with a valuable introduction and instructive notes by Célestin Bouglé and Elie Halévy was published in the series *Collection des économistes et réformateurs français* (Paris: M. Rivière, 1924). It is to this edition that all the page references below refer. [Hayek made reference to the Bouglé-Halévy edition in chapter 13, note 58, and also in note 5 of the present chapter.—Ed.]

[23] Célestin Bouglé in his introduction to Halévy, *L'ère des tyrannies*, p. 9. [See Halévy, *The Era of Tyrannies*, p. xxi.—Ed.]

[24] (Abel Transon), *De la religion saint-simonienne: Aux élèves de l'Ecole polytechnique*. First published in the (second) *Organisateur* (July–September 1829 [1830]), and reprinted separately (Paris: Au

It is difficult without tiresome repetition to give an adequate idea of this most comprehensive expression of Saint-Simonian thought, since much of it is of course a more or less faithful reproduction of views we have already met. It is, however, not merely, as it claims to be, the sole publication in which the whole of the contribution of Saint-Simon (and, we should add, the young Comte) has been brought into a comprehensive system; but it also develops it further, and it is these developments by Enfantin and his friends which we must mainly consider.

A large part of the more important first volume of the *Exposition* is given to a broad philosophic survey of history and of the "law of development of humanity revealed to the genius of Saint-Simon",[25] which, based on the study of mankind as a "collective being",[26] shows us with certainty what its future will be.[27] This law asserts in the first instance the alternation of *organic* and *critical* states, in the former of which "all aspects of human activity are ordered, foreseen and co-ordinated by a general theory", while in the critical states society is an agglomeration of isolated individuals struggling against each other.[28] The final destiny towards which we are tending is a state where all antagonism between men will have entirely disappeared and the exploitation of men by men is replaced by their joint and harmonic action upon nature.[29] But this definite state, where the "systematisation of effort",[30] the "organisation of labour"[31] for a common purpose[32] is perfected, is reached only in stages. The basic fact of the ever-decreasing antagonism between men, which will lead in the end to the "universal association",[33] implies a "steady diminution of the exploitation of men by men"—a phrase which forms the leitmotif of the whole *Exposition*.[34] While the positive advance towards the universal

---

bureau de l'Organisateur, 1830; Brussels: Laurant frères, 1831), and at the end of the second edition of the *Exposition, deuxième année, 1829–1830*. A German translation appeared at Göttingen in 1832. [Three of Transon's five lectures, which were unsigned, appeared in July 1830 issues of *L'Organisateur*, the other two in September 1830 issues. The first *L'Organisateur* appeared in 1819–20; the second, to which Hayek refers above, began weekly publication in August 1829 and ran through August 1831. A book containing a photocopy of all the issues from the second *L'Organisateur* was published under the auspices of the Burt Franklin Research and Source Work Series (New York: Lennox Hill, 1973). The German edition of Transon's lectures is more fully referenced in chapter 15, note 19.—Ed.]

[25] *Exposition, première année*, p. 127.
[26] Ibid., pp. 131, 160.
[27] Ibid., p. 89.
[28] Ibid., p. 27 [127].
[29] Ibid., p. 162.
[30] Ibid., p. 206.
[31] Ibid., pp. 89, 139.
[32] Ibid., pp. 73, 124 [142], 153 [156].
[33] Ibid., pp. 203, 206, 234, 253 [235].
[34] Ibid., pp. 236, 350.

association is marked by the stages of the family, town, nation, and the federation of nations having a common creed and church,[35] the decrease of exploitation is shown by the changing relations between the classes. From the stage when cannibalism was practised on the captive, through slavery and serfdom to the present relations between proletarians and proprietors, there has been a constant decrease of the degree of exploitation.[36] But men are still divided into two classes, the exploiters and the exploited.[37] There is still a class of disinherited proletarians.[38] As the eloquent Abel Transon put it to the young polytechnicians in a passage of his lectures which better than anything in the *Exposition* sums up the main argument:

> The peasant or craftsman is no longer attached to the man or to the soil, he is not subjected to the whip like the slave; he owns *a greater part* of his labour than the serf, but still, the law is cruel at his expense. All the fruit of his labour does not belong to him. He has to share it with other people who are not useful to him either by their knowledge or by their power. In short, there are no *masters* for him nor *lords*, but there are bourgeois, and so that's what a bourgeois is.
>
> As the owner of land and capital the bourgeois disposes of these at his will and does not place them in the hands of the workers except on condition that he receive a premium from the price of their work, a premium that will support him and his family. Whether a direct heir of the man of conquest or else an emancipated son of the peasant class, this difference of origin merges into the common character which I have just described; only in the first case is the title of his possession based on a fact which is now condemned, on the action of the sword; in the second case the origin is more honourable, it is the work of industry. But *in the eyes of the future* this title is in either case illegitimate and without value because it hands over to the mercy of a privileged class all those whose fathers have not left them any instruments of production.[39]

The cause of this still existing state of affairs is the "constitution of property, the transmission of wealth by inheritance within the family".[40] But the institution of "property is a social fact, subject, as all other social facts, to the law of progress".[41] According to the *Exposition*, the new order will be created by

---

[35] Ibid., pp. 208–9.
[36] Ibid., pp. 214–16, 238.
[37] Ibid., p. 225.
[38] Ibid., pp. 239, 307.
[39] Transon, *De la religion saint-simonienne*, in the *Organisateur*, pp. 48–49.
[40] *Exposition, première année*, Bouglé and Halévy, eds, p. 243.
[41] Ibid., p. 244.

the transfer to the state, which will become an *association of workers*, of the right of inheritance which today is confined to the members of the family. The privileges of birth which have already received such heavy blows in so many respects must entirely disappear.[42]

If, as we proclaim, humanity moves towards a state where all the individuals will be classed according to their capacities and remunerated according to their work, it is evident that the right of property, as it exists, must be abolished, because, by giving to a certain class of men the possibility to live on the work of others and in complete idleness, it preserves the exploitation of one part of the population, the most useful one, that which works and produces, in favour of those who only destroy.[43]

They explain that to them land and labour are merely "instruments of work; and the proprietors and capitalists . . . are the depositaries of these instruments; their function[44] is to distribute them among the workers".[45] But they perform this function very inefficiently. The Saint-Simonians had studied Sismondi's *Nouveaux principes d'économie politique* which in 1826 had appeared in a new edition, in which the author for the first time describes how the ravages of economic crises were caused by "chaotic competition". But while Sismondi had no real remedy to propose and later seems even to have deplored the effects of his teaching,[46] the Saint-Simonians had one. Their description of the defects of competition is almost entirely taken from Sismondi:

In the present state of affairs, where the distribution [of the instruments of production—FAH] is effected by the capitalists and proprietors, none of these functions is performed except after much groping, experimenting, and many

---

[42] Ibid., pp. 253–54.

[43] Ibid., p. 255.

[44] The French word *fonction*, of course, also means 'office'.

[45] *Exposition, première année*, Bouglé and Halévy, eds, p. 257.

[46] In a letter to Channing in 1831 he admitted, "I have shown the defects of the system of free competition; I have demolished, but I lack the strength to reconstruct", in Jean Charles Léonard Simonde de Sismondi, *Fragments de son journal et correspondance* (Geneva: J. Cherbuliez, 1857), p. 130. On the general influence of Sismondi, which can here not be adequately discussed, see Jean Rudolphe de Salis, *Sismondi 1773–1842, la vie et l'œuvre d'un cosmopolite philosophe* (Paris: H. Champion 1932). [Hayek refers to the Swiss economist and historian Jean-Charles-Léonard Simonde de Sismondi (1773–1842) who, though at first a follower of Adam Smith and Jean-Baptiste Say, broke with their views in his *Nouveau principes d'économie politique*, 2nd ed. (Paris: Delaunay, 1827). Sismondi is best remembered today for his underconsumptionist theory of economic fluctuations. He was writing to William Ellery Channing (1780–1842), a liberal American Unitarian minister who, as minister of the Federal Street Church in Boston from 1803–42, was a spokesman for free speech, the abolition of slavery, poor relief, and social reform. Note that the second edition of Sismondi's book appeared a year later than was stated by Hayek in the text.—Ed.]

unfortunate experiences; and even so the result obtained is always imperfect, always temporary. Each person is left to act on his own individual knowledge; no general conspectus guides production; it takes place without judgement, without foresight; it is deficient at one point and excessive at another.[47]

The economic crises are thus due to the fact that the distribution of the instruments of production is effected by isolated individuals, ignorant of the requirements and needs of industry and of the people, and of the means that can satisfy them.[48] The solution which the Saint-Simonians propose was at the time completely new and original. In the new world which they invite us to contemplate

> there will be no longer any proprietors, no isolated capitalists, who by their habits are strangers to industrial activity, yet who decide the character of the work and the fate of the workers. A *social* institution is charged with these functions which today are so badly performed; it is the *depository* of all the instruments of production; it presides over the exploitation of all the material resources; from its point of vantage it has a comprehensive view of the whole which enables it to perceive at one and the same time all the parts of the industrial *workshop*; through its ramifications it is in touch with all the different places, with all kinds of industries, and with all the workers; it can thus take account of all the general and individual wants, bring men and instruments to where the need for them makes itself felt; in a word, it can direct the production and put it in harmony with consumption and entrust the tools to the most deserving industrialists, because it incessantly endeavours to discover their capacity and is in the best position to develop them. . . . In this new world . . . the disturbances which follow from the lack of general accord and from the blind distribution of the agents and instruments of production would disappear and with them also the misfortunes, the reverses and failures of firms against which today no peaceful worker is protected. In a word, industrial activity is *organised*, everything is connected, everything foreseen; the division of labour is perfected and the combination of efforts becomes every day more powerful.[49]

The 'social institution' which is to perform all these functions is not left vague and undetermined as it was by most later socialists. It is the banking system, properly reconstructed and centralised and crowned by a single *banque unitaire, directrice*, which is to serve as the planning body:

---

[47] *Exposition, première année*, Bouglé and Halévy, eds, p. 258.
[48] Ibid., pp. 258–59.
[49] Ibid., p. 261.

The social institution of the future will direct all industries in the interest of the whole society and specially of the peaceful workers. We call this institution provisionally the general system of banks, making all reservations against the too narrow interpretations which one might give to this term.

The system will comprise in the first instance a central bank which constitutes the government in the material sphere; this bank will become the depository of all wealth, of the whole productive fund, of all the instruments of production, in short of everything that today makes up the whole mass of private property.[50]

We need not follow the *Exposition* further into the detail of the proposed organisation.[51] The main points given will suffice to show that in their description of the organisation of a planned society they went much further than later socialists until quite recent times, and also how heavily later socialists have drawn on their ideas. Till the modern discussion of the problem of calculation in a socialist community this description of its working has not been further advanced. There was very little justification for dubbing this very realistic picture of a planned society 'utopian'. Marx, characteristically, added to it the one part of classical English economics which was out of tune with its

---

[50] Ibid., pp. 272–73. It may be noted that this seems to be the first occurrence of the term 'central bank'.

[51] The following passage from the *Exposition, deuxième année* (Première séance, résumé de l'exposition de la première année [1854], pp. 338–39) [p. 9], deserves, however, to be quoted: "Pour que cette *association industrielle* soit réalisée et produise tous ses fruits, il faut qu'elle constitue une hiérarchie, il faut qu'une vue générale préside à ses travaux et les harmonise . . . il faut absolument que l'Etat soit en possession de tous les instrumens de travail qui forment aujourd'hui le fond de la propriété individuelle, et que les directeurs de la société industrielle soient chargés de la distribution de ces instrumens, fonction que remplissent aujourd'hui, d'une manière si aveugle et à si grands frais les *propriétaires et capitalistes* . . . alors seulement on verra cesser le scandale de la concurrence illimitée, cette grande négation de la critique dans l'ordre industriel, et qui, considérée sous son respect le plus saillant, n'est autre chose qu'une guerre acharnée et meurtrière que, sous une forme nouvelle, continuent de se faire entre eux les individus et les nations". The opening of the passage shows clearly that at this stage they were using the term *association* in precisely the sense in which two years later they introduced the term *socialism*. [The passage may be translated as follows, "In order for this *industrial association* to be realised and bring forth all its fruit, it is necessary that the association set up a hierarchy, that a general view presides over its works and harmonise them . . . it is absolutely necessary that the State be in possession of all the instruments of labour which form the basis for individual property today, and that the directors of the industrial society be charged with the distribution of these instruments, a function that *owners* and *capitalists* fill today in such a blind and costly way . . . only then will cease the scandal of unlimited competition, this great critical negation in the industrial order, which, in its most striking aspect, is nothing but an unremitting and murderous war in a new form, that continues to divide individuals and nations".—Ed.]

general analysis of competition, the 'objective' or labour theory of value. The general results of the fusion of Saint-Simonian and Hegelian ideas, of which Marx is of course the best-known exponent, will occupy us later.[52]

But insofar as that general socialism which today is common property is concerned, little had to be added to Saint-Simonian thought. As a further indication of how profoundly the Saint-Simonians have influenced modern thought, it need only be mentioned to what a great extent all European languages have drawn from their vocabulary. "Individualism",[53] "industrialist",[54] "positivism",[55] and the "organisation of labour"[56] all occur first in the *Exposition*. The concept of the class struggle and the contrast between the bourgeoisie and the proletariat in the special technical sense of the terms are Saint-Simonian creations. The word *socialism* itself, although it does not yet appear in the *Exposition* (which uses 'association' in very much the same sense), appears in its modern meaning for the first time[57] a little later in the Saint-Simonian *Globe*.[58]

[52] See below, part 3.

[53] *Exposition, première année*, Bouglé and Halévy, eds, p. 377. See, however, Comte, *Lettres d'Auguste Comte à M. Valat*, pp. 164–65, for an informal use of the term in a letter dated March 30, 1825. [The phrases Comte used in his letter were "abjecte individualité" and "l'esprit d'individualité", both of which he linked with egoism.—Ed.]

[54] Ibid., p. 275. *Industrialism* was coined by Saint-Simon himself to describe the opposite of liberalism. See *OSSE*, vol. 37, pp. 178, 195.

[55] *Exposition, première année*, Bouglé and Halévy, eds, pp. 183, 487.

[56] Ibid., pp. 98 [89], 139.

[57] Strictly speaking, both the terms *socialist* and *socialism* had already been used in Italian (by Giacomo Giuliani) in 1803, but had been forgotten. Independently of this, *socialist* occurs once in the Owenite *Co-operative* magazine for November 1827, and *socialism* (although in a different sense) in a French Catholic journal in November 1831. But it was only with its appearance in the *Globe* that it was immediately taken up and frequently used, particularly by Leroux and Reybaud. See Carl Grünberg, "Der Ursprung der Worte 'Sozialismus' und 'Sozialist'", *Archiv für die Geschichte des Sozialismus und der Arbeiterbewegung*, vol. 2, 1912, p. 378. See also *Exposition, première année*, Bouglé and Halévy, eds, p. 205, note. [The French literary critic and philosopher Pierre Leroux (1797–1871), advocate of 'humanitarianism', was also a co-founder of the liberal journal *Le Globe*, and the editor who turned it over to the Saint-Simonians in 1831. He split with them over Enfantin's views later that year. In 1841 the French writer and economist Marie-Roch-Louis Reybaud (1799–1845) received a prize from *l'Académie Française* for his book describing the socialist systems of Saint-Simon, Owen, Fourier, and Cabet.—Ed.]

[58] *Globe*, February 2, 1832 [February 13, 1832, p. 176]. The word occurs in an article by H. [X.] Joncières and the context in which it occurs is so significant that the whole sentence must be quoted: "Nous ne voulons pas sacrifier la personnalité aux socialisme, pas plus que ce dernier à la personnalité". [This translates as, "We no more want to sacrifice personality to socialism, than to sacrifice socialism to personality". The phrase appeared in Joncières' review of Victor Hugo's collection of poems, *Les feuilles d'Automne* (1831).—Ed.]

V

With the appearance of the *Exposition*, and of a number of articles by Enfantin[59] and others in the new Saint-Simonian journals *Organisateur* and *Globe* which we need not further consider, the development of their ideas which is of interest to us came more or less suddenly to an end. If we cast a quick glance over the further history of the school, or rather the Saint-Simonian church, as it presently became, it will show why its immediate influence was not greater, or rather, why that influence was not more clearly recognised. The reason is that under Enfantin's influence the doctrine was turned into a religion;[60] the sentimental and mystic elements gained the upper hand over the ostensibly scientific and rational, just as they did in the last phases of Saint-Simon's and later of Comte's life. Already the second year of the *Exposition* shows an increasing tendency in that direction. But in its further career the literary activities are of less importance and it is to the organisation of the church and to the practical application of its doctrines that we must look for the picturesque qualities and sensational doings of the new church which have attracted more attention than the earlier and more important phase of its activity.[61]

The new religion consisted at first merely of a vague pantheism and a fervent belief in human solidarity. But the dogma was much less important than the cult and the hierarchy. The school became a family over which Enfantin and Bazard presided as the two supreme fathers—new popes with a college of apostles and various other grades of members below them. Services were organised at which not only the doctrine was taught, but at which the members soon began publicly to confess their sins. Itinerant preachers spread the doctrine all over the country and founded local centres.

For a time the success was considerable, not only in Paris but throughout France and even in Belgium. Among their group they counted then Pierre Leroux, Adolphe Blanqui, Pacqueuer, and Cabet.[62] Le Play was also a mem-

[59] Some of the articles of Enfantin in the *Globe* which have been collected in a separate volume under the title *Economie politique et politique*, 2nd ed. (Paris: Au Bureau du Globe, 1832) deserve, however, to be specially mentioned.

[60] A curious account of the motive for this is given by Eduard Gans, "Paris in Jahre 1830", in *Rückblicke auf Personen und Zustände* (Berlin: Veit, 1836), p. 92: "Benjamin Constant erzählte mir, dass, als die St.-Simonisten ihn vor etwa einem Jahre um Rath gefragt hätten, wie sie ihre Grundsätze verbreiten könnten, er ihnen gesagt habe: macht eine Religion daraus". [Benjamin Constant recounted to me that when, approximately a year ago, the Saint Simonians asked for his advice on how to spread their principles, he told them: Make a religion out of them.—Ed.]

[61] See Henry René d'Allemagne, *Les saint-simoniens 1827–1837* (Paris: Gründ, 1930).

[62] [For Pierre Leroux, see this chapter, note 57. French political activist Louis Auguste Blanqui (1805–81) was a member of the Charbonnerie and a contributor to *Le Globe*. Blanquism, the doctrine that became associated with his name, is the idea that a social revolution is best under-

ber[63] and in Brussels they gained a new enthusiast for social physics in the astronomer and statistician A. Quetelet, who had already been profoundly influenced by the circle of the *Ecole polytechnique*.[64]

The July revolution of 1830 found them altogether unprepared but naïvely assuming that it would place them into power. It is said that Bazard and Enfantin even requested Louis Philippe to hand over to them the Tuileries since they were the only legitimate power on earth. One effect of the revolution on their doctrines appears to have been that they felt compelled to make some concessions to the democratic tendencies of the age. The originally authoritarian socialism thus began its temporary partnership with liberal democracy. The reasons for this step were explained by the Saint-Simonians with an amazing frankness, rarely equalled by later socialists: "We demand at this moment liberty of religious practice in order that a single religion can be more easily erected on the ruins of the religious past of humanity; . . . the liberty of the press, because this is the indispensable condition for the subsequent creation of a legitimate direction of thought; the liberty of teaching, in order that our doctrine can be more easily propagated and become one day the only one loved and followed by all; the destruction of the monopolies as a means of arriving at the definite organisation of the industrial body".[65] Their real views,

---

taken by a small, well-organised group of conspirators. Constantin Pecqueur (1801–87) began as a Saint-Simonian, later switched to Fourierism, and ultimately became known as a founder of French collectivist socialism. Etienne Cabet (1788–1856), influenced by Robert Owen, was the author of *Voyage en Icarie* (1840) which depicted a utopia in which an elected government controlled all economic activity. Icarian communities sprang up on the Red River in Texas, in Illinois, and in Iowa.—Ed.]

[63] See Pinet, *Ecrivains et penseurs polytechniciens*, p. 176, and Charléty, *Histoire du saint-simonisme*, p. 29 [77]. [Though trained as a metallurgist, Pierre Guillaume Frédéric Le Play (1806–82) is also remembered for developing the case-study method in his research on the family life of European workers. Hayek discusses his work briefly in chapter 16, p. 277.—Ed.]

[64] See Georges Weill, "Le saint-simonisme hors de France", *Revue d'histoire économique et sociale*, vol. 9, 1921, p. 105. A Saint-Simonian mission consisting of P. Leroux, H. Carnot, and others had visited Brussels in February 1831; and although, apart from the remarks of Weill referred to, there is no direct evidence for the influence of the Saint-Simonians on Quetelet, it is remarkable how precisely from this date his ideas developed in a direction very similar to Comte's. On this, see Joseph Lottin, *Quetelet: statisticien et sociologue* (Louvain: Institut supérieur de philosophie, 1912), pp. 123, 356–67; also pp. 10, 21. [An astronomer and statistician, the Belgian Lambert-Adolphe-Jacques Quetelet (1796–1874) famously applied statistical theory to social questions. His 'average man' became a slogan in the social sciences. Hayek discusses Quetelet in chapter 16, p. 267.—Ed.]

[65] *Organisateur*, vol. 2, pp. 202, 213, quoted by Charléty, *Histoire du saint-simonisme*, p. 83. [Although the quotation that Hayek translates is indeed found in Charléty as indicated, the page numbers that Charléty provides for the source of the original quotation in *L'Organisateur* are wrong, and I could not locate the correct pages for the quotation.—Ed.]

however, are better shown by their early discovery of, and enthusiasm for, the organising genius of Prussia[66]—a sympathy which, as we shall presently see, was reciprocated by the 'Young Germans', one of whom, with some justification, remarked that the Prussians had long been Saint-Simonians.[67] The only other doctrinal development during this period which we need mention is their increasing interest in railways, canals, and banks, to which so many of them were to give their lifework after the dispersal of the school.

Already Enfantin's early attempt to turn the school into a religion had created a certain tension among the leaders and caused some desertions. The main crisis came when he began to develop new theories about the position of women and the relation between the sexes. There was virtually nothing in the teaching of Saint-Simon himself to justify this new departure, and the first elements of this doctrine were probably an importation from Fourierism, with its theory of the couple, man and woman, constituting the true social individual. For Enfantin there was only a short step from the principle of the emancipation of women to the doctrine of the 'rehabilitation of the flesh' and the distinction between the 'constant' and 'inconstant' types among both sexes, which both should be able to have it their own way. These doctrines and the rumours which got around about their practical application (for which, it must be admitted, the Saint-Simonians gave ample cause in their writings)[68] created a considerable scandal. A break between Enfantin and Bazard followed, and the latter left the movement and died nine months later. His chair was left vacant for the Mère suprême, an honour which George Sand had declined.[69] With Bazard some of the most eminent members, Carnot, Leroux, Lechevalier, and Transon, seceded, the last two becoming Fourierists; and a few

---

[66] *Globe*, June 3 and 8, 1831, quoted by Charléty, *Histoire du saint-simonisme*, p. 110.

[67] Karl Gutzkow, *Briefe eines Narren an eine Närrin* (Hamburg: Hoffmann und Campe, 1832), p. 119, quoted in Eliza Marian Butler, *The Saint-Simonian Religion in Germany: A Study of the Young German Movement* (Cambridge: Cambridge University Press, 1926), p. 263.

[68] Duveyrier, for example, one of the oldest members, wrote in the *Globe* of January 12, 1832, p. 46: "On verrait sur la terre ce qu'on n'a jamais vu. On verrait des hommes et des femmes unis par un amour sans exemple et sans nom, puisqu'il ne connaîtrait ni le refroidissement, ni la jalousie; des hommes et des femmes se donneraient à plusieurs sans jamais cesser d'être l'un à l'autre et dont l' [leur] amour serait au contraire comme un divin banquet augmentant en magnificence en raison du nombre et du choix des convives". [One would see on the earth what one has never seen. One would see men and women united by an unequalled and nameless love, with no hint of cooling down or jealousy; men and women would give themselves to several without ever ceasing to be the one to the other, and to them, love would on the contrary be like a heavenly banquet, gaining in magnificence with the number and choice of partners.—Ed.]

[69] [The French feminist novelist George Sand (1804–76) was known for her unconventional lifestyle and her uncompromising attacks upon the institution of marriage. She encountered the Saint-Simonians in the 1830s, with Pierre Leroux being a notable influence, and she maintained a lifelong sympathy for socialist ideals.—Ed.]

months later even Rodrigues, the living link with Saint-Simon, broke with Enfantin.

Faced with a serious setback, since financial difficulties made it necessary to discontinue the *Globe*, and as they had begun to attract the attention of the police, Enfantin with forty faithful apostles withdrew to a house at Ménilmontant, at the outskirts of Paris, to begin a new life in accordance with the precepts of the doctrine. The forty men started there a community life without servants, dividing the menial tasks between them, and observing, to silence the ugly rumours, strict celibacy. But if their life was half modelled on that of a monastery, in other respects it was more like that of a Nazi *Führerschule*.[70] Athletic exercises and courses in the doctrine were to prepare them for a more active life in the future.

Although they voluntarily confined themselves to their estate, they did not cease in their attempts to attract notoriety. The forty apostles who in their fantastic costumes cultivated their garden and tended their home became for a while the sensation of the Parisians, who flocked there in thousands to watch the spectacle. In consequence the 'retreat' by no means reassured the police. Proceedings were instituted against Enfantin, Chevalier, and Duveyrier for outraging public morality and ended with their being condemned to imprisonment for one year. The march of the whole group to the law courts in their peculiar costumes and with their spades and other implements on their shoulders, and the sensational defence of the accused, was almost the last public appearance of the group. When Enfantin entered the St. Pelagier prison to serve his sentence the movement began rapidly to decline and the establishment in Ménilmontant soon broke up. A group of disciples still gave the people much to talk about by their journey to Constantinople and the East *pour chercher la femme libre*.[71] But when Enfantin left the prison, although he organised another journey to the East, it was for a more sensible purpose. He and a group of Saint-Simonians spent some years in Egypt, trying to organise the piercing of the Isthmus of Suez. And although they at first failed to obtain support, it is largely due to their efforts that later the Suez Canal Company was founded.[72] As we shall have occasion to mention again, most of them con-

---

[70] [*Führerschule* refers to the Nazi officer training schools set up by Heinrich Himmler, leader of the SS.—Ed.]

[71] Apparently the expression *chercher la femme* derives from this. [Look for the woman. The *Oxford English Dictionary* demurs, stating that Alexandre Dumas the elder first used the phrase in his *Les Mohicans de Paris* (1864) "to indicate that the key to a problem or mystery is a woman, and that she need only be found for the matter to be solved". In any event, the woman sought by the Saint-Simonians was to be the counterpart to the male leader of the cult, and when found, would preside with him over the new religious order.—Ed.]

[72] See Jacques Lajard de Puyjalon, *L'Influence des saint-simoniens sur la réalisation de l'Isthme de Suez* (Paris: L. Chauny et L. Quinsac, 1926).

tinued to devote their lives to similar useful efforts—Enfantin to founding the Paris-Lyon-Méditerranée railway system and many of his disciples to organising railway and canal constructions in other parts of France and elsewhere.[73]

[73] See Maurice Wallon, *Les saint-simoniens et les chemins de fer* (Paris: A. Pedrone, 1908), and Henry René d'Allemagne, *Prosper Enfantin et les grandes entreprises du XIX siècle* (Paris: Gründ, 1935).

FIFTEEN

SAINT-SIMONIAN INFLUENCE[1]

I

It is not easy today to appreciate the immense stir which the Saint-Simonian movement caused for a couple of years, not only in France, but throughout Europe, or to gauge the extent of the influence which the doctrine has exercised. But there can be little doubt that this influence was far greater than is commonly realised. If one were to judge that influence by the frequency with which the Saint-Simonians were mentioned in the literature of the time, it would seem that their celebrity was as short-lived as it was great. We must not forget, however, that in its later years the school had covered itself with ridicule by its pseudo-religious harlequinades and its various escapades and follies, and that in consequence many men who had absorbed most of its social and philosophical teaching might well have been ashamed to admit their association with the cranks of Ménilmontant and the men who went to the East in search of the *femme libre*. It was only natural that people should come to treat their Saint-Simonian period as a youthful folly of which they did not wish to boast. But that did not mean that the ideas they had then absorbed did not continue to operate in and through them, and a careful investigation, which has yet to be undertaken, would probably show how surprisingly wide that influence has extended.

[1] [In the original *Economica* article, this chapter carried the following note:
This is the third and last instalment of the series of articles of which the earlier parts have appeared in the preceding issues of *Economica*. While, however, the first four sections of this essay were sufficiently self-contained to make unnecessary any reference to the fact that the series is intended as part of a larger work, it was less easy to avoid such references in the two sections which follow. Although this may be somewhat irritating to the reader, the author has decided to let stand various references to other parts of the larger investigation, as they serve to mark gaps which otherwise would be difficult to justify. It should, perhaps, be explained that in the intended larger work the present historical account of the 'French phase' of the influence of 'scientistic' views on social thought will be preceded by two theoretical studies of the character of individualism in social studies, and of the general nature of the influences exercised on them by the natural sciences and technology, and immediately followed by a series of chapters on the 'German phase', beginning with a chapter on 'Comte and Hegel'.—Ed.]

Here we are not primarily interested in tracing the influence of persons or groups. From our point of view it would be even more significant if it could be shown that a similar situation has produced similar ideas elsewhere without any direct influence from the Saint-Simonians. Yet any study of similar contemporaneous movements elsewhere soon reveals a close connection with the French prototypes. Even if it is doubtful whether in all these cases we are really entitled to speak of influence, and whether we should not rather say that all those who happened to have similar ideas soon found their way to Saint-Simonism, it will be worth while to cast a rapid glance over the variety of channels through which this influence acted, since the extent of it is yet so little understood, and particularly because the spreading of Saint-Simonism also meant a spreading of Comtian positivism in its early form.

The first point which it is important to realise is that this influence was by no means confined to people mainly interested in social and political speculation, but that it was even stronger in literary and artistic circles, which often became almost unconsciously the medium of spreading Saint-Simonian conceptions on other matters. In France the Saint-Simonian ideas about the social function of art made a deep impression on some of the greatest writers of the time, and are held responsible for the profound change in the literary atmosphere which then took place.[2] The demand that all art should be tendentious, that it should serve social criticism and for this purpose represent life as it is in all its ugliness, led to a veritable revolution in letters.[3] Not only authors who like George Sand or Béranger had been closely associated with the Saint-Simonians, but some of the greatest writers of the period such as Honoré de Balzac, Victor Hugo, and Eugène Sue absorbed and practised much of the Saint-Simonian teaching.[4] Among composers Franz Liszt had been a frequent

---

[2] On this and the following, see Marguerite Thibert, *Le rôle social de l'art d'après les saint-simoniens* (Paris: Rivière, 1926); Herbert James Hunt, *Le socialisme et le romantisme en France: Etude de la presse socialiste de 1830 à 1848* (Oxford: Clarendon, 1935); and J. M. Gros, *Le mouvement littéraire socialiste depuis 1830* (Paris: A. Michel, 1904).

[3] For the development of the Saint-Simonian theory of art, see particularly Emile Barrault, *Aux artistes: Du passé et de l'avenir des beaux arts* (Paris: A. Mesnier, 1830).

[4] See Ernst Robert Curtius, *Balzac* (Bonn: F. Cohen, 1923). [For Honoré de Balzac, see chapter 11, note 41, and for Sand, see chapter 14, note 69. In his works the popular French poet and song-writer Pierre-Jean de Béranger (1780–1857) mocked and satirised the government of the Restoration and the reactionary clergy. Copies of one of his songs were circulated during the early days of the July Revolution of 1830. Remembered today for his novels *Notre Dame de Paris* (1831) and *Les Misérables* (1862), the romantic poet, novelist, and playwright Victor Hugo (1802–85) became acquainted with writers for the newspaper *Le Globe* in the early 1830s. A lifelong political activist, he moved from monarchist to republican and following the coup of 1851 lived in exile in Brussels until the restoration of the French Republic in 1870. Eugène Sue's (1804–57) republican and socialist views are best represented in his serial novels *Les mystères de Paris* (1842–43), which is set in the Paris slums, and *Le Juif errant* (1844–45).—Ed.]

visitor to their meetings and Berlioz with a *Chant d'inauguration des chemins de fer* applied Saint-Simonian precepts to music.[5]

II

The influence of Saint-Simonism in England was also partly in the literary field. The main expositor of their ideas here became for a time Thomas Carlyle, whose indebtedness to Saint-Simonian doctrine is well known and who even translated and attempted to publish with an anonymous introduction Saint-Simon's *Nouveau christianisme*.[6] He is the first of the many instances we

[5] [Franz Liszt (1811–86) was a Hungarian composer and pianist, and the French composer Hector Berlioz (1803–69) is generally regarded as one of the founders of the romantic movement. Liszt and Heinrich Heine were witnesses at Berlioz's wedding in 1833; Sand and Liszt were romantically involved.—Ed.]

[6] See David Brooks Cofer, *Saint-Simonism in the Radicalism of Thomas Carlyle* (College Station, TX: Von Boeckmann-Jones, 1931); Muckle, *Henri de Saint-Simon*, pp. 345–80; Eugène d'Eichthal, "Carlyle et le saint-simonisme", *Revue historique*, vol. 79, 1903, pp. 82–83, English translation in *New Quarterly* (London: J. M. Dent, April 1909); Emery Edward Neff, *Carlyle and Mill: Mystic and Utilitarian*, 2nd ed. (New York: Columbia University Press, 1926), p. 210; Hill Shine, *Carlyle and the Saint-Simonians: The Concept of Historical Periodicity* (Baltimore: Johns Hopkins Press, 1941), and the same author's "Carlyle and Fraser's 'Letter on the Doctrine of Saint-Simon'", *Notes & Queries*, vol. 171, October 24, 1936, pp. 290–93 [291–93]. Why in the case of Carlyle, as with so many others, the influence of the Saint-Simonians blended so readily with that of the German philosophers will become clearer later. An interesting contrast to Carlyle's sympathetic reception of Saint-Simonian ideas is the exceedingly hostile reaction of R. Southey, who contributed to the *Quarterly Review*, vol. 45, July 1831, pp. 407–50, under the heading "New Distribution of Property", a very full and intelligent account of the *Doctrine de Saint-Simon*. See also his letter of June 31, 1831, in Edwin Hodder, *The Life and Work of the 7th Earl of Shaftesbury, K. G.*, vol. 1 (London: Cassell and Company, 1886), p. 126. Tennyson, in a letter written in 1832, still says that "reform and St. Simonism are, and will continue to be, subjects of the highest interest . . . the existence of the sect of the St. Simonists is at once a proof of the immense mass of evil that is extant in the nineteenth century, and a focus which gathers all its rays. This sect is rapidly spreading in France, Germany, and Italy, and they have missionaries in London", in Hallam Lord Tennyson, *Alfred Lord Tennyson: A Memoir by His Son*, vol. 1 (London: Macmillan and Co., 1897), p. 99 [pp. 98–99]. It is a striking fact that the social novel begins in England with Disraeli just at the time when one would expect Saint-Simonian influences to work in this direction; but there is, as far as I am aware, no evidence of any influence of the Saint-Simonians on Disraeli. [Hayek identifies four great men of letters of nineteenth-century Britain. Historian and essayist Thomas Carlyle (1795–1881), critic of modern liberal society, was noted for his praise of heroes and of the 'organic' societies of the Middle Ages. As noted in chapter 14, note 15, Gustave d'Eichthal introduced Carlyle to the work of Bazard and Enfantin by sending him copies of *L'Organisateur*. The romantic poet and essayist Robert Southey (1774–1843) was, with Wordsworth and Coleridge, one of the Lake Poets, and for thirty years the poet laureate. Though a radical youth—his epic poem "Joan of Arc", published in 1796, revealed revolutionary sympathies—in his later years he became increasingly conservative. Another poet laureate, Alfred, Lord Tennyson (1809–92), is remembered today for "In Memorium" (1850), "The Charge of the Light Brigade" (1855),

shall meet where Saint-Simonism or Comtian and German influences so readily blended. Carlyle's views on the philosophy of history, his exposition of the law of progress in *Sartor Resartus*, his division of history into positive and negative periods, are all mainly of Saint-Simonian origin, and his interpretation of the French Revolution is penetrated with Saint-Simonian thought. The influence which he in turn exercised need not be stressed here, but it is worth pointing out that the later English positivists recognised that his teaching had largely prepared the way for them.[7]

Better known is the influence which the Saint-Simonians exercised on J. S. Mill. In his *Autobiography*[8] he describes them as "the writers by whom, more than by any others, a new mode of thinking was brought home" to him and recounts how particularly one of their publications, which seemed to him far superior to the rest, Comte's early *System of Positive Policy*,

> harmonised well with my existing notions, to which it seemed to give a scientific shape. I already regarded the methods of physical science as the proper models for political. But the chief benefit which I derived at this time from the trains of thought suggested by the Saint-Simonians and by Comte, was, that I obtained a clearer conception than ever before of the peculiarities of an era of transition in opinion, and ceased to mistake the moral and intellectual characteristics of such an era, for the normal attributes of humanity.[9]

---

and *Idylls of the King* (1885) on the Arthurian legend. Benjamin Disraeli (1805–81) was a Tory Prime Minister and opponent of Gladstone, but in his early years was known for his biting satirical novels.—Ed.]

[7] See Charles Gaskell Higginson, *Auguste Comte: An Address on His Life and Work* (London: Reeves and Turner, 1887), p. 6, and Malcolm Quinn [Quin], *Memoirs of a Positivist* (London: G. Allen and Unwin, 1924), p. 38. [The London Positivist Society was formed by Dr. Richard Congreve (1818–91) in 1867 with the goal of establishing an English Positivist church, one based on scientific conviction rather than supernatural belief, along lines laid out by Comte in his later writings. In 1878 members who wanted to maintain closer ties with the Positivist world organisation established a second group, the London Positivist Committee. It was before this second group that Charles Gaskell Higginson delivered his address at Newton Hall, London, on September 5, 1887; the address was later printed as a one-penny pamphlet. Malcolm Quin (1854–1946) was consecrated to the Positivist priesthood by Congreve and spent thirty years trying to establish a Positivist church and priesthood in Newcastle-upon-Tyne, England.—Ed.]

[8] J. S. Mill, *Autobiography* (London: Longmans, Green, Reader, and Dyer, 1873), pp. 164–67 [163–68; the quoted passage is found on p. 163]. See also ibid., p. 61, where Mill describes how in 1821, at the age of fifteen, he had met in J. B. Say's house Saint-Simon himself, "not yet the founder either of a philosophy or a religion, and considered only as a clever *original*". [See *Autobiography and Literary Essays*, John Robson and Jack Stillinger, eds, vol. 1 (1981) of *Collected Works of John Stuart Mill*, pp. 171–75, and p. 63, respectively. The passage quoted in the text is found on p. 171, and there the word "political" precedes "thinking".—Ed.]

[9] [Mill, *Autobiography and Literary Essays*, p. 173.—Ed.]

Mill goes on to explain how, although he lost sight for a time of Comte, he was kept *au courant* of the Saint-Simonians' progress by Gustave d'Eichthal (who had also introduced Carlyle to Saint-Simonism),[10] how he read nearly everything they wrote and how it was "partly by their writings that [his— FAH] eyes were opened to the very limited and temporary value of the old political economy, which assumes private property and inheritance as indefeasible facts, and freedom of production and exchange as the *dernier mot* of social improvement".[11] From a letter to d'Eichthal[12] it appears that he became so far convinced as to be "inclined to think that [their—FAH] social organisation, under some modification or other . . . is likely to be the final and permanent condition of our race", although he differed from them in believing that it would take many or at least several stages till mankind would be capable of realising it. We have here undoubtedly the first roots of J. S. Mill's socialist leanings. But in Mill's case, too, this was largely a preparation for the still more profound influence which Comte was later to exercise on him.

III

In no other country outside France, however, did the Saint-Simonian doctrine arouse greater interest than in Germany.[13] This interest began to show itself

[10] Gustave d'Eichthal and Charles Duveyrier came in 1831 to London on an official Saint-Simonian mission. See *An Address to the British Public by the Saint-Simonian Missionaries* (London: Rolandi, 1832), and Charléty, *Histoire du saint-simonisme*, p. 93. See also *St. Simonism in London*, by Fontana, Chief, and Prati, Preacher of the St. Simonian Religion in England (London: E. Wilson, 1834), reviewed by J. S. Mill in the *Examiner*, February 2, 1834, pp. 68–69. [Mill's review may be found in *Newspaper Writings, August 1831–October 1834*, Ann Robson and John Robson, eds, vol. 23 (1986) of *Collected Works of John Stuart Mill*, pp. 674–80.—Ed.]

[11] [See *Autobiography and Literary Essays*, p. 174. Hayek added the bracket to replace Mill's "my" with "his".—Ed.]

[12] *The Letters of John Stuart Mill*, ed. Hugh Samuel Roger Elliot, vol. 1 (London: Longmans, Green and Co, 1910), p. 20. [See *The Earlier Letters, 1812 to 1848*, ed. Francis E. Mineka, vol. 12 (1963) of *The Collected Works of John Stuart Mill*, p. 88. The last words of Mill's sentence should read "of the human race" rather than "of our race".—Ed.] See also J. S. Mill, *Correspondance inédite avec Gustave d'Eichthal, 1828–1842, 1864–1871*, translated by Eugène d'Eichthal (Paris: F. Alcan, 1898); and, in part in the original English, in *Cosmopolis* (London, 1897–98), esp. vol. 5 [6], pp. 356, 359–60. [The quoted passage, from a letter from Mill to d'Eichthal dated 30 November 1831, is found on p. 356. The international journal *Cosmopolis* was published in London from 1896 to 1898. The Mill-d'Eichthal correspondence appeared in vol. 6, April (pp. 19–38) and May (pp. 348–66) 1897, and in vol. 9, February (pp. 368–81) and March (pp. 780–90) 1898.—Ed.]

[13] The *Globe*, March 16, 1832, p. 302, already reports that "nul pays n'a consacré une attention plus profonde au saint-simonisme" than Germany. [The passage may be translated as follows, "no country has paid more profound attention to Saint-Simonism" than Germany.—Ed.]

surprisingly early. Already the first *Organisateur* seems to have reached a considerable number of readers in that country.[14] Some years later it seems to have
been Comte's pupil Gustave d'Eichthal who, even before his similar efforts in
England, on a visit to Berlin in 1824, succeeded in interesting several people in
Comte's *Système de politique positive*, with the result that a fairly detailed review,
the only one the book ever received in any language, appeared in the *Leipziger
Literatur-Zeitung*.[15] And in Friedrich Buchholz, then a well-known political
writer, d'Eichthal gained Comte a warm admirer, who not only in a flatter-
ing letter to Comte expressed complete agreement,[16] but who also in 1826 and
1827 published in his *Neue Monatsschrift für Deutschland* four anonymous articles
on Saint-Simon's work, followed by a translation of the concluding part of the
Système industriel.[17]

It was, however, only in the autumn of 1830 that general interest in the
Saint-Simonian movement awoke in Germany; and during the next two or
three years it went like wildfire through the German literary world. The July
revolution had made Paris once more the centre of attraction for all progres-
sives, and the Saint-Simonians, then at the height of their reputation, were the
outstanding intellectual movement in that Mecca of all liberals. A veritable
flood of books, pamphlets, and articles of the Saint-Simonians[18] and transla-

---

[14] See Henri Fournel, *Bibliographie saint-simonienne* (Paris: A. Johanneau, 1833), p. 22.

[15] See Pierre Lafitte [Laffitte], "Matériaux pour la biographie d'Auguste Comte. I. Relations
d'Auguste Comte avec l'Allemagne", *La revue occidentale philosophique, sociale et politique*, vol. 8, 1882,
p. 227; and "Correspondance d'Auguste Comte et Gustave d'Eichthal", ibid., new series, vol.
12, 1891 [1896], pp. 186–276.

[16] Laffitte, "Materiaux pour la biographie d'Auguste Comte", p. 228 and pp. 223 [233] et seq.,
where the review of September 27, 1824, is reprinted. It gives among other things an adequate
account of the "law of three stages". [Representative of the many words of praise in Buchholz'
letter to Comte of September 28, 1825, are these: "la vérité me presse de vous dire que jamais
je n'ai lu ouvrage qui ait fait sur moi une impression aussi agréable que le vôtre", which might
be rendered, "in truth, I must tell you that I have never read any work that impressed me so
favourably".—Ed.]

[17] *Neue Monatsschrift für Deutschland*, vol. 21, 1821 (three articles), and vol. 22, 1827 (three articles); see also vols. 34 and 35 for later articles on the same subject. On Friedrich Buchholz,
who for a period earlier in the century had been one of the most influential political writers
of Prussia, and who in 1802 had published *Darstellung eines neuen Gravitationsgesetzes für die moralis-
che Welt*, see Kurt Bahrs, *Friedrich Buchholz, ein preussischer Publizist 1768–1843* (Berlin: E. Ebering,
1907), and on d'Eichthal's relations to him particularly, see Laffitte, "Correspondance d'Auguste
Comte et Gustave d'Eichthal". [Noted Francophile Paul Ferdinand Friedrich Buchholz (1768–
1843) was a pro-Napoleonic political activist, writer, and editor; the title of his 1802 book may
be translated as *Presentation of a New Law of Gravitation for the Moral World*.—Ed.]

[18] See the list of some fifty publications on Saint-Simonism which appeared in Germany
between 1830 and 1832, given by Butler, *The Saint-Simonian Religion in Germany*, pp. 52–59; the list
is, however, by no means complete. On this, see Rodolphe Palgen's review of this book in *Revue
de littérature comparée*, vol. 9, 1929, pp. 196–201; also Werner Suhge, *Der Saint-Simonismus und Junges
Deutschland* (Berlin: E. Ebering, 1935).

tions of some of their writings[19] appeared in German and there was little that could not be learned about them from German sources. The wave of excitement even reached the old Goethe, who subscribed to the *Globe* (probably since its liberal days) and who, after he had warned Carlyle as early as October 1830, "to keep away from the Société St. Simonienne",[20] and after several recorded conversations on the subject, in May 1831, still felt impelled to spend a day reading to get at the bottom of the Saint-Simonian doctrine.[21]

The whole German literary world seems to have been agog for news about the novel French ideas and to some, as Rahel von Varnhagen describes it, the Saint-Simonian *Globe* became the indispensable intellectual daily bread.[22] The news about the Saint-Simonian movements appears to have been the decisive factor which in 1831 drew Heinrich Heine to Paris,[23] and, as he later said, he had not been twenty-four hours in Paris before he sat in the midst of the Saint-Simonians.[24] From Paris he and Ludwig Börne did much to spread information about the Saint Simonians in German literary circles.[25] Another important source of information for those who had stayed behind, particularly the Varnhagens, was the American Albert Brisbane, then not yet a Fourierist, but already spreading socialist ideas on his travels.[26] How profoundly

[19] See (Abel Transon), *Die Saint-Simonistische Religion: Fünf Reden an die Zöglinge der polytechnischen Schule, nebst einem Vorberichte über das Leben und den Charakter Saint-Simons* (Göttingen: Kübler, 1832).

[20] Quoted in Butler, *Saint-Simonian Religion in Germany*, from *Briefe: Weimarer Ausgabe*, vol. 42, p. 300, letter dated October 17, 1830. [Butler does not have Goethe's letter to Carlyle, but it may be found in Goethe's collected works: see *Goethes Werke: Weimarer Ausgabe* [1887–1919] (Munich: Deutscher Taschenbuch Verlag, 1987), vol. 140, pp. 299–300.—Ed.]

[21] See Johann Peter Eckermann, *Gespräche mit Goethe in den letzten Jahren seines Lebens*, vol. 3 (Leipzig: F. A. Brockhaus, 1885), pp. 236–38, under date of October 20, 1830, and Goethe's *Tagebücher*, under dates of October 31, 1830, and May 30, 1831. [For the latter two entries in Goethe's diaries, see *Goethes Werke*, vol. 89, p. 324, and vol. 90, pp. 82–83, respectively.—Ed.]

[22] Rahel Varnhagen, *Rahel: Ein Buch des Andenkens für ihre Freunde* (Berlin: Duncker und Humblot, 1834), vol. 3, p. 568, under date of April 25, 1832. [Rahel Antonie Friederike Levin Varnhagen von Ense's (1771–1833) salon was frequented by the most eminent intellectuals of Europe; she was later the subject of a biography by Hannah Arendt titled *Rahel Varnhagen: The Life of a Jewess*, ed. Liliane Weissberg (Baltimore: Johns Hopkins University Press, 1997).—Ed.]

[23] See Butler, *Saint-Simonian Religion in Germany*, p. 70. [The lyrical poems of Heinrich Heine (1797–1856) were set to music by composers such as Schumann and Schubert. Heine was viewed as one of the leaders of the Young Germany movement, a loosely affiliated group of progressive writers in the 1830s whose ideas were deemed dangerous and banned by the German authorities.—Ed.]

[24] Karl Grün, *Die soziale Bewegung in Frankreich und Belgien* (Darmstadt: C. W. Leske, 1845), p. 90 [117].

[25] [The journalist and political writer Karl Ludwig Börne (1786–1837) frequently attacked the illiberal policies of the Frankfurt government. Like Heine he went to Paris after the 1830 revolution, hoping that it presaged a new society, but returned home disappointed. Börne's political writings eventually led to his identification with the Young Germany movement.—Ed.]

[26] See Margaret A. Clarke, *Heine et la monarchie de juillet* (Paris: Rieder, 1927), especially appendix 2, pp. 242–71; Butler, *Saint-Simonian Religion in Germany*, p. 71. It seems that some overen-

these ideas were affecting the Young German poets Laube, Gutzkow, Mundt, and Wienbarg has been well described by Miss E. M. Butler in her book *Saint-Simonian Religion in Germany*, where with much justification she describes the whole Young German school as a Saint-Simonian movement.[27] In their short but spectacular existence as a group between 1832 and 1835 they persistently, if more crudely than their French contemporaries, applied the Saint-Simonian principle that art must be tendentious, and in particular popularised their feminist doctrines and their demands for the "rehabilitation of the flesh".[28]

---

thusiastic German admirers of Saint-Simon even compared him to Goethe, which enthusiasm induced Metternich (in a letter to Prince Wittgenstein, November 30, 1835) to make the tart comment that Saint-Simon, whom he had known personally, "had been as complete a cynical fool as Goethe was a great poet". See Otto Draeger, *Theodor Mundt und seine Beziehungen zum jungen Deutschland* (Marburg: N. G. Elwert, 1909), p. 156 [154]. [American Albert Brisbane (1809–90) was an early socialist theoretician. While in Europe he studied with Fourier for two years and on returning to America helped spread the Fourierist doctrine. His book *Social Destiny of Man* (1840) and his newspaper articles in the *New York Tribune* touting what he called 'Associationism' led to the establishment of a number of Fourierist societies.—Ed.]

[27] Butler, *Saint-Simonian Religion in Germany*, p. 430 [pp. 431–32]. In addition to the book by Suhge already cited, see also Fritz Gerathewhol [Geratherwohl], *Saint-Simonistische Ideen in der deutschen Literatur, Ein Beitrag zur Vorgeschichte des Sozialismus* (Munich: G. Birk, 1920); Hugo von Kleinmayr, *Welt- und Kunstanschauung des 'Jungen Deutschland'* (Vienna: Österreichischer Bundesverlag für Unterricht, Wissenschaft und Kunst, 1930); and Joseph Dresch, *Gutzkow et la jeune Allemagne* (Paris: Société nouvelle de librarie et d'édition, 1904), on another German poet, Georg Büchner, who was not a member of the Young German group, but who seems also to have been influenced by Saint-Simonian ideas. It is perhaps worth mentioning that he was the elder brother of Ludwig Büchner, author *of Kraft und Stoff* (1855), and one of the main representatives of extreme materialism in Germany. On G. Büchner, see also Georg Adler, *Die Geschichte der ersten sozialpolitischen Arbeiterbewegung in Deutschland* (Breslau: E. Trewendt, 1885), pp. 8 et seq. [7–10], which should also be consulted for some other early German socialists, particularly Ludwig Gall and later Georg Kuhlmann and Julius Treichler, whose relations to Saint-Simonism need investigation (ibid., pp. 6, 67, 72). [In the text, Hayek mentions a number of artists and writers who were identified with the Young Germany movement: the dramatist, novelist, and theatre director Heinrich Laube (1806–84); novelist and journalist Theodor Mundt (1808–61); novelist and dramatist Karl Ferdinand Gutzkow (1811–78); and the journalist and writer Ludolf Wienbarg (1802–72). Though the term Young Germany was first used by Wienbarg in his 1834 book *Ästhetische Feldzüge (Aesthetic Campaigns)*, its usage as a term of opprobrium became widespread when the German government banned the work of Heine, Laube, Mundt, Gutzkow, and Wienbarg in December 1835. As a result, many of its putative members denied their membership, or even that anything like a Young Germany movement actually existed. The effects were real enough, however: both Laube and Gutzkow spent time in prison for their political views.—Ed.]

[28] An interesting testimony to the extent of Saint-Simonian influence in Germany is a circular directed against it by the archbishop of Trier, dated February 13, 1832. See the *Allgemeine Kirchenzeitung* (Darmstadt), March 8, 1832.

IV

Much more important for our purpose, but unfortunately much less explored,[29] is the relation of the Saint-Simonians to another connected German group, the Young Hegelians. The curious affinity which existed between the Hegelian and the Saint-Simonian ideas and which was strongly felt by the contemporaries will occupy us later. Here we are concerned only with the actual extent to which the younger Hegelian philosophers were directly affected by Saint-Simonian ideas, and how much therefore the decisive change which led to the separation of the Young Hegelians from the orthodox followers of the philosopher may have been partly due to that influence. Our actual knowledge on this point is small, yet, as there existed close personal contacts between the Young Germans and the members of what later became the Young Hegelian group, and as some of the former as well as some of the authors of the German works on Saint-Simon were Hegelians,[30] there can be little doubt that in the group as a whole the interest in Saint-Simonism cannot have been much smaller than that among the Young Germans.

The period of German thought which is still so little explored and yet so crucial for the understanding of the later developments is the 1830s, during which it seems the seeds were sown which bore fruit only in the next decade.[31] We meet here with the difficulty that after the Saint-Simonians had discredited themselves, people became most reluctant to acknowledge any indebtedness, especially as the Prussian censorship was likely to object to any reference to that dangerous group. As early as 1834, Gustav Kühne, a Hegelian philosopher closely connected with the Young Germans, said of Saint-Simonism,

---

[29] See Benedetto Croce, *History of Europe in the Nineteenth Century* (London: George Allen and Unwin, 1934), p. 147.[The Young Hegelians, a group of students and younger academics at the University of Berlin, used dialectical reasoning to call for reform of Prussian government and society and thus opposed the more orthodox and conservative interpretations of the Right Hegelians. The Young Hegelians included such writers as Ludwig Feuerbach, who was introduced in chapter 10, note 15; David Friedrich Strauss (1804–74), author of *Life of Jesus* (1835), whose search for 'the historical Jesus' both scandalised Europe and transformed Biblical exegesis; and, of course, Karl Marx, hence their importance in Hayek's narrative of the rôle of the Young Hegelians in the spread of socialist ideas.—Ed.]

[30] Of the Young Germans, T. Mundt and G. Kühne were both Hegelian University lecturers of philosophy, and the same is true of the authors of most of the books reporting on the philosophical aspects of Saint-Simonism, particularly Moritz Veit, *Saint-Simon und der Saint-Simonismus* (Leipzig: Brockhaus, 1834); Friedrich Wilhelm Carové, *Der Saint-Simonismus und die neuere französische Philosophie* (Leipzig: T. C. Hinrichssche Buchhandlung, 1831). I have been unable to procure another work of the same period, S. R. Schneider, *Das Problem der Zeit und dessen Lösung durch die Association* (Gotha: n.p., 1834), which, judging from its title, seems to contain an account of the socialist aspects of Saint-Simonism.

[31] See B. Groethuysen, "Les jeunes Hégéliens et les origines du socialisme contemporain en Allemagne", *Revue philosophique*, vol. 95, no. 5/6, 1923, especially p. 379.

"the French counterpart of Hegelianism", that "it will scarcely any longer be permissible to mention the name, yet the basic feature of this view of life, which in this particular form has become a caricature, will prove to have been completely embedded in social relations".[32] And when we remember that the men who were to play the decisive rôle in the revolt against orthodox Hegelianism and in the birth of German socialism, Arnold Ruge, Ludwig Feuerbach, David Friedrich Strauss, Moses Hess, and Karl Rodbertus, were all in their twenties when the rage for Saint-Simonism swept through Germany,[33] it seems almost certain that they all imbibed Saint-Simonian doctrine at the time. Only of one of them, although the one from whom socialist doctrines are known to have spread more than from anybody else in the Germany of the time, Moses Hess, is it definitely known that he visited Paris in the early thirties,[34] and the traces of Saint-Simonian and Fourierist doctrines can easily be seen in his first book of 1837.[35] In the case of some of the others, as particularly in that of the most influential of the Young Hegelians, Ludwig Feuerbach, in whom positivism and Hegelianism were so completely combined and who exercised great influence on Marx and Engels, we have no direct evidence of his having known the Saint-Simonian writings. It would be even more significant if this Hegelian, who in providing a positivist *Weltanschauung* for the next generations of German scientists was to play a rôle similar to that of Comte in France, had arrived at his view independently of the contemporary movements in that country. But it seems practically certain that he must have come to know them in the formative period of his thought. It is hard to believe that the young university lecturer in philosophy, who, in the summer of

[32] In a review of his friend Mundt's *Lebenswirren*, quoted in Walter Grupe, *Mundts und Kühnes Verhältnis zu Hegel und seinen Gegnern* (Halle: M. Niemeyer, 1928), p. 76. [Ferdinand Gustav Kühne (1806–88), author of the novel *Eine Quarantäne im Irrenhause* (1835), was from 1835 to 1842 the editor of the *Zeitung für die elegante Welt*, during which time he frequently promoted Mundt's views.—Ed.]

[33] In 1831, when the German Saint-Simonian movement began, Ruge was 29, Feuerbach 27, Rodbertus 26, Strauss 23, Hess 19, and Karl Marx 12 years of age. The corresponding ages of the leading Young Germans were Laube 25, Kühne 25, Mundt 23, and Gutzkow 20. [Strauss was introduced in note 29 above, and Feuerbach in chapter 10, note 15. Arnold Ruge (1802–80) was a Hegelian philosopher, political writer, and activist; he briefly co-edited the *Deutsch-Französische Jarbücher* in Paris with Karl Marx, but was better known as a radical democrat than as a socialist. Karl Johann Rodbertus (1805–75) believed that the gradual transition to a fully socialist society should be carried out by a strong monarchy in a united Germany. Though Moses Hess (1812–75) collaborated with Marx and is credited with converting Friedrich Engels to communism, he later was attacked by them. In his later work Hess laid the groundwork for Zionist socialism.—Ed.]

[34] See Theodor Zlocisti, *Moses Hess, der Vorkämpfer des Sozialismus und Zionismus* (Berlin: Weltverlag, 1920), p. 13 [pp. 99–100].

[35] Moses Hess, *Die heilige Geschichte der Menschheit* (Stuttgart: Halberger, 1837). [For an English translation, see Moses Hess, *The Holy History of Mankind and Other Writings*, translated by Shlomo Avineri (Cambridge: Cambridge University Press, 2004).—Ed.]

1832, when Germany was reverberating with discussions of Saint-Simonism, spent months in Frankfurt reading to prepare himself for an intended visit to Paris,[36] should, almost alone among men of his kind, have escaped their influence. It seems much more likely that, as in the case of others, it was precisely the fame of this school which attracted him to Paris. And although the intended visit did not take place, Feuerbach probably absorbed much of Saint-Simonian thought at that time and thus prepared himself to replace the Saint-Simonian influence among his younger contemporaries. If one reads his work with this probability in mind, it becomes difficult to believe that the obvious resemblances between his work and that of Comte are accidental.[37]

An important rôle in spreading French socialist thought in Germany during this period was also played by various members of the large colony of German journeymen in Paris, whose organisations became so important for the growth of the socialist movement and among whom for a time Wilhelm Weitling was the outstanding figure.[38] He and numerous other travellers must have provided a continuous stream of information about the development of French doctrine, even before, in the beginning of the forties, Lorenz von Stein and Karl Grün went to Paris for a systematic study of French socialism.[39] With the appearance of the two books[40] which were the results of these

---

[36] See Adolph Kohut, *Ludwig Feuerbach, sein Leben und seine Werke* (Leipzig: F. Eckardt, 1909), p. 77; and *Ausgewählte Briefe von und an Feuerbach*, ed. Wilhelm Bolin (Leipzig: O. Wigand, 1904), vol. 1, p. 256, where in a letter to his brother, written from Frankfurt and dated March 12, 1832, Feuerbach explains that "Paris ist ein Ort, an den ich längst hinstrebte, für den ich mich längst in einem unwillkürlichen Drange, mit dem ich das Französische schon früher und besonders seither betrieb, vorbereitet, ein Ort, der ganz zu meiner Individualität, zu meiner Philosophie passt, an dem sich daher meine Kräfte entwickeln und selbst solche, die ich noch nicht kenne, hervortreten können". [Paris is a place to which I have long been drawn, for which I have long prepared myself with instinctive urgency, in that I have pursued my French studies from an early age and even more so lately, a place totally congenial to my individuality, my philosophy, and so it will let my abilities develop, even those I don't yet know I have.—Ed.]

[37] See Tomáš Garrigue Masaryk, *Die philosophischen und sociologischen Grundlagen des Marxismus* (Vienna: C. Konegen, 1899), p. 35.

[38] See Adler, *Die Geschichte der ersten sozialpolitischen Arbeiterbewegung in Deutschland*, and Karl Mielcke, *Deutscher Frühsozialismus* (Stuttgart: Cotta, 1931), pp. 185–89. [The German tailor, inventor, and Pre-Marxian communist writer and agitator Wilhelm Weitling (1808–71) was well known in radical circles in Paris, Switzerland, and Germany in the 1830s and 1840s. After emigrating to America following the revolution of 1848, he founded a socialist society, the *Arbeiterbund*, and newspaper, *Die Republik der Arbeiter*, and later became involved with the utopian community of Communia, Iowa.—Ed.]

[39] [Hayek refers to the German economist Lorenz von Stein (1815–90) and to the German translator of Proudhon's work Karl Grün (1817–87). Stein taught public administration at the University of Vienna from 1855 to 1885, where he was (from 1873) a colleague of Carl Menger.—Ed.]

[40] Lorenz von Stein, *Der Socialismus und Communismus des heutigen Frankreich* (Leipzig: O. Wigand, 1842), and Grun, *Die soziale Bewegung in Frankreich und Belgien*. Concerning the latter, cf. Karl Marx

visits, particularly with Lorenz von Stein's most detailed and sympathetic account in his widely read *Socialism and Communism in Present-Day France* (1842), the whole of Saint-Simonian doctrine became common property in Germany. That Stein—incidentally another Hegelian who was most ready to absorb and spread Saint-Simonian ideas—was, with Feuerbach, one of the strongest influences that were brought to bear on Karl Marx's early development is well known.[41] Yet the belief that it was only through Stein and Grün (and later, perhaps, Thierry and Mignet) that Marx made his acquaintance with Saint-Simonian ideas and that he studied them firsthand only later in Paris, is probably mistaken. It seemed certain that he was directly affected by the early wave of Saint-Simonian enthusiasm when he was a boy of thirteen or fourteen. He himself told his friend, the Russian historian Maxim Kowalewski, how his paternal friend and later father-in-law, Baron Ludwig von Westphalen, had been infected by the general enthusiasm and had talked to the boy about the new ideas.[42] The fact, often noted by German scholars,[43] that many parts of Marx's doctrine, particularly the theory of the class struggle and certain aspects of this interpretation of history, bear a much closer resem-

---

and Friedrich Engels, *The German Ideology*, Marxist Leninist Library (London: Lawrence and Wishart, 1938), pp. 118–79. [In addition to their mocking attack on Grün as a derivative expositor of Saint-Simonism and Fourierism in *The German Ideology*, Grün was dismissed by Marx and Engels in *The Communist Manifesto* (1848) as a leader of the 'True Socialism' movement. In their view, this movement emasculated the ideas of French socialists by separating them from their concrete historical development and reinterpreting them using the categories of the 'German ideology' (that is, the idealistic philosophy of Hegel and Feuerbach).—Ed.]

[41] Cf. Béla Földes, "Bemerkungen zu dem Problem Lorenz Stein-Karl Marx", *Jahrbücher für Nationalökonomie und Statistik*, vol. 102, no. 1, 1914, pp. 289–99, and Heinz Nitschke, "Die Geschichtsphilosophie Lorenz von Steins", supplement no. 26, *Historische Zeitschrift* (Munich: R. Oldenbourg, 1932).

[42] See Maxim Kowalewski, "Erinnerungen an Karl Marx", in *Karl Marx, Eine Sammlung von Erinnerungen und Aufsätzen* (Zurich: Ring, 1934), p. 223. Judging from a remark by Walter Sulzbach in *Die Anfänge der materialistischen Geschichtsauffassung* (Karlsruhe: G. Braun, 1911), p. 3, there seems also to be other independent evidence of Marx having studied Saint-Simonian writings while still at school. But I have been unable to trace it. [Maxim Kowalewski (1851–1916) was an historian of social and state structure and a correspondent of both Marx and Engels. Of Marx's father-in-law, the Baron von Westphalen, Edmund Wilson wrote that "he used to take young Karl Marx for walks among the vineyard-covered hills of the Moselle and tell him about the Frenchman, Saint-Simon, who wanted society organised scientifically in the interests of Christian charity". See *To the Finland Station: A Study in the Writing and Acting of History* (Anchor Books Edition, New York: Doubleday, 1953), p. 113.—Ed.]

[43] Apart from various earlier works by Muckle, Eckstein, Cunow, and Sulzbach, see particularly Kurt Breysig, *Vom geschichtlichen Werden* (Stuttgart: Cotta, 1926), vol. 2, pp. 64 et seq., 84; and Werner Heider, *Die Geschichtslehre von Karl Marx*, in *Forschungen zur Geschichts- und Gesellschaftslehre*, ed. Kurt Breysig, no. 3 (Stuttgart: Cotta, 1931), p. 19. These suggestions have been confirmed by the careful investigation by V. Volgin, "Über die historische Stellung St.-Simons", *Marx-Engels Archiv*, vol. 1, no. 1, 1926, pp. 82–118.

blance to those of Saint-Simon than to those of Hegel, becomes even more interesting when we realise that the influence of Saint-Simon on Marx seems to have preceded that of Hegel.

Friedrich Engels, in whose separate writings Saint-Simonian elements are perhaps even more conspicuous than in those of Marx, was at one time closely associated with some of the members of the Young German movement, particularly Gutzkow, and later received his first introduction to socialist theory from Moses Hess.[44] The other leaders of German socialist thought are similarly indebted. How closely most of Rodbertus's doctrines resemble those of the Saint-Simonians has often been noticed and, in view of the whole situation, there can be little doubt about the direct derivation.[45] Among the leading members of the active socialist movement in Germany, we know at least of Wilhelm Liebknecht that he steeped himself in Saint-Simonian doctrine when still very young,[46] while Lassalle received most of it from his masters Lorenz von Stein and Louis Blanc.[47]

[44] Cf. Gustav Mayer, *Friedrich Engels, Eine Biographie* (Berlin: J. Springer, 1920), vol. 1, pp. 40, 108.

[45] See Heinrich Dietzel, *Karl Rodbertus* (Jena: G. Fischer, 1888), vol. 1, p. 5, vol. 2, pp. 40, 44, 51, 66, 132 et seq., 184–89; Charles Andler, *Les origines du socialisme d'état en Allemagne* (Paris: F. Alcan, 1897), pp. 107, 111; Charles Gide and Charles Rist, *Histoire des doctrines économiques depuis les Physiocrates jusqu'à nos jours* (Paris: L. Larose and L. Tenin, 1909), pp. 481, 484, 488, 490; Friedrich Muckle, *Die großen Sozialisten* (Leipzig: B. G. Teubner, 1920), vol. 2, p. 77; Walter Eucken, "Zur Würdigung Saint-Simons", *Schmollers Jahrbuch für Gesetzgebung, Verwaltung und Volkswirtschaft im Deutschen Reich*, vol. 45 (1921), p. 1052. The objections which have recently been raised against this contention by Erich Thier, *Rodbertus, Lassalle, Adolf Wagner: Ein Beitrag zur Theorie und Geschichte des deutschen Staatssozialismus* (Jena: G. Fischer, 1930), pp. 15–16, seem to arise from an inadequate knowledge of the Saint-Simonian writings.

[46] See Franz Mehring, *Geschichte der deutschen Sozialdemokratie*, 4th ed. (Stuttgart: J. H. W. Dietz, 1909), vol. 2, p. 180. [The German socialist Wilhelm Liebknecht (1826–1900) was with August Bebel a founder of the Social Democratic Worker's Party of Germany.—Ed.]

[47] See Andler, *Origines du socialisme d'état*, p. 101. [The German state socialist Ferdinand Lassalle (1825–64) was the founder of the General German Workers Association and, for a time, a rival of Karl Marx. The French historian and socialist thinker Louis Blanc (1811–82) laid out the principles of his system in his 1839 essay "The Organisation of Labour", where he advanced the principle of "from each according to his ability, to each according to his needs" and advocated the formation of 'national workshops', producer co-operatives that would eventually replace the competitive market system.—Ed.] Another curious and yet completely unexplored case where Saint-Simonian influence on German thought seems to have been at work is that of the economist Friedrich List. There is at least evidence of his direct contact with Saint-Simonian circles. List came to Paris, where he had already visited in 1823–24, on his return from America in December 1830. On his earlier visit he had already made the acquaintance of the first editor of the *Revue encyclopédique*, which during his second visit came into the hands of the Saint-Simonians and from August 1831 onwards was edited by Hippolyte Carnot. List's interest, like that of the Saint-Simonians, was largely in railway projects and any attempt to make contact with people of similar interests during his visit must have led him straight to the Saint-Simonians. We know that List met Chevalier early and that he at least tried to make the acquaintance of d'Eichthal. (See

V

We have not yet said anything about the relations of Saint-Simonism to later French socialist schools. But this part of their influence is on the whole so well known that we can be brief. The only one of the early French socialists who was independent of Saint-Simon was of course his contemporary Charles Fourier[48]—who, with Robert Owen and Saint-Simon, is usually regarded as one of the three founders of socialism.[49] But although the Saint-Simonians borrowed from him some elements of their doctrines—particularly with respect to the relations between the sexes—neither he nor, for that matter, Robert Owen contributed much to that aspect of socialism which is relevant here: the deliberate organisation and direction of economic activity. His contribution there is more of a negative character. A fanatic for economy, he

---

Friedrich List, *Schriften, Reden, Briefe*, ed. Friedrich List Gesellschaft (Berlin: Hobbing, 1927), vol. 4, p. 8). Two of his articles on railways appeared in the *Revue encyclopédique*. I have not been able to ascertain whether the *Globe*, from which he quotes in one of these articles (a passage for which the unsuspecting editor of the *Schriften* searched in vain in the English *Globe and Traveller*), was not, as seems much more likely, the Saint-Simonian journal of that name. (See List, *Schriften*, vol. 5, 1928, pp. 62, 554). Some years later List translated Louis Napoleon's *Idées Napoléoniennes* (1839), the Saint-Simonian tendencies of which we yet have to note. It is now known that he wrote the first version of his chief work, *Das nationale System der Politischen Ökonomie* (1841), during a third and much more extended stay in Paris in the thirties, as a prize essay, and that in the essay he felt himself compelled to defend himself against any suspicion of 'Saint-Simonism' in the sense of communism, in which it was then generally understood (List, *Schriften*, vol. 4, p. 294). There can be little doubt that any marked resemblance to Saint-Simonian ideas we find in his later work is likely to derive from that essay. And such similarities are not wanting. Particularly List's conception of 'natural laws of historical development' is most likely of Saint-Simonian origin; according to this view, social evolution necessarily passes through definite stages, an idea readily accepted by the historical school of German economists. How strong in general the French influence on List was, his declamations against 'ideology' bear witness.

That the other German author from whom the historical school of German economists derived its preoccupation with the discovery of definite stages of economic development, B. Hildebrand, derived his ideas from Saint-Simonians has been pointed out by Johann Plenge, *Die Stammformen der vergleichenden Wirtschaftstheorie* (Essen: G. D. Baedeker, 1919), p. 15. [Hayek refers in this long note to the journalist and author Friedrich List (1789–1846), who offered his 'national system of political economy' as an alternative to the 'cosmopolitan doctrine' of Adam Smith, and to Bruno Hildebrand (1812–78), a member of the older German historical school of economics and founder in 1863 of the journal *Jahrbücher für Nationalökonomie und Statistik*.—Ed.]

[48] See H. Louvancour, *De Henri de Saint-Simon à Charles Fourier* (Chartres: Durand, 1913), and Hubert Bourgin, *Fourier: Contribution à l'étude du socialisme français* (Paris: Société nouvelle de librairie et d'édition, 1905), esp. pp. 415 et seq. [For more on Fourier, see chapter 11, note 45.—Ed.]

[49] [Believing that character is formed by one's social environment, the Welsh social reformer and textile mill owner Robert Owen (1771–1858) established a model community in New Lanark, Scotland, with improved housing and working conditions for his employees. New Harmony, Indiana was one of the many Owenite co-operatives that formed, but none was successful. Later in life Owen also played a rôle in the formation of the British trade union movement.—Ed.]

could see nothing but waste in the competitive institutions and surpassed even the Saint-Simonians in his belief in the unbounded possibilities of technological progress. There was indeed much of the engineer mentality in him and, like Saint-Simon, he recruited his pupils largely among the polytechnicians. He is probably the earliest representative of the myth of 'scarcity in the midst of plenty', which to the engineering mind seemed as obvious 120 years ago as it does now.

Victor Considérant, the leader of the Fourierist school which gave their doctrines more coherence than did their master, was a polytechnician, and most of the influential members, like Transon and Lechevalier, were old Saint-Simonians.[50] Of the rival socialist sects nearly all the leaders were former Saint-Simonians who had developed particular aspects of that doctrine: Leroux, Cabet, Buchez, and Pecqueur, or, like Louis Blanc, whose *Organisation du travail* is pure Saint-Simonism, had borrowed extensively from it.[51] Even the most original of the later French socialists, Proudhon, however much he may have contributed to political doctrine, was in his properly socialist doctrines largely Saint-Simonian.[52] It can be said that by about 1840 Saint-Simonian ideas had ceased to be the property of a particular school and had come to form the basis of all the socialist movements. And the socialism of 1848—apart from the strong democratic and anarchistic elements which by then had been carried into it as new and alien elements—was in doctrine and personnel still largely Saint-Simonian.

VI

Although there is already some danger that we may appear unduly to exaggerate the importance of that little group of men, we have by no means yet sur-

[50] See Maurice Dommanget, *Victor Considérant, sa vie, son œuvre* (Paris: Editions sociales internationales, 1929). [For more on Considérant, see chapter 11, note 45. Transon and Lechevalier were mentioned in chapter 14, note 16, and Transon's lectures before the Polytechnicians were noted in chapter 14, note 24.—Ed.]

[51] [For more on Pierre Leroux, see chapter 14, note 57, and for Etienne Cabet and Constantin Pecqueur, see chapter 14, note 62. A co-founder with Bazard of the Charbonnerie, Philippe Buchez (1796–1865) was another Saint-Simonian who would leave the group after the split with Enfantin. He would later advocate Christian socialism in his journal *l'Européen*, and edit, with Pierre Celéstin Roux-Lavergne, a 40-volume parliamentary history of the French revolution.—Ed.]

[52] On the Saint-Simonian elements in Proudhon's doctrine, see particularly Karl Diehl, *P. J. Proudhon: Seine Lehre und seine Leben* (Jena: G. Fischer, 1896), vol. 3, pp. 159, 176, 280. [The French printer and anarchist Pierre-Joseph Proudhon (1809–65) answered the query that formed the title of his most famous work *What is Property?* (1840) with "Property is theft". Though Saint-Simon is referenced in various places in Diehl's book, including the chapter on Proudhon's social philosophy, the page references provided by Hayek do not match up.—Ed.]

veyed the full extent of their influence. To be inspirers of practically all socialist movements[53] during the past hundred years would be enough to secure
them an important place in history. The influence which Saint-Simon exercised on the study of social problems through Comte and Thierry, and the
Saint-Simonians through Quetelet and Le Play is hardly less important and
will occupy us again. A full account of the spreading of their ideas through
Europe would have to give considerable attention to the profound influence
they exercised on Giuseppe Mazzini,[54] the whole young Italian movement, Silvio Pellico, Gioberti, Garibaldi, and others[55] in Italy, and to trace their effects

[53] There may even have been a direct influence on early English socialism. At least one of
T. Hodgskin's letters, written in 1820 soon after his return from France, shows fairly definite
traces of Saint-Simonian ideas. See Elie Halévy, *Thomas Hodgskin* (Paris: Société nouvelle de
librairie et d'édition, 1903), pp. 58–59. I owe this reference to Dr. W. Stark. [British naval officer, journalist and lecturer Thomas Hodgskin (1787–1869) used Ricardo's labour theory of
value to criticise the appropriation by capitalists of value produced by workers in *Labour Defended
against the Claims of Capital* (1825). Because this tract was often cited by Karl Marx, Hodgskin
was often identified as a Ricardian socialist. In other works, however, he defended free trade
and criticised state intervention, leading some to identify him as an individualist anarchist. See
George Smith, "Thomas Hodgskin (1787–1869)", in *The Encyclopedia of Libertarianism*, ed. Ronald
Hamowy (Thousand Oaks, CA: SAGE, 2008), pp. 227–28. Historian of economic thought Werner Stark (1909–85) mentions some of Hodgskin's debts to Saint-Simon in his essay "The End
of Classical Economics, or Liberalism and Socialism at the Crossroads", in his *The Ideal Foundations of Economic Thought: Three Essays on the Philosophy of Economics* (London: Kegan Paul, Trench,
Trubner and Co., 1943), pp. 61, 80.—Ed.]

[54] Mazzini was in the years between 1830 and 1835, particularly during his exile in France, in
intimate contact with the Saint-Simonians Pierre Leroux and Jean Reynaud, and the effect of
this can be traced throughout his work. On this, see Gaetano Salvemini, *Mazzini*, in *La Giovine
Europa*, ed. G. d'Acandia, no. 2 (Rome: n.p., 1920), *passim*; Otto Vossler, *Mazzini's politisches Denken und Wollen in den geistigen Strömungen seiner Zeit*, supplement no. 11, *Historische Zeitschrift* (Munich:
R. Oldenbourg, 1927), pp. 42–52; and Croce, *History of Europe*, pp. 118, 142. On Mazzini's
later critical attitude towards Saint-Simonism, see his "Thoughts upon Democracy in Europe",
in Emilie Ashurst Venturi, *Joseph Mazzini: A Memoir by E. A. V.* (London: H. S. King, 1875), esp.
pp. 205–17. [The Italian nationalist and full-time revolutionary Giuseppe Mazzini (1805–72)
was a member of the Carbonari, the founder while in exile in Marseilles of Young Italy (a movement that helped spawn similar groups in Germany and Poland), and a leader of the *Risorgimento*
movement for an independent and unified Italy.—Ed.]

[55] See Weill, "Le Saint-Simonisme hors de France", p. 109, and Vossler, *Mazzini's politisches
Denken*, p. 44. [The Italian author and playwright Silvio Pellico (1788–1854) spent most of the
1820s in prison on suspicion of his being a member of the Carbonari; his diary of his imprisonment *Le mie Prigioni (My Prisons)* was said to have done more to damage the cause of Austrian
domination of Italy than any battlefield victory. Vincenzo Gioberti (1801–52) was an Italian philosopher, politician, and nationalist. Giuseppe Garibaldi (1807–82) was an Italian nationalist,
adventurer, and revolutionary who fought a lifelong struggle to expel foreigners from Italy and
unite it under a single government. His greatest success was to liberate Sicily and Naples with his
'thousand red shirts' in 1860.—Ed.]

on such diverse figures as August Strindberg in Sweden,[56] Alexander Herzen in Russia,[57] and others in Spain and South America.[58] Nor can we stop here to consider the frequent occurrence of similar types who sometimes rallied to the Saint-Simonian flag as did the Belgian industrialist, sociologist, and benefactor Ernest Solvay,[59] or the *Néo-Saint-Simoniens* who in postwar France published a new *Producteur*.[60] Such conscious or unconscious rebirths we meet throughout the last hundred years.[61]

There is, however, one direct effect of Saint-Simonian teaching which deserves more consideration: the founders of modern socialism also did much to give Continental capitalism its peculiar form; 'monopoly capitalism', or 'finance capitalism', growing up through the intimate connection between banking and industry (the banks organising industrial concerns as the largest

[56] See Nelly Mehlin [Melin], "Auguste Strindberg", *La revue de Paris*, vol. 16 [19], 1912, p. 857. [Many of the works of the Swedish dramatist, novelist, and poet Johan August Strindberg (1849–1912) were tragedies centring on constricting gender rôles within the institution of marriage in bourgeois society.—Ed.]

[57] See Aleksandr Hertzen, *Le monde Russe et la révolution: Memoires de A. Hertzen* (Paris: E. Dentu, 1860–62), vol. 6, pp. 195 et seq. [The discussion of Saint-Simonism is found in volume 1, chapter 6, on pp. 235–41 of the Russian political writer and activist Alexander Herzen's (1812–70) three-volume memoirs. Chapter 6 concerns his university days, and on p. 238 he wrote, "Le saint-simonisme forma le fond de nos croyances, et il en compose toujours la partie essentielle", which translates as, "Saint-Simonism provided the grounds for our Credo, and always composed its essential part". Exiled for a time to the provinces for his anti-tsarist views, Herzen hurried to Paris when the Revolution of 1848 was launched, but was soon chastened by the outcome. Moving to London, in the 1850s and 1860s he established the Free Russian Press (devoted to printing and sending to Russia censored Russian writings), the literary magazine the *Polar Star*, and the journal the *Bell*, which offered up political criticism of the Tsar, the Russian bureaucracy, and such social institutions as serfdom.—Ed.]

[58] See Weill, "Saint-Simonisme hors de France", and J. F. Normano, "Saint-Simonian America", *Social Forces*, vol. 9 [11], October 1932, 8–14.

[59] See Ernest Solvay, *A propos de saint-simonisme* (Principes libérosocialistes d'action sociale). Project de lettre au journal *Le Peuple*, 1903 (printed 1916). Cf. Paul Héger and Charles Lefebure, *Vie d'Ernest Solvay* (Brussels: Lamertin, 1929), pp. 77, 150. [The first rather obscure entry in this note is taken from a list of Solvay's publications in the book by Héger and Lefebure. They state that the letter was never sent to *Le Peuple*, but that the text of it was published in March 1916. For more on Solvay, see chapter 5, note 12.—Ed.]

[60] The postwar *Le Producteur* was published in Paris from 1919 by a group which included G. Darquet, G. Gros, H. Clouard, M. Leroy, and F. Delaisi. On this, see Marc Bourbonnais, *Le néo saint-simonisme et la vie sociale d'aujourd'hui* (Paris: Presses universitaires de France, 1923).

[61] See also C.-J. Gignoux, "L'Industrialisme de Saint-Simon à Walther Rathenau", *Revue d'histoire économiques et sociale*, vol. 11, 1923, pp. 200–17, and Gottfried Salomon, "Die Saint-Simonisten", *Zeitschrift für die gesamte Staatswissenschaft*, vol. 82, 1927, pp. 550–76. On the influence Saint-Simonian ideas had in the conception of the corporativist theories of fascism, see Hans Reupke, *Unternehmer und Arbeiter in der faschistischen Wirtschaftsidee* (Berlin: R. Hobbing, 1931), pp. 14, 18, 22, 29–30, 40.

shareholders of the component firms), the rapid development of joint-stock enterprises and the large railway combines are largely Saint-Simonian creations.

The history of this is mainly one of the *Crédit mobilier* type of bank, the kind of combined deposit and investment institution which was first created by the brothers Pereire in France and then imitated under their personal influence or by other Saint-Simonians almost all over the European continent.[62] One might almost say that after the Saint-Simonians had failed to bring about the reforms they desired through a political movement, or after they had grown older and more worldly, they undertook to transform the capitalist system from within and thus to apply as much of their doctrines as they could by individual effort. And it cannot be denied that they succeeded in changing the economic structure of the Continental countries into something quite different from the English type of competitive capitalism. Even if the *Crédit mobilier* of the Pereires ultimately failed, it and its industrial concerns became the model on which the banking and capital structures in most of the industrial countries of Europe were developed, partly by other Saint-Simonians. For the Pereires the aim of their *Crédit mobilier* was most definitely to create a centre of administration and control which was to direct according to a coherent program the railway systems, the town planning activities, and the various public utilities and other industries which by a systematic policy of mergers they attempted to consolidate into a few large undertakings.[63] In Germany Gustav von Mevissen and Abraham Oppenheim, who had early come under Saint-Simonian influence, went similar ways with the foundation of the Darmstädter Bank and

---

[62] [For more on the brothers Pereire, see chapter 14, note 15.—Ed.]

[63] See Johann Plenge, *Gründung und Geschichte des Crédit Mobilier* (Tübingen: H. Laupp, 1903), esp. pp. 79 et seq., and the passage quoted on p. 139 from the Annual Report of the *Crédit mobilier* for 1854: "Quand nous touchons à une branche de l'industrie, nous désirons surtout obtenir son développement non par la voie de la concurrence, mais par voie *d'association et de fusion*, par l'emploi le plus économique des forces et non par leur opposition, leur déstruction réciproque". [When we enter a branch of industry, we want most of all to achieve its development not through competition, but by way of *association and merger*, by the most economical use of forces, instead of their opposition and reciprocal destruction.—Ed.]

There is no space here for the discussion of the Saint-Simonian theories of credit in the hands of the Pereires and we must refer in this respect to J. B. Vergeot, *Le crédit comme stimulant et régulateur de l'industrie, la conception saint-simonienne, ses réalisations, etc.* (Paris: Jouve et cie, 1918), and Kurt Moldenhauer, *Kreditpolitik und Gesellschaftsreform* (Jena: G. Fischer, 1932). But it may just be mentioned that the Pereires, after acquiring the *Banque de Savoy* with its note-issuing privilege, in order to be in a position to put their theories into practice, became ardent advocates of 'free banking' and the cause of the great controversy between the 'free banking' and the 'central banking' school which raged in France in and after 1864. On this, see Vera C. Smith, *The Rationale of Central Banking* (London: P. S. King and Son, 1936), pp. 33 et seq.

other banking ventures.[64] In Holland other Saint-Simonians worked in the same direction,[65] and in Austria,[66] Italy, Switzerland, and Spain[67] the Pereires or their subsidiaries or connections created similar institutions. What is known as the 'German' type of bank with its close connection with industry and the whole system of *Effektenkapitalismus* as it has been called is essentially the realisation of Saint-Simonian plans.[68] This development was closely connected with the other favourite activity of the Saint-Simonians in later years, railway construction,[69] and their interest in public works of all kinds,[70] which, as years went by, became more and more their chief interest. As Enfantin organised the Paris-Lyon-Méditerranée railway system, the Pereires built railways in Austria, Switzerland, Spain, and Russia, and Paulin Talabot in Italy, employing as engineers on the spot other Saint-Simonians to carry out their directions.[71] Enfantin, looking back at the works of the Saint-Simonians in late life, was well entitled to say that they had "covered the earth with a network of railways, gold, silver, and electricity".[72]

If with their far-flung plans for industrial organisation they did not succeed in creating large combines, as was later done with the assistance of the

---

[64] See Joseph Hansen, *Gustav von Mevissen, ein rheinisches Lebensbild 1815–1889* (Berlin: G. Reimer, 1906), vol. 1, pp. 60, 606, 644–46, 655, and Walther Däbritz, *Gründung und Anfänge der Discontogesellschaft Berlin* (Munich: Duncker und Humblot, 1931), pp. 34–36. [German financiers Gustav von Mevissen (1815–99) and Abraham Oppenheim (1804–78) were partners in the Darmstädter National Bank, about which Rondo Cameron has written that "the inspiration, the idea, most of the capital, and large part of the practical experience both in promoting it and organising its operations came from the Crédit Mobilier". See Rondo Cameron, *France and the Economic Development of Europe: 1800–1914* (Princeton: Princeton University Press, 1961), pp. 150–51.—Ed.]

[65] See H. M. Hirschfeld, "Le saint-simonisme dans les Pays-Bas: Le Crédit Mobilier Néerlandais", *Revue d'économie politique*, 37th année, 1923, pp. 364–74.

[66] See Fritz G. Steiner, *Die Entwicklung des Mobilbankwesens in Oesterreich von den Anfängen bis zur Krise von 1873* (Vienna: C. Konegan, 1913), pp. 38–78.

[67] See H. M. Hirschfeld, "Der Crédit Mobilier Gedanke mit besonderer Berücksichtigung seines Einflusses in den Niederlanden", *Zeitschrift für Volkswirtschaft und Sozialpolitik*, n. f. vol. 3, 1923, pp. 438–65.

[68] See Gerhart von Schulze-Gaevernitz, *Die deutsche Kreditbank*, in *Grundriß der Sozialökonomik* (Tübingen: J. C. B. Mohr, 1915), vol. 2, p. 146.

[69] See Maurice Wallon, *Les Saint-Simoniens et les chemins de fer* (Paris: A. Pedone, 1908), and Henry René D'Allemagne, *Prosper Enfantin et les grandes entreprises du XIX siecle* (Paris: Gründ, 1935).

[70] See the *Vues politiques et pratiques sur les travaux publics de France* (Paris: Impr. d'Everat, 1832), published in 1832 by the four Saint-Simonian engineers, Gabriel Lamé, B. P. E. Clapeyron, and Stéphane and Eugène Flachat.

[71] [Polytechnician Paulin Talabot (1799–1885) was an ironmaster and railway magnate. In addition to directing many engineering and railway projects in southern France, he provided the plans for the development of the port facilities in Trieste and participated in the construction of the Lombard-Venetian and Central Italian Railway.—Ed.]

[72] Quoted in Pinet, *Ecrivains et penseurs polytechniciens*, p. 165.

governments in the process of cartellisation, this was largely due to the policy of free trade on which France had embarked and of which some of the old Saint-Simonians, particularly Michel Chevalier, but also the Pereires, were still among the chief advocates.[73] But already others from the same circle, notably Pecqueur,[74] were agitating in the same direction as their friend Friedrich List in Germany. Yet they could not succeed till another branch from the same stem, positivism and 'historicism', had succeeded in effectively discrediting 'orthodox' political economy. The arguments, however, which were later to justify a policy of supporting the growth of cartels were already created by the Saint-Simonians.

However far their practical influence extended, it was greatest in France during the second empire. During this period they had not only the support of the press because some of the leading journalists were old Saint-Simonians;[75] but the most important fact was that Napoleon III himself was so profoundly influenced by Saint-Simonian ideas that Sainte-Beuve could call him "Saint-Simon on horseback".[76] He remained on friendly terms with some of its members and even committed himself to part of their ideas in his programmatic *Idées Napoléniennes* and some other pamphlets.[77] It is thus not surprising that the years of the second empire became the great period of the Saint-Simonian

---

[73] [For more on Chevalier, see chapter 14, note 17, and for the Perieres, see chapter 14, note 15.—Ed.]

[74] See Constantin Pecqueur, *Economie sociale: Des intérêts du commerce, de l'industrie et de l'agriculture, et de la civilisation en général, sous l'influence des applications de la vapeur* (Paris: Desessart, 1838). [For more on Pecqueur, see chapter 14, note 62.—Ed.]

[75] Particularly Jourdan, an intimate friend of Enfantin, and Guérault. [Guéroult]. On the latter, cf. Charles Augustin Sainte-Beuve, *Nouveaux Lundis* (Paris: Michel Lévy Frères, 1865), vol. 4, pp. 140–62 and on Sainte-Beuve's own relations to Saint-Simonism, Maxime Leroy, "Le Saint-Simonisme de Sainte-Beuve", *Zeitschrift für Sozialwissenschaft*, vol. 7, 1938, pp. 132–47. [Hayek refers to the French journalists Louis Jourdan (1810–81), who collaborated with Enfantin in producing the journal *L'Algerie*, and Adolphe Guéroult (1810–72), who contributed articles to *Le Globe* and later became the founder of the political paper *L'Opinion nationale*. Jourdan was indeed an 'intimate friend'; Enfantin was the father of a child by Jourdan's wife. The child was raised by Jourdan and his wife and named 'Prosper' after Enfantin. The literary critic Charles-Augustin Sainte-Beuve (1804–69) contributed to *Le Globe* both in its liberal days and after it had become under Leroux a Saint-Simonian organ, though later in his life he denied any Saint-Simonian influence. Hayek refers to his review of Guéroult's *Etudes de politique et de philosophie religieuse* (1863).—Ed.]

[76] See Albert Léon Guérard, *Napoleon III* (Cambridge, MA: Harvard University Press, 1943), p. 215, where this description of Napoleon III is called "strikingly accurate"; and Hendrik Nicolaas Boon, *Rêve et réalité dans l'œuvre économique et sociale de Napoléon III* (The Hague: M. Nijhoff, 1936).

[77] *Des idées Napoléoniennes* (1839), *L'idée Napoléonienne* (1840), and *Extinction du paupérisme* (Paris: Pagnerre, 1844).

réalisations. So closely indeed did they become associated with the regime that its end meant more or less also the end of their direct influence in France.[78] When to this influence of the French empire we add the facts that Bismarck's social policy and ideas were largely derived from Lassalle and thus via Louis Blanc, Lorenz von Stein, and Rodbertus from Saint-Simon,[79] and that the theory of the *soziale Königtum* and state socialism, which guided the execution of that policy, can be traced, through L. von Stein and Rodbertus and others, to the same source,[80] we begin to get the measure of this influence in the nineteenth century. Even if this influence was tempered by others which in any case would have worked in the same direction, the statement of the German Karl Grün, which may conclude this survey, appears certainly in no way to exaggerate their importance. "Saint-Simonism", he wrote in 1845, "is like a seed pod that has been opened and whose husk has been lost, while the individual seeds have found soil everywhere and have come up, one after the other". And in his enumeration of all the different movements which have been thus fertilised, we find for the first time the term "scientific socialism"[81] applied to the work of Saint-Simon, who "had throughout his life been searching for the new science".

[78] On this whole phase of their activities, see Georges Weill, "Les Saint-Simoniens sous Napoléon III", *Revue des études Napoléoniennes*, May 1931 [1913], pp. 391–406.

[79] Cf. Halévy, "La doctrine économique saint-simonienne", in *L'Ere des tyrannies*, p. 91. [See Halévy, *The Era of Tyrannies*, p. 101.—Ed.]

[80] See L. Brentano, "Die gewerbliche Arbeiterfrage", in Gustav Schonberg, *Handbuch der politischen Ökonomie*, vol. 1 (Tübingen: Laupp, 1882), pp. 935 et seq.

[81] Grün, *Die soziale Bewegung in Frankreich und Belgien*, p. 182 [82]. It is interesting to compare this statement with a manuscript note by Lord Acton (Cambridge University Library, Acton Collection, MS add 5487, f. 135) in which, apropos Bazard, Acton says: "A system is shut in. It is the broken fragments of it, dissolved, that fructify". Cf. also John Stuart Mill, *Principles of Political Economy*, 2nd ed. (London: J. W. Parker, 1849), vol. 1, p. 250 [See *Principles of Political Economy, Books I, II*, ed. John Robson, vol. 2 (1965) of *Collected Works of John Stuart Mill*, p. 203]: St. Simonism, "during the few years of its public promulgation, sowed the seeds of nearly all the Socialist tendencies which have since spread so widely in France"; and Wilhelm Roscher, *Geschichte der Nationalökonomik in Deutschland* (Munich: R. Oldenbourg, 1874), p. 845: "Und es lässt sich nicht leugnen, wie diese Schriftsteller [Bazard, Enfantin, Comte, Considérant—FAH] an praktischem Einfluss auf ihre Zeit mit den heutigen Sozialistenführern gar nicht verglichen werden können, ebenso sehr überragen sie die letzteren an wissenschaftlicher Bedeutung. Es kommen in der neuesten sozialistischen Literatur sehr wenige erhebliche Gedanken vor, die nicht bereits von jenen Franzosen ausgesprochen wären, noch dazu meist in einer viel würdigern, geistreichen Form". [It cannot be denied that the practical impact of these authors (Bazard, Enfantin, Comte, Considérant) on their time far exceeds that of contemporary socialist leaders. Similarly, their scientific significance outstrips these contemporaries. There are very few important ideas in the newest socialist literature that were not already expressed by those Frenchmen, and often in a more dignified and witty style.—Ed.]

SIXTEEN

SOCIOLOGY: COMTE AND HIS SUCCESSORS

I

Eight years after the first *Système de politique positive*[1] there began to appear that work of Comte to which his fame is mainly due. The *Cours de philosophie positive*, the literary version of the series of lectures which he had first started in 1826, and then, after recovery from his mental illness, delivered in 1829, extended to six volumes, which appeared between 1830 and 1842.[2] In devoting the best years of his manhood to this theoretical task, Comte remained

---

[1] Originally published in 1822 under the title *Plan des travaux nécessaires pour réorganiser la société* and republished under the above title only in 1824. [Comte reprinted his 1822 essay in an appendix to volume 4 of *Système*. For an English translation, see "Plan of the Scientific Operations Necessary for Reorganising Society", in Auguste Comte, *System of Positive Polity*, translated by John Henry Bridges, Frederic Harrison, Edward Spencer Beesly, Richard Congreve, and Henry Dix Hutton (London: Longmans, Green, and Co., 1875–77; reprinted, New York: Burt Franklin, 1968), vol. 4, pp. 527–89.—Ed.]

[2] Page references to the *Cours* will be to the second edition, edited by Emile Littré (Paris: J. B. Baillière et fils, 1864), the pagination of which is identical with that of the third and fourth, but not with that of the first and fifth editions. English quotations in the text will be taken, wherever practicable, from the admirable condensed English version by Miss Martineau, *The Positive Philosophy of Auguste Comte*, freely translated and condensed by Harriet Martineau, 3rd ed. (London: Kegan Paul, Trench, Trübner and Co., 1893), 2 vols. In references to this edition the title will be abbreviated *PP*, as distinguished from the French original, referred to as *Cours*.

Although the coincidence of the exact date is no more than an accident, it is perhaps worth pointing out that the year 1842, in which the concluding volume of the *Cours* appeared and which for our purposes thus marks the conclusion of the 'French phase' of the strand of thought with which we are here concerned, is also the year which more than any other may be regarded as the beginning of the 'German phase' of the same development, with which we hope to deal on another occasion. In 1842 Lorenz von Stein's *Der Socialismus und Communismus des heutigen Frankreichs* and J. K. Rodbertus' first work *Zur Erkenntnis unserer staatswirtschaftlichen Zustände* appeared, and Karl Marx sent his first essays to the publisher. In the preceding year Friedrich List had published his *Das Nationale System der politischen Oekonomie*, and Ludwig Feuerbach his *Das Wesen des Christentums*. In the following year there appeared Wilhelm Roscher's *Grundriss zu Vorlesungen über die Staatswirthschaft nach geschichtlicher Methode*. The special significance of this date in German intellectual history is well brought out by Hans Freund, *Soziologie und Sozialismus: Ein Beitrag zur Geschichte der deutschen Sozialtheorie um 1842* (Würzburg: K. Triltsch, 1934).

faithful to the conviction which had led to his break with Saint-Simon: that the political reorganisation of society could be achieved only after the spiritual foundation had been laid by a reorganisation of all knowledge.[3] But he never lost sight of the political task. The main philosophical work was duly followed by the definitive *Système de politique positive* (4 vols., 1851–54) which, in spite of all its bizarre excrescences, is a consistent execution of the plans of his youth. And if his death in 1857 had not prevented it, this would have been followed by the third part of the original plan, a similarly elaborate treatise on technology or 'the action of man upon nature'.[4]

No attempt can be made here to give an adequate summary of the whole of Comte's philosophy or of its evolution. We are concerned only with the birth of the new discipline, of which Saint-Simon and the younger Comte had only dreamed but which the latter's mature works brought into existence. Yet, as the whole of Comte's work is directed towards this end, this is not a sufficient restriction of our task. We shall have to confine ourselves to a consideration of those aspects of his immense work which, either because of their influence on other leading thinkers of the period, or because they are particularly representative of the intellectual tendencies of the age, are of special significance. They concern mainly the methods appropriate to the study of social phenomena, a subject which is extensively treated in the *Cours*. But it should perhaps be pointed out that it is because the subjects which mainly concern us are treated in that work that we shall confine ourselves to its contents, and that we cannot accept the belief, at one time widely held, that there is a fundamental break between it and Comte's later work, brought about by the increasingly pathological state of his mind.[5]

A few further facts of Comte's life may be recalled here which will help us to understand his views and the extent and limits of his influence. The most important feature of his career is, perhaps, that trained as a mathematician he remained one by profession. Through the greater part of his life he derived his income from coaching and examining in mathematics for the *Ecole polytechnique*—but the professorship at the institution which he coveted remained denied to him. The repeated disappointments and the quarrels caused by his

---

[3] *Cours*, vol. 2, p. 438.

[4] [This was laid out by Comte in the 1822 essay Hayek mentions above. See "Plan of the Scientific Operations Necessary for Reorganising Society", p. 550, where Comte promises "a general exposition of the Collective Action which civilised men, in the present state of their knowledge, can exercise over Nature so as to modify it for their own advantage".—Ed.]

[5] The essential unity of Comte's thought, which had always had its defenders, has since Georges Dumas's investigations in *Psychologie de deux messies positivistes: Saint-Simon et Auguste Comte* (Paris: F. Alcan, 1905) been accepted by practically all French scholars concerned with these questions. See on this the survey of the discussion in Gouhier, *La jeunesse d'Auguste Comte*, vol. 1, pp. 18–29, and the two works by Pierre Ducassé, *Méthode et intuition chez Auguste Comte* (Paris: F. Alcan, 1939) and *Essai sur les origines intuitives du positivisme* (Paris: F. Alcan, 1939).

recriminations, which in the end lost him even the modest positions which he held, explain to some extent his increasing isolation, his outspoken contempt for most of his scientific contemporaries, and the almost complete neglect of his work in his own country during his lifetime. Although in the end he found a few enthusiastic disciples, it is on the whole not difficult to see why to most people he seems to have appeared a singularly unattractive figure, whose whole intellectual style has often repelled those who have most in common with him.[6] The man who prided himself that in a few years of his youth he had absorbed all the knowledge from which he could construct a grandiose systematisation of all human science and who, through a great part of his life, practised a 'cerebral hygiene' consisting in not reading any new publications, was not likely to be readily accepted as that *preceptor mundi et universae scientiae* he claimed to be. The excessive length and prolixity and the clumsy style of his mature works were a further bar to its popularity. Yet if this restricted the number of people who became directly acquainted with his work, it was made up for by the profound effect it had on some of the most influential thinkers of the age. Although largely indirect, his influence was among the most potent in the nineteenth century, certainly where the study of social phenomena was concerned.

II

The whole of Comte's philosophy hinges, of course, upon the celebrated law of the three stages which we have already met in his early essays. His very task is determined for him by that law: all the simpler sciences like physics, chemistry, and biology having reached the positive stage, it was reserved for Comte to do the same for the crowning science of the human race and thus to complete the main development of the human mind. The stress which Comte himself and still more his interpreters have put on the *three* separate stages is, however, rather misleading. The great contrast is between, on the one hand, the theological and the metaphysical stage (the latter being a mere "modification"[7] of the first), and, on the other, the positive stage. What he is concerned with is the continuous and gradual emancipation from the anthropomorphic inter-

---

[6] See the interesting confession by H. G. Wells in his *Experiment in Autobiography* (London: V. Gollancz, 1934), p. 658: "Probably I am unjust to Comte and grudge to acknowledge a sort of priority he had in sketching the modern outlook. But for him, as for Marx, I have a real personal dislike". [For more on Wells, see chapter 10, note 7.—Ed.]

[7] See *Cours*, vol. 1, p. 9: "L'état métaphysique, qui n'est au fond qu'une simple modification générale du premier". [The metaphysical stage, which is basically nothing else than a simple general modification of the first (stage).—Ed.] See also vol. 4, p. 213.

pretation of all phenomena[8] which each science completely achieves only as it reaches the positive stage. The metaphysical stage is no more than the phase of dissolution of the theological stage, the critical phase in which man has already abandoned the cruder personalistic view which seeks spirits and deities in all phenomena, but has merely replaced them with abstract entities or essences which have as little place in the truly positivist view of science. In the positive phase every attempt to explain phenomena by causes or a statement of the "mode of production" is abandoned;[9] it aims at directly connecting the observed phenomena by rules about the coexistence or sequence or, to use a modern phrase not yet used by Comte, at merely 'describing' their interrelations by general and invariable laws.[10] In other words, since the habits of thought which man had acquired in interpreting the actions of his own kind had long held up the study of external nature, and the latter had only made real progress in proportion as it got rid of this human habit, the way to progress in the study of man must be the same: we must cease to consider man anthropomorphically and must treat him as if we knew about him as little as we know about external nature. Although Comte does not say so in so many words, he comes very near doing so, and therefore one cannot help wondering how he could have failed to see the paradoxical nature of this conclusion.[11]

---

[8] Cf. Lucien Lévy-Bruhl, *La philosophie d'Auguste Comte*, 4th ed. (Paris: F. Alcan, 1921), p. 42, and *Cours*, vol. 5, p. 25.

[9] *Cours*, vol. 2, p. 312, and vol. 4, p. 469.

[10] [That scientific theories only *describe* phenomena was a basic tenet of operationalism, a view associated with the physicist Percy Bridgman, from whose work Hayek quoted in chapter 1, note 11. Bridgman's influence on economics is perhaps most evident in the methodological writings of Paul Samuelson, who in a reply to Fritz Machlup once said, "Scientists never 'explain' any behaviour, by theory or by any other hook. Every description that is superseded by a 'deeper explanation' turns out upon careful examination to have been replaced by still another description". Paul Samuelson, "Theory and Realism: A Reply", *American Economic Review*, vol. 54, September 1964, p. 737.—Ed.]

[11] Ibid., vol. 3, pp. 188–89: "Le véritable esprit général de toute philosophie théologique ou métaphysique consiste à prendre pour principe, dans l'explication des phénomènes du monde extérieur, notre sentiment immédiat des phénomènes humains; tandis que, au contraire, la philosophie positive est toujours caractérisée, non moins profondément, par la subordination nécessaire et rationnelle de la conception de l'homme à celle du monde. Quelle que soit l'incompatibilité fondamentale manifestée, à tant de titres, entre ces deux philosophies, par l'ensemble de leur développement successif, elle n'a point, en effet, d'autre origine essentielle, ni d'autre base permanente, que cette simple différence d'ordre entre ces deux notions également indispensables. En faisant prédominer, comme l'esprit humain a dû, de toute nécessité, le faire primitivement, la considération de l'homme sur celle du monde, on est inévitablement conduit à attribuer tous les phénomènes à des *volontés* correspondantes, d'abord naturelles, et ensuite extra-naturelles, ce qui constitue le système théologique. L'étude directe du monde extérieur a pu seule, au contraire, produire et développer la grande notion des lois de la nature, fondement indispensable de toute philosophie positive, et qui, par suite de son extension graduelle et continue à des phénomènes de moins en moins réguliers, a dû être enfin appliquée à l'étude même de l'homme

But that in the positive treatment of social phenomena man must not be treated differently from the way in which we approach the phenomena of inanimate nature is only a negative characteristic of the character which the new "natural science"[12] of society will assume. We have yet to see what the positive characteristics of the 'positive' method are. This is a far more difficult task, as Comte's statements on most of the epistemological problems involved are distressingly naïve and unsatisfactory. The basis of Comte's views is the apparently simple contention that "the fundamental character of all positive philosophy is to regard all phenomena as subject to invariable natural *laws*, whose precise discovery and reduction to the smallest number possible is the aim of all our effort".[13] All science deals with observed facts,[14] and, as he states in a sentence which he quotes with pride from his essay of 1825, "any proposition which does not admit of being reduced to a simple enunciation of fact, special or general, can have no real or intelligible sense".[15] But the question to which it is exceedingly difficult to find an answer in Comte's work is what precisely is meant by the 'phenomena' which are all subject to invariable laws, or what he regards as 'facts'. The statement that all phenomena are subject to invariable natural laws clearly makes sense only if we are given some guidance on what individual events are to be regarded as the same phenomena. It

---

et de la société, dernier terme de son entière généralisation. . . . L'étude positive n'a pas de caractère plus tranché que sa tendance spontanée et invariable à baser l'étude réelle de l'homme sur la connaissance préalable du monde extérieur". See also vol. 4, pp. 468–69. [The real general spirit of all theological or metaphysical philosophy consists in taking for its principle, in the explanation of the external world, our immediate sense of human phenomena; whereas, to the contrary, positive philosophy is always characterised, no less profoundly, by the necessary and rational subordination of the conception of man to that of the world. Whatever the fundamental inadequacy manifested, regardless of titles, between these two philosophies in the whole of their successive processes, it is nothing more, in effect, than this simple difference of order between these two equally indispensable notions. In making pre-dominant, as the primitive human mind necessarily had to do, the observation of man over that of the world, one is inevitably driven to attribute to all phenomena the corresponding *purposes*, first natural and then supernatural, which constitute the theological system. The direct study of the external world alone could have, on the contrary, produced and developed the great notion of the laws of nature, fundamentally indispensable to all positive philosophy, by following its gradual and continuous extension to phenomena less and less regular until finally it had to be applied to the very study of man and of society, the last stage of its entire generalisation . . . . The positivist method has no character more clearly defined than its spontaneous and invariable tendency towards basing the real study of man on the previous knowledge of the external world.—Ed.]

[12] Ibid., vol. 4, p. 256.

[13] Ibid., vol. 1, p. 16; see also vol. 2, p. 312, vol. 4, p. 230.

[14] Ibid., vol. 1, p. 12.

[15] Ibid., vol. 6, p. 600. Cf. *Early Essays on Social Philosophy*, p. 223. As it is of some interest that nearly all the basic ideas were already clearly stated in Comte's *Early Essays*, references to the corresponding passages in these will occasionally be added to the references to the *Cours*.

evidently cannot mean that everything which appears the same to our senses must behave in the same manner. The task of science is precisely to reclassify the sense impressions on the basis of their coexistence with or succession to others so as to make it possible to establish regularities for the behaviour of the newly constructed units of reference. But this is exactly what Comte objects to. The construction of such new entities as the 'ether' is definitely a metaphysical procedure and any attempt to explain the 'mode of production' of the phenomena as distinct from the study of the laws which connect the directly observed facts is to be proscribed. The emphasis lies on the establishment of direct relationship among the immediately given facts. But what these facts (which may be 'particular' or 'general'!) are seems to constitute no problem for Comte, who approaches the question with an entirely naïve and uncritical realism. As in the whole of nineteenth-century positivism,[16] this concept is left exceedingly obscure.

III

The only indication of what is meant by the term *fact* as used by Comte we obtain from its regular conjunction with the adjective *observed*, together with his discussion of what he means by observation. This is of great importance for its meaning in the field with which we are concerned, the study of human and social phenomena. "True observation", we are told, "must necessarily be external to the observer" and the "famous internal observation is no more than a vain parody of it", which pre-supposes the "ridiculously contradictory situation of our intelligence contemplating itself during the habitual performance of its own activity".[17] Comte accordingly consistently denies the possibility of all psychology, that "last transformation of theology",[18] or at least of all introspective knowledge of the human mind. There are only two ways in which the phenomena of the individual mind can properly become the object of positive study: either through the study of the organs which produce them, that is, through "phrenological psychology";[19] or, since "affective and intellectual functions" have the peculiar characteristic of "not being subject to direct

---

[16] See Lucia Grunicke, *Der Begriff der Tatsache in der positivistischen Philosophie des 19. Jahrhunderts* (Halle: Heinrich John, 1930).

[17] *Cours*, vol. 6, pp. 402–3; cf. also vol. 1, pp. 30–32: "L'organe observé et l'organe observateur étant, dans ce cas, identiques, comment l'observation pourrait-elle avoir lieu?" [This translates as, "The observed organ and the observing one being, in this case, identical, how could the observation occur?" This sentence is found on p. 32 of vol. 1 of the *Cours*.—Ed.] and vol. 3, pp. 538–41; *PP*, vol. 2, p. 385, and vol. 1, pp. 9–10, 381–82.

[18] *Cours*, vol. 1, p. 30.

[19] Ibid., vol. 3, p. 535.

observation during their performance", through the study of "their more or less immediate and more or less durable results"[20]—which would seem to mean what is now called the behaviourist approach. To these only two legitimate ways of studying the phenomena of the individual mind is later added, as the result of the creation of sociology, the study of the 'collective mind', the only form of psychology proper which is admitted into the positive system.

As regards the first of these aspects we need here say no more than that it is remarkable that even Comte should have fallen so completely under the influence of the founder of 'phrenology', the "illustrious Gall" whose "immortal works are irrevocably impressed upon the human mind",[21] as to believe that his attempt at localising particular mental 'faculties' in particular parts of the brain should provide an adequate substitute for all other forms of psychology.

The 'behaviourist' approach in Comte deserves rather more attention, because in this primitive form it shows particularly clearly its weakness. Only a few pages after Comte has confined the study of the individual mind to the observation of its "more or less immediate and more or less durable results" this becomes the direct observation of "the series of intellectual and moral acts, which belongs more to natural history proper" and which he seems to regard as in some sense objectively given and known without any use of introspection or any other means different from "external observation".[22] Thus Comte not only tacitly admits intellectual phenomena among his 'facts', which are to be treated like any objectively observed facts of nature; he even admits, to all intents and purposes, that our knowledge of man, which we possess only because we are men ourselves and think like other men, is an indispensable condition of our interpretation of social phenomena. It can only mean this when he emphasises that wherever we have to deal with 'animal' life (as distinguished from merely vegetative life, that is, those phenomena which appear only in the higher part of the zoological scale),[23] investigation cannot succeed unless we begin with "the consideration of man, the sole being where this order of phenomena can ever be directly intelligible".[24]

---

[20] Ibid., p. 540.

[21] Ibid., pp. 533, 563, 570. [See chapter 12, note 8, for more on Gall.—Ed.]

[22] [Ibid., pp. 540ff.—Ed.]

[23] Ibid., pp. 429–30, 494; *PP*, vol. 1, p. 354.

[24] *Cours*, vol. 3, pp. 336–37; see also pp. 216–17 and *Early Essays*, p. 219. It is interesting to note that while the passage in the early work (see Auguste Comte, *Opuscules de philosophie sociale, 1819–28* (Paris: E. Leroux, 1883), p. 182), states simply, "L'action personnelle de l'homme sur les autres êtres est la seule dont il comprenne le mode, par le sentiment qu'il en a" [The personal actions of man towards other beings are the only ones he can understand the process of, according to the manner in which he senses it.—Ed.], this becomes in the corresponding passage of the *Cours*, vol. 4, p. 468: "ses propres actes, les seuls dont il *puisse jamais croire comprendre* le mode essentiel de production" (italics added) [his own actions, the only ones about which *he might ever think that he understands* their fundamental mode of production.—Ed.].

IV

Comte's theory of the three stages is closely connected with the second main characteristic of his system, his classification, or the theory of the 'positive hierarchy', of the sciences. In the beginning of the *Cours* he still plays with the Saint-Simonian idea of the unification of all sciences by reducing all phenomena to one single law, the law of gravitation.[25] But gradually he abandons this belief and in the end it becomes even the subject of violent denunciation as an "absurd utopia".[26] Instead, the 'fundamental' or theoretical sciences (as distinguished from their concrete applications) are arranged in a single linear order of decreasing generality and increasing complexity, beginning with mathematics (including theoretical mechanics) and leading through astronomy, physics, chemistry, and biology (which includes all study of man as an individual) to the new and final science of social physics or sociology. As each of these fundamental sciences is 'based' on those preceding it in the hierarchical order, in the sense that it makes use of all the results of the preceding sciences *plus* some new elements peculiar to itself, it is an "indispensable complement of the law of the three stages" that the different sciences can reach the positive stage only successively in this "invariable and necessary order".[27] But as the last of these sciences has for its object the growth of the human mind and therefore particularly the development of science itself, it becomes, once established, the universal science which will progressively tend to absorb all knowledge in its system, although this ideal may never be fully realised.

Here we are interested only in the meaning of the assertion that sociology 'rests' on the results of all other sciences and therefore could only be created after all the other sciences had reached the positive stage. This has nothing to do with the undeniable contention that the biological study of man as one of the most complicated organisms will have to make use of the results of all the other natural sciences. Comte's sociology, as we shall see presently, does not deal with man as a physical unit but with the evolution of the human mind as a manifestation of the 'collective organism' which mankind as a whole constitutes. It is the study of the organisation of society and the laws of the evolution of the human mind which are supposed to require the use of the results of all the other sciences. Now this would be justified if Comte really contended that the aim of sociology (and that part of biology which in his system replaces individual psychology) was to explain mental phenomena in physical terms, that is, if he wanted seriously to carry out his early dreams of unifica-

[25] *Cours*, vol. 1, pp. 10, 44.
[26] Ibid., vol. 6, p. 601.
[27] [Ibid., pp. 654ff.—Ed.]

tion of all sciences on the basis of some single universal law.[28] But this he has explicitly abandoned. His schematism leads him indeed to assert that none of the phenomena belonging to any of the sciences higher up in his hierarchy can ever fully be reduced to, or explained in terms of, the preceding sciences. It is just as impossible to explain sociological phenomena purely in biological terms as, in his opinion, it will remain forever impossible to reduce chemical phenomena altogether to physical. While there will always be sociological laws which cannot be reduced to mechanical or biological laws, this break between sociology and biology is no different from the presumed difference between chemistry and physics.

When, however, Comte tries to prove his contention that sociology depends on a sufficient development of the other sciences, he fails completely, and the examples he gives as illustrations are almost childish. That in order to understand any social phenomena we have to know the *explanation* of the change of day and night and of the changes of the seasons "by the circumstances of the earth's daily rotation and annual movements", or that "the very conception of the stability in human association could not be positively established till the discovery of gravitation",[29] is simply not true. The results of the natural

---

[28] Cf. Menger, *Untersuchungen über die Methoden der Sozialwissenschaften*, p. 15 [pp. 157–58], note, where he argues that in the exact social sciences "sind die menschlichen *Individuen* und ihre *Bestrebungen*, die letzten Elemente unserer Analyse, empirischer Natur und die exacten theoretischen Socialwissenschaften somit in großem Vortheil gegenüber den exacten Naturwissenschaften. Die 'Grenzen des Naturerkennens' und die hieraus für das theoretische Verständniss der Naturphänomene sich ergebenden Schwierigkeiten bestehen in Wahrheit nicht für die exacte Forschung auf dem Gebiete der Socialerscheinungen. Wenn A. Comte die 'Gesellschaften' als reale Organismen und zwar als Organismen komplicierterer Art, denn die natürlichen, auffaßt und ihre theoretische Interpretation als das unvergleichlich kompliciertere und schwierigere wissenschaftliche Problem bezeichnet, so befindet er sich somit in einem schweren Irrthume. Seine Theorie wäre nur gegenüher Socialforschern richtig, welche den, mit Rücksicht auf den heutigen Zustand der theoretischen Naturwissenschaften, geradezu wahnwitzigen Gedanken fassen würden, die Gesellschaftsphänomene nicht in specifisch socialwissenschaftlich-, sondern in naturwissenschaftlich-atomistischer Weise interpretiren zu wollen". [See Menger, *Investigations*, book three, chapter 2, p. 142, note 51, where this passage is translated as follows: "Here the human *individuals* and their *efforts*, the final elements of our analysis, are of empirical nature, and thus the exact theoretical social sciences have a great advantage over the exact natural sciences. The 'limits of knowledge of nature' and the difficulties resulting from this for the theoretical understanding of natural phenomena do not really exist for exact research in the realm of social phenomena. When A. Comte conceives of 'societies' as real organisms and to be sure as organisms of a more complicated nature than the natural ones and designates their theoretical interpretation as the incomparably more complicated and more difficult scientific problem, he exposes himself forthwith to a serious error. His theory would be correct only as against sociologists who might get the idea, which is really insane in the light of the present state of the theoretical natural sciences, of wanting to interpret social phenomena not in a specifically sociological way, but in the atomistic way of the natural sciences".—Ed.]

[29] *Cours*, vol. 4, pp. 356–57; *PP*, vol. 2, p. 97.

sciences may be essential data for sociology to the extent to which they actually affect the actions of the men who use them. But that is true, whatever the state of natural knowledge is, and there is no reason why the sociologist need know more of natural science than those whose actions he tries to explain, and therefore no reason why the development of the study of society should have to wait on the natural sciences having reached a certain stage of development.

Comte claims that with the application of the positive method to social phenomena the unity of method of all sciences is established. But beyond the general characteristic of the positive method, "to abandon, as necessarily vain, all search for causes, be it primary or final, and to confine itself to the study of the invariable relations which constitute the effective laws of all observable events",[30] it is difficult to say in what precisely this positive method consists. It certainly is not, as one might expect, the universal application of mathematical methods. Although mathematics is to Comte the source of the positive method, the field where it appeared first and in its purest form,[31] he does not believe that it can be usefully applied in the more complicated subjects, even chemistry[32], and he is scornful about the attempts to apply statistics to biology[33] or the calculus of probability to social phenomena.[34]

Even observation, the one common element of all sciences, does not appear in the same form in all of them. As the sciences become more complicated, new methods of observation become available while others appropriate to the less complicated phenomena cease to be useful. Thus, while in astronomy the mathematical method and pure observation rule, in physics and chemistry the experiment comes in as a new help. And as we proceed further, biology brings the comparative method and sociology, finally, the "historical method", while mathematics and the experiment become in turn inapplicable.[35]

There is one more aspect of the hierarchy of the sciences which must be briefly mentioned, as it is relevant to points which we shall presently have to consider. As we ascend the hierarchical scale of the sciences, and the phenomena with which they deal become more complex, they also become more subject to modification by human action and at the same time less 'perfect' and therefore more in need of improvement by human control. Comte has nothing but contempt for people who admire the "wisdom of nature", and he is quite certain that a few competent engineers in creating an organism

---

[30] *Cours*, vol. 6, p. 599 [pp. 598–99].

[31] Ibid., vol. 1, p. 122; vol. 3, p. 295.

[32] Ibid., vol. 3, p. 29.

[33] Ibid., p. 291.

[34] Ibid., vol. 4, pp. 365 367; *Early Essays*, pp. 193–98.

[35] *Cours*, vol. 3, 40ᵉ leçon; vol. 6, p. 671. [The 40ᵉ leçon is found on pp. 187–338 of volume 3.—Ed.]

for a particular task would do infinitely better.[36] And the same applies necessarily to the most complicated and therefore most imperfect of all natural phenomena, human society. The paradox that the instrument of the human mind, which according to this theory should be the most imperfect of all phenomena, should yet at the same time have the unique power to control and improve itself, does not trouble Comte in the least.

V

There is one respect in which Comte not only admits but even stresses a difference in the method, not only of sociology, but of all organic sciences from that of inorganic sciences. Yet, although this break occurs between chemistry and biology, the importance of this 'inversion' of procedure, as Comte calls it himself, is of even greater importance with respect to sociology and we shall quote in full the passage in which he himself explains it with direct reference to the study of social phenomena. "There exists necessarily", he explains, "a fundamental difference between the whole of inorganic philosophy and the whole of organic philosophy. In the first, where solidarity between the phenomena, as we have shown, is little pronounced, and can only little affect the study of the subject, we have to explore a system where the elements are better known than the whole, and are usually even alone directly observable. But in the second, on the contrary, where man and society constitute the principal object, the opposite procedure becomes most often the only rational one, as another consequence of the same logical principle, because the whole of the object is here certainly much better known and more immediately accessible".[37]

This astounding assertion that where we have to deal with social phenomena the whole is better known than the parts is put forward as an indisputable axiom without much explanation. It is of crucial importance for the understanding of the new science of sociology as created by Comte and accepted by his direct successors. Its significance is further enhanced by the fact that this collectivist approach is characteristic of most of the students who approach such phenomena from what we have called a 'scientistic' point of view.[38] But it must be admitted that it is not easy to see why this should be so, and Comte gives us little help in this respect.

One possible justification of this view which would occur first to the mod-

[36] Ibid., vol. 3, pp. 321–22.

[37] Ibid., vol. 4, p. 258; cf. *Early Essays*, p. 239.

[38] This has often been noted and commented upon. See particularly Ernst Bernheim, *Geschichtsforschung und Geschichtsphilosophie* (Göttingen: R. Peppmüller, 1880), p. 48 [pp. 48–49], and *Lehrbuch der historischen Methode*, index Sachverzeichnis: "Sozialistisch-naturwissenschaftliche beziehungsweise kollektivistische Geschichtsauffassung", p. 835.

ern mind, played at best a very minor rôle in Comte's thought: the idea that mass phenomena may show statistical regularities while the composing elements seem to follow no recognisable law.[39] This idea, made familiar by Comte's contemporary Quetelet,[40] is certainly not the foundation of Comte's own argument. It is indeed more than doubtful whether Comte ever took notice of Quetelet's work beyond showing indignation about the latter using, in the subtitle of a work dealing with "mere statistics"[41] the term "social physics", which Comte regarded as his intellectual property. But though Quetelet seems thus to have been indirectly responsible for the substitution of the new word *sociology*,[42] for what Comte till well on in the fourth volume of the *Cours* still describes as "social physics",[43] his main idea, which should have fitted so well into Comte's general approach and which was to play so important a rôle in later scientistic sociology, found no place in Comte's system.

We shall probably have to seek the explanation in Comte's general attitude of treating whatever phenomena a science had to deal with as immediately given 'things' and in his desire to establish a similarity between biology, the science immediately beneath sociology in the positive hierarchy, and the science of the 'collective organism'. And since in biology it was unquestionably true that the organisms were better known to us than their parts, the same had to be asserted of sociology.

VI

The exposition of Comte's sociology, which was to constitute the fourth volume of the *Cours*, extended in fact to three volumes, each considerably longer than any of the first three dealing with all the other sciences. The fourth volume, published in 1839, contains mainly the general considerations on the new science and its static part. The two remaining ones contain a very full and detailed exposition of sociological dynamics, that general theory of the history of the human mind, which was the main aim of Comte's labours.

The division of the subject into statics and dynamics,[44] a division Comte believes to be appropriate to all sciences, he takes over, not directly from mechanics, but from biology to which it had been applied by the physiologist de Blainville, whose work had influenced Comte to an extent equalled

---

[39] There is one vague reference to this aspect in *Cours*, vol. 4, pp. 270–71.

[40] See below, pp. 276–77.

[41] *Cours*, vol. 4, p. 15, note 1.

[42] Maurice Defourny, *La sociologie positiviste. Auguste Comte* (Paris: F. Alcan, 1902), p. 57.

[43] *Sociologie* is introduced in *Cours*, vol. 4, p. 185; *lois sociologiques* appears first a few pages earlier, ibid., p. 180.

[44] Ibid., vol. 1, p. 29; vol. 4, pp. 230–31.

only by Lagrange, Fourier, and Gall.[45] The distinction, which according to De Blainville in biology corresponds to that between anatomy and physiology, or organisation and life, is made to correspond in sociology with the two great watchwords of positivism, order and progress. Static sociology deals with the laws of coexistence of social phenomena, while dynamic sociology is concerned with the laws of succession in the necessary evolution of society.

When it comes to the execution of this scheme it proves, however, that Comte has extraordinarily little to say on the static part of his subject. His disquisitions about the necessary *consensus* between all the parts of any social system, the *idée mère* of solidarity as he often calls it, which in social phenomena is even more marked than in biological, remain pretty empty generalisations, as Comte has no way (or intention) of establishing why particular institutions, or which kinds of institutions, should necessarily go together, or others be incompatible. The comments on the relations between the individual, the family, and society, in the single chapter devoted to social statics, rise little above the commonplace.[46] In the discussion of the division of labour, although a distant echo of Adam Smith,[47] there is no trace of a comprehension of the factors

---

[45] *Cours* is dedicated to Fourier and de Blainville, the two men among these four who were still alive at the time of its publication. [For more on Fourier, see chapter 11, note 45. Henri Marie Ducrotay de Blainville (1777–1850) was a French naturalist and physician. He studied under Cuvier and later assumed Cuvier's chair in comparative anatomy at the Jardin des Plantes. —Ed.]

[46] It may, however, be mentioned, since it does not seem to have been noticed before, that the distinction between *Gemeinschaft* and *Gesellschaft*, popularised by the German sociologist Ferdinand Tönnies, already appears in Comte, who stresses the fact that "domestic relations do not constitute an association but a *union*" (*Cours*, vol. 4, p. 419; *PP*, vol. 2, p. 116). [In *Gemeinschaft und Gesellschaft* (1887) Ferdinand Tönnies (1855–1936) contrasted the community (*Gemeinschaft*), which includes organic groups like the family, tribe, or religious orders, and that are typified by adherence to tradition and solidarity with group goals, with society (*Gesellschaft*), which includes organisations such as clubs or corporations in which relations are voluntary, often contractual, and in which individuals instrumentally pursue narrow and well-defined aims.—Ed.]

[47] Smith's influence appears in a clear and rather surprising form when Comte asks: "Peut-on réellement concevoir, dans l'ensemble des phénomènes naturels, un plus merveilleux spectacle que cette convergence régulière et continue d'une immensité d'individus, doués chacun d'une existence pleinement distincte et, à un certain degré, indépendante, et néanmoins tous disposés sans cesse, malgré les différences plus ou moins discordantes de leurs talents et surtout de leurs caractères, à concourir spontanément, par une multitude de moyens divers, à un même développement général, sans s'être d'ordinaire nullement concertés, et le plus souvent à l'insu de la plupart d'entre eux, qui ne croient obéir qu'à leurs impulsions personnelles?" (*Cours*, vol. 4, pp. 417–18). [Is it possible to conceive of any sight, amidst all of the natural phenomena, more satisfactory than the regular and sustained convergence of a multitude of individuals, each of them endowed with a fully distinct and to some extent, independent existence, and nevertheless altogether constantly prone, in spite of more or less acute discrepancies in their talents and especially in their characters, to concur by different means and without previous concertation, to their common development, whilst most of them are even unaware of it and think they are solely driven by their own impulses?—Ed.]

which regulate it; and how little he understands them becomes evident when he expressly denies that a division of intellectual labour similar to that applying to material labour is possible.[48]

The whole of his statics is, however, no more than a brief sketch and of minor importance compared with the dynamic part of sociology, the fulfilment of his main ambition. It is the attempt to prove the basic contention, which Comte, as a young man of twenty-six, had expressed in a letter to a friend when he promised to show that "there were laws governing the development of the human race as definite as those determining the fall of a stone".[49] History was to be made a science, and the essence of all science is that it should be capable of prediction.[50] The dynamic part of sociology was therefore to become a philosophy of history, as it is commonly but somewhat misleadingly called, or a theory of history as it would be more correctly described. The idea which was to inspire so much of the thought of the second half of the nineteenth century, was to write "abstract history", "history without the names of men or even people".[51] The new science was to provide a theoretical scheme, an abstract order in which the major changes of human civilisation must necessarily follow each other.

The basis of this scheme is of course the law of the three stages and the main content of dynamic sociology is a detailed elaboration of the law. It is thus a curious feature of the Comtean system that this same law which is supposed to prove the necessity of the new science is at the same time its main and almost sole result. We need not trouble here with its elaboration in detail, beyond saying that in Comte's hands human history becomes largely identified with the growth of the natural sciences.[52] What are relevant to us are only the general implications of the idea of a natural science which deals with the laws of intellectual development of the human race, and the practical conclusions drawn from it with regard to the future organisation of society. The idea of recognisable laws, not only of the growth of individual minds, but of the development of the knowledge of the human race as a whole, pre-supposes that the human mind could, so to speak, look down on itself from a higher plane and be able not merely to understand its operation from the inside, but

[48] Ibid., p. 436; *PP*, vol. 2, p. 121.

[49] *Lettres d'Auguste Comte à M. Valat*, pp. 138–39 (letter dated September 8, 1824).

[50] *Cours*, vol. 1, p. 51; vol. 2, p. 20; vol. 6, p. 618; *Early Essays*, p. 191.

[51] *Cours*, vol. 5, p. 14; see also p. 188, where it is explained that "ces dénominations de grec et romain ne désignent point ici essentiellement des sociétés accidentelles et particulières; elles se rapportent surtout à des situations nécessaires et générales, qu'on ne pourrait qualifier abstraitement que par des locutions trop compliquées". [Labels such as 'Greek' and 'Roman' do not essentially designate actual contingent and specific societies, they rather refer to general situations brought about by sheer necessity, and to define them conceptually would require formulae that are too complicated.—Ed.]

[52] Ibid., vol. 1, p. 65.

also to observe it, as it were, from the outside. The curious thing about this proposition, particularly in its Comtean form, is that although it explicitly recognises that the interactions of individual minds may produce some thing in a sense superior to what an individual mind can ever achieve, it yet claims for the same individual mind not only the power to grasp this development as a whole and to recognise the principle on which it works and even the course it must follow, but also the power to control and direct it and thereby to improve upon its uncontrolled working.

What this belief really amounts to is that the products of the process of mind can be comprehended as a whole by a simpler process than the laborious one of understanding them, and that the individual mind, looking at these results from the outside, can then directly connect these wholes by laws applying to them as entities, and finally, by extrapolating the observed development, achieve a kind of shortcut to the future development. This empirical theory of the development of the collective mind is at the same time the most naïve and the most influential result of the application of the procedure of the natural sciences to social phenomena, and of course based on the illusion that the phenomena of the mind are in the same sense given as objective things, and subject to external observation and control as physical phenomena. It follows from this approach that our knowledge is to be regarded as 'relative' and conditioned by assignable factors—not merely from the point of view of some hypothetical, more highly organised mind, but from our own point of view. It is from this point of view that the belief springs that we ourselves can recognise the "mutability"[53] of our mind and of its laws and the belief that the human race can undertake to control its own development. This idea that the human mind can, as it were, lift itself up by its own bootstraps, has remained a dominant characteristic of most sociology to the present day,[54] and we have here the root (or rather one of the roots, the other being Hegel) of that modern hubris which has found its most perfect expression in the so-called sociology of knowledge. And the fact that this idea—the human mind controlling its *own* development—has from its beginning been one of the leading ideas of sociology also provides the link which has always connected it with socialist ideals so that in the popular mind sociological and socialist often mean the same thing.[55]

[53] Cf. ibid., vol. 6, pp. 620, 622.

[54] Cf. the concluding sentences in Professor Morris Ginsberg's recent *Sociology*, in the Home University Library series (Oxford: Oxford University Press, 1934), p. 244, "The conception of a self-directed humanity is new, and as yet vague in the extreme. To work out its full theoretical implications, and, with the aid of other sciences, to inquire into the possibilities of its realisation, may be said to be the ultimate object of sociology".

[55] This was, perhaps, even more true of the Continent, where it was generally known that the various 'sociological societies' consisted almost exclusively of socialists.

It is this search for the "general laws of the continuous variations of human opinions"[56] which Comte calls the "historical method", the "indispensable complement of the positive logic".[57] But although, partly under Comte's influence, this is what the term *historical method* increasingly came to mean in the second half of the nineteenth century, we cannot leave this subject without pointing out that it is, of course, nearly the opposite of what *historical approach* really means or did mean to the great historians who in the beginning of the century tried by the application of the historical method to understand the genesis of social institutions.[58]

VII

It is hardly surprising that, with this ambitious conception of the task of the single theoretical science of society which he admits into his system, Comte should have nothing but contempt for the already existing social disciplines. It would hardly be worth while to dwell on this attitude if it were not so characteristic of the view taken at all times of the social sciences by men blinded by the scientistic prejudice, and if his own efforts had not, at least in part, to be explained by his almost complete ignorance of the achievements of the then existing social sciences. Some, as particularly the study of language, he regards

[56] *Cours*, vol. 6, p. 670.

[57] Ibid., p. 671.

[58] See herein, pp. 294–95.

[In the original 1941 essay in *Economica*, the paragraph continued at this point as follows: "As the contrast between the two approaches which are both described as 'historical method' corresponds in many ways to the general contrast between the scientistic or naturalistic approach to social phenomena and the specific methods developed by the social sciences, and as the use of the same term for two so very different views has so greatly obscured the conflict, it is, perhaps, not inappropriate if we conclude this discussion of Comte's method with a brief summary of the difference. The real historical method (perhaps better described as genetic method) attempts to understand essentially unique historical situations as the result of all the circumstances which have contributed to its developments—using whatever laws of social phenomena we know in very much the same sense in which we can explain the peculiarities of an individual as the joint result of many independent factors. There is no attempt to constitute these complex situations into wholes which as such obey separate laws. The other, which is now usually meant when the 'idea of evolution', the *Entwicklungsgedanke*, is brought in as a sort of incantation, attempts to treat historical situations as a species of a genus, as instances of the same type of fact, and it believes that these facts can be treated as phenomena of the kind, which according to the basic maxim of positivism, must all be 'subject to laws'".

The last sentence carried as a note the following: "On all these problems connected with the two kinds of 'historism' see the excellent article by Walter Eucken, "Die Überwindung des Historismus", *Schmollers Jahrbuch*, vol. 63 [62], 1938, pp. 191–14".

It makes sense that he dropped these lines, given his clarification in the 1952 edition of the difference between 'historicism' and 'historism' at the beginning of chapter 7.—Ed.]

as hardly worth mentioning.[59] But he takes the trouble to denounce political economy at some length, and here his severity stands in a strange contrast to his exceedingly slender knowledge of the object of his abuse. Indeed, as even one of his admirers, who has devoted a whole book to Comte's relation to economics,[60] could not help emphasising, his knowledge of economics was virtually nonexistent. He knew and even admired Adam Smith, partly for his descriptive work in economics, but mainly for his *History of Astronomy*.[61] In his early years he had made the acquaintance of J. B. Say and some other members of the same circle, particularly Destutt de Tracy. But the latter's treatment of economics in his great treatise on 'ideology' between logic and morals appeared to Comte merely a frank admission of the 'metaphysical' character of economics.[62] For the rest, the economists did not seem to Comte to be worth bothering about. He knew *a priori* that they had merely performed their necessary destructive rôle, typical representatives of the negative or revolutionary spirit which was characteristic of the metaphysical phase. That no positive contribution to the reorganisation of society could be expected from them was evident from the fact that they had not been trained as scientists: "Being almost invariably lawyers or literary men, they had no opportunity of discipline in that spirit of positive rationality which they suppose they have introduced into their researches. Precluded by their education from any idea of scientific observation of even the smallest phenomena, from any notions of natural laws, from all perception of what demonstration is, they must obviously be incapable of applying a method in which they had no practice to the most difficult of all analyses".[63] Comte indeed would admit to the study of sociology only men who had successively and successfully mastered all the other sciences and thus properly prepared themselves for the most difficult task of the study of the most complex of all phenomena.[64] Although the further development of the new science could not again present difficulties as great as those he had himself surmounted in first creating it,[65] only the very

---

[59] The "grammarians are even more absurd than the logicians". See Comte, *Système de politique positive*, vol. 2, pp. 250–51 [p. 255].

[60] Roger Mauduit, *Auguste Comte et la science économique* (Paris: F. Alcan, 1929), especially pp. 48–69 [48–70]. A full reply to Comte's strictures on political economy has been given by John Elliott Cairnes in the essay "M. Comte and Political Economy", *Fortnightly Review*, new series, vol. 7, May 1870, pp. 579–602; reprinted in *Essays in Political Economy* (London: Macmillan, 1873 [reprinted, New York: Kelley, 1965]), pp. 265–311.

[61] Adam Smith, "The History of Astronomy". [Hayek provides no edition; the modern reader should consult the essay in *Essays on Philosophical Subjects*, W. P. D. Wightman and J. C. Bryce, eds, vol. 3 of *Works and Correspondence of Adam Smith*, pp. 31–105.—Ed.]

[62] *Cours*, vol. 4, p. 196.

[63] Ibid., p. 194 [pp. 194–95]; *PP*, vol. 2, p. 51.

[64] *Cours*, vol. 1, p. 84; vol. 4, pp. 144–45, 257, 306, 361.

[65] Ibid., vol. 6, p. 547; *PP*, vol. 2, p. 412.

best minds could hope successfully to grapple with them. The special difficulty of this task arises from the absolute necessity of dealing with all aspects
of society at the same time, a necessity dictated by the particularly close 'consensus' of all social phenomena. To have sinned against this principle and to
have attempted to deal with economic phenomena in isolation, "apart from
the analysis of the intellectual, moral, and political state of society",[66] is one
of his main reproaches against the economists. Their "pretended science"
presents to "all competent and experienced judges most decidedly the character of purely metaphysical concepts".[67] "If one considers impartially the
sterile disputes which divide them concerning the most elementary concepts
of value, utility, production, etc., one may fancy oneself attending the strang-
est debates of medieval scholastics on the fundamental attributes of their
metaphysical entities".[68] But the main defect of political economy is its conclusion, "the sterile aphorism of absolute industrial liberty",[69] the belief that
there is no need of some "special institution immediately charged with the
task of regularising the spontaneous co-ordination" which should be regarded
as merely offering the opportunity for imposing real organisation.[70] And he
particularly condemns the tendency of political economy to "answer to all
complaints that in the long run all classes, and especially the one most injured
on the existing occasion, will enjoy a real and permanent satisfaction; a reply
which will be regarded as derisive, as long as man's life is incapable of being
indefinitely lengthened".[71]

VIII

It cannot be too much emphasised in any discussion of Comte's philosophy
that he had no use for any knowledge of which he did not see the practical
use.[72] And "the purpose of the establishment of social philosophy is to re-
establish order in society".[73] Nothing seems to him "more repugnant to the
real scientific spirit, not even the theological spirit",[74] than disorder of any

[66] *Cours*, vol. 4, pp. 197–98 [197–99], 255.
[67] Ibid., p. 195.
[68] Ibid., p. 197.
[69] Ibid., p. 203 [202]; *PP*, vol. 2, p. 54.
[70] *Cours*, vol. 4, pp. 200–1.
[71] Ibid., p. 203 [pp. 202–3]; *PP*, vol. 2, p. 54.
[72] Cf. *Lettres d'Auguste Comte à Valat*, p. 99 (letter dated September 28, 1819): "J'ai une souveraine
aversion pour les travaux scientifiques dont je n'aperçois pas clairement l'utilité, soit directe, soit
éloignée". [I feel a supreme distaste for those scientific works which do not clearly appear to me
as being of some utility, whether immediate or delayed.—Ed.]
[73] *Cours*, vol. 1, p. 42.
[74] Ibid., vol. 4, p. 139.

kind, and nothing is perhaps more characteristic of the whole of Comte's work than "the inordinate demand for 'unity' and 'systematisation'", which J. S. Mill described as the *fons errorum* of all Comte's later speculation.[75] But even if the "frenzy for regulation"[76] is not quite as preponderant in the *Cours* as it became in the *Système de philosophie positive*, the practical conclusions to which the *Cours* leads, just because they are still free from the fantastic exaggeration of the later work, show this feature already in a marked degree. With the establishment of the "definitive"[77] philosophy, positivism, the critical doctrine which has characterised the preceding period of transition, has completed its historic mission and the accompanying dogma of the unbounded liberty of conscience will disappear.[78] To make the writing of the *Cours* possible was, as it were, the last necessary function of "the revolutionary dogma of free enquiry",[79] but now that this is achieved, the dogma has lost its justification. All knowledge being once again unified, as it has not been since the theological stage began to decay, the next task is to set up a new intellectual government where only the competent scientists will be allowed to decide the difficult social questions.[80] Since their action will in all respects be determined by the dictates of science, this will not mean arbitrary government, and "true liberty", which is nothing else than "a rational submission to the preponderance of the laws of nature",[81] will even be increased.

The detail of the social organisation which positive science will impose need not concern us here. So far as economic life is concerned, it still resembles in many respects the earlier Saint-Simonian plans, particularly insofar as the leading rôle of the bankers in guiding industrial activity is concerned.[82] But he dissents from the later outright socialism of the Saint-Simonians. Private property is not to be abolished, but the rich become the "necessary depositaries of the public capitals"[83] and the owning of property is a social function.[84] This is not the only point in which Comte's system resembles the later authoritarian socialism which we associate with Prussia rather than socialism as we used to know it. In fact, in some passages this resemblance to Prussian socialism, even down to the very words used, is really amazing. Thus when he argues that in the future society the "immoral" concept of individual rights

---

[75] J. S. Mill, *Auguste Comte and Positivism*, 2nd ed. (London: N. Trübner, 1866), p. 141. [See the reprint of the essay in *Essays on Ethics, Religion, and Society*, ed. J. M. Robson, vol. 10 (1969) of *Collected Works of John Stuart Mill*, p. 336.—Ed.]

[76] Ibid., p. 196. [In the *Collected Works* edition, p. 366.—Ed.]

[77] *Cours*, vol. 1, p. 15. Cf. *Early Essays*, p. 132.

[78] *Cours*, vol. 4, p. 43.

[79] Ibid., p. 43; *PP*, vol. 2, p. 12.

[80] *Cours*, vol. 4, p. 48.

[81] Ibid., p. 147; *PP*, vol. 2, p. 39.

[82] *Cours*, vol. 6, p. 495.

[83] Ibid., p. 511.

[84] *Système de politique positive*, vol. 1, p. 156.

will disappear and there will be only duties,[85] or that in the new society there will be no private persons but only state functionaries of various units and grades,[86] and that in consequence the most humble occupation will be enno-bled by its incorporation into the official hierarchy just as the most obscure soldier has his dignity as a result of the solidarity of the military organism,[87] or finally when, in the concluding section of the first sketch of the future order, he discovers a "special disposition towards command in some and to-wards obedience in others" and assures us that in our innermost heart we all know "how sweet it is to obey",[88] we might match almost every sentence with identical statements of recent German theoreticians who laid the intellectual foundations of the doctrines of the Third Reich.[89] Having been led by his phi-losophy to take over from the reactionary Bonald the view that the individual is "a pure abstraction"[90] and society as a whole a single collective being, he is of necessity led to most of the characteristic features of a totalitarian view of society.

The later development of all this into a new religion of humanity with a fully developed cult is outside our subject. Needless to say that Comte, who was so completely a stranger to the one real cult of humanity, tolerance (which he would admit only in indifferent and doubtful matters),[91] was not the man to make much of that idea, which in itself does not lack a certain greatness. For the rest we cannot better summarise this last phase of Comte's thought than by the well-known epigram of Thomas Huxley, who described it as "Catholi-cism *minus* Christianity".[92]

---

[85] *Cours*, vol. 6, p. 454; *Système de politique positive*, vol. 1, pp. 151, 361–66; vol. 2, p. 87.

[86] *Cours*, vol. 6, pp. 482–85.

[87] Ibid., p. 484.

[88] Ibid., vol. 4, p. 437; *PP*, vol. 2, p. 122.

[89] This applies particularly to the writings of Oswald Spengler and Werner Sombart. [For more on Spengler and Sombart, see chapter 7, note 15.—Ed.]

[90] *Cours*, vol. 6, p. 590; Comte, *Discours sur l'esprit positif* [1844] (Paris: Société positiviste inter-nationale, 1914), p. 118.

[91] *Cours*, vol. 4, p. 51.

[92] [British biologist Thomas Huxley (1825–95), 'Darwin's Bulldog', was an early and passion-ate defender of Darwin's theory of evolution by natural selection. Huxley's remark, which in full read, "In so far as my study of what specially characterises the Positive Philosophy has led me, I find therein little or nothing of any scientific value, and a great deal, which is as thor-oughly antagonistic to the very essence of science as anything in ultramontane Catholicism. In fact, M. Comte's philosophy in practice might be compendiously described as Catholicism *minus* Christianity", appeared in his article "On the Physical Basis of Life", *Fortnightly Review*, vol. 5, February 1869, p. 141. His remark drew criticism from Richard Congreve, a leading En-glish positivist, and in his reply Huxley said that he would "refuse to recognise anything which deserves the name of grandeur of character in M. Comte, unless it be his arrogance, which is undoubtedly sublime". Bulldog indeed. See Thomas Huxley, "The Scientific Aspects of Positiv-ism", *Fortnightly Review*, vol. 5, June 1869, p. 656.—Ed.]

IX

Before we cast a glance on the direct influence of Comte's main work we must briefly consider certain simultaneous and in a sense parallel efforts which, from the same intellectual background, but by a different route, produced an impression which tended to strengthen the tendencies of which Comte's work is the main representative. The Belgian astronomer and statistician Quetelet, who must be mentioned here in the first place, differs from Comte not only by being a great scientist in his own field but also by the great contributions which he has made to the methods of social study. He did this precisely by that application of mathematics to social study which Comte condemned. Through his application of the 'Gaussian' normal curve of error to the analysis of statistical data he became, more than any other single person, the founder of modern statistics and particularly of its application to social phenomena. The value of this achievement is undisputed and indisputable. But in the general atmosphere in which Quetelet's work became known the belief was bound to arise that the statistical methods, which he had so successfully applied to some problems of social life, were destined to become the sole method of study. And Quetelet himself contributed not a little to create that belief.

The intellectual environment out of which Quetelet rose[93] is exactly the same as that of Comte: it was the French mathematicians of the circle of the *Ecole polytechnique*,[94] above all Laplace and Fourier, from whom he drew the inspiration for the application of the theory of probability to the problem of social statistics, and in most respects he, much more than Comte, must be regarded as the true continuer of their work and of that of Condorcet. His statistical work proper is not our concern. It was the general effect of his demonstration that something like the methods of the natural sciences could be applied to certain mass phenomena of society and of his implied and even explicit demand that all problems of social science should be treated in a similar fashion, which operated in a direction parallel to Comte's teaching. Nothing fascinated the ensuing generation so much as Quetelet's 'average man' and the celebrated conclusion of his studies of moral statistics that "we pass from one year to another with the sad perspective of seeing the same crimes reproduced in the same order and calling down the same punishments in the same proportions. Sad conditions of humanity! . . . We might enumerate in advance how many individuals will stain their hands in the blood of their fellows, how many will be forgers, how many will be poisoners, almost we can enumerate in advance the births and deaths that should occur. There is a budget which we

---

[93] The fullest account of Quetelet's life and work is by Lottin, *Quetelet: Statisticien et sociologue.*
[94] On the reputed influence of the Saint-Simonians on Quetelet, compare above, p. 231, note 64.

pay with a frightful regularity; it is that of prisons, chains and the scaffold".[95] His views on the application of the mathematical methods have become more characteristic of later positivist method than anything deriving directly from Comte: "The more advanced the sciences have become, the more they have tended to enter the domain of mathematics, which is a sort of centre towards which they converge. We can judge of the perfection to which a science has come by the facility, more or less great, with which it may be approached by calculation".[96]

Although Comte had condemned this view and particularly all attempts to find social laws by means of statistics, his and Quetelet's general endeavours to find natural laws of the development of the human race as a whole, to extend the Laplacean conception of universal determinism to cultural phenomena, and to make mass phenomena the sole object of the science of society were sufficiently akin to lead to a gradual fusion of their doctrines.

In the same category of contemporary efforts with similar methodological tendencies we must at least briefly mention the work of Frédéric Le Play, polytechnician and ex-Saint-Simonian, whose descriptive social surveys became the model of much later sociological work. Though differing from Comte as well as Quetelet in more respects than they have in common, he contributed like them to the reaction against theoretical individualism, classical economics, and political liberalism, thus strengthening the particular effects of the scientistic influences with which we are here concerned.[97]

X

The tracing of influences is the most treacherous ground in the history of thought, and we have in the last chapter already so much sinned against the canons of caution in this field that we shall now be brief. Yet the curious course which Comte's influence took is so important for the understanding of the intellectual history of the nineteenth century, and the cause of so many still prevailing misconceptions about his rôle, that a few more words about it are indispensable. In France, as already observed, Comte's immediate influence on thinkers of importance was small. But, as J. S. Mill points out, "the great treatise of M. Comte was scarcely mentioned in French literature or criticism, when it was already working powerfully on the minds of many Brit-

---

[95] The English translation of this passage is from Helen M. Walker, *Studies in the History of Statistical Method* (Baltimore: Williams and Wilkins Co., 1929), p. 40 [pp. 40–41].

[96] Ibid., p. 29 [39].

[97] Cf. Louis Dimier, *Les maîtres de la contre-révolution aux dix-neuvième siècle* (Paris: Nouvelle librarie nationale, 1917), pp. 215–35. [Le Play was first mentioned in chapter 14, note 63.—Ed.]

ish students and thinkers".[98] It was this influence on Mill himself and a few other leading English thinkers which became decisive for Comte's effect on European thought.[99] Mill himself, in the sixth book of his *Logic*, which deals with the methods of the moral sciences, became little more than an expounder of Comtean doctrine. The philosopher George Lewes and George Eliot are some of the better-known names of Comte's English adherents.[100] And nothing could be more characteristic of the tremendous impact of Comte on England than that the same Miss Martineau who in her younger years had been the faithful and most successful populariser of Ricardo's economics, should become, not only the translator and most skilful condenser of Comte's work, but also one of his most enthusiastic disciples.[101] As important almost as Mill himself for the spreading of positivist views among students of social phenomena was their adoption by the historian Henry Thomas Buckle, although in this case the influence of Comte was reinforced and perhaps outweighed by that of Quetelet.[102]

It was largely through the medium of these English writers that Comtian

---

[98] Mill, *Auguste Comte and Positivism*, p. 2. [In the *Collected Works* version, p. 263.—Ed.]

[99] For a full account of English positivism, see Rudolf Metz, *A Hundred Years of British Philosophy* (London: G. Allen and Unwin, 1938), pp. 171–234 [171–83], and John Edwin McGee, *A Crusade for Humanity: The History of Organised Positivism in England* (London: Watts and Co., 1931). On Comte's influence in the United States, see the two studies by Richmond Laurin Hawkins, *Auguste Comte and the United States (1816–1853)* (Cambridge, MA: Harvard University Press, 1936), and *Positivism in the United States (1853–1861)* (Cambridge, MA: Harvard University Press, 1938).

[100] [The British philosopher, biographer, journalist, and scientist George Henry Lewes (1817–78) expressed his debt to Comte in *Comte's Philosophy of the Sciences* (1853), though in his article (a review of J. S. Mill's 1865 book, *Auguste Comte and Positivism*), "Auguste Comte", *Fortnightly Review*, vol. 3, January 1866, p. 404, he also identified himself as a "reverent heretic". His departure from Comte is most evident in Lewes's psychological writings, where he argued that introspection is a valid method. George Eliot (1819–80) was the pen name of Mary Ann (later Marian) Evans, one of England's most famous novelists: her works include *The Mill on the Floss* (1860), *Silas Marner* (1861), and *Middlemarch* (1871–72). Though Lewes was married to someone else, he and Eliot lived as extramarital partners from 1854 until Lewes death in 1878. For more on Eliot and positivism, see J. B. Bullen, "George Eliot's *Romola* as a Positivist Allegory", *Review of English Studies*, vol. 26, November 1975, pp. 425–35.—Ed.]

[101] [Before her conversion to positivism, the English essayist and novelist Harriet Martineau (1802–76) was famous for her multivolume series *Illustrations of Political Economy* (1832–34) which, through stories, fables, and parables, illuminated the economic principles of writers like James Mill, David Ricardo, and Thomas Robert Malthus. Comte himself endorsed her translation of his *Cours*.—Ed.]

[102] [English historian Henry Thomas Buckle (1821–62) claimed to have applied the inductive method to history, which allowed him to discover its universal laws. He attacked both narrative history and the history of exceptional individuals, arguing that truly scientific history makes generalisations about social aggregates. Many historians found this unpersuasive, but social reformers took Buckle's work as a radical critique of the old order.—Ed.]

positivism made its entry into Germany.[103] Mill's *Logic*, Buckle's and Lecky's historical works, and later Herbert Spencer, made Comte's ideas familiar to many who were often completely unaware of their source.[104] And although it is perhaps doubtful whether many of the German scholars who in the second half of the nineteenth century professed views closely similar to Comte's had derived them directly from him, there were probably in no other country a greater number of influential men who tried to reform the social sciences on essentially Comtean lines. No other country seems at that time to have been more receptive of new ideas, and positivist thought together with Quetelet's new statistical methods was definitely the fashion of the period and was accepted in Germany with corresponding enthusiasm.[105] The curious phenomenon that there (and elsewhere) positivist influences should have so readily combined with that of Hegel will require separate investigation.

We have no space here more than briefly to mention the successors who

[103] This penetration of Comtean positivism into Germany through the medium of English authors is a curious reversal of the earlier processes when English seventeenth- and eighteenth-century thought had become known to Germany largely through the instrumentality of French writers, from Montesquieu and Rousseau down to J. B. Say. This fact largely explains the belief, widely held in Germany, that there exists a fundamental contrast between 'Western' naturalist and German idealist thought. In fact, if such a contrast can at all be drawn, it is much more between English thought, as represented, say, by Locke, Mandeville, Hume, Smith, Burke, Bentham, and the classical economists, and, on the other hand, Continental thought, as represented by the two parallel and very similar developments that went from Montesquieu through Turgot and Condorcet to Saint-Simon and Comte, and from Herder through Kant, Fichte, Schelling, and Hegel to the later Hegelians. The French school of thought, which indeed was closely related to English thought, that of Condillac and the 'ideologues', had disappeared by the time with which we are now concerned.

[104] [For more on Spencer, see the Prelude, note 21. The Irish historian William Lecky (1838–1903) traced the emergence of modern scientific thought in his *History of the Rise and Influence of the Spirit of Rationalism in Europe* (1865). In his *History of European Morals from Augustus to Charlemagne* (1869) he sought to show the natural origins of religious and moral belief.—Ed.]

[105] The infiltration of positivist thought into the social sciences in Germany is a story by itself which cannot be told here. Among its most influential representatives were the two founders of *Völkerpsychologie*, Moritz Lazarus and H. Steinthal (the former important because of his influence on Wilhelm Dilthey), Emil du Bois-Reymond (see particularly his lecture "Kulturgeschichte und Naturwissenschaft", 1877), and the Viennese circle of Theodor Gomperz and Wilhelm Scherer, later Wilhelm Wundt, Hans Vaihinger, Wilhelm Ostwald, and Karl Lamprecht. On this, see Erich Rothacker, *Einleitung in die Geisteswissenschaften* (Tübingen: J. C. B. Mohr, 1920), pp. 200–6 [200–9], 253 et seq.; Clara Dilthey Misch, *Der junge Dilthey* (Leipzig: B. G. Teubner, 1933); Bernheim, *Geschichtsforschung und Geschichtsphilosophie* and *Lehrbuch der historischen Methode*, pp. 699–716. And for the influence on some of the members of the younger historical school of German economists, see particularly Heinrich Waentig, *Auguste Comte und seine Bedeutung für die Entwicklung der Socialwissenschaft* (Leipzig: Duncker und Humblot, 1894), pp. 279 et seq. [On Lazarus and Steinthal, the English reader may wish to consult Ivan Kalmar, "The *Völkerpsychologie* of Lazarus and Steinthal and the Modern Concept of Culture", *Journal of the History of Ideas*, vol. 48, October–December 1987, pp. 671–90.—Ed.]

in France at last took up the Comtean tradition. Before we mention the sociologists proper we must at least mention the names of Taine and Renan, both, incidentally, representatives of that curious combination of Comtean and Hegelian thought to which we have just referred.[106] Of the sociologists almost all the best-known ones (with the exception of Tarde), Espinas, Lévy-Bruhl, Durkheim, Simiand, stand directly in the Comtean tradition, although in their case, too, this has in part come back to France via Germany and with the modifications which it there experienced.[107] To attempt to trace this later influence of Comte on French thought during the Third Republic would mean writing a history of sociology in the country where for a time it gained the greatest influence. Many of the best minds who devoted themselves to social studies were here attracted by the new science, and it is perhaps not too much to suggest that the peculiar stagnation of French economics during that period is at least partly due to the pre-dominance of the sociological approach to social phenomena.[108]

That Comte's direct influence remained confined to comparatively few, but that through these very few it extended exceedingly far, is even more true of the present generation than it was of earlier ones. There will be few students of the social sciences now who have ever read Comte or know much about

---

[106] [French polymath scholar Hippolyte-Adolphe Taine (1828–93) sought to apply the scientific method of positivism to such diverse fields as literary criticism, psychology, and cultural history. His argument that a writer's ideas are a result of heredity, historical position, and immediate environment affected the naturalistic movement in French literature. His contemporary the historian and biblical scholar Ernest Renan (1823–92) caused considerable outrage when he provided an historical rather than a theological approach to his subject in his *Life of Jesus* (1863).—Ed.]

[107] Cf. Simon Deploige, *Le conflit de la morale et de la sociologie* (Louvain: Institut supérieur de philosophie, 1911), especially chapter 6 [4], on the genesis of Durkheim's system. [For more on Alfred Victor Espinas, see chapter 3, note 3. In his book *Laws of Imitation* (1890) the French sociologist and social psychologist Gabriel Tarde (1843–1904) argued that invention is the source of human progress, and that the imitation and adaptation of inventions is a continuing process by which social history unfolds. Philosopher and anthropologist Lucien Lévy-Bruhl (1857–1939), author of *The Philosophy of Auguste Comte* (1903), took a Comtean approach to the study of morals in his *Ethics and Moral Science* (1903). Emile Durkheim (1858–1917) is generally viewed as a successor to Comte in the sense that he disdained all metaphysics, thought that the social sciences should search for the laws governing phenomena rather than first or final causes, and trumpeted a new science of politics based on 'physique sociale'. Durkheim made both specific contributions (e.g., to the study of suicide and primitive religion) as well as more general theoretical contributions on the nature of sociology and of the social reality that it studies. François Simiand (1873–1935) was a French economic historian whose work had a strong sociological flavour. He was a member of the editorial board of *Anneé sociologique*, a journal founded by Durkheim to promote the sociological approach to the study of society.—Ed.]

[108] The direct influence of Comte on Charles Maurras should perhaps also be mentioned here. [The influential French journalist and critic Charles Maurras (1868–1952) was introduced to Comtean ideas while studying philosophy in Paris.—Ed.]

him. But the number of those who have absorbed most of the important elements of his system through the intermediation of a few very influential representatives of his tradition, such as Henry Carey and Thorstein Veblen[109] in America; John Kells Ingram, William Ashley, and L. T. Hobhouse[110] in England; and Karl Lamprecht[111] and Kurt Breysig in Germany, is very large indeed.[112] Why this influence of Comte should so frequently have been much more effective in an indirect manner, those who have attempted to study his work will have no difficulty in understanding.

[109] Cf. William Jaffé, *Les théories économiques et sociales de Thorstein Veblen* (Paris: M. Giard, 1924), p. 35, and Richard Victor Teggart, *Thorstein Veblen: A Chapter in American Economic Thought* (Berkeley: University of California Press, 1932), pp. 15, 43, 49–53. [In his book on Veblen, Teggart claimed that "though he did not announce it as such", Veblen's turn of the century essay "The Preconceptions of Economic Science" was "an effort to show the 'development' of the science of economics *according to the ideal series of stages outlined by Comte*" (p. 49). The American economist Henry Carey (1793–1879) favoured tariffs to promote economic development, arguing that the classical economists had reached incorrect policy conclusions due to their preoccupation with the static case.—Ed.]

[110] Cf. Francis Sydney Marvin, *Comte, The Founder of Sociology*, in the series, *Modern Sociologists* (London: Chapman and Hall, 1936), p. 183. [For more on Sir William J. Ashley and John Kells Ingram see chapter 7, note 4, and for more on Leonard Trelawny Hobhouse, see chapter 9, note 3.—Ed.]

[111] Cf. Bernheim, *Lehrbuch der historischen Methode*, pp. 710 et seq. [Economic and cultural historian Karl Lamprecht (1856–1915), founder of an institute in Leipzig for the study of comparative world and cultural history, was a prominent member of a group of Leipzig positivists who sought the unity of science and promoted evolutionary models of group psychology and cultural development. Philosopher of history Kurt Breysig (1866–1940) sought to establish, through empirical research, universal laws of world history.—Ed.]

[112] [In the original text in *Economica*, only Veblen, Hobhouse, and Lamprecht were mentioned here as examples.—Ed.]

PART III

COMTE AND HEGEL

["Comte and Hegel" was originally published in F. A. Hayek, *The Counter-Revolution of Science: Studies on the Abuse of Reason* (Glencoe, IL: Free Press, 1952; reprinted, Indianapolis, IN: Liberty Fund, 1979), pp. 365–400.—Ed.]

SEVENTEEN

COMTE AND HEGEL

I

The discussions of every age are filled with the issues on which its leading schools of thought differ. But the general intellectual atmosphere of the time is always determined by the views on which the opposing schools agree. They become the unspoken pre-suppositions of all thought, and common and unquestioningly accepted foundations on which all discussion proceeds.

When we no longer share these implicit assumptions of ages long past, it is comparatively easy to recognise them. But it is different with regard to the ideas underlying the thought of more recent times. Here we are frequently not yet aware of the common features which the opposing systems of thought shared, ideas which for that very reason often have crept in almost unnoticed and have achieved their dominance without serious examination. This can be very important because, as Bernard Bosanquet once pointed out, "extremes of thought may meet in an error as well as in a truth".[1] Such errors sometimes become dogmas merely because they were accepted by the different groups who quarreled on all the live issues, and may even continue to provide the tacit foundations of thought when most of the theories are forgotten which divided the thinkers to whom we owe that legacy.

When this is the case, the history of ideas becomes a subject of eminently practical importance. It can help us to become aware of much that governs our own thought without our explicitly knowing it. It may serve the purposes of a psychoanalytical operation by bringing to the surface unconscious elements which determine our reasoning, and perhaps assist us to purge our minds from influences which seriously mislead us on questions of our own day.

My purpose is to suggest that we are in such a position. My thesis will be that in the field of social thought not only the second half of the nineteenth

---

[1] Bernard Bosanquet, *The Meeting of Extremes in Contemporary Philosophy* (London: Macmillan, 1921), p. 100. [Bernard Bosanquet (1848–1923) was, along with Francis Herbert Bradley (1846–1924), the leading exponent of the philosophy of Absolute Idealism in Great Britain.—Ed.]

century but also our own age owes much of its characteristic approach to the agreement between two thinkers who are commonly regarded as complete intellectual antipodes: the German 'idealist' Georg Wilhelm Friedrich Hegel and the French 'positivist' Auguste Comte. In some respects these two men do indeed represent such complete extremes of philosophical thought that they seem to belong to different ages and scarcely even to talk about the same problems. But my concern here will be only incidentally with their philosophical systems as a whole. It will be chiefly with their influence on social theory. It is in this field that the influence of philosophical ideas can be most profound and most lasting. And there is, perhaps, no better illustration of the far-reaching effects of the most abstract ideas than the one I intend to discuss.

II

The suggestion that in these matters we have to deal with a common influence of Hegel and Comte has still so much the air of a paradox that I had better say at once that I am by no means the first to notice similarities between them. I could give you a long list, and shall presently mention a few outstanding examples, of students of the history of ideas who have pointed out such resemblances. The curious fact is that these observations have again and again been made with the air of surprise and discovery, and that their authors always seem a little uneasy about their own temerity and afraid of going beyond pointing out a few isolated points of agreement. If I am not mistaken, these coincidences go much further, however, and, in their effects on the social sciences, were much more important than has yet been realised.

Before I mention some instances of such earlier notice I must, however, correct a common mistake which is largely responsible for the neglect of the whole issue. It is the belief that the similarities are due to an influence which Hegel exercised on Comte.[2] This belief is due mainly to the fact that the publication of Comte's ideas is commonly dated from the appearance of the six volumes of his *Cours de philosophie positive* from 1830 to 1842, while Hegel died in 1831. All the essential ideas of Comte were, however, expounded by him

---

[2] See James Hutchinson Stirling, "Why the Philosophy of History Ends with Hegel, and Not with Comte", in "Supplementary Notes" to Albert Schwegler's *Handbook of the History of Philosophy*, translated by James Hutchison Stirling (Edinburgh: Edmundston and Co., 1877), pp. 446–68; and John Tulloch, "The Positive Philosophy of M. Auguste Comte", *Edinburgh Review*, vol. 127, no. 260, April 1868, pp. 303–57. Ernst Troeltsch, *Der Historismus und seine Probleme*, volume 3 of his *Gesammelte Schriften* (Tübingen: J. C. B. Mohr, 1922), p. 24, is inclined to ascribe even Comte's celebrated law of the three stages to the influence of Hegel's dialectics, although it derives in fact from Turgot. See also Rudolf Levin, *Der Geschichtsbegriff des Positivismus* (Leipzig: J. Moltzen, 1935), p. 20.

as early as 1822 in his youthful *System of Positive Policy*,[3] and this *opuscule fonda-mentale*, as he later called it, appeared also as one of the works of the Saint-Simonian group and as such probably reached a wider audience and exercised a greater influence than the *Cours* immediately did. It seems to me to be one of the most pregnant tracts of the nineteenth century, infinitely more brilliant than the now better-known, ponderous volumes of the *Cours*. But even the *Cours*, which is little more than an elaboration of the ideas sketched in that small tract, was planned as early as 1826 and delivered as a series of lectures before a distinguished audience in 1828.[4] Comte's main ideas were thus published within a year of Hegel's *Philosophy of Law*, within a couple of years of the *Encyklopaedie*, and of course before the posthumous appearance of the *Philosophy of History*, to mention only Hegel's main works which are relevant here.[5] In other words, although Comte was Hegel's junior by twenty-eight years, we must regard them to all intents and purposes as contemporaries, and there would be about as much justification for thinking that Hegel might have been influenced by Comte, as that Comte was influenced by Hegel.

You will now appreciate the significance of the first, and in many ways the most remarkable, instance in which the similarity between the two thinkers was noticed. In 1824 Comte's young pupil Gustave d'Eichthal went to study in Germany. In his letters to Comte he soon reported excitedly from Berlin about his discovery of Hegel.[6] "There is", he wrote with regard to Hegel's lectures on the philosophy of history, "a marvelous agreement between your results, even though the principles are different, at least in appearance". He went on to say that "the identity of results exists even in the practical principles, as Hegel is a defender of the governments, that is to say, an enemy of the liberals". A few weeks later d'Eichthal was able to report that he had presented a copy of Comte's tract to Hegel, who had expressed satisfaction

[3] First published in 1822 in Henri de Saint-Simon's *Catéchisme des industrielles* as *Plan of the Scientific Operations Necessary for Reorganising Society* and two years later republished separately as *System of Positive Policy*—"a title premature indeed, but rightly indicating the scope" of his labours, as Comte wrote much later when he reprinted his early works as an appendix to his *Systéme de politique positive*. A translation of this appendix by D. H. Hutton was published in 1911 under the title *Early Essays in Social Philosophy* in Routledge's New Universal Library, and it is from this little volume that the above English titles and the later quotations are taken. [Cf. Hayek's discussion in chapter 13, section 4, and Chapter 16, section 1.—Ed.]

[4] On Comte's early history and his relation to Saint-Simon, see the comprehensive account in Gouhier, *La jeunesse d'Auguste Comte*, 3 vols.

[5] [Hayek refers here to three of Hegel's works, *Encyklopädie der philosophischen Wissenschaften im Grundrisse* (1817), *Naturrecht und Staatswissenschaft im Grundrisse* (1821), and *Vorlesungen über die Philosophie der Geschichte* (1837).—Ed.]

[6] Gustave d'Eichthal to Auguste Comte, November 18, 1824, and January 12, 1825. Pierre Lafitte [Laffitte], "Matériaux pour servir à la biographie d'Auguste Comte: Correspondance d'Auguste Comte et Gustave d'Eichthal", *La revue occidentale*, pp. 186ff. [The two quotations in the text are from the November 18 letter and may be found on p. 259 of the article.—Ed.]

and greatly praised the first part, although he had doubts about the meaning of the method of observation recommended in the second part. And Comte not much later even expressed the naïve hope that "Hegel seemed to him in Germany the man most capable to push the positive philosophy".[7] The later instances in which the similarity has been noticed are numerous, as I have already said. But although such widely used books as R. Flint's *Philosophy of History*[8] and J. T. Merz's *History of European Thought*[9] comment upon it, and such distinguished and diverse scholars as Alfred Fouillée,[10] Emile Meyerson,[11] Thomas Wittaker,[12] Ernst Troeltsch,[13] and Eduard Spranger[14] have discussed it—I will keep for a note a score of other names I could mention[15]—little attempt has yet been made at a systematic examination of these similarities,

[7] Auguste Comte, *Lettres d'Auguste Comte à divers* (Paris: Fonds typographique de l'exécution testamentaire d'Auguste Comte, 1905), vol. 2, p. 86, letter of April 11, 1825 [April 6, 1825].

[8] Robert Flint, *The Philosophy of History in France and Germany* (Edinburgh: W. Blackwood and Sons, 1874), vol. 1 [book 1], pp. 262, 267, 281 [262–64 only].

[9] Merz, *History of European Thought*, vol. 4, pp. 186, 481ff., 501–3.

[10] Alfred Fouillée, *Le mouvement positiviste et la conception sociologique du monde* (Paris: F. Alcan, 1896), pp. 268, 366.

[11] Emile Meyerson, *De l'explication dans les sciences* (Paris: Payot, 1921), vol. 2, pp. 122–38.

[12] Thomas Wittaker [Whittaker], *Reason: A Philosophical Essay with Historical Illustrations* (Cambridge: Cambridge University Press, 1934), pp. 7–9.

[13] Troeltsch, *Historismus und seine Probleme*, p. 408.

[14] Eduard Spranger, "Die Kulturzyklentheorie und das Problem des Kulturverfalls", *Sitzungsberichte der Preussischen Akademie der Wissenschaften, Philosophisch-Historische Klasse* (Berlin: Akademie der Wissenschaften, 1926), pp. xlii ff.

[15] William Ashley, *An Introduction to English Economic History and Theory*, 3rd ed. (London: Longmans, Green and Co., 1914), vol. 1, pp. ix–xi. Alfred William Benn, *The History of English Rationalism* (London: Longmans, Green, and Co., 1906), vol. 1, pp. 412, 449; vol. 2, p. 82. [Though Benn mentions both Comte and Hegel in vol. 2, p. 82, the reference is not about their similarities but to the reception of their ideas in Oxford.—Ed.] Edward Caird, *The Social Philosophy and Religion of Comte*, 2nd ed. (Glasgow: Maclehose, 1893), p. 51. Morris R. Cohen, "Causation and Its Application to History", *Journal of the History of Ideas*, vol. 3, January 1942, p. 12. Rudolf Eucken, "Zur Würdigung Comte's und des Positivismus", in *Philosophische Aufsätze: Eduard Zeller zu seinem fünfzigjährigen Doctor-Jubiläum gewidmet* (Leipzip: Fues, 1887), p. 67 [pp. 67–68], and also in *Geistige Strömungen der Gegenwart* (Leipzig: Veit, 1904), p. 164. Reinhold Geijer, "Hegelianism och Positivism", *Lunds Universitets Års-skrift*, vol. 18 (1883). Georges Gourvitch [Gurvitch], *L'idée du droit social* (Paris: Librarie du Recueil Sirey, 1932), pp. 271, 297. Harald Høffding, *Der menschliche Gedanke, seine Formen und seine Aufgaben* (Leipzig: O. R. Reisland, 1911), p. 41 [pp. 121–22]. Maurice Mandelbaum, *The Problem of Historical Knowledge* (New York: Liveright Pub., 1938), pp. 312ff. Georg Mehlis, "Die Geschichtsphilosophie Hegels und Comtes", *Jahrbuch für Soziologie*, vol. 3, 1927, pp. 91–110. Joseph Rambaud, *Histoire des doctrines économiques* (Paris: Librairie de la Société du recueil général des lois et des arrêts et du Journal du palais, 1899), pp. 485, 542 [327–28, 338]. Rothacker, *Einleitung in die Geisteswissenschaften*, pp. 190, 287. Albert Salomon, "Tocqueville's Philosophy of Freedom: A Trend Towards Concrete Sociology", *Review of Politics*, vol. 1, October 1939, p. 400. Max Schinz, *Die Anfänge des französischen Positivismus*, p. 2. Wilhelm Windelband, *Lehrbuch der Geschichte der Philosophie*, new ed. (Tübingen, J. C. B. Mohr, 1935), pp. 554ff. An article by G. Salomon-Delatour, "Comte ou Hegel", in *Revue positiviste internationale*, vol. 52, 1935,

though I must not omit mention of Friedrich Dittmann's comparative study of the philosophies of history of Comte and Hegel,[16] on which I shall draw in some measure.

III

More significant, perhaps, than any list of the names of those who have noticed the similarities is the long series of social thinkers of the last hundred years who testify to this kinship in a different and more effective manner. Indeed, still more surprising than the neglect of the similarities in the two original doctrines is the similar failure to notice the surprising number of leading figures who succeeded in combining in their own thought ideas derived from Hegel and Comte. Again, I can quote only a few of the names which belong here.[17] But if I tell you that the list includes Karl Marx, Friedrich Engels, and probably Ludwig Feuerbach in Germany, Ernest Renan, Hippolyte Taine, and Emile Durkheim in France, Giuseppe Mazzini in Italy—and I should probably add Benedetto Croce and John Dewey from the living—you will begin to see how far this influence reaches.[18] When later I shall have occasion to show how we can trace to the same source such widespread intellectual movements as that peculiarly unhistorical approach to history which paradoxically is called historicism, much of what has been known as sociology during the last hundred years, and especially its most fashionable and most ambitious branch, the sociology of knowledge, you will perhaps understand the importance which I attach to this combined influence.

Before addressing myself to my main task, I must go through one more preliminary: I ought, in fairness, to acquaint you with a serious deficiency with

---

pp. 220–27, and vol. 53, 1936, pp. 110–18, became available to me only after the present essay was in the hands of the printer.

[16] Friedrich Dittmann, "Die Geschichtsphilosophie Comtes und Hegels", *Vierteljahrsschrift für wissenschaftliche Philosophie und Soziologie*, vol. 38, 1914, pp. 281–312, and vol. 39, 1915, pp. 38–81.

[17] The list of additional names, which could be extended almost indefinitely, would include Eugen Dühring, Arnold Ruge, Pierre-Joseph Proudhon, Vilfredo Pareto, L. T. Hobhouse, Ernst Troeltsch, Wilhelm Dilthey, Karl Lamprecht, and Kurt Breysig.

[18] [The Italian idealist philosopher and historian Benedetto Croce (1866–1952) wrote a commentary on Hegel titled *What Is Living and What Is Dead in the Philosophy of Hegel* (1907). The American pragmatist philosopher and educational reformer John Dewey (1859–1952) was introduced to Hegel's thought in graduate school at Johns Hopkins. He would later write that Hegel's ideas had left "a permanent deposit" on his thinking: "The form, the schematism, of his system now seems to me artificial to the last degree. But in the content of his ideas there is often an extraordinary depth; in many of his analyses, taken out of their mechanical dialectical setting, an extraordinary acuteness". See John Dewey, *The Structure of Experience*, ed. John J. McDermott, vol. 1 of *The Philosophy of John Dewey* (New York: G. P. Putnam's Sons, 1973), p. 8.—Ed.]

which I approach it. So far as Comte is concerned, it is true that I strongly disagree with most of his views. But this disagreement is still of a kind which leaves room for profitable discussion because there exists at least some common basis. If it is true that criticism is worth while only when one approaches one's object with at least this degree of sympathy, I am afraid I cannot claim this qualification with regard to Hegel. Concerning him I have always felt, not only what his greatest British admirer said, that his philosophy was "a scrutiny of thought so profound that it was for the most part unintelligible",[19] but also what John Stuart Mill experienced, who "found by actual experience . . . that conversancy with him tends to deprave one's intellect".[20] I ought to warn you, therefore, that I do not pretend to understand Hegel. But, fortunately for my task, a comprehension of his system as a whole is not necessary. I think I know well enough those parts of his doctrines which have, or are supposed to have, influenced the development of the social sciences. Indeed, they are so well known that my task will consist largely in showing that many of the developments commonly ascribed to Hegel's influence might well in fact be due to Comte's. It seems to me that it is largely the support which the Hegelian tradition received from this quarter that accounts for the otherwise inexplicable fact that in the social sciences Hegelian thought and language continued to rule long after, in the other fields of science, the rule of his philosophy had been superseded by that of exact science.

IV

There is one feature, however, which their general theories of knowledge have in common, and which I must mention—for its own sake as well as because it will give me an opportunity to refer to an interesting question which I shall not have time to consider elsewhere in this chapter: the original source of their common ideas.

[19] Quoted in Karl Popper, *The Open Society and Its Enemies*, vol. 2, p. 25. [Hegel's "greatest British admirer" is the Scottish philosopher James Hutchison Stirling (1820–1909), author of *The Secret of Hegel* (1865). Though it was influential, many found his book to be as difficult as Hegel's own work, which prompted one wag to report that the secret had been well kept. The passage from Stirling makes up part of the epigraph of chapter 12 of Popper's *Open Society*, which is titled "Hegel and the New Tribalism".—Ed.]

[20] J. S. Mill to A. Bain, November 4, 1867, *The Letters of John Stuart Mill*, ed., Hugh S. R. Elliot (London: Longmans, Green and Co., 1910), vol. 2, p. 93. [See *The Later Letters of John Stuart Mill, 1849–1873*, Francis Mineka and Dwight Lindley, eds, vol. 16 (1972) of *Collected Works of John Stuart Mill*, p. 1324. In an interview later in life Hayek said that one reason he never completed the Abuse of Reason project was that he could not stomach the idea of having to work through the writings of Hegel and Marx, which he termed "that dreadful stuff". See the editor's introduction, this volume, p. 31.—Ed.]

The point of their doctrines to which I refer is one on which at first they may appear to hold diametrically opposed views: their attitude to empirical research. For Comte this constitutes the whole of science; for Hegel it is entirely outside what he calls science, although he by no means underrates the importance of factual knowledge within its sphere. What brings them together is their belief that empirical science must be purely descriptive, confined to establishing regularities of the observed phenomena. They are both strict phenomenalists in this sense, denying that empirical science can proceed from description to explanation. That the positivist Comte regards all explanation, all discussion of the manner in which the phenomena are produced, as futile metaphysics, while Hegel reserves it to his idealistic philosophy of nature, is a different matter. In their views on the functions of empirical research they agree almost completely, as Emile Meyerson has beautifully shown.[21] When Hegel argues, for example, that "empirical science has no business to assert the existence of anything that is not given to sense perception",[22] he is as much a positivist as Comte.

Now this phenomenalist approach to the problems of empirical science derives in modern times without question from Descartes, to whom both philosophers are directly indebted. And the same is, I believe, true of the second basic feature which they have in common and which will show up strongly in the more detailed points on which they agree: their common rationalism, or better, intellectualism. It was Descartes who first combined these apparently incompatible ideas of a phenomenalist or sensualist approach to physical science and a rationalist view of man's task and functions.[23] With respect to the points in which we are chiefly interested, it was mainly through Montesquieu,[24] d'Alembert,[25] Turgot, and Condorcet in France, Herder,[26] Kant, and Fichte in Germany, that the Cartesian heritage was passed on to Hegel and Comte.[27] But what in those men had been merely bold and stimu-

[21] Meyerson, *De l'explication dans les sciences*, vol. 2, especially chapter 13.

[22] Ibid., p. 50.

[23] Jean Laporte, *Le rationalisme de Descartes*, new ed. (Paris: Presses universitaires de France, 1950).

[24] E. Buss, "Montesquieu und Cartesius: Ein Beitrag zur Geschichte der französischen Aufklärungsliteratur", *Philosophische Monatshefte*, vol. 4, 1869 [1869/70], pp. 1–37 [1–38], and Hildegard Trescher, "Montesquieus Einfluss auf die philosophischen Grundlagen der Staatslehre Hegels" *Schmollers Jahrbuch*, vol. 42, 1918, pp. 471–501, 907–44.

[25] Cf. Schinz, *Geschichte der französischen Philosophie*, and Misch, "Zur Entstehung des französischen Positivismus", *Archiv für Geschichte der Philosophie*.

[26] In a letter of August 5, 1824, Comte writes of Herder as "prédécesseur de Condorcet, mon prédécesseur immédiat". [the predecessor of Condorcet, who was my immediate predecessor.— Ed.] See Lettres *d'Auguste Comte*, vol. 2, p. 56.

[27] [Among those Hayek mentions as having passed Cartesian ideas on to Hegel and Comte are the German poet, critic, and philosopher Johann Gottfried von Herder (1744–1803), who emphasised the importance of language and cultural traditions in determining a *Volk*, and the

lating suggestions became with our two philosophers the bases of the two ruling systems of thought of their time. In thus stressing the common Cartesian origin of what I believe to be the common errors of Hegel and Comte, I wish, of course, not in the least to depreciate the great service which Descartes has rendered to modern thought. But as has been true with so many fertile ideas, a stage is often reached when their very success brings about their application to fields in which they are no longer appropriate. And this, I believe, is what Comte and Hegel have done.

V

When we turn to the field of social theory we find that the central ideas which Hegel and Comte have in common are so closely related that we can almost express them all in one sentence, if we give due weight to every single word. Such a statement would have to run somewhat like this: the central aim of all study of society must be to construct a universal history of all mankind, understood as a scheme of the necessary development of humanity according to recognisable laws. It is characteristic of the extent to which their ideas have entered into the whole intellectual makeup of our time, that, thus baldly stated, they now sound almost commonplace. Only when we analyse in greater detail the meaning and the implications of this statement do we become aware of the extraordinary nature of the undertaking which it proposes.

The laws which both seek—and it makes little difference that Comte presents them as "natural laws"[28] while for Hegel they are metaphysical principles—are in the first instances laws of the development of the human mind. They both claim, in other words, that our individual minds, which contribute to this process of development, are at the same time capable of comprehending it as a whole. It is the necessary succession of stages of the human mind determined by these dynamic laws which accounts for a corresponding succession of different civilisations, cultures, *Volksgeister*, or social systems.

Their common stress on the pre-dominance of the intellectual development in this process, incidentally, in no way conflicts with the fact that the most influential tradition which they both inspired came misleadingly to be called the 'materialist' interpretation of history. Comte, in this as in many

---

German philosopher Johann Gottlieb Fichte (1762–1814), who attempted to reconstruct the foundations of Kantian philosophy with his own *Wissenschaftslehre*.—Ed.]

[28] Comte, *Cours de philosophie positive*, 5th ed. (identical with 1st) (Paris: Société positiviste, 1893), vol. 4, p. 253; see also *Early Essays*, p. 150. [Note that Hayek is using the 5th edition of Comte's *Cours* for this chapter, whereas in earlier chapters he used the 2nd edition.—Ed.]

other points nearer to Marx than Hegel, laid the foundation for this development with his stress on the pre-dominant importance of our knowledge of nature; and the basic contention of the so-called materialist (or better, technological) interpretation of history is, after all, merely that it is our knowledge of nature and of technological possibilities which governs the development in other fields. The essential point, the belief that one's own mind should be capable of explaining itself, and the laws of its past and future development—I cannot explain here why to me this seems to involve a contradiction[29]—is the same with both, and it is derived by Marx, and through him by his disciples, from Hegel and Comte.

The conception of laws of succession of distinct stages in the development of the human mind in general, and in all its particular manifestations and concretisations, of course implies that these wholes or collectives can be directly apprehended as individuals of a species: that we can directly perceive civilisations or social systems as objectively given facts. Such a claim is not surprising in a system of idealism like Hegel's, that is, as a product of a conceptual realism or of 'essentialism'.[30] But it seems at first out of place in a naturalist system like Comte's. The fact is, however, that his phenomenalism which eschews all mental constructions and allows him to admit only of what can be directly observed, forces him into a position very similar to Hegel's. Since he cannot deny the existence of social structures, he must claim that they are immediately given to experience. In fact, he goes so far as to claim that the social wholes are undoubtedly better known and more directly observable than the elements of which they consist,[31] and that therefore social theory must start from our knowledge of the directly apprehended wholes.[32] Thus he, no less than Hegel, starts from intuitively apprehended abstract concepts of society or civilisation, and then deductively derives from it his knowledge of the structure of the object. He even goes so far, surprisingly enough in a positivist, as to claim explicitly that from this conception of the total we can derive *a priori* knowledge about the necessary relations of the parts.[33] It is this which justifies it if Comte's positivism has sometimes been described as a system of

---

[29] For a systematic analysis and criticism of these ideas, see part 1 of this volume. [Hayek refers here to his "Scientism" essay.—Ed.]

[30] Cf. Karl R. Popper, "The Poverty of Historicism", *Economica*, n.s., vol. 11, May 1944, p. 94. [Popper's essay later appeared as a book; the discussion above may be found in *The Poverty of Historicism*, section 10.—Ed.]

[31] *Cours*, vol. 4, p. 286: "L'ensemble du sujet est certainement alors beaucoup mieux connu et plus immédiatement abordable que les diverses parties qu'on distinguera ultérieurement". [The whole topic is certainly far better known and directly apprehensible than its diverse components, which are subsequently discernible.—Ed.]

[32] Ibid., p. 291. [Probably a better reference for this is p. 286.—Ed.]

[33] Ibid., p. 526.

idealism.[34] Like Hegel, he treats as "concrete universals"[35] those social structures which in fact we come to know only by composing them, or building them up, from the familiar elements; and he even surpasses Hegel in claiming that only society as a whole is real and that the individual is only an abstraction.[36]

VI

The similarity of the treatment of social evolution by Hegel and Comte goes far beyond these methodological aspects. For both, society appears as an organism in a fairly literal sense. Both compare the stages through which social evolution must pass with the different ages through which individual man passes in his natural growth. And for both, the growth of the conscious control of his destiny by man is the main content of history.

Neither Comte nor Hegel was of course a historian, properly speaking— although it is not so very long since it was the fashion to describe them, in contrast to their predecessors, as 'true historians'[37] because they were 'scientific', which, presumably, meant that they aimed at the discovery of laws. But what they presented as the 'historical method' soon began to displace the approach of the great historical school of a Niebuhr or a Ranke.[38] It is customary to trace to Hegel the rise of the later historicism[39] with its belief in the necessary succession of 'stages' which manifest themselves in all fields of social life; but Comte's influence had probably more to do with it than Hegel's.

In the confused state of terminology on these matters,[40] it is perhaps necessary to say explicitly that I draw a sharp distinction between the 'historical

[34] See, e.g., Eugène de Roberty, *La philosophie du siècle: Criticisme, positivisme, évolutionnisme* (Paris: F. Alcan, 1891), p. 29, and Schinz, *Die Anfänge des französischen Positivismus*, p. 255.

[35] Salomon, "Tocqueville's Philosophy of Freedom", p. 400.

[36] *Cours*, vol. 6, p. 590; *Discours sur l'esprit positif*, p. 118.

[37] Cf., e.g., Dittmann, "Die Geschichtsphilosophie Comtes und Hegels", vol. 38, 1914, p. 310, and Merz, *History of European Thought*, vol. 4, p. 500.

[38] [German historian Barthold Georg Niebuhr (1776–1831) insisted on the importance of checking historical accounts against contemporary and documentary evidence, applying these principles in his writings on Roman history. Leopold von Ranke (1795–1886), whose goal as an historian was "to show what really happened", sought to apply Niebuhr's methods in the writing of modern history. Through his historical seminars in Berlin Ranke trained most of the influential German historians of the nineteenth century.—Ed.]

[39] Cf. Popper, *The Open Society and its Enemies*, and Karl Löwith, *Von Hegel bis Nietzsche* (Zürich: Europa, 1941), p. 302.

[40] This long-standing confusion has been accentuated recently by the fact that so distinguished a historian as Friedrich Meinecke devoted his great work, *Die Entstehung des Historismus*, entirely to that earlier historical school, in contradistinction to which the term *historicism* was coined during the second half of the nineteenth century. See also Walter Eucken, "Die Überwindung des

school' of the early nineteenth century and the majority of the later professional historians, and the historicism of a Marx, a Schmoller, or a Sombart.[41] It was the latter who believed that with the discovery of laws of development they had the only key to true historical understanding, and who in an altogether unjustified arrogance claimed that the earlier writers, and particularly those of the eighteenth century, had been 'unhistorical'. It seems to me that in many respects David Hume, for example, had much more justification when he believed his "to be the historical age and [his—FAH] to be the historical nation"[42] than the historicists who tried to turn history into a theoretical science. The abuses to which this historicism ultimately led are best seen by the fact that even a thinker so close to it as Max Weber was once driven to describe the whole *Entwicklungsgedanke* as a "romantic swindle".[43] I have little to add to the masterly analysis of this historicism by my friend Karl Popper, hidden away in a wartime volume of *Economica*,[44] except that the responsibility for it seems to me to rest at least as much with Comte and positivism as with Plato and Hegel.

This historicism, let me repeat, was much less an affair of the historians proper than of the representatives of the other social sciences who applied what they believed to be the 'historical method'. Gustav Schmoller, the founder of the younger historical school of economics, is perhaps the best example of one who was clearly guided by the philosophy of Comte rather than that of Hegel.[45] But if the influence of this kind of historicism was perhaps most marked in economics, it was a fashion which, first in Germany and then elsewhere, affected all the social sciences. It could be shown to have influenced the history of art[46] no less than anthropology or philology. And the great popularity which 'philosophies of history' have enjoyed during the last hundred years, theories which ascribed to the historical process an intelligible 'meaning' and which pretended to show us a recognisable destiny of mankind, is essentially the result of this joint influence of Hegel and Comte.

Historismus". [Cf. Hayek's discussion of historicism in chapter 7, note 1, and chapter 16, note 58.—Ed.]

[41] [For more on Schmoller, see chapter 4, note 4, and for Sombart, see chapter 7, note 15. —Ed.]

[42] Quoted in Gladys Bryson, *Man and Society: The Scottish Inquiry of the Eighteenth Century*, p. 78.

[43] Quoted in Troeltsch, *Historismus und seine Probleme*, pp. 189–90 note.

[44] Popper, "Poverty of Historicism". [Popper's essay appeared in three parts in *Economica*, n.s., vol. 11, May 1944, pp. 86–103; August 1944, pp. 119–37; and vol. 12, May 1945, pp. 69–89. —Ed.]

[45] On Comte's influence on the growth of the younger historical school in German economics, see particularly Franz Raab, *Die Fortschrittsidee bei Gustav Schmoller* (Freiburg: T. Kehrer, 1934), p. 72, and Waentig, *Auguste Comte und seine Bedeutung für die Entwicklung der Sozialwissenschaft*.

[46] Most clearly seen in the person of Wilhelm Scherer. See also Rothacker, *Einleitung in die Geisteswissenschaften*, pp. 190–250.

VII

I will not dwell here on another and perhaps only superficial resemblance between their theories: the fact that with Comte the necessary development proceeds according to the famous law of the three stages, while with Hegel a similar threefold rhythm is the result of the growth of mind as a dialectical process which proceeds from thesis to antithesis and synthesis. More important is the fact that for both men history leads to a pre-determined end, that it can be interpreted teleologically as a succession of achieved purposes.

Their historical determinism—by which is meant, not merely that historical events are somehow determined, but that *we* are able to recognise why they were bound to take a particular course—necessarily implies a thorough fatalism: man cannot change the course of history. Even the outstanding individuals are, with Comte, merely "instruments"[47] or "organs of a pre-destined movement",[48] or with Hegel *Geschäftsführer des Weltgeistes*, managers of the World-spirit whom Reason cunningly uses for its own purposes.

There is no room for freedom in such a system: For Comte freedom is "the rational submission to the domination of natural laws",[49] that is, of course, his natural laws of inevitable development; for Hegel it is the recognition of necessity.[50] And since both are in possession of the secret of the "definitive and permanent intellectual unity"[51] to which evolution is tending according to Comte, or of the "absolute truth" in Hegel's sense, they both claim for themselves the right to impose a new orthodoxy. But I have to admit that in this as in many other respects the much-abused Hegel is still infinitely more liberal than the 'scientific' Comte. There are in Hegel no such fulminations against the unlimited liberty of conscience as we find throughout the work of Comte, and Hegel's attempt to use the machinery of the Prussian state to impose an

---

[47] *Early Essays*, p. 15 [pp. 154–57].

[48] *Cours*, vol. 4, p. 298.

[49] Ibid., p. 157: "Car la vraie liberté ne peut consister, sans doute, qu'en une soumission rationnelle à la seule prépondérance, convenablement constatée, des lois fondamentales de la nature". [Because it is likely that true freedom consists in nothing other than a rational submission to the duly established precedence of the fundamental laws of nature.—Ed.]

[50] Hegel, *Philosophie der Geschichte* (Leipzig: Reclam, 1924), p. 77: "Notwendig ist das Vernünftige als das Substantielle, und frei sind wir, indem wir es als Gesetz anerkennen und ihm als der Substanz unseres eigenen Wesens folgen: der objektive und der subjektive Wille sind dann ausgesöhnt und ein und dasselbe ungetrübte Ganze". [In G. W. F. Hegel, *Lectures on the Philosophy of History, Introduction: Reason in History*, translated by H. B. Nisbet (Cambridge: Cambridge University Press, 1975), p. 97, this passage is translated as follows: "The Rational, as the substance of things, is necessary, and we are free in so far as we recognize it as law and follow it as the substance of our own being; the objective and the subjective will are then reconciled, forming a single, undivided whole".—Ed.]

[51] *Cours*, vol. 4, p. 144; cf. *Early Essays*, p. 132.

official doctrine[52] appears very tame compared with Comte's plan for a new 'religion of humanity' and all his other thoroughly anti-liberal schemes for regimentation which even his old admirer John Stuart Mill ultimately branded as "liberticide".[53]

I have not the time to show in any detail how these similar political attitudes are reflected in equally similar evaluations of different historical periods or of different institutions. I will merely mention, as particularly characteristic, that the two thinkers show the same dislike of Periclean Greece and of the Renaissance, and the same admiration for Frederick the Great.[54]

VIII

The last major point of agreement between Hegel and Comte which I will mention is no more than a consequence of their historicism. But it has exercised so much independent influence that I must discuss it separately. It is their thorough moral relativism, their conviction either that all moral rules can be recognised as justified by the circumstances of the time, or that only those are valid which can be thus explicitly justified—it is not always clear which they mean. This idea is, of course, merely an application of historical determinism, of the belief that we can adequately explain why people at different times believed what they actually did believe. This pretended insight into the manner in which people's thought is determined implies the claim that we can know what they ought to believe in given circumstances, and the dismissal as irrational or inappropriate of all moral rules which cannot be thus justified.

In this connection historicism shows most clearly its rationalist or intellectualist character:[55] since the determination of all historical development is to be intelligible, only such forces as can be fully understood by us can have been at work. Comte's attitude on this is really not very different from Hegel's

---

[52] For references, see Meyerson, *De l'explication dans les sciences*, vol. 2, p. 130, and cf. Popper, *Open Society*, vol. 2, p. 40.

[53] J. S. Mill to Harriet Mill, Rome, January 15, 1855: "Almost all the projects of social reformers of these days are really liberticide—Comte's particularly so", quoted in F. A. Hayek, *John Stuart Mill and Harriet Taylor: Their Friendship and Subsequent Marriage* (Chicago: University of Chicago Press, 1951), p. 216. [A *Collected Works* edition of this title is anticipated.—Ed.] For a fuller statement of Comte's political conclusions, whose anti-liberal tendencies go far beyond anything Hegel ever said, see herein, pp. 273–75.

[54] In Comte's 'Positivist Calendar,' the 'Month of Modern Statesmanship' is given the name of Frederick the Great!

[55] See Hugo Preller, "Rationalismus und Historismus", *Historische Zeitschrift*, vol. 126, 1922, pp. 207–41.

statement that all that is real is rational and all that is rational is also real[56]—only that instead of rational Comte would have said historically necessary and therefore justified. Everything appears to him as in this sense justified in its time, slavery and cruelty, superstition and intolerance, because—this he does not say but it is implied in his reasoning—there are no moral rules which we must accept as transcending our individual reason, nothing which is a given and unconscious pre-supposition of all our thought, and by which we must judge moral issues. Indeed, he significantly could not conceive of any other possibility except either a system of morals designed and revealed by a higher being, or one demonstrated by our own reason.[57] And between these two the necessary superiority of the 'demonstrated morals' seemed to him unquestionable. Comte was both more consistent and more extreme than Hegel. He had indeed already stated the main conception in his very first publication when, at the age of nineteen, he wrote: "There is nothing good and nothing bad, absolutely speaking; everything is relative, this is the only absolute statement".[58]

It is possible, however, that with regard to this particular point I am attributing too much importance to the influence of our two philosophers, and that they were merely following a general fashion of their time which fitted in with their systems of thought. How rapidly moral relativism was then spreading we can see clearly in an interesting exchange of letters between Thomas Carlyle and John Stuart Mill. As early as January 1833 we find Carlyle writing to Mill with reference to a recently published *History of the French Revolution*:[59] "Has not M. Thiers a most wonderful system of Ethics *in petto?* He will prove to you that the power to have done a thing almost (if not altogether) gave you the right to do it: every hero of his turns out to be perfectly justified in doing whatsoever—he has succeeded in doing".[60] To which Mill replied: "You have characterised Thiers's system of ethics most accurately. I am afraid it is too just a specimen of the young French *littérateurs*, and that *this* is all they have made, ethically speaking, of their attempt to imitate the Germans in identifying themselves with the *past*. By dint of shifting their point of view to make it accord with that of whomsoever they are affecting to judge, coupled with their historical fatalism, they have arrived at the annihilation of all moral dis-

---

[56] G. W. F. Hegel, *Grundlinien der Philosophie des Rechts*, volume 124 in the series *Philosophische Bibliothek* (Leipzig: Felix Meiner, 1911), p. 14.

[57] *Système de politique positive*, vol. 1, p. 356: "La supériorité nécessaire de la morale démontrée sur la morale révélée". [The necessary superiority of demonstrated over revealed moral standards.—Ed.]

[58] *L'Industrie*, ed. Saint-Simon, vol. 3, 2me cahier. [Cf. chapter 13, note 7.—Ed.]

[59] Adolphe Thiers, *Histoire de la révolution française* (Paris: Lecointe et Durey, 1823–27).

[60] T. Carlyle to J. S. Mill, January 12, 1833, in *Letters of Thomas Carlyle to John Stuart Mill, John Sterling, and Robert Browning*, ed. Alexander Carlyle (London: T. F. Unwin, 1923; [reprinted, New York: Haskell House, 1970]), p. 34.

tinctions except *success* and *not success*".[61] It is interesting that Mill, who knew very well how these ideas had been spread in France by the Saint-Simonians, yet explicitly ascribes their appearance in a young French historian to German influence.

That these views lead both Comte and Hegel to a complete moral and legal positivism[62]—and at times desperately close to the doctrine that Might is Right—I can mention only in passing. I believe that quite a good case could be made out that they are among the main sources of the modern tradition of legal positivism. It is, after all, only another manifestation of the same general attitude that refuses to admit anything as relevant which cannot be recognised as the expression of conscious reason.

IX

This brings me back to the common central idea which underlies all these particular similarities of the doctrines of Comte and Hegel: the idea that we can improve upon the results of the earlier individualist approaches with their modest endeavour to understand how individual minds interact, by studying human Reason, with a capital *R*, from the outside as it were, as something objectively given and observable as a whole, as it might appear to some supermind. From the belief that they had achieved the old ambition of *se ipsam cognoscere mentem*, and that they had reached a position where they were able to predict the future course of the growth of Reason, it was only one step more to the still more presumptuous idea that Reason should now be able to pull itself up by its own bootstraps to its definitive or absolute state.[63] It is in the last analysis this intellectual *hubris*, the seeds of which were sown by Des-

---

[61] J. S. Mill to T. Carlyle, February 2, 1833 (unpublished, National Library of Scotland). [This letter is now in print; for the quoted passage, see *The Earlier Letters, 1812 to 1848*, ed. Francis E. Mineka, vol. 12 (1963) of *Collected Works of John Stuart Mill*, p. 139.—Ed.]

[62] On Hegel's legal positivism, see particularly Herman Heller, *Hegel und der nationale Machstaatsgedanke in Deutschland* (Leipzig: B. G. Teubner, 1921), p. 166, and Popper, *Open Society*, vol. 2, p. 39. For Comte, see *Cours*, vol. 4, pp. 266ff. [In Hayek's view, legal positivism is the doctrine that what counts as legally valid is simply that which has been created by a lawmaker—all law is 'posited' rather than being 'derived from nature' or 'discovered'—so that there is no necessary connection between what is legal and what is morally just. In this it stands in opposition to natural law doctrines. Hayek offered his assessment of the (in his view, pernicious) effects of legal positivism in *The Constitution of Liberty*, pp. 236–39, and in *The Mirage of Social Justice*, vol. 2 of *Law, Legislation, and Liberty*, pp. 44–48.—Ed.]

[63] [At the end of his *Lectures on the History of Philosophy*, translated by Elizabeth S. Haldane and Francis H. Simson (London: Kegan Paul, Trench, Trübner and Co., 1896), p. 546, Hegel describes the movement of the World-spirit becoming conscious of itself as follows: "To this point the World-spirit has come, and each stage has its own form in the true system of Philosophy; nothing is lost, all principles are preserved, since Philosophy in its final aspect is the

cartes, and perhaps already by Plato, which is the common trait in Hegel and Comte. The concern with the movement of Reason as a whole not only prevented them from understanding the process through which the interaction of individuals produced structures of relationships which performed actions no individual reason could fully comprehend, but it also made them blind to the fact that the attempt of conscious reason to control its own development could only have the effect of limiting this very growth to what the individual directing mind could foresee.[64] Although this aspiration is a direct product of a certain brand of rationalism, it seems to me to be the result of a misunderstood rationalism, better called intellectualism—a rationalism which fails in its most important task, namely, in recognising the limits of what individual conscious reason can accomplish.[65]

Hegel and Comte both singularly fail to make intelligible how the interaction of the efforts of individuals can create something greater than they know. While Adam Smith and the other great Scottish individualists of the eighteenth century—even though they spoke of the 'invisible hand'—provided such an explanation,[66] all that Hegel and Comte give us is a mysterious teleological force. And while eighteenth-century individualism, essentially humble in its aspirations, aimed at understanding as well as possible the principles by which the individual efforts combined to produce a civilisation in order to learn what were the conditions most favourable to its further growth, Hegel and Comte became the main source of that hubris of collectivism which aims at 'conscious direction' of all forces of society.

X

I must now attempt to illustrate briefly, by a few more examples, the hints I have already given about the course which the common influence of Hegel and

---

totality of forms. This concrete idea is the result of the strivings of spirit during almost twenty-five centuries of earnest work to become objective to itself, to know itself:

Tantæ molis erat, se ipsam cognoscere mentem.

All this time was required to produce the philosophy of our day; so tardily and slowly did the World-spirit work to reach this goal". The Latin phrase invokes Virgil's summation of the hardships suffered by the Trojan Aeneas in the journey that ultimately resulted in the founding of Rome: *Tantæ molis erat Romanam condere gentem*—So vast was the effort to found the race of Rome. (*Aeneid*, 1.33)—Ed.]

[64] See herein, chapter 9, pp. 150–55.

[65] [Hayek later settled on the term 'rationalist constructivism' to describe this tendency. See F. A. Hayek, "Kinds of Rationalism" [1964] in *Studies in Philosophy, Politics, and Economics* (Chicago: University of Chicago Press, 1967), p. 85.—Ed.]

[66] See my *Individualism and Economic Order* (Chicago: University of Chicago Press, 1948), p. 7. [Hayek refers here to his essay, "Individualism: True and False", which is reprinted as the Introduction to the present volume. The discussion he references is on pp. 52–54.—Ed.]

Comte took. One of the most interesting to study in detail would be that once very famous but now largely forgotten German philosopher Ludwig Feuerbach. It would be even more significant if that old Hegelian who became the founder of German positivism had arrived at that position without any knowledge of Comte; but circumstances make it very probable that he too had at an early stage become acquainted with Comte's first *Système*.[67] How enormous his influence was, not only on the other radical Young Hegelians but on the whole rising generation, is best seen in the account given by Friedrich Engels, who describes how they "all became at once Feuerbachians".[68]

The blend of Hegelianism and positivism which Feuerbach provided[69] became characteristic of the thought of the whole group of German social theorists who appeared in the 1840s. Only one year after Feuerbach had broken away from Hegel because, as he later said, he had recognised that the absolute truth meant merely the absolute professor,[70] the same year in which the last volume of Comte's *Cours* appeared and when, incidentally, the young Karl Marx sent his first work to the printers, namely, in 1842, another author, who was very influential and representative of the time, Lorenz von Stein, published his *Socialism and Communism in France*, which admittedly attempted a fusion of Hegelian and Saint-Simonian and therefore Comtian thought.[71] It has often been noticed that in this work Stein anticipated much of the historical theories of Karl Marx.[72] This fact becomes even more suggestive when we find that another man who was later discovered as a precursor of Karl Marx, the Frenchman Jules Lechevalier, was an old Saint-Simonian who had actually studied under Hegel in Berlin.[73] He preceded Stein by ten years, but

---

[67] See herein, pp. 256 et seq.

[68] Friedrich Engels, *Ludwig Feuerbach and the Outcome of Classical German Philosophy* (New York: International Publishers, 1941), p. 18.

[69] On Feuerbach, see Simon Rawidowicz, *Ludwig Feuerbachs Philosophie* (Berlin: Reuther und Reichard, 1931); Löwith, *Von Hegel bis Nietzsche*; Albert Lévy, *La philosophie de Feuerbach et son influence sur la littérature allemande* (Paris: F. Alcan, 1904); and Franco Lombardi, *Ludovico Feuerbach* (Florence: Nuova Italia, 1935). A recent English study of Feuerbach by William Benton Chamberlain, *Heaven Wasn't His Destination: The Philosophy of Ludwig Feuerbach* (London: G. Allen and Unwin, 1941), is unfortunately quite inadequate. For the widespread positivistic tendencies among the Young Hegelians, see particularly David Koigen, *Zur Vorgeschichte des modernen philosophischen Socialismus in Deutschland* (Bern: Sturzenegger, 1901).

[70] Ludwig Feuerbach to Wilhelm Bolin, October 20, 1860, in Bolin, *Ausgewählte Briefe von und an Feuerbach*, vol. 2, 246–47.

[71] Stein, *Der Socialismus und Communismus des heutigen Frankreichs*.

[72] See Nitschke, "Die Geschichtsphilosophie Lorenz von Steins", esp. p. 136, for the earlier literature on the subject; and Masaryk, *Die philosophischen und sociologischen Grundlagen des Marxismus*, p. 34.

[73] On Jules Lechevalier, see Heinrich Ahrens, *Naturrecht, oder Philosophie des Rechts und des Staates*, 6th ed. (Vienna: C. Gerold's Sohn, 1870), vol. 1, p. 204 [pp. 204–05]; Charles Pelarin [Pellarin], *Notice sur Jules Lechevalier et Abel Transon* (Paris: Impr. nouvelle, Association ouvrière, 1877); Adolph von Wenckstern, *Marx* (Leipzig: Duncker und Humblot, 1896), pp. 205ff. [240–52]; and

remained for some time an isolated figure in France. But in Germany Hegelian positivism, if I may so call it, became the dominant trend of thought. It was in this atmosphere that both Karl Marx and Friedrich Engels formed their now famous theories of history, largely Hegelian in language but, I believe, much more indebted to Saint-Simon and Comte than is commonly realised.[74] And it was those similarities which I have discussed which made it so easy for them to retain Hegelian language for the exposition of a theory which, as Marx himself said, in some respects turned Hegel upside down.

It is probably also more than an accident that it was almost at the same time, in 1841 and in 1843, that two men who were much nearer to a natural science approach to social study than they were to Hegel, Friedrich List[75] and Wilhelm Roscher[76], began the tradition of historicism in economics which became the model that the other social sciences soon eagerly followed. It was in those fifteen or twenty years following 1842[77] that the ideas developed and spread which gave Germany for the first time a leading position in the social

---

Stephan Bauer, "Henri de Saint-Simon nach hundert Jahren", *Archiv für die Geschichte des Sozialismus*, vol. 12, 1926, p. 172.

[74] A careful analysis of the positivist influence on Marx and Engels would require a separate investigation. A direct influence extending to surprising verbal similarities could be shown in the writing of Engels, while the influence on Marx is probably more indirect. Some material for such a study will be found in Masaryk, *Die philosophischen und sociologischen Grundlagen des Marxismus*, p. 35, and Lucie Prenant, "Marx et Comte", in *A la lumière de marxisme* (Paris: Cercle de la Russie neuve, 1935) vol. 2, part 1. In a late letter to Engels (July 7, 1866), Marx who was then reading Comte, apparently for the first time consciously (as distinguished from his probable acquaintance with Comte's Saint-Simonian writing), describes him as "lamentable" compared with Hegel.

[75] Friedrich List, *Das Nationale System der Politischen Oekonomie* (1841).

[76] Wilhelm Roscher, *Grundriss zu Vorlesungen über die Staatswirthschaft nach geschichtlicher Methode* (1843).

[77] The special significance of the year 1842 in this connection is well brought out by Koigen, *Zur Vorgeschichte des modernen philosophischen Socialismus*, pp. 236ff., and by Hans Freund, *Soziologie und Sozialismus* (Würzburg: K. Triltsch, 1934). Particularly instructive on the influence of positivism on the German historians of the period are the letters of Johann Gustav Droysen. See particularly his letter of February 2, 1851 [1852], to T. v. Schön, in which he writes: "Die Philosophie ist durch Hegel und seine Schule für geraume Zeit nicht bloss diskreditiert, sondern in ihrem eigensten Leben zerrüttet. Die Götzendienerei mit dem konstruierenden, ja schöpferischen Denken hat, indem alles ihm vindiziert wurde, zu dem Feuerbachschen Wahnwitz getrieben, der methodisch und ethisch jener polytechnischen Richtung völlig entspricht" [Not only has philosophy long been externally discredited thanks to Hegel and his school, but has also been unhinged in its own internal 'private life'. The idolatry of both derivative and creative thought, in that it affirms everything, has led to the Feuerbachian delusion that totally accords, methodologically and ethically, with that engineering tendency.—Ed.]; and the letter of July 17, 1852, to M. Duncker, which contains the following passage: "Weh uns und unserm deutschen Wesen, wenn diese polytechnische *Misère*, an der Frankreich seit 1789 verdorrt und verfault, diese babylonische Mengerei von Rechnerei und Lüderlichkeit in das schon entartende Geschlecht noch tiefer einreißt! Jener brute Positivismus, den man in Berlin betreibt, setzt diese Revolution des geistigen Lebens ins Treibhaus" [Pity on us and our German nature if this engineering *Misère*

sciences; and it was to some extent by way of re-export from Germany (though partly also from England through Mill and Buckle) that French historians and sociologists such as Taine[78] and Durkheim[79] became familiar with the positivist tradition at the same time as with Hegelianism.

It was under the banner of this historicism made in Germany that in the second half of the nineteenth century the great attack on individualist social theory was conducted, that the very foundations of individualist and liberal society came to be questioned, and that both historical fatalism and ethical relativism became dominant traditions. And it was particularly under its influence that, from Marx to Sombart and Spengler, 'philosophies of history' became the most influential expression of the attitude of the age to social problems.[80] Its most characteristic expression, however, is probably the so-called sociology of knowledge, which to the present day in its two distinct yet closely similar branches still shows how the two strands of thought emanating from Comte and Hegel operate sometimes side by side and sometimes in combination.[81] And, last but not least, most of modern socialism derives its theoretical foundation from that *Alliance intellectuelle franco-allemande*, as Celestin Bouglé has called it,[82] which was in the main an alliance of German Hegelianism and French positivism.

Let me conclude this historical sketch with one more remark. After 1859, as far as the social sciences are concerned, the influence of Darwin could do little more than confirm an already existing tendency. Darwinism may have assisted the introduction into the Anglo-Saxon world of ready-fashioned evolutionary theories. But if we examine such scientific 'revolutions' as were attempted in the social sciences under the influence of Darwin, for example by Thorstein Veblen and his disciples, they appear in fact as little more than a revival of the ideas which German historicism had developed under the influence of Hegel and Comte. I suspect, though I have no proof, that on closer investigation even this American branch of historicism would prove to have more direct connections with the original source of these ideas.[83]

---

that has enervated and defiled France since 1789, this Babylonian jumble of precise calculation and careless disorder, penetrates even deeper into the already degenerate kind! That gross positivism that is practiced in Berlin shunts this revolution of intellectual life into the greenhouse. —Ed.], both in Johann *Gustav Droysen, Briefwechsel*, ed. Rudolf Hübner (Berlin: Deutsche Verlags-Anstalt, 1929), vol. 2, pp. 48, 120.

[78] Cf. Dumitru D. Rosca, *L'influence de Hegel sur Taine* (Paris: J. Gamber, 1928), and Otto Engel, *Der Einfluss Hegels auf die Bildung der Gedankenwelt Hippolyte Taines* (Stuttgart: F. Frommann, 1920).

[79] See Simon Deploige, *The Conflict Between Ethics and Sociology*, translated by Charles Miltner (St. Louis, MO: B. Herder, 1938), chapter 4.

[80] See Paul Barth, *Die Philosophie der Geschichte als Soziologie* (Leipzig: O. R. Reisland, 1922).

[81] See Ernst Grünwald, *Das Problem der Soziologie des Wissens* (Vienna: Wilhelm Braumüller, 1934).

[82] Célestin Bouglé, *Chez les prophètes socialistes* (Paris: F. Alcan, 1918), chapter 3.

[83] That Comte's ideas influenced Veblen seems fairly clear. See Jaffé, *Les théories économiques et sociales de Thorstein Veblen*, p. 35.

XI

It is impossible in this one chapter to do full justice to so big a subject. Least of all can I hope, with the few remarks I have been able to make on the filiation of ideas, to have convinced you that they are correct in every detail. But I trust I have at least provided sufficient evidence to persuade you of the burden of my argument: that we are still, largely without knowing it, under the influence of ideas which have almost imperceptibly crept into modern thought because they were shared by the founders of what seemed to be radically opposed traditions. In these matters we are to a great extent still guided by ideas which are at least a century old, just as the nineteenth century was mainly guided by the ideas of the eighteenth. But whereas the ideas of Hume and Voltaire, of Adam Smith and Kant, produced the liberalism of the nineteenth century, those of Hegel and Comte, of Feuerbach and Marx, have produced the totalitarianism of the twentieth.

It may well be true that we as scholars tend to over-estimate the influence which we can exercise on contemporary affairs. But I doubt whether it is possible to over-estimate the influence which ideas have in the long run. And there can be no question that it is our special duty to recognise the currents of thought which still operate in public opinion, to examine their significance, and, if necessary, to refute them. The first part of this duty I have attempted to outline in this chapter.

APPENDIX: RELATED DOCUMENTS

Some Notes on Propaganda in Germany (1939)[1]

Second draft 12/9/39[2]

Without attempting to be systematic or exhaustive I propose to outline here certain suggestions concerning propaganda in Germany. The main purpose of those notes is to show why, to be effective, such propaganda must be based on the most intimate knowledge of German psychology and conditions in Germany. At the same time it should always be remembered that there has existed in Germany for a long time a certain gulf which separated the Jewish and socialist intelligentsia from the rest of the community, and that in consequence the typical refugee may not always be the most reliable guide on these matters.

1. *Political.* Effective propaganda must be prepared frankly to explain and defend the principles of liberal democracy and to show how these principles have consistently guided the policy of the Western Democracies. One of the main difficulties here is that many concepts and expressions which in English have a familiar and time honoured ring will, if translated into German, sound meaningless and empty phrases, while others, which in English are worn commonplaces, will in German have all the attraction and freshness of a new idea. While, for instance, the words liberty or militarism, or their equivalents mean little or nothing to the average German and are more likely to be misunderstood, it would be most effective to explain the fundamental liberal principle 'to tolerate everything but intolerance'—and of course exceedingly appropriate to make the Germans understand the causes of the present conflict.

   The main asset of any propaganda directly aimed against the political principles of the Hitler regime would however be that it would not be difficult to show that it is Great Britain and France which now stand for all the principles

---

[1] [This document may be found in the Hayek papers, box 61, folder 4, Hoover Institution Archives.—Ed.]

[2] [American readers should note that Hayek was following the British convention of expressing dates. This draft was executed September 12, 1939.—Ed.]

which were dear to the great German poets and thinkers whose names are still sacred in Germany although their relevant writings are largely unknown. Here as in other respects it is of the greatest importance that so far as possible German sources should be quoted to explain the ideals for which Great Britain and France are fighting. There is a wealth of material in the writings of the German classics which, if skilfully selected, could be used to the greatest effect. As an instance of the sort of thing I have in mind I will here mention only Schiller's appraisal of the relative values of the civilisation of Athens and Sparta which almost word for word could be applied to the present clash of ideologies.[3]

There are also certain analogies from recent history of which in this connection much greater use should be made. To the complaint, which in recent months has been expressed even by the most reasonable Germans, that Great Britain interferes in parts of Europe which are no immediate concern to her, the obvious answer is of course to point to German intervention in Spain—but no use appears to have been made of this yet. Another historical parallel, familiar to every German, which might be effectively used is that the importance of the German Danzig to Poland is exactly analogous to the importance of the Italian Trieste to Austro-Hungary.

2. *Historical.* The extent to which the political views not only of the more intelligent Germans but even of the ordinary citizen of Germany are based on the distorted view of history, on which they have been brought up during the past sixty years, can hardly be exaggerated: even in so far as the common people are concerned, the long run effect of any propaganda will depend on now far it succeeds in dispelling the main misconceptions in this respect; and the influence which we can hope to exert in the long run on the more intelligent classes and their belief in the justice of their cause, which in the end will surely be decisive, will depend perhaps primarily on the extent to which we succeed in correcting this distorted view of historical events by which they are guided.

If such 'historical instruction' is to have a chance of success it is absolutely essential that all historical references should be scrupulously and even pedantically correct, that, in so far as is at all possible, German sources should be used and quoted literally, and, of course, that under no circumstances different versions of the same historical events must be allowed to be used. At the same time it would of course be important to limit this kind of historical instruction to the most important facts and constantly to repeat the correct version with respect to them in all possible forms. This can only be achieved if all historical information to be used in propaganda work (including that of French and other propaganda agencies) is based on some sort of official handbook, a compendium to which all

---

[3] [Hayek refers to "The Laws of Lycurgus and Solon" in which the German poet, dramatist, philosopher, and historian Friedrich Schiller (1759–1805) contrasted the Athenian Solon's republican government with the totalitarian regime of the Spartan Lycurgus. See Friedrich Schiller, "Die Gesetzgebung des Lycurgus und Solon", *Historische Schriften*, vol. 4 of *Friedrich Schiller Sämtliche Werke* (Munich: Carl Hanser, 1960), pp. 805–36.—Ed.]

concerned with propaganda work can refer, giving the most reliable information and the confirmation of the facts from German sources. Such a handbook can of course not be produced in a day but will have to be built up gradually. The main point is that the active propaganda work will have to be supported by the systematic and slower work of a panel of historians and persons specially familiar with the German literature of a technical as well as a popular kind.

In so far as the pre-1914 history is concerned, H. Kantorowicz' book on the *Spirit of British Policy and the Spectre of Encirclement* (in the German Original) provides an almost perfect sourcebook for the purpose.[4] But with respect to the period since the last war and particularly the last six years, nothing similar is available and the work of collecting the information which can be effectively used in propaganda will be of considerable magnitude and difficulty. It must never be forgotten, however, that the German people are almost completely ignorant of the more discreditable acts of the Nazi regime, from the Reichstag fire and the events of June 30th, 1934, down to the more recent developments.[5] But while they are to some extent anxious to know the facts and while nothing is more apt to shake them in their beliefs than incontrovertible evidence in this respect, they are of course profoundly suspicious of any information from foreign sources and will often be able to check some of the facts presented to them. One single fact convincingly established and, so far as possible, proved from German sources, will count more than many more indefinite allegations.

3.   *Facts about the Nazi Regime.* That so little is reliably known about the recent internal history of Germany is mainly due to the fact that on the one hand no person could hope single-handed to collect and sift the available evidence, while private or public bodies which might have organised such investigations, have (with one or two exceptions) been naturally reluctant to interfere in the internal affairs of another state. These considerations no longer count and it would certainly pay now to devote considerable expense and trouble to obtain all the facts which can be established in as much concrete and circumstantial detail as possible. In this connection systematic research will have to be done as an essential complement of propaganda if any effective use is to be made of the more ghastly aspects of the Nazi regime in peace time.

The preparation of such a full and truthful account of events inside Germany during the Nazi Regime will be of the greatest importance not only for propa-

---

[4] [Hayek refers to Hermann Kantorowicz, *Der Geist englischen Politik und das Gespenst der Einkreisung Deutschlands* (Berlin: E. Rowohlt, 1929), which was translated as *The Spirit of British Policy and the Myth of the Encirclement of Germany*, translated by W. H. Johnson (New York: Oxford University Press, 1932).—Ed.]

[5] [Hayek refers to the Reichstag fire of February 27, 1933, which led the next day to the Reichstag Fire Decree that suspended most civil liberties in Germany and ultimately led to the Enabling Act (March 23, 1933) that allowed Hitler to enact laws without the consent of the Reichstag. On June 30, 1934, known as the 'Night of the Long Knives', Hitler had a number of rivals executed, thereby solidifying the power of the SS.—Ed.]

ganda inside Germany during the war but equally for propaganda in the neutral countries (and even Great Britain and France) and perhaps later in occupied territory and among prisoners of war. And it will be absolutely invaluable when once the problem arises of finally extirpating Naziism in Germany after the war.

Great as the difficulties of compiling such a history of the Nazi regime will be, the task is by no means an impossible one. There are now in this country and elsewhere outside Germany a considerable number of persons who at one time or another occupied high positions in Nazi Germany and consequently possess a great deal of inside knowledge. Most of them can of course not be considered as reliable or expected to give much active help. But examined and re-examined by persons who have studied the published evidence and with their statements checked against one another and the already known facts, they could undoubtedly be used to establish most of the more important facts.

I believe that the task of producing such a handbook of recent German history should be entrusted to a small committee consisting largely of (non-Jewish) German scholars including the one or two persons who have already produced fairly reliable accounts of these events. It might be desirable to invite a few neutral scholars of notoriously pro-German leanings (such as, e.g., Sven Hedin) to sit in and control the proceedings.[6] The question under whose auspices such a publication should appear will have to be very carefully considered. Once such a handbook is compiled it should be produced in tenths [tens] of thousands of copies of small size and on thin paper so that all possible channels, including in particular the organisations of the German opposition, could be used to get as many copies as possible into Germany.

4. *To whom propaganda to be mainly addressed*. It must not be objected that these methods are too 'academic' to be effective propaganda. With the type of mind of those with whom we can hope to have any success we cannot be too pedantically exact and circumstantial with respect to fact. I should even, in the historical propaganda, freely give references to German sources and recommend German books. If they then find that these are promptly banned, this will only increase their suspicion against the official information. Of course there must be no lengthy disquisition. What I have in mind are mainly broadcasts of fifteen to twenty minutes duration (if that medium remains available) or printed material which takes about the same time to read and in which the contents of the 'handbook' are broadcast piecemeal.

In general it seems important not to place too much reliance on propaganda directly aimed at the broad masses. In Germany as in every other country ideas only take root if they gradually filter through from above. The persons at which to aim would be mainly the leading circles outside the Nazi organisations, partic-

---

[6] [The Swedish explorer and geographer Sven Anders Hedin (1865–1952) was a noted Germanophile who had advocated a Swedish alliance with the German Empire during the First World War.—Ed.]

ularly the army, the industrialists, and the civil service. These circles will to some extent have access to information from neutral sources and will form their views about the chances of Germany partly on this information. This will be particularly true with respect to economic problems and it is important here to prevent that these circles derive too much encouragement from such information. During the last war, for instance, the Swedish economist Professor G. Cassel has contributed a great deal to strengthen the belief in Germany's invincibility by his—as it proved mistaken—appraisal of *Germany's Economic Power of Resistance*.[7] This can only be prevented if real information on these questions is provided to neutral experts.

There are many special points which propaganda aimed at the ruling classes inside and outside the party must carefully take into account. There is the predominant desire in German army circles to preserve at any price the German army—not so much as an instrument of war but because they sincerely believe that it is an essential ingredient for the preservation of the stability of the nation. Special caution is necessary not to be misled by the idea, wrongly held not only by many refugees but also by leftish circles in this country, that Naziism is a reactionary, capitalist movement. In so far as the possible effects of propaganda on the intelligent classes outside the Nazi party are concerned it would be much more effective, and much truer, to stress the communist tendencies in the Nazi movement and to underline its kinship with Bolshevism.

In connection with this propaganda directed mainly to the more intelligent classes, it is necessary to return for a moment to the historical side of it. Here it will not be enough to tell the Germans the truth. It will be essential to prove to them how and why they have been deliberately misled by the official teaching of history. This again can and must be done from German sources. It is a long story however since Bismarckian times, when a famous scientist and president of the Prussian Academy of Science could boast that the German scholars were proud to regard themselves as the 'spiritual bodyguard of the Hohenzollerns' certain sections of the German scholars have placed themselves in the service of the political ambitions of the Government at the time.[8] But I know from experience that if one can prove how history has been deliberately falsified this does more than almost anything else to make German minds disposed to listen to the truth.

It cannot be sufficiently emphasised that this kind of propaganda should in form and character be altogether different from the German propaganda and rather aim to emphasise its sober, dispassionate, and matter-of-fact nature. And it should not only be different from the propaganda to which the German is used to from his own Government. It would probably be well worth while clearly to distinguish the considered historical information disseminated for propaganda purposes from the more hastily prepared ephemeral news on current events. The

---

[7] [Gustav Cassell, *Germany's Economic Power of Resistance* (New York: Jackson Press, 1916).—Ed.]

[8] [Hayek refers to Emil du Bois-Reymond; for more on the episode, see the editor's introduction, p. 16.—Ed.]

German recipient must gradually learn to trust the former implicitly. It will be advisable occasionally to explain what trouble we are taking to establish the truth. And, in general, any mistakes made, either by policy or in particular statements made in the course of propaganda activities, should be frankly admitted.

5. *Liaison between propaganda and intelligence services.* Although this is probably unnecessary, the importance of adequate contacts between the agencies collecting information from Germany and those disseminating propaganda to Germany must be mentioned here. If the propaganda material to be given out at any moment is to be rightly selected, those responsible for it must have full knowledge of the intellectual dope which at the time is administered to the German people by their official propaganda, of their moods and their material position. This means that those drafting propaganda material should not only keep informed about the German press and German broadcasting, but should also be supplied with all the important information available in this country which is relevant to their work.

6. *Propaganda in neutral countries.* Although this lies outside the scope of these notes except in so far as the repercussions in Germany are concerned, I should like to stress the opportunity that the influence of information emanating from Great Britain will be considerable only if it comes to be considered the best information available. This may imply an almost complete reversal of the politics of the first few days of the war.

7. *War aims.* The importance of a clear statement of war aims in connection with propaganda in Germany need hardly be mentioned. If I allude to it here at all it is merely to emphasise the importance that in formulating any pronouncement on this subject some person really familiar with German psychology should be consulted. The turn of a phrase can make all the difference with regard to its effect on the German people.

8. *Some suggestions concerning the technique of propaganda.*

   a. *One-sentence broadcasts on German wavelength in the intervals of German announcements.* If these are technically feasible they might be used with great effect, without actually disturbing German broadcasts, to disseminate news, to direct attention to other forms of propaganda, or to neutralise the effect of German propaganda. If skilfully prepared and spoken by a person of great presence of mind, not merely announcements, as, say "Die Franzosen haben Saarbrücken besetzt", but also such slogans, familiar to every child in Germany, as "Noch is Polen nicht verloren" might prove very effective.[9] As the Germans have apparently already violated the existing conventions in this respect, we probably need feel no compunction on this point, particularly as the purpose is not deception and the German broadcasts are not disturbed in a technical sense.

   b. Further with regard to broadcasting, it is important to take account of certain

---

[9] [The news announcement translates as "The French have occupied Saarbrücken", and the slogan is "Poland has not yet perished", which is the first line of the Polish national anthem. —Ed.]

German susceptibilities and particularly not to forget that even anti-Nazis are to a certain degree anti-Semite and are exceedingly quick in recognizing a Jewish accent. The recent broadcasts by some French stations specially directed to Austrians have almost certainly been deprived of all effects and have perhaps even done harm by being spoken by a person with a pronounced Jewish accent. The same, I believe, is or was true, though to a lesser extent, of the press review broadcast by the BBC in German in the late evening.

c. Printed propaganda material to be smuggled into Germany can be usefully disguised by binding it as if it were a volume of one of the popular series corresponding to the *Penguin* or *Everyman* series (in Germany *Reclam, Inselbücherei, Sammlung Göschen*, etc.). It will frequently be possible to give such publications such a form that even the recipient will not know, or at least cannot be presumed to know, that it is foreign propaganda. This will apply particularly to the selection from the German classics which I have suggested above and which it would even for the Nazis be difficult to suppress since even the most enthusiastic Nazi would only become curious if he were not allowed to see genuine writings of authors like Schiller whom he has always heard praised.

d. As regards the technique of smuggling propaganda material, or in fact any information, into Germany I would like to draw special attention to the possibilities of the German-Jugoslaw border with its overlapping nationalities and intense small frontier traffic. Without claiming any intimate knowledge of the conditions there I might yet be able to give some useful advice concerning personnel, etc.

In conclusion I should like to point out that much more use might be made of certain passages in Hitler's speeches and writings, such as the passage in *Mein Kampf* which was recently quoted in the correspondence column of the *Times* and of which I give the original at the foot of this page.

F. A. von Hayek

"So liegt schon in der Tatsache eines Abschlusses eines Bündnisses mit Russland die Anweisung für den nächsten Krieg. Sein Ausgang wäre das Ende Deutschlands". (A. Hitler, *Mein Kampf*, vol. 2., 41st ed., p. 749)[10]

[10] [Adolf Hitler, *Mein Kampf*, 41st ed. (Munich: Franz Eher Nachfolger, 1933), vol. 2, p. 749. For an English translation, see Adolf Hitler, *Mein Kampf*, translated by Ralph Manheim (Boston: Houghton Mifflin, 1943), p. 660, where the quoted passage reads: "And so the very fact of the conclusion of an alliance with Russia embodies a plan for the next war. Its outcome would be the end of Germany". Hitler's warning that an alliance with the Russians would be disastrous—they would be a weak ally, and the alliance would cause the French and English to attack them—presumably could be used against his decision to sign a non-aggression pact with the Soviet Union.—Ed.]

Selected Correspondence, F. A. Hayek to Fritz Machlup (1940–41)

June 21, 1940
8, Turner Close
London, N. W. 11
Tel. Speedwell 7861

My dear Machlup,

Although things look pretty grim life here still goes on in its normal course. I am alone here in the house, Hella and the children are with the Robbins family in the country, and I am immersed in examination scripts, as Lionel Robbins has now at last joined a Government Dept. and I have to do all the examining for him in addition to my own. We are trying to get it over before bombing starts in earnest. Of the first raids of the last few days we have here noticed nothing and in the peace of one's house and garden it is still difficult to believe how near the war has now come. One looks of course with a certain amount of 'Wehmut'[11] on one's things and books which may go at any moment. But in the meantime one just carries on with one's work, hoping that there will soon be an opportunity to do something more immediately useful.

My main anxiety at the moment is whether Mises and Roepke got away from Geneva in time.[12] As you probably know Penrose had secured for them almost at a moment's notice appointments in California and the problem was merely whether the formalities could be settled before Italy's entry into the war. The last letter I had from M. was from the end of May and he hoped then to leave almost any day. I have done my best through my French friend to secure him a French transit visa but I fear this will have come too late and the only hope is that he and R. got out by the Locarno-Barcelona air line before it was stopped.[13]

The very last news I had from him was in fact his book which must have got out of Geneva almost with the last parcel post. I am reading it now and reviewing it for the Economic Journal. We have asked Knight to do it for ECONOMICA and hope he will accept. My own book is in the press and I have already the first page proofs, so I hope it will appear in spite of all. In fact, so far as my time permits, I am already at work on my new book, a history of the influence of scientific and technological development on social thought and policy (to be called The Abuse and Decline of Reason) and I have in the course of the last year already worked out a fairly definite

---

[11] [Wistfulness or ruefulness.—Ed.]

[12] [Both Ludwig von Mises and Wilhelm Roepke were at the Graduate Institute of International Studies in Geneva when the war began. Roepke remained there throughout the war, but Mises escaped. E. F. Penrose (1896–1984) worked at the International Labour Office in Geneva and had been on the faculty of the University of California at Berkeley.—Ed.]

[13] [The identity of Hayek's "French friend" remains unknown. The French composer Darius Milhaud wrote a letter on behalf of Mises to the French Embassy, and this enabled Mises and his wife to secure French transit visas. Their escape to the United States, which involved a bus trip across occupied France, a delayed border crossing into Spain, and a brief stay in Lisbon, is recounted in Margit von Mises, *My Years with Ludwig von Mises* (Cedar Falls, IA: Center for Futures Education, 1984), pp. 51–56.—Ed.]

plan and done a good deal of preliminary reading. It is a great subject and one could make a great book of it. I believe indeed I have now found an approach to the subject through which one could exercise some real influence. But whether I shall ever be able to write it depends of course not only on whether one survives this but also on the outcome of it all. If things go really badly I shall certainly not be able to continue it here and since I believe that it is really important and the best I can do for the future of mankind, I should then have to try to transfer my activities elsewhere. Since at a later stage it may be difficult to write about it, I have already sent copies of the outline of the first part to Haberler and Lipmann[14] as a basis of any future application to one of the foundations for funds, and I am enclosing another copy with this letter. I am afraid it gives only the historical skeleton round which the main argument is to be developed, but I have not the peace of mind at the present moment to put the outline of the argument itself on paper. The second part would of course be an elaboration of the central argument of my pamphlet on Freedom and the Economic System.

If it were at all possible I would of course like to send Hella and the children away while it is possible. But with the impossibility of sending money out of the country I do not see much chance. In the Dominions, to which it might be possible to send them, we do not know anybody, and in the States the Immigration regulations are of course an obstacle. It might however be a help if I got some sort of pro forma invitation on the basis of which I might get a visa for the whole family which would be helpful if the worst came. I myself have no intention of running away while the war lasts, at least if I still succeed in getting into some useful work or so long as the School goes on. But I must confess that I am getting really annoyed by the refusal to use a person like myself on any useful work and if this goes on I shall probably sooner or later feel that I am more in the way than anything else.

If you hear from Mises please let me know. If you see him, please ask him whether he wishes me to send him books (old books which retain their value) for at least part of the money which I owe him. It is the only legal way in which he now can get an equivalent and a way which is not even an evasion of the regulation and certainly in no way unpatriotic, since it does nobody any harm and may indeed save the books from destruction. I had mentioned this in my last letter to him, but I doubt whether this has reached him.

The enclosed exam papers will perhaps interest you. The war has not lowered our standards!
With the best wishes to everybody,
Very cordially yours,

F. A. Hayek

I have now made an attempt to sketch the main argument of the book rapidly on a page, but I am afraid not very successful. I also enclose the plan of a volume of more technical economic studies I had been contemplating.

---

[14] [See the editor's introduction, p. 4, for more on Gottfried Haberler and Walter Lippmann.—Ed.]

October 13, 1940
8, Turner Close
London, N. W. 11
Tel. Speedwell 7861

My dear Machlup,

Many thanks for your letter of precisely one month ago which I found a few days ago on my return from my first regular visit to Cambridge. As you may already have heard, the School is continuing there, probably for the duration, and since my own movements are a bit uncertain, you had better write in future to me at the School, New Court, Peterhouse, Cambridge.

Apart from the three nights I am now regularly spending in Cambridge, I am however for the time being continuing in my London home. My family is now permanently in the country, at the moment still in the same cottage with the Robbins but we have some hope of finding a separate cottage not very far distant. It is so far in the heart of the country that I have after long hesitation decided that this involves less, even for a long period, than a single Atlantic crossing. I may have been wrong—but when one takes in account that a parting of the family now would probably mean a separation for years, I found it very difficult to decide otherwise.

Life here in London is amazingly unchanged. Some nights have been unpleasant, and once or twice even we out here have had bombs uncomfortably close. But on the whole the effects of the German attacks are—at least in the parts of London which I regularly see—extraordinarily small. I think any visitor who did not know would think that London had been bombed for one night rather than for one month. And after a certain amount of disorganisation caused by the raids of the first two nights (which were also the severest) life has returned very much to normal. One gets used to sleeping in a basement or, as in our case, a strengthened ground floor room and just hopes for the best. It is of course by no means excluded that things may get worse—in which case I shall probably also change my present habits. But so far the advantage of being able to continue my work in my own study and among my own books still seems to outweigh the slight danger attaching to it.

I have, in fact, done more work this summer than ever before in a similar period. After finishing with the proofs of my book on capital (which Macmillan is now hesitating to bring out—it is all ready) I have completed five historical chapters of my new book and am now deep in the most difficult first, theoretical chapters. Only during the last fortnight have I been able to do little, partly because the various beginning-of-term occupations and partly because of a miserable cold which under the present conditions is a greater nuisance than usual.

During the day one can here almost completely forget that a war is on and few people take any notice of the sirens (which are going this very moment). We out here at least have not yet seen a German plane during the day. It is of course a different matter during the night. But even then the most noticeable thing is the din of the AA

314

guns and even the most serious danger outdoors are the splinters from AA shells. This means that after dark one is really strictly confined to one's home which, as nights become longer, is of course irksome. If, of course, as seems now likely, this continues indefinitely, the chances of one's house being hit earlier or later increase and I shall try to find a possibility of transferring at least my more valuable possessions including part of my library elsewhere. But this is really difficult.

I am very anxious for further news about Mises. The two letters I had from him since he escaped (one still from Lisbon) were extremely laconic, and I want more definite information because I hope that now that he is definitely established in the States I may succeed in obtaining permission to transfer at least part of his account.

I have heard practically nothing from any of our other friends in the States, except of course Haberler. But I assume that Schütz, Fröhlich, Fürth, Vögelin, etc. are all well?[15]

I hope that you will be getting on with your book on *Monopoly and Competition*.[16] It seems to me a subject excellently suited for your genius and one on which a competent survey is badly needed.

The people here are really magnificent, and if they have awoken late to the grimness of the task before them, they certainly are more resolute than ever. I only hope it will be the same with the Americans. While I have no doubt about our capacity to defend ourselves, I find it difficult to see how we can actually win without real American help. Many people here believe that all we need is more complete material help—but I find it difficult to see how the war can be finally decided without American participation—unless the German collapse which would ultimately happen, but by then the civilisation of Europe will be destroyed.

With the kindest regards and the best wishes yours ever,

F. A. Hayek

Well, well, one must not be too confident. I have just heard a distant bomb, almost the first here at day-time!

---

[15] [Alfred Schütz (1899–1959), Walter Fröhlich (1901–75), J. Herbert Fürth (1899–1995), and Eric Vögelin (1901–85) were all friends from university days in Vienna or from Mises' *Privatseminar*.—Ed.]

[16] [Machlup's book on monopoly and competition ultimately appeared as two separate volumes, one on theory, the other on policy: *The Economics of Sellers' Competition: Model Analysis of Sellers' Conduct* (Baltimore: Johns Hopkins Press, 1952), and *The Political Economy of Monopoly: Business, Labor, and Government Policies* (Baltimore: Johns Hopkins Press, 1952).—Ed.]

December 14, 1940
Kings College
Cambridge

My dear Machlup,
Your letter of November 12th, which reached me some time ago, was very welcome. We hear so little nowadays from our friends overseas that every bit of news is gratefully received. And that all the news from you was so satisfactory made it doubly pleasant.

As you will see from the notepaper, I am now, during term-time, living here in College. To live alone in London became gradually too uncomfortable and the offer of rooms here provided the perfect solution. The term is of course mostly over now and I am on the point of leaving to join my family and to go with them to Cornwall for the vacation. I do not want to bring the children to London, although so far our district has on the whole been spared. But any part of London is fairly noisy and although one gets used to it and the children did not seem to mind during the first few days of September when they just happened to be in London, it can't be good for their nerves, quite apart from the danger. We shall therefore probably be continuing this sort of life for the duration—Hella and the children staying with Mrs. Robbins and their children during term-time and we rejoining for vacations.

Apart from being separated from my family my life is as satisfactory as possible and from the external circumstances of my life I would not know that there is a war on. Cambridge itself is of course completely peaceful and apart from the reduced numbers of staff and students academic life is also very much the same as in normal times. In a way I even resent this complete seclusion: not only the feeling that one cannot do something more important is depressing; I also feel it sometimes as somehow not right that even intellectually one should be so very much separated from the really important problems of the time. But this feeling is completely irrational and so long as one is not wanted the best thing one can do is to go on with one's normal work, and that is what I am doing.

January 2, 1941
Tintagel (Cornwall)

I did not succeed finishing this in Cambridge and I am now continuing after nearly a fortnight of a most pleasant holiday here in Cornwall. The North Cornish Coast is one of the most beautiful parts of the country—I discovered this on a very short holiday in September and we shall now probably spend all our war holidays here. It is a fine rocky coast, the climate very pleasant and we have so far been very fortunate with the weather. I have not done much work here, but since, after having worked through practically all last summer I was rather tired, I was perhaps entitled to treat this as a real vacation. But I have now started to get on with some of my work and I hope in the remaining week to get something done.

My capital book is now at last due within the next few weeks. A few historical

316

chapters of the new book I am planning will appear in the forthcoming numbers of ECONOMICA. And at the moment I am mainly concerned with an enlarged and somewhat more popular exposition of the theme of my *Freedom and the Economic System* which, if I finish it, may come out as a sixpence Penguin volume.

Did I already urge you in one of my earlier letters to let us have something for ECONOMICA? I am now practically solely responsible for it and as so many people are not available, it is rather difficult to keep up the standard and to continue regularly, which we want to do as long as possible.

Since with you I need not be diplomatic, I may as well tell you how impatient in more than one respect I am now with the Americans. Every time I see an American newspaper I am in a rage. They pride themselves to have the best press in the world and in fact even the best papers succumb to sensationalism of the worst sort. The account of the effect of the air raids here, particularly in the first few weeks were simply scandalous. That early in October a reputable American paper should estimate the reduction of production due to air raid damages at 10 per cent (in October, mind you) when including all indirect and temporary effects (like stoppage of electricity) it cannot have been more than about 1 per cent suggests that people over there have got things altogether out of perspective. I can quite believe that even without such exaggerations it must be difficult enough to believe that on the whole life in London proceeds very much like normal—I experience this myself when on my visits to town I am every time amazed how little damage one sees. But I am certain that the Americans as a whole must have a completely wrong picture. On the other hand, the American reports don't seem to give at all an adequate idea how completely indiscriminate the bombing is—which is of course part of the explanation of its ineffectiveness. The best proof of this indiscriminate character is probably the fact that so far by far the greatest destruction has been done by land-mines dropped by parachute where of course any attempt at deliberate aim is out of the question.

Much more upsetting is of course the American attitude on the bigger issues. That before the collapse of France the Americans may have felt that the Allies will win without them is of course partly the fault of people over here. That immediately after they may have felt that it was too late I can understand—although it is difficult enough to understand it over here. But that now, when nobody can have any illusions about what a victory of Hitler would mean for America and when it is so clear that every day may be decisive, and with the elections out of the way things should still move no faster, is incomprehensible to me. I say this even after Roosevelt's last speech and in full knowledge of the 'political difficulties'. It is the blindness of the American isolationists which I cannot understand. Compared with them Baldwin and Chamberlain were marvels of foresight.[17] It would be too long to discuss all this more fully—but in what I see of current American discussions I find hardly a sentence which does not

[17] [Hayek refers to British Prime Ministers Stanley Baldwin (1867–1947) and Neville Chamberlain (1869–1940), both of whom many blamed for Britain's state of military unpreparedness at the beginning of the Second World War.—Ed.]

prove that people are yet completely unaware of what is at stake now—and how irrevocable the days lost are.

But, to return to more private matters, I am very glad that nearly all of our friends are settled and I very much hope that something will also soon be found for Mises. Although there is of course much in his book with which I disagree, and much else is so familiar to us that it is boring, I think it is in many ways a great achievement and I cannot understand Haberler's harsh judgement. I believe one can still learn more real economics from it than from many a modern textbook.

I have now got sufficiently over my first reaction to say that the offer from the New School which I owe to Haberler has really caused me some indignation. Not only proves it such a complete misconception of conditions here—I could not help regarding its nature as a personal slight. I wonder what a professor at Harvard or Chicago would say if in similar circumstances he were offered without asking for anything a nondescript job at about a fourth of his present salary? There is of course the possibility that someday many of us may have to transfer their activities elsewhere, but even then I should think twice before accepting an offer of this kind. And although I fully see the particular difficulty of the Mises problem, I fully share his dislike of joining that particular crowd. I did not want to hurt Haberler so I never let him know what I felt about it—and I have of course declined the offer with all due expressions gratitude, etc. I now feel rather too politely. But I don't think I should have acted differently even if I knew that the war would last for ten years.

I am now called away and if I don't post the letter to-day, it will again be held up.

Yours ever,
F. A. Hayek

October 19, 1941
The Hostel
Peterhouse
Cambridge

Dear Machlup,

There is no special excuse why both your letters of August 3rd and September 17th are still unanswered. But the process of first settling down here in Cambridge and then the beginning of term have taken up much of my time and till I had disposed of all the really urgent jobs I did not feel like settling down to my correspondence.

You will have heard in the meantime from the ECONOMICA offices about your article—but in case this letter should overtake the other one, I will repeat here that, as your article will have to appear in two parts and as we shall have to change to smaller type (to save paper) between November and February, we thought it better to hold it over till February. I found it exceedingly interesting and most useful. I hope the book will come out fairly soon.

I have not yet had time carefully to consider what you say about the confusion in chapter IX of my book, but I am afraid at least so far as the sentence on page 108 is concerned you are right. Professor Smithies has sent me a carbon of his article on my book, but I am afraid I shall hardly have time now to reply to it, although it is a careful work which would deserve more serious attention than I can give it at the moment.[18]

As you will gather from this, even my theoretical interests are still elsewhere than the theory of capital. If you have seen the series of articles which have appeared in ECONOMICA (a reprint is on the way to you) you will have some idea of my plans, although they will become clearer only after the theoretical section which will ultimately precede it has been published. It is far advanced, but at the moment I am not even getting on with that because I have decided that the applications of it all to our own time, which should some day form volume II of the ABUSE AND DECLINE OF REASON, are more important. I have therefore resumed my plan of expanding my pamphlet on Freedom and the Economic System into a book. If one cannot fight the Nazis one ought at least to fight the ideas which produce Naziism; and although the well-meaning people who are so dangerous have of course no idea of it, the danger which comes from them is none the less serious. The most dangerous people here are a group of socialist scientists and I am just publishing a special attack on them in NATURE—the famous scientific weekly which in recent years has been one of the main advocates of 'planning'.[19] The Final Report of the TNEC was one of the few

---

[18] [The "confusion in chapter IX of my book" refers to a comment Machlup had made in his August 3rd letter about a problem he had discovered in Hayek's *The Pure Theory of Capital*. In his letter of September 17 Machlup had urged Hayek to reply to Arthur Smithies's review article, "Professor Hayek on *The Pure Theory of Capital*", *American Economic Review*, vol. 31, December 1941, pp. 767–79.—Ed.]

[19] [For more on this, see the editor's introduction, p. 7.—Ed.]

grains of comfort I have recently had—can you tell me how far it is representative and important?[20]

Many thanks for your readiness to send me some of the Monographs published by the Committee. They have not yet arrived. If I may trouble you for one more official publication which seems to be of considerable importance in connection with my study of the influence of the engineering mentality on social policy? I should very much like to get Alexander Gourvitch, *Survey of Economic Theory on Technological Change and Employment*. Philadelphia, Works Projects Administration. 1940 (National Research Project Report No. G-6).

As our school library is largely evacuated and spread all over the country, and the Cambridge libraries are not too good in our field, serious work is getting more and more difficult. I am somewhat better off now I have my own books all here—but one needs of course always things one has not got.

We are quite comfortable in our house here—at least at the moment, but we dread the winter since the problem of heating the one enormous room (the size of a minor college hall) of which it mainly consists may well prove insoluble this winter. But the advantages of having the family once again together are of course great. The children have happily settled down in their new schools and they as well as Hella are as comfortable as one can wish—although the problem of coping with this house with little help is rather a big one for Hella.

Last week we had a flying visit from Alvin Hansen[21] who did impress me even less than on earlier occasion but who was full of praise for your teaching capacities. Of my English colleagues, including some of my closest colleagues, I see now very little and I fear we shall lose even one or two of the few still left at the School. But as far as I know they are all well and now fairly satisfied with the work they are doing.

With the best regards to all of you from Hella and myself, yours ever,

F. A. Hayek

[20] [*Final Report and Recommendations of the Temporary National Economic Committee*, United States of America, 77th Congress, 1st Session, Senate Document No. 35, 1941. The Committee's report was on concentrations of economic power, and one of its findings was that, contrary to popular belief of the day, the greater efficiency of large scale production does not necessarily lead to the end of competition. Hayek discusses the report in *The Road to Serfdom*, pp. 92–93.—Ed.]

[21] [Alvin Hansen (1887–1975), after initial scepticism, would become the leading American advocate of Keynesian economics. In 1945 he would write a strongly critical review of Hayek's *The Road to Serfdom*; for more on this, see the editor's introduction to F. A. Hayek, *The Road to Serfdom*, p. 23.—Ed.]

Preface to the U. S. Edition (1952)

The studies united in this volume, although in the first instance published separately in the course of a number of years, form part of a single comprehensive plan. For this republication the exposition has been slightly revised and a few gaps have been filled in, but the main argument is unchanged. Their arrangement is now systematic, in the order in which the argument develops, rather than the accidental one of their first appearance. The book thus begins with a theoretical discussion of the general issues and proceeds to an examination of the historical rôle played by the ideas in question. This is not mere pedantry or a device for avoiding unnecessary repetition but, it seems to me, essential in order to show the true significance of the particular development. But I am quite aware that as a result the opening sections of the book are relatively more difficult than the rest, and that it might have been more politic to put the more concrete matter in the forefront. I still believe that most readers who are interested in this kind of subject will find the present arrangement more convenient. But any reader who has little taste for abstract discussion may do well to read first the second part which has given the title to this volume. I hope he will then find the general discussion of the same problems in the first study more interesting.

These two major sections of the volume were first published in parts in *Economica* for 1942–44 and for 1941, respectively. The third study, written more recently as a lecture, appeared first in *Measure* for June 1951 but was prepared from notes collected at the same time as those for the first two essays. I have to thank the editors of both of these journals and the London School of Economics and Political Science and the Henry Regnery Company of Chicago as their respective publishers for permission to reprint what first appeared under their auspices.

F. A. Hayek

Preface to the German Edition (1959)[22]

The essays assembled in this volume were written as a part of a greater work that, if it ever should be finished, pursues the history of the abuse and decline of reason in modern times. I wrote the first two essays in London in relative leisure, which the early years of the last war afforded me. I wrote them on a remote subject matter in a state of intensive concentration with which I reacted to my impotence against the continuous disruptions of falling bombs. The first two appeared in the journal *Economica* in 1941 to 1944. The third was written later from notes on a lecture given at the same time and was published in *Measure* in June 1951. I am indebted to the publishers of these journals as well as to the London School of Economics and the Henry Regnery Company in Chicago for their permission to reproduce these works in essentially unaltered form.

Other investigations that do not follow directly, but belong to the same area of interest, disrupted my labours on the original plan. A sense of urgency then led me to prepare a summary of my analyses that were to constitute the main argument of the second part of that greater work on the decline of reason. But I became more and more aware that a satisfactory execution of the original plan pre-supposes extensive philosophical studies, which occupied me during the greater part of the intervening years. I readily accepted the friendly offer of the American publisher to reprint the essays because of the public interest they generated and because the time I had hoped to publish the complete work has not drawn any closer.

The train of thought of such a fragmentary discourse is determined, of course, by the wider setting in which it belongs. Therefore, the reader may welcome a brief explanation of the objectives of the greater task. The essays were to be preceded by a study on the individualistic theories of the eighteenth century. Some preliminary results of this undertaking were published in the meantime in the first chapter of my book *Individualism and Economic Order* (Chicago: University of Chicago Press, 1948). The first part of the present volume pursues the intellectual sources of the hostility against this individualism. The historical development of these views, that to me seem to reflect an abuse of reason, was to follow in four more sections. The second part of the present volume dealing with the earlier French phase of this development would have been the first of these sections. And the third part was to be the beginning of the second section, which deals with the German continuation of this movement that originated in France. There was to follow a similar section on the retreat of liberalism that took place in England towards the end of the nineteenth century, due primarily to intellectual influences that came from France and Germany. And finally there was to be a section on a similar development in the United States.

---

[22] This preface originally appeared in the German edition of *The Counter-Revolution of Science*, published under the title *Mißbrauch und Verfall der Vernunft* (Frankfurt: Fritz Knapp) in 1959. [Helene Hayek, Hayek's second wife, was the translator.—Ed.]

This overview of the progressive abuse of reason, or socialism, was to be followed by a discussion of the decay of reason under totalitarianism, be it fascism or communism. The basic thought of this second major part was initially presented in popular form in my book *The Road to Serfdom* (Chicago: University of Chicago Press, 1944).

Perhaps I should not have retained the original order in this reprint of an excerpt. A detailed theoretical introduction into "Scientism and the Study of Society" probably presents a better systematic analysis than this small volume, in which it may create an unnecessary obstacle to the easier terrain that follows. The reader who has little taste for abstract discussion, therefore, would do well to read first the second part on "The Counter-Revolution of Science". He will find it easier then to perceive the significance of the abstract discussion of the same problems in the first part.

I should like to add that the work of which this is a part will not be continued in the form originally conceived. I now hope to present the body of thought in another volume that is less historical but more systematic.

F. A. Hayek

ACKNOWLEDGMENTS

I gratefully acknowledge the staff of the Interlibrary Loan Department at Jackson Library, UNC–Greensboro, who obtained some two hundred books and articles for me so that I could check the accuracy of Hayek's citations. Gaylor Callahan's assistance was especially notable.

A number of individuals helped me in tracking down some of Hayek's more obscure references. These include Alain Alcouffe, Guido Erreygers, Dan Hammond, Helena Rosenblatt, Malcolm Rutherford, Mark Schumacher, Martin Staum, Nicholas Theocarakis, Yuri Tulupenko, Bernhard Walpen, John Wells, and Terry Wright.

The passages in German and French found in the 1952 version of *The Counter-Revolution of Science* often contained typos, and not all were translated into English. Oscar Camy did a meticulous job both in checking all of the French passages and in rendering historically appropriate translations of the words of Henri de Saint-Simon, Auguste Comte, and others from earlier periods. Georg Vanberg, Viktor Vanberg, and Dan Kirklin checked for typos and provided translations for the German passages. Finally, Susan Shelmerdine and Linda Danford checked the Greek and Latin passages, respectively.

Columbia University archivist Jocelyn Wilk provided Wesley Clair Mitchell's course schedule for the 1923–24 academic year that is noted in the editor's introduction.

Professor Peter Klein did a good deal of initial work on the footnotes prior to my taking over responsibility for the volume, and this was of great help.

On November 8–11, 2007, the Liberty Fund sponsored a colloquium entitled "Hayek, Scientism, and Liberty" at which a group of scholars critically examined Hayek's texts for this volume. The participants included Brandon Beck, Peter Boettke, Evelyn Forget, Jerry Gaus, Wade Hands, Dan Hammond, Ronald Hamowy, Paul Lewis, Leonard Liggio, Gene Miller, Claire Morgan, Jerry Z. Muller, Sandy Peart, Ben Powell, Viktor Vanberg, and Amy Willis. Those who know an author well are usually his most perceptive critics, and this was no exception. The observations shared at the meeting were invaluable to me in preparing the final draft of my editor's introduction.

I gratefully acknowledge the assistance of Brandon Beck in preparing the manuscript and thank two anonymous readers for their perceptive comments and suggestions. Finally, I thank David Pervin of the University of Chicago Press for his advice and guidance through the editorial process and Rhonda Smith of the Press for her skilled copyediting.

Bruce Caldwell

INDEX